CW00545875

MIXING IT

MIXING IT

DIVERSITY IN WORLD WAR TWO BRITAIN

WENDY WEBSTER

OXFORD
UNIVERSITY PRESS

OXFORD
UNIVERSITY PRESS

Great Clarendon Street, Oxford, OX2 6DP,
United Kingdom

Oxford University Press is a department of the University of Oxford.
It furthers the University's objective of excellence in research, scholarship,
and education by publishing worldwide. Oxford is a registered trade mark of
Oxford University Press in the UK and in certain other countries

© Wendy Webster 2018

The moral rights of the author have been asserted

First Edition published in 2018

Impression: 1

All rights reserved. No part of this publication may be reproduced, stored in
a retrieval system, or transmitted, in any form or by any means, without the
prior permission in writing of Oxford University Press, or as expressly permitted
by law, by licence, or under terms agreed with the appropriate reprographics
rights organization. Enquiries concerning reproduction outside the scope of the
above should be sent to the Rights Department, Oxford University Press, at the
address above

You must not circulate this work in any other form
and you must impose this same condition on any acquirer

Published in the United States of America by Oxford University Press
198 Madison Avenue, New York, NY 10016, United States of America

British Library Cataloguing in Publication Data
Data available

Library of Congress Control Number: 2017950133

ISBN 978–0–19–873576–2

Printed in Great Britain by
Clays Ltd, St Ives plc

Links to third party websites are provided by Oxford in good faith and
for information only. Oxford disclaims any responsibility for the materials
contained in any third party website referenced in this work.

For Rick

Acknowledgements

This book is part of a wider project, funded by a Leadership Fellowship award from the Arts and Humanities Research Council, that included a display at Imperial War Museum North. I am grateful to the AHRC for the Fellowship award and to Gillian Gray at the AHRC for all her support. The data collected from this project is available at http://eprints.hud.ac.uk/26657/

In the early stages of the project, I developed the research through two other Fellowships—one at Australian National University and the other at the University of Tasmania. Thanks are due to both institutions for these awards. I am also very grateful to the University of Huddersfield and to my colleagues there for all the support I was given in the middle and later stages of the project.

I owe a great debt to Janette Martin and Rob Light for the brilliant work they did on the project in 2015. Thanks also to all the people interviewed by Janette and Rob—Ray Costello, Maria Cunningham, Joseph Drylaga, Zbigniew and Genia Dzeurman, Richard and Elizabeth Flammer, Yvonne Foley, Susanne Medas, Jan Niczyterowizc, Sue Pearson, Fred Sichert, Zbigniew Siemaszko, Peter and Edith Sinclair, Jack and Doreen Stang, and Irena Zientek. I was provided with invaluable information, suggestions, and support by Suzanne Bardgett, John Belchem, Nick Chapman, Peter Devitt, Peter Elliott, Robert Faber, Frank Grombir, Thomas Hajkowski, Steven O'Connor, Liz Pente, Wendy Ugolini, and Paul Ward. Thanks also to the people who sent me photographs and documents about members of their family and gave me permission to use them—Michael Jaffé, Kathy Lowe, Kawana Pohe, John and Jane Sheppard, Anna Siemaszko, and Peter Zimmermann. I am particularly grateful to Anna Siemaszko for translating passages from her father's published work into English.

I presented earlier versions of this work at seminars and conferences held by Australian National University, the Centre for Contemporary British History, the Institute for War, Holocaust and Genocide Studies in Amsterdam, and at the Universities of Leeds, London, Huddersfield, Nottingham, Sheffield, Strathclyde, Sussex, Tasmania, Texas at Austin, and York. Presenting a paper drawn from the project at John MacKenzie's Festschrift was a particular pleasure. My thanks go to all those who organized and participated in these events and helped me to clarify and refine my ideas. At Oxford University Press, Stephanie Ireland and Cathryn Steele provided excellent support. For their work on the display at Imperial War Museum North, I am particularly grateful to Sophie Loftus and Claire Wilson. Will Kaufman came up with a title when I was struggling to find one.

Chapter 3 draws on an article in *Twentieth Century British History*: 'Enemies, Allies and Transnational Histories: Germans, Irish and Italians in Second World War Britain'. Chapter 6 draws on an article in *Women's History Review*: ' "Fit to Fight, Fit to Mix": Sexual Patriotism in Second World War Britain'.

Contents

List of Illustrations

Figure 0.1 Porokuru Patapu 'Johnny' Pohe (by kind permission of Kawana Pohe).

Introduction
'The Big Proposition'

In 2015, a display opened at Imperial War Museum North, telling the story of people who arrived in Britain during the Second World War—chiefly from continental Europe, America and the British Empire—and of what happened to them when the war was over.[1] A museum visitor commented, 'People post-war wanted Polish fighters to leave despite the help we were given—sad reflection of "Brexit Britain"'. The comment was prompted by a panel in the display on Polish soldiers and airmen. Many were in Britain during the Second World War and lost their lives fighting alongside British forces. But when a Gallup Poll was held in Britain in June 1946, asking people whether they agreed with a government decision to allow Poles who wanted to remain in Britain to do so, more than half answered 'no'.[2]

'Brexit Britain' saw a rising number of hate crimes after the vote to leave the European Union in the referendum of June 2016. In the aftermath of an attack on the Polish Cultural Centre in London, Jan Black, who was a Polish gunner in the Royal Air Force (RAF), during the Second World War, commented:

> I was so proud of what we did together, my countrymen and my British colleagues, and I don't know why these sudden changes are happening with the referendum. That makes me so sad, because I saw so many of my countrymen give their lives in order to change Europe for the better... I think the problem is, people just don't know their history.[3]

The far-right British National Party had demonstrated their ignorance of this history in 2009, when they produced a poster for the European elections that showed a Spitfire, above the slogan, 'Battle for Britain'. The picture of the iconic British plane flown in the Battle of Britain was evidently intended to portray Britain in its finest hour. It was only after the poster went on display that someone pointed out that the Spitfire featured on it had been flown by the RAF's 303 Squadron—a Polish Squadron that fought in the Battle of Britain and brought down 126 enemy planes.

Right-wing nationalist propaganda like the British National Party poster often uses images from the Second World War to evoke pride in past national greatness. It identifies membership of the European Union and immigration as two key developments that have brought national decline since 1945. The British National Party's policy is to stop all immigration—'mass immigration and artificially promoted miscegenation is destroying Britain and the British'.[4] This narrative places the history of the Second World War—a symbol of British greatness in the past—in opposition to subsequent immigration, which destroys the nation. But as *Mixing It* demonstrates, movements of migrants, refugees, and troops to Britain not only took place during the Second World War, but were on an unprecedented scale. Between 1939 and 1945, the population of Britain became more diverse by nationality and ethnicity than it had ever been before.

This book charts the history of multinational, multi-ethnic Britain during the Second World War, focusing particularly on stories that are little known. They include the story of German refugees—most of them Jewish— who arrived in Britain before the war, were arrested and interned by the British government in 1940 as enemy aliens, and were subsequently released to join the British army. Those who re-entered Germany as victors in 1945 experienced a dramatic reversal of power, occupying positions of considerable authority over Nazis who had been their persecutors before the war. Another dramatic story told here is of Czech airmen who, as France was collapsing in 1940, 'borrowed' aeroplanes without the preliminary formality of asking the French and flew to Britain to continue the fight. After serving in the RAF and returning to Prague when the war was over, some went on to 'borrow' planes from Czechoslovakia—again without the preliminary formalities of asking—to fly back to Britain.[5] Their journeys back were prompted by the actions of the newly installed Communist regime in Czechoslovakia, which was arresting and imprisoning airmen who had fought in the West.

A book about multinational and multi-ethnic Britain during the Second World War needs to cover a wide range of different groups, but readers will also encounter many individual stories. Each chapter of *Mixing It* begins with one—this chapter, with the little-known story of the first Maori pilot to serve in the RAF.

Porokuru Pohe (Figure 0.1) was one of many volunteers from the British Empire who arrived in Britain during the Second World War. He served as a pilot in the RAF, where he was known as 'Johnny'. In 1943, returning from a flight over Germany, he had to ditch his plane and was captured and taken to Stalag Luft III—a German prisoner-of-war camp that subsequently became famous as the setting for what was called 'the Great Escape'. Pohe participated in this 'Great Escape', later to become the subject of numerous books and the Hollywood film of the same name, starring Steve McQueen.

Before the Second World War, an RAF rule stated that 'only men who are British subjects and of pure European descent are accepted for enlistment or commission in the RAF and they must be the sons of parents both of whom have British nationality'.[6] The rule about 'pure European descent' also applied in the Royal New Zealand Air Force and was still in operation when Pohe filled in his application form, on 12 September 1939—only nine days after New Zealand, along with Australia, Britain, Canada, France, and India, had declared war on Germany after the German invasion of Poland. To a question on the application form that asked him to state whether he was 'of pure European descent', Pohe answered 'no'. A version of his pre-war life is filtered through the conventions of other application form questions. Place of birth—Wanganui (which is on New Zealand's North Island); date of birth—10 December 1914; sports and games played—'Football, Cricket, Tennis, Golf (occasionally)'. Under the question about the nationality of his parents, Pohe gives both as New Zealander and adds that his father is 'Maori' and his mother 'half-caste Maori'.

The rule that recruits had to be 'of pure European descent' was lifted on 19 October 1939, and Pohe (shown in Figure 0.2 with his younger brother) enlisted on 1 September 1940 at the Ground Training School in Levin, on New Zealand's North Island. He gained his flying badge in January 1941 and promotion to Sergeant in March. A month later he sailed for Britain on a ship with a Maori name—the *Aorangi*. After his arrival, Pohe was stationed in Berkshire, where he took part in his first operational flight. He was then posted to No. 51 Squadron, based at Dishforth in Yorkshire, and completed twenty-two missions flying Whitley bombers over the next eight months. Various other postings followed before he returned to No. 51 Squadron in September 1943. Pohe rose rapidly up the ranks from Sergeant

Figure 0.2 Porokuru Pohe with his young brother Kawana (by kind permission of Kawana Pohe).

to Flight Sergeant, then Warrant Officer, Pilot Officer, and Flying Officer. Recommending Pohe for promotion, an RAF officer wrote, 'He is a good pilot, and a steady and reliable captain. He is immensely keen and a hard worker, and when not actually flying is nearly always to be found with his crew in or around his aircraft. Both on and off duty, a number of the other Sergeants seem to regard him as a natural leader'.[7]

Pohe was nicknamed 'Lucky Johnny', but on his return to No. 51 Squadron his luck ran out. On a bombing raid over Germany, his Halifax was hit by flak and caught fire. His crew bailed out and he had to ditch the plane in the English Channel, off the French coast. Tom Thomson, the Canadian tail gunner in the Halifax, remembers:

> He did an excellent job of ditching. The aircraft broke in half but the front part floated for quite a while. Johnny had hit his head on the aircraft when we landed. Those aren't soft landings. The aircraft sunk pretty shortly after that. We were hoping that we were just off Cornwall, but it wasn't to be. We floated in a dinghy for almost 48 hours then were spotted by a Luftwaffe fighter from a training base in France.[8]

A German patrol boat picked them up and they were taken initially to an interrogation camp in Frankfurt. Pohe was sent from there to Stalag Luft III, where he wrote to his parents, 'I am quite alright but very disappointed that my career should end in a POW camp'. He also sent letters using Maori words that the German censors would not understand. 'Glowing pictures of a POW's life in Germany have been published in England and perhaps in New Zealand', he wrote, 'and you can believe them as being *tito*'.[9] '*Tito*' is the Māori word for lies. Pohe's assumption that German censors would not understand the meaning of *tito* proved correct—the letter arrived at his parents' home in New Zealand with this sentence intact.

Pohe's journey, which had taken him from New Zealand to Britain, ended far from home. He was one of the seventy-six Allied airmen who escaped from Stalag Luft III in March 1944, but was recaptured after six days. Fifty escapees were executed by the Gestapo and Pohe was one of these fifty. He is commemorated on the memorial at Stalag Luft III erected by fellow-prisoners in memory of the fifty officers who were murdered.

Despite Steve McQueen's starring appearance as an American airman in the Hollywood film of the escape from Stalag Luft III, no Americans were actually involved in the escape. The film pays little attention to the many escapees from the British Empire and from continental Europe, but off screen the escape demonstrates that the war fought from Britain was a multinational effort. The memorial for those who were murdered lists Allied airmen of many different nationalities—Australian, Belgian, British, Canadian, Czechoslovakian, French, Greek, Lithuanian, New Zealander, Norwegian, Polish, and South African. Most were serving with the wartime RAF. Only three Allied airmen escaped successfully—Per Bergsland and Jens Müller, who were both Norwegian pilots and Bram van der Stok, a Dutch pilot. Before capture, all had been serving in the RAF in Britain.

Movements to Britain

The diversity of airmen serving in the wartime RAF was one aspect of the unprecedented diversity of the population in Britain during the Second World War. Figures for wartime arrivals give some sense of the scale of movements to Britain. Half a million Canadians disembarked in Britain, most of them troops. By 1945, over half a million German and Italian prisoners of war were held in Britain. Over a quarter of a million Irish men and women left Southern Ireland (Éire) for Britain between 1939 and 1945, some to do war work and others as volunteers for the British armed forces.[10] Nearly three million Americans, mainly troops, arrived in Britain between 1942 and 1945.[11] (See Figure 0.3)

In *The True Glory* (1945)—an Anglo-American documentary film telling the story of the Allied victory in Europe from D-Day to German surrender—an American voice calls the diverse wartime population in Britain 'the big proposition'. 'Funny thing', he says 'on the way over you felt like you were the whole works...but then all over the UK you'd see things that made you begin to realise you were just part of a hell of a big proposition'. The American voice speaks over shots which make clear that the 'big proposition' which Americans encounter in Britain is a war effort undertaken by allies from all over the world. The range of Allied nationalities involved is shown in shots of men and women walking British streets in a wide variety of uniforms and headgear. Street signs advertising clubs and other organizations indicate where some of them come from—America, Canada, India, Newfoundland, New Zealand, Yugoslavia. The final sign shown in this sequence is for the United Nations Forces Club.[12]

Two weeks before the D-Day landings, when the numbers of American troops in Britain reached a high point, Mollie Panter-Downes, the journalist

Figure 0.3 United States army nurses leave their transport ship in England after crossing the Atlantic (© Imperial War Museum, EA 18096).

and novelist, in her regular 'Letter from London' for the *New Yorker*, provided a vivid description of a country full to capacity:

> Living on this little island just now uncomfortably resembles living on a vast combination of an aircraft carrier, a floating dock jammed with men, and a warehouse stacked to the ceiling with material labelled 'Europe'. It's not at all difficult for one to imagine that England's coastline can actually be seen bulging and trembling.[13]

Around 130,000 of the Americans who disembarked in Britain were African-American and there was ethnic diversity within many other groups.[14] Germans in wartime Britain included not only Jewish German refugees—most arriving before war was declared—but also German prisoners of war. New Zealander contingents were white and Maori. West Indian troops and war workers included African Caribbeans, Indo-Caribbeans, and white Caribbeans. The countries of origin of people arriving were so varied that writing about 'the big proposition' risks becoming a long list of different nationalities.

The First World War had brought almost a quarter of a million refugees to Britain from Belgium. The number of Belgian refugees in Britain during the Second World War was much smaller—some 15,000—and the Home Office estimated that the total number of refugees in Britain in 1943 was around 150,000.[15] But if Second World War refugees arriving were not as numerous as those who had arrived in the First World War, they were far more diverse by nationality. By 1939, 78,000 refugees from Austria, Germany, and Czechoslovakia had escaped to Britain.[16] In 1940, as German forces overran much of Europe, they were joined by a further wave of refugees, including Albanians, Belgians, Czechoslovakians, Danes, Dutch, French, Norwegians, and Poles. There were also British refugees—some 30,000 came from the Channel Islands before they were occupied by Germany, including 4,000 schoolchildren.[17] Most of the civilian population of Gibraltar, numbering some 15,000, were also evacuated, the majority bound for Britain.[18]

The numbers of troops and war workers who arrived from overseas were far greater in the Second World War than in the First World War and, like refugees, these arrivals were very diverse. In 1940, six European armies-in-exile were stationed in Britain—Belgian, Czech, French, Dutch, Norwegian, and Polish. This, like the arrival of a range of European governments-in-exile, was completely unprecedented. People who came from the British

Empire and Commonwealth to serve in the armed forces and as war workers included not only the half-million Canadians but also Africans, Australians, Indians, Newfoundlanders, New Zealanders, Maltese, and West Indians. Since Éire remained in the Commonwealth during the war—leaving in 1949—it could be argued that volunteers and war workers from Éire belong in this list. Éire was the only Commonwealth country to remain neutral throughout the war.

The American voice in *The True Glory* comments that the 'big proposition' could be seen 'all over the UK' and is right about this. *Mixing It*, charting the history of multinational, multi-ethnic wartime Britain, takes the reader to the four nations of the United Kingdom and to a number of the islands in the British Isles. German and Italian prisoner-of-war camps were sited in England, Northern Ireland, Scotland, and Wales. American contingents were concentrated in English counties, particularly in East Anglia and the South West, but the first American contingent sent to the United Kingdom disembarked in Northern Ireland. (Figure 0.4 shows African-American troops in Northern Ireland.)

In 1940 almost half the Belgian fishing fleet sailed for Britain, where it was spread out from the Dartmouth–Brixham area (south-west England) to Milford Haven (Wales) and to Fleetwood (Northern England).[19] A school for refugee children established by the Czechoslovakian government-in-exile was located from 1943 in Llanwrtyd Wells (Wales).[20] The Commando's X troop, made up predominantly of Jewish Austrians and Germans, trained in Aberdovey (Wales). When Dutch soldiers arrived, they were quartered at first in Porthcawl (Wales). Belgian soldiers were quartered in Tenby (Wales), French and Czechs in England. Most of the Polish and Norwegian armies-in-exile were in Scotland. Lumbermen from British Honduras recruited to do forestry work also went to Scotland.

Before the war, racial diversity in Britain had been most apparent in London and in seaport towns and cities like Liverpool, Bristol, Cardiff, and South Shields where seamen included Africans, Arabs, Caribbeans, Chinese, and South Asians. Some settled. Others came and went. They were counted in census figures if they were temporarily ashore or on board ships moored in British docks on census day.[21] In wartime, racial diversity continued to be characteristic of the merchant navy. The *Manchester Guardian*, covering King George VI's visit in 1941 to Liverpool, where he spent several hours with men of the merchant navy, reported that he met 'Norwegian and Dutch skippers and men as well as British and Indian sailors'. One Indian

Figure 0.4 African–American soldiers in Northern Ireland (by kind permission of the National Archives at College Park, Maryland).

told the King that he had been at sea for forty years. A Dutch captain told the King that in his crew lined up on the dockside were 'representatives of four of "our allies"—Dutch, Javanese, Chinese, and lascars'.[22] But wartime racial diversity extended well beyond seaport towns like Liverpool. Black American soldiers and black and South Asian British soldiers, airmen/women and war workers, including volunteers from the Empire, were stationed throughout the United Kingdom.

Many of the islands of the British Isles also became increasingly diverse. When the government introduced a policy of mass internment of enemy aliens in May 1940, many internees were sent to the Isle of Man. Hotels and boarding houses along its coastline were converted into the largest internment camp in Britain, surrounded by barbed wire. Internees travelled there by ferry from Liverpool. In 1940, they were mainly Austrian, German, and Italian, with some Japanese and Finnish internees arriving in 1941. There was also a substantial German presence in the Channel Islands, but for a very different reason—the Channel Islands were the only British territory to be invaded and occupied by Germany. German occupation led to the arrival of some 16,000 foreign workers on the Channel Islands, many of them slave labourers. They included Belgians, French Jews, Poles, Russians, and Ukrainians, as well as German, Czech, Dutch, and French political prisoners.[23]

On the Shetland Isles, off the north coast of Scotland, there was a substantial Norwegian presence. Small boats manned by Norwegian sailors sailed regularly in wartime from the Shetland Isles to Norway, to land weapons and supplies for the Norwegian resistance and to bring back refugees. This traffic was known in Norway as 'the Shetland Bus'.[24] On the Orkney Islands, also off the north coast of Scotland, Italian prisoners of war, brought in at the request of the Admiralty to construct the so-called 'Churchill Barrier' defences, also constructed the beautiful Orkney Italian Chapel on the previously uninhabited island of Lamb Holm, in two of the prison camp's Nissen huts.[25] They used materials retrieved from the hulks of German ships scuttled at Scapa Flow during the First World War.[26]

Historians of migrant and refugee movements to Britain often comment on the neglect of these topics in national history and public memory.[27] Such neglect is particularly apparent in histories and memories of Britain during the Second World War. There were no precedents for the scale of movements to Britain. But when the war ended, awareness of the diverse wartime population in Britain was lost and has played little part in public memories of the war. Some groups that fought with the British were forgotten not only by the British, but also by their compatriots.

Transnational Mixing

Michelle Hilmes, writing about the cultural relationship between British and American broadcasting, comments that 'the unthinking national preoccupation of historians simply overlooks the presence of the transnational or sweeps it under the rug'.[28] Her book is an example of an increasing 'transnational turn' in historical research in recent years concerned with movements across national boundaries—of peoples, ideas, media, commodities, technologies— with networks and connections that cross national boundaries, and with 'the ways in which past lives and events have been shaped by processes and relationships that have transcended the borders of nation states'.[29] *Mixing It* traces some of the rich histories that are sidelined in work that is dominated by a national frame of reference, demonstrating the many ways in which people of varied nationalities in Britain during the Second World War were connected with each other across national boundaries and connected with a multinational war effort in Britain.

Transnational themes are prominent in the story of the 'big proposition'. Journeys to Britain were often circuitous, involving people in crossing many national borders. They include the epic journey made by Zbigniew Siemaszko to join the Polish army, beginning on a horse-drawn sleigh from a village in Kazakhstan and reaching Scotland via Iran, Iraq, and South Africa. Some journeys—especially those from occupied Europe—were daring, improvised, and entirely unauthorized. Bram van der Stok, the Dutch pilot who later escaped successfully from Stalag Luft III, arrived in Scotland after stowing away on board a Swiss merchant ship sailing from Rotterdam. In 1941, *The Times*, recording the arrival of Belgians, Czechs, Dutch, French, Norwegians, and Poles to serve in the RAF, told a compelling story of journeys from occupied Norway:

> Many of these Norwegian flyers crossed the North Sea in small fishing vessels, others flew over. One 'escape' story is worth repeating. A Norwegian pilot, wearing civilian clothes, overheard some German airmen talking about a Heinkel 115 which they had left near by. He went straight to the machine and flew it to England.[30]

Other stories about daring escapes from occupied Europe featured in a
BBC radio series in 1942—*Escape to Freedom*. One episode, scripted by Louis
de Jong, a Jewish Dutch refugee who worked in the wartime BBC, described
three Dutch students making off with a Nazi seaplane 'practically under the
eyes of those who were guarding it' to fly to Britain.[31]

The unprecedented scale of movements meant that people mingled and
mixed in Britain across a range of national boundaries. They did so in a
variety of public and private places—on buses and trains, in the forces and
workplaces, in hospitals and schools, in places of leisure such as pubs and
dance halls, in the domestic space of private houses. *Mixing It* looks at the
experiences of those who arrived—their journeys to Britain; what they
made of the British and of each other; their service in the military and in
war work; and their contributions to British wartime culture, particularly to
film and broadcasting.

Through mixing and mingling, many people, including Britons, were
involved in multinational communities. When Jean Offenberg, a Belgian
pilot in the RAF's No. 145 Squadron, told an Australian that there were three
Belgians in B flight, as well as a Czech and an Anglo-Argentine, the Australian
responded, 'Well, that's fine. I'm a Digger. We shall be a fine bloody Russian
salad and there won't be any chance of getting bored'.[32] The 'fine bloody
Russian salad' in 145 Squadron was even more mixed than the one Offenberg
experienced in B flight, incorporating not only Argentinians, Australians,
Belgians, and Czechs, but also Americans, Britons, Canadians, New Zealanders,
Trinidadians, Poles, and South Africans.

Mixing across national boundaries brought many novel experiences, both
for the British and for those who arrived. Pierre Lefranc, a Parisian student,
travelled to Britain via Spain with fellow students to join the Free French.
He records, 'we arrived in a London full of people in uniform including
many women, a fact which amazed us'. Not all these uniforms were
military. Lefranc remembers 'WVS [Women's Voluntary Service] ladies' who
'smiled at us, handing out cake, chocolate—and cups of tea'.[33] Tadeusz
Szumowski, a Polish pilot, also remembers a welcome from the Women's
Voluntary Service when his ship docked at Plymouth in 1940 and he
encountered fish paste for the first time:

> It was pouring with rain—we had always known that it rained all the time in
> England—but our welcome was warm and friendly even if we could not
> understand a word that was said. As we disembarked ladies in green overalls
> handed each of us a mug of hot tea and some sandwiches... It was the first

hot drink we had had for days and we were glad of it. The sandwiches contained a thin filling of a peculiar pink spread which we found later to be fish paste—we were not hungry enough to take more than an experimental bite and threw them discreetly away.[34]

The Women's Voluntary Service welcome provided Alwyn Pindar— a volunteer for the RAF from the West Indies—with his first experience of being served by white people. When he disembarked at Greenock in 1945, he remembers:

> The WVS were there in full strength to greet us...These were the first white people we'd seen in such a capacity, that is, serving us, rather than the other way round. They were extremely pleasant, pouring out cups of hot brew and dishing out the biscuits with gusto, chatting, singing and joking as they did so. Their ebullience became contagious to such an extent that it buoyed us up, contributing a great deal to the reduction of our homesickness and melancholy.[35]

Others had different reactions to 'cups of hot brew'. Jean Offenberg—the Belgian pilot—wrote in his diary 'I shall never get used to this hideous beverage'.[36]

In the early stages of the war, members of the Women's Voluntary Service were as unfamiliar with offering tea and biscuits to West Indian servicemen as the West Indian servicemen were with being served by white women. A forester from British Honduras (now Belize), recruited to fell timber in Scotland, remembers:

> Some people had never seen coloured people before. In some parts of Scotland never seen a black man before...they really looked at you. They thought we were all from Africa. We never seen Africa, never knew anything about Africa. They said 'where did you learn to speak English'? I said 'that's my native tongue'.[37]

White Britons became increasingly familiar with meeting black servicemen, servicewomen and war workers as the war progressed. In 1943, a report on 'Feelings about America and the Americans' found that '44% of those questioned had at some time met American Negro soldiers...men three times as much as women'. The report was by Mass Observation—one of the main organizations collecting information on people's experiences and attitudes during the Second World War. It went on to comment, 'Among those who had met Negro troops, opinions were very strongly favourable, though women tended to be rather more critical than men'. Such meetings could challenge stereotypes. The report quoted from an interviewee who said, 'they are not like we've seen on the films... not stupid and dull... they are educated, some of them'. The report noted similar responses from other interviews, 'Bristol people who have come into contact with them [African-American troops] have little but praise. Impressed by their politeness and their standard of education'.[38] Another Mass Observation report also noted that mixing changed British attitudes to non-white people. 'This change', the report stated, 'has usually been brought about through personal meetings with either American Negro troops or Indian troops. A few speak of meeting other coloured people since the war. Nearly all who admit a change in attitude have become more friendly and more pro-colour'.[39]

There are similar accounts by people who arrived in wartime Britain of the way mixing could change attitudes to the British. Columbanus Deegan, an Irish volunteer for the RAF from Dublin, records a sea change in his view of them:

> I was educated by the Christian Brothers and their education was totally Ireland, patriotic, that English had fought and starved us, the famine, we'd all this history of antiBrits because that was the nature of our education... And then you found to your surprise, the English—and I'm saying it in all sincerity—were lovely people and they weren't the people you thought they were... they were kind and they were helpful and you made some tremendous friends.[40]

But mixing and mingling did not always lead to friendships. This book argues that although there is much evidence of welcome and hospitality from Britons for those arriving and of close friendships formed between allies of a range of nationalities, there was also considerable inter-allied tension, sometimes extending to violence. It considers not only the good relationships that often characterized mixing in the forces and in domestic settings, but also some of the main causes of tension and conflict.

Throughout the war, the British media paid little attention to inter-allied conflict, celebrating a multinational community fighting with or alongside the British and inviting Britons to imagine themselves as members of this community. The True Glory, with its enthusiasm for the 'big proposition', provides a late example of such celebration. But even in 1940—a year subsequently remembered as one when Britain stood alone—the media publicized the arrival of troops from the British Empire and from the continent and began to promote a vision of a multinational community united in a common fight for freedom and civilization against Nazi tyranny and barbarity. As other countries entered the war, this vision expanded to include new allies. Although the government sponsored a great deal of wartime propaganda celebrating what I call here an 'allies' war', the private records of government policy-makers are often at odds with the image that the government promoted. This image was one of British liberality and tolerance, explicitly or implicitly in contrast to that of Nazi Germany. How tolerant was wartime Britain?

Tolerant Britain?

The question of how far Britain lived up to the image of a decent, tolerant nation that was widely disseminated in wartime has been the subject of a considerable literature, but has no easy answers.[41] *Mixing It* is concerned not only with the histories of people who journeyed to Britain, but also with the history of British responses to them, which were complex and varied.

In mid-1940, when imminent invasion by Germany was widely expected, hostility to foreigners in Britain was intense and widespread. According to wartime surveys, the government policy of mass internment of people of enemy nationality, introduced in May 1940, had considerable popular support. Hostility often extended to all foreigners, regardless of their nationality. Suspicions that they worked as spies and fifth columnists were fostered by allegations in the press and by some politicians. A report from Birmingham in early June 1940 noted that spies were 'seen all over the place'.[42] Two days later, following Italy's declaration of war, there were anti-Italian riots in many British towns and cities.

After mid-1940, there is much evidence of the persistence of hostility, discrimination, and racism. There were many instances of the operation of a colour bar in Britain, often blamed on white Americans. Mass Observation and Home Intelligence—the two main organizations collecting information on public opinion—regularly reported the persistence of anti-Semitism. This book traces two main shifts within varied and sometimes contradictory popular attitudes. It argues that after 1940, there was a shift towards greater tolerance, away from the intense anti-alienism of the mid-1940 moment, but that, as the war was ending and in its aftermath, the climate shifted again to one of increased hostility to foreigners.

Mixing It focuses on three key factors that shaped the experience of those arriving and British responses to them. The first is speech and language.

The arrival of refugees, exiles, troops, and war workers made Britain increasingly multilingual—their voices and accents changed British soundscapes. When physical markers of difference such as skin colour were absent, it was language and speech that marked people out as different, and as foreigners. Changing soundscapes could provoke hostility. A cartoon in the *Sunday Dispatch* in 1943 showed an encounter between two Englishmen wearing bowler hats in a London square which is full of foreigners. It offered a vision of the English as strangers within their capital city, surrounded by foreigners speaking other languages. Only a small enclave is left, in a corner of the square labelled 'English spoken here'.[43] But the presence of people in Britain who spoke a very wide range of languages was an asset to the war effort, particularly to wartime propaganda. At the BBC, their work as translators, scriptwriters and speakers was indispensable for the rapid expansion of services broadcasting to Europe and the wider world, giving BBC messages their global reach.

A second factor shaping attitudes and experiences was British women's relationships with men of Allied and enemy nationality in Britain, both white and black. The government assigned the Women's Voluntary Service a key role in welcoming troops and in welfare work with refugees—providing cups of tea and clothing, finding accommodation—but when women's relationships with non-British men went beyond the provision of hospitality, they attracted criticism and hostility and were a main cause of inter-allied violence. A man interviewed by Mass Observation offered a different version of the multinational community of allies from the one projected and celebrated in the British media:

> I went for a walk with my wife on Wimbledon Hill last weekend. Americans everywhere with a girl on each arm. Free Frenchies the same. But if ever there was one of our own Tommies to be seen, he'd be walking all on his lonesome. No girls for him, poor chap; he's got no money. The other night, we walked out on Clapham Common. Just the same thing there. I saw one free Frenchman with <u>three</u> girls hanging round him. And a good many Americans, all with girls too. And one of our poor old Tommies sitting all by himself on a seat, watching them. I'm sometimes sorry for the younger chaps who see it all— they must wonder sometimes what they're fighting for, with the women all going off with the aliens.[44]

I have coined the term 'sexual patriotism' to describe what popular opinion demanded. It was generally hostile to interracial sex and often laid down further and more extensive rules and requirements for British women—the avoidance of sexual relationships with all men who were not native-born Britons. These rules were generally female only—British men's relationships with non-British women attracted little attention. *Mixing It* traces women's diverse responses to the demands that they should be sexually patriotic— many flouted the rules that popular opinion laid down for them.

Uniforms also played a significant role in responses to those arriving and in answers to the question of which people in wartime Britain were enemies and which were allies. Were Germans enemies when they were wearing British military uniform? *Mixing It* argues that 'enemy' and 'neutral' were categories with unstable meanings and that many people shifted their place on a spectrum that had 'enemy' at one end and 'ally' at the other. Germans and Italians were positioned at the 'enemy' end of this spectrum in 1940, when they faced internment by the British government. But those who joined the British forces on release from internment found that a British uniform eroded the idea that they were enemies and brought them some recognition as allies.

Military uniforms worn by men and women of Allied nationalities were increasingly regarded as a sign that they were fighting with or alongside the British and were therefore welcome—more welcome than those who came as civilians or refugees. Cy Grant, from British Guiana (now Guyana), volunteered for the RAF and arrived in Britain in 1941. He records, 'A war was on and I was wearing a uniform. People were generally friendly'.[45] According to Tadeusz Szumowski—the Polish airman who encountered fish paste for the first time on arrival in Britain—the uniform did not even have to be smart. Szumowski's uniform was battered during his journey from Poland via Bucharest and Malta to Marseilles. In France, he was issued with the dark blue uniform of the French Air Force. As France fell, this uniform was battered in its turn in his journey to Britain on a collier. After arriving in Britain, he was sent to a training camp in West Kirby, and records, 'Here we met up with colleagues who had arrived in England by various routes and basked in the smiling, obviously admiring faces of English people looking at us over the perimeter fencing. We might have worn uniforms which were dirty and decidedly past their best but at least we were recognised as sturdy welcome allies'.[46]

Even though many wartime arrivals departed when the war was over, the population in Britain in the aftermath of war continued to be more multi-national and multi-ethnic than it had been pre-war. However, the reception given to people who stayed on when the war was over or arrived in its aftermath was increasingly frosty. Most West Indians who had served in Britain were demobbed back home. Those who returned were no longer in uniform, but in civvies, no longer 'allies', but 'immigrants'. Alan Wilmot, from Jamaica, who served with RAF Sea Rescue, went back to Jamaica when the war was over, but subsequently returned to Britain. He records of this return:

> It was frightening because you feel...you have been here before, so you should be more or less able to fit in. But being a civilian was a completely different thing from being in the services...The thing was 'What you come back here for? The war's over. What you come back here for? Why didn't you stay home'? That was the attitude...For instance, you could go into a pub, and the pub would go dead quiet as you walk in...because you were a novelty then...'Why you come back here'?[47]

When the war was over, walls near Polish Air Force stations were daubed with 'Poles Go Home' and 'England for the English'.[48] Tony Sosna, who served in the Polish army in Scotland, remembers:

> After the war there were some people in Scotland already, mostly politically motivated, who...were hostile towards us...these people who try to be hostile to us, they had the support of the press in many instances...we are not needed any more, we are alright when we are fighting for our and your freedoms—that was alright, but now some of them think that our usefulness has ceased, so we should go...It would be unfair to say that it was all—all the society—we had a lot, a lot of friends here, but...some part of—of the community.[49]

The findings of the Gallup Poll held in Britain in June 1946 suggest that the view that Poles were not needed any more and should go back home was held by a substantial proportion of the community. Only 30 per cent of those questioned agreed with the government scheme that allowed Poles to remain.[50] Allies were also increasingly forgotten in the media in the aftermath of war, when attention shifted to the war fought by the British and the vision of an 'allies' war', so prominent in wartime, rapidly receded.

Individual Stories

The individual stories told in *Mixing It* are very varied. Some of those who arrived felt welcome, others were interned or faced discrimination and hostility. Some found wartime Britain exciting, others were bored. Many stories are strongly informed by a sense of exile and a longing to return home. There are accounts of homesickness and loneliness. Max Herrmann-Neiße, a German poet, came to Britain in 1933 after Hitler's rise to power, because of his revulsion against a regime which he described as 'aggressive, lawless, intolerant... hostile to freedom and ruthless in its worship of power'. One of his poems, written in Hyde Park soon after his arrival, reads, in translation:

> I sat opposite Byron
> On the park bench
> Cars hurtled wildly past
> And my heart was sick for home.[51]

Jimmy Hyde, a pilot from Trinidad, had 'no friend, no girl, no one in all England. I am alone and the only time I feel at all happy is when I am in my Spitfire alone in the clouds'.[52] Hyde was killed in action in a dogfight over Holland in 1944.

Many journeys, like those made by Jimmy Hyde and Porokuru Pohe, ended in death far away from home and family. In an entry in his diary in 1941, Jean Offenberg, the Belgian pilot, recorded the death of a fellow pilot from New Zealand who had fought in the Battle of Britain:

> A veteran of twenty, little Langdon from New Zealand... has been brought down over Malta. He was a quiet boy whose face had not yet lost the traces of childhood. He had been brought down far from home, defending a strip of island which he knew only from having seen it on the school maps at Wellington in his own country. He died as a pilot of twenty with 1,000 flying hours and more than 100 combats to his credit.[53]

Pilot Officer Charles Langdon, commemorated in this diary entry by a Belgian pilot, is also commemorated on the Commonwealth Air Forces Memorial at Floriana in Malta, along with many other airmen who have no known grave.

In a later diary entry, Offenberg records that he told a British colleague, '[T]he difference between us is that I've no longer a home, so I want to get on with the job and finish the war as quickly as possible... Each time we go up we ought to shoot down as many as possible. The more we do the quicker I shall return home'.[54] This conversation suggests Offenberg's confidence that he would get home eventually. At other times, he wondered if he would ever see Belgium again. On a sortie to the French coast, realizing how close he was to Belgium, he flew further and saw Dixmude, Roulers, and Nieuport, but only from the air. In January 1942, Offenberg was killed in a crash with another Spitfire and was buried in Digby—a small village in Lincolnshire.[55] Frank Ziegler, a fellow officer in No. 609 Squadron, wrote an epitaph:

> Here in a corner of an English shire
> Far from the homeland that he fought to save,
> A Belgian pilot sleeps.[56]

Many graves and cemeteries in Britain bear witness to the presence of a multinational community in wartime. When the war was over this community was largely forgotten, and it rarely features in the countless histories, radio and television programmes, novels, films, and websites that tell the story of Britain during the Second World War. There are many studies of particular national and ethnic groups in wartime Britain, but no work that has taken the 'big proposition' as its subject and traced the rich histories involved in the movements of refugees and exiles, servicemen and servicewomen, war workers and prisoners of war to Britain.[57] *Mixing It* is the first book to chart this history.

A Note on Sources

Mixing It draws on a range of studies of particular national groups in wartime Britain and is very indebted to them. For evidence about transnational journeys and encounters and for the experiences of migrants, refugees, troops, and war workers of diverse nationalities and ethnicities in wartime Britain, *Mixing It* draws on personal narratives. These include autobiographies, biographies, diaries, letters, and oral accounts given in interviews. There are many more by men than by women. Most of the autobiographies and memoirs were written when the war was over and their accounts may be coloured by the passage of time. The same applies to oral history that has been collected in the post-war period. Diaries and letters that were written in wartime do not pose this problem, but their authors may not be representative of wider groups. Even so, personal narratives offer insights into people's experiences, anxieties, and hopes, and expand and complicate our understanding of life in Britain during the conflict.

For attitudes to those arriving, Mass Observation directives and surveys are invaluable. They provide evidence, often vividly expressed, about public opinion on different groups in wartime Britain, with titles that include 'Public feeling on aliens', 'Feelings about Americans', 'Feelings about Australians', 'Feelings about Czechs', 'Feelings on Foreigners'.[58] These surveys and directives did not always focus on people in Britain, but the survey on 'Feelings about Czechs' chose Leamington as one of the places where interviews were conducted. The reason for this choice was that 'Czech forces were stationed there for a period, and thus the population of Leamington might be presumed to have more than an average acquaintance with Czechs'.[59] The survey on 'Feelings on Foreigners' was designed to gather information about attitudes to foreigners in Britain, asking, 'How has the presence of all these troops of different nationalities affected your feelings about foreigners? Have you personally met (foreign soldiers)? If so what do you think of them'?[60] When interviewed, people often mentioned experience of contact with foreigners, either at first or at second hand. In the survey on 'Feelings about Czechs', one man responded, 'There's a whole camp of Czechs near Banbury, where my people live, and I hear on all hands how popular they are with the townspeople. And Banbury is very fussy indeed: it couldn't stand our own evacuees at any price'.[61]

Mass Observation directives asked for written answers to questions from a panel that Mass Observation described as 'biased in a middle-class direction, consisting of people of more than average intelligence and broad-mindedness'.[62] But street interviews conducted in a range of places were with people of all classes. What had been said in short interviews was later typed onto small pieces of paper with information that gave the gender, age, and social class to which the interviewer assigned the interviewee. Interviewers may have asked the age and occupation of interviewees, but it seems likely that what they recorded under these headings was sometimes guesswork. Social class D was at the bottom and Social Class A at the top. For example, 'F 40 C' indicated the interviewer's record of the age and class of a woman interviewed in Hampstead on her 'feelings about foreigners', including whether the presence of troops of different nationalities had affected these feelings. She said, 'I feel very proud of them. And, yes I expect it has really made me like foreigners better'.[63] When Mass Observation street interviews are quoted in Mixing It, the interviewer's record of the gender, social class, and age of the person speaking is given in the footnotes for each.

During the war, the British state amassed information on public opinion and attitudes, including information on attitudes to those arriving as refugees, troops, war workers, and prisoners of war. The Ministry of Information, set up in September 1939, compiled daily Home Intelligence reports on the state of popular morale from May to September 1940, and weekly summaries after that. Its early activities prompted a short-lived press campaign which named people conducting its investigations as 'home-made Gestapo', 'spies', and 'snoopers'—the name 'Cooper's snoopers' after Duff Cooper, Minister of Information, quickly caught on.[64]

In 1940, Home Intelligence daily reports frequently mentioned popular opinion of foreigners in Britain—including refugees and troops—as well as responses to the government's policy of mass internment.[65] Later weekly reports offer considerable evidence about popular attitudes to war workers from Éire, German and Italian prisoners of war in Britain, and American troops. Since Home Intelligence reports drew on the work of Mass Observation, it is not surprising that their findings were often similar. The methods used by Home Intelligence and Mass Observation, such as eavesdropping on people's conversations and reporting on them, fell far short of those deployed by social scientists. Even so, their findings provide rich evidence that demonstrates the diversity of British popular opinion. *Mixing It* attempts to do justice to this diversity.

The Ministry of Information directly sponsored many publications and documentary films and its wartime files in the National Archives at Kew therefore include some film scripts. Many of these scripts are for films celebrating a multinational community of allies. There was often considerable divergence between this government-sponsored celebration of allies and the views that policy-makers recorded confidentially. Divergent opinion can also be found within these confidential records. Different Ministries did not always see eye to eye and officials within the same Ministry sometimes held different views. For example, policy-makers at the Colonial Office generally sought to avoid policies that were discriminatory against black troops and war workers recruited from the empire to serve in Britain. Other government Ministries often advocated covert discrimination, attempting to ensure that black troops and war workers from the empire were demobbed back home and did not settle in Britain when the war was over.[66]

Mixing It draws on a range of British media, including films, BBC broadcasts, and national, regional, and local newspapers to look at the wartime vision of a war fought by a multinational community of allies. Media archives demonstrate that men and women from continental Europe, the Empire, and America, who worked in the wartime British media, made a considerable contribution to the development of this vision and that it was extensively disseminated. Given the size and diversity of the audiences for newspapers, film, and radio, evidence on the reception of British media is necessarily problematic, but there was considerable wartime research. The government's efforts to find out how British media were received at home and overseas included audience research conducted by the Ministry of Information. Home Intelligence reports also supplied information on the reception of BBC programmes, often drawing on BBC research. This BBC research developed in wartime, when its Listener Research Section was expanded, and upgraded to the status of a Department. Research done through local correspondents' reports, panel reports, and special investigations provided the basis for weekly Listener Research Reports and Bulletins, which often quoted individual comments that had been collected.[67]

Postal Censorship was one of the sources used by Home Intelligence in compiling its reports. Postal Censorship reports were seen at the highest levels of government and always quoted from letters that had been intercepted. Since many people were aware that their letters were censored, what they wrote cannot always be taken at face value. Were some letters written to curry favour with the authorities which censored them? This was a possibility raised by a Postal Censorship report on letters written by internees held in British internment camps after the introduction of mass internment of enemy aliens. The report noted 'a large number of pro-British letters which may or may not be genuine and a small proportion of bitter and anti-British comments'.[68] It is also possible that people used the knowledge that their letters would be read by censors to address appeals and protests to the authorities. A letter written in August 1940 by an internee seems likely to have been one of these. He protested, 'It is beyond all reason that Nobel prize-winners, clergymen, professors and invalids up to 65 years should live in tents in the English climate'.[69]

A Polish soldier addressed the censor directly in a letter of February 1944, shortly after the signing of the Yalta agreement by the so-called 'Big Three' leaders of Britain, the Soviet Union, and the United States—an agreement that consigned much of Poland to the Soviet sphere of influence. His letter reverses the usual direction of censorship, issuing instructions to the censor on what can and what cannot be said about Poland, as well as instructions not to cut out the truth about Poland. The view he takes of censorship anticipates twenty-first century debates about nations that see themselves as 'great democracies' but practise surveillance on a wide scale.

Never, never congratulate our people of Warsaw and Poland being 'liberated'. This sounds like the most cruel irony and is deeply resented by every Pole. You could speak about a lamb being liberated from a bear by a tiger. A day will come when most if not all of the British people I like and love so much, will understand full meaning of what I am saying—including the censor who is probably wondering if he has to cut out certain sentences of this letter or destroy it as a whole. Don't do it, it is not propaganda—it is truth and remember that the only countries where we Poles can express our thoughts and feelings are your great democracies Great Britain and United States. If you order us to close our mouths—I ask you—what are we fighting for?[70]

Figure 1.1 Mary Mulry (by kind permission of Kathy Lowe).

I

1940

In September 1940, Mary Mulry (see Figure 1.1) wrote in her diary:

> There is a marvellous feeling of international camaraderie in London—everybody pulling together—and there is great friendliness. We talked with a young Polish airman on the bus. His English was very limited but we gathered that he and many other of his compatriots are training to fly Spitfires and Hurricanes.[1]

Mary Mulry was from County Galway in Southern Ireland (Éire), which remained neutral during the war. She wrote this diary entry when she was on a trip to London with Pierre—a Frenchman she met while nursing him at the Kent and Sussex hospital. Mulry arrived in Britain at the age of eighteen, in August 1939, to begin training as a nurse at Guy's—one of the large teaching hospitals in London. She moved to the Kent and Sussex hospital in Tunbridge Wells when Guy's evacuated its staff and patients to hospitals in the country.

The year 1940 is widely regarded as a momentous one in British history—the year of Dunkirk, the Battle of Britain, and the Blitz. Mulry nursed people who were injured in all these events. Her diary dates the beginning of the 'real war', as she experienced it, to 31 May, 1940:

> It was about 2 p.m. that the ambulances started to arrive. I was ordered to report to Casualty Sister, a being who terrifies me...As I entered the Casualty department, I was astounded to see so many wet, dirty and injured people there. Some were soldiers (I guessed they must be Dunkirk survivors), the others were civilians...Several of the men had their skin flayed by oil burns, a very painful condition, others were injured by bomb splinters, and some were injured by machine-gun fire from the air as they came across the Channel.[2]

One of Mulry's patients, called John, with a fractured tibia and fibula, was the captain of the *Brighton Belle*—a steamer which had once taken holidaymakers on pleasure trips. John had taken the *Brighton Belle* to Dunkirk to evacuate troops and told Mulry that 'it was on the return journey [from Dunkirk], with four hundred exhausted soldiers aboard, that she [the *Brighton Belle*] struck the wreck of a ship and slowly sank'. John had managed to transfer the soldiers on board to another ship. Mary's diary records what John told her about the vessels involved in evacuating troops, 'It was apparently the queerest and most nondescript flotilla that ever was, and manned by all kinds of people, English, Belgian, French'.[3]

Mulry describes Pierre—her companion on the bus journey in London where she noticed the 'marvellous feeling of international camaraderie'—as 'slim and dark, with beautiful brown eyes and masses of Gallic charm' and comments that 'his fractured English is delightful'. While she was nursing him, Pierre told her about his plans to remain in Britain and become a member of the Free French Army, and invited her to dinner. Accepting such an invitation was against hospital rules, which also forbade speaking to patients about anything other than their treatment—a rule that Mulry broke regularly. She also broke the rule against accepting an invitation from a patient, 'Pierre is charming. I shall go out with him'.[4] Mulry's meeting with Pierre did not go unnoticed. It was reported by senior nurses and she was reprimanded by the hospital Matron, who told her that in her work report she was criticized for spending too much time talking to the patients and that she was 'far too flighty'.

Mulry continued to see Pierre intermittently until 1942, when he told her that he would be returning to France to join the French resistance. The last entry in her diary for 1940 records a visit to London on leave, where she met Pierre. Together they witnessed a sight which subsequently became an iconic symbol of the London Blitz:

> We could hear planes overhead but it was not until we walked across Westminster Bridge that we realised the full horror of the situation. The whole city was ablaze. It was like bright daylight and had we felt so inclined it would have been possible to read a newspaper. We could see the dome of St Paul's standing out against an awesome background of flame.

In August, Mulry had witnessed the Battle of Britain in the skies over Kent, watching dogfights, planes bursting into flame, and white parachutes opening and dropping—sometimes becoming entangled in trees or even a church tower. 'All this has become a commonplace everyday event now', she wrote. She nursed Battle of Britain pilots, 'most of them with burns'. She also nursed German prisoners of war who had been captured after parachuting into Kent. They included Helmut, described in her diary as 'a typical blond Aryan German youth'. His parachute had landed on top of a church steeple and he refused to come down, despite ladders provided by the Fire Brigade. The Local Defence Force and the Air Raid Precautions were also on the scene and decided to ignore him, getting out their flasks of tea and sandwiches. Helmut came down eventually, when he was hungry.[5]

By October, Mulry was nursing victims of the London Blitz:

> In the lonely hours of the night they tell me over and over again how awful the days and nights of bombing have been for them. Some have lost their homes and their relatives and are still in a state of severe shock. Harry Smith lost his wife and daughter in a raid and is here for the amputation of his left foot. He is remarkably cheerful. It will be difficult for Hitler to break the spirit of people like Harry.[6]

The term 'multinational' was not widely used in the 1940s, but Mulry uses it on several occasions in her diary. In 1944, she became one of the thousands of Irish volunteers for the British armed forces, joining Queen Alexandra's Imperial Military Nursing Service—the British Army's nursing branch. Figure 1.2 shows Mary Mulry in uniform. Posted to Normandy, she nursed casualties of the D-day landings and described her ward as a 'multi-national microcosm of a Europe at war'.

In 1940, Mulry wrote about a trip to London with Pierre, 'We mingled with the multi-national crowd in the West End for a couple of hours. There are many Polish and Czech soldiers here at present and the raucous voices of the Aussies are still recognisable'.[7] Mulry's presence as an Irishwoman—accompanied by a Frenchman—contributed to the multinational composition of this crowd, as well as to the 'international camaraderie' she experienced on the London bus.

The multinational crowd witnessed by Mulry was a result of extensive movements to Britain in 1940, including troops from Australia, Canada, and New Zealand. After France fell and Germany overran and occupied much of Europe, many European nationals began arriving from the continent. The evacuation from Dunkirk, named Operation Dynamo, which brought more than 338,000 troops and refugees to Britain, is well known. There were some Belgians, French, and Poles among those evacuated, although the majority were British. But under subsequent lesser-known evacuations—named Operations Aerial and Cycle—many more European nationals embarked from French ports, mainly in Western France. Troops and civilians

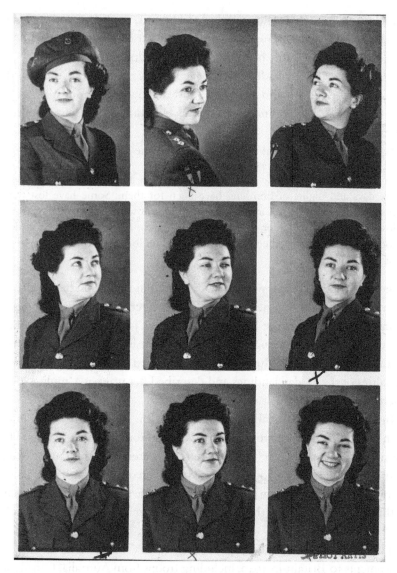

Figure 1.2 Mary Mulry in uniform after joining Queen Alexandra's Imperial Military Nursing Service (by kind permission of Kathy Lowe).

brought to Britain under Operation Aerial numbered some 150,000, including 24,352 Poles, 17,062 French, 4,398 Czechs, and 163 Belgians.[8] Many other European nationals, including Belgians, Czechs, Danes, Dutch, French, Norwegians, and Poles, acted on their own initiative to make their way to Britain.

These movements to Britain involved the development of multinational communities—particularly in the armed forces—and the 'international camaraderie' that Mulry experienced on the London bus. But there was also a great deal of hostility to foreigners in Britain in 1940, which began to build in the early months of the year and reached a high point in May and June, when the invasion of Britain by Germany was widely anticipated.

The targets of particular hostility were people whose nationality identified them as 'enemies'—Austrian and German refugees who had escaped to Britain before war was declared, and the Italian community in Britain. Such hostility was evident in the introduction of mass internment of people of enemy nationality—which had considerable public support—and in the anti-Italian riots of June. But there was also widespread suspicion of all foreigners as potential spies and fifth columnists, which meant that refugees arriving from the continent in mid-1940 were given a mixed reception. People arriving in military uniforms were generally exempted from hostility and often warmly welcomed. This chapter traces the beginnings of a change of climate as the threat of imminent invasion began to recede—a shift away from the intense hostility and suspicion directed at many foreigners in mid-1940 toward greater tolerance.

Journeys to Britain

The 'real war' started for Mary Mulry as a result of the evacuations of soldiers and civilians from Dunkirk. The name of this French port features prominently in British memories of 1940, where it stands for what was described by Churchill as a 'miracle of deliverance'.[9] The idea of a merciful deliverance was taken up in the press and quickly developed, in a celebration of what the *Daily Express* called 'the amateur sailors of England' and their 'ragged armada'.[10] J. B. Priestley, broadcasting about Dunkirk on 5 June, defied Ministry of Information instructions that a focus on England, rather than Britain, should be avoided in wartime propaganda:

> But here at Dunkirk is another English epic. And to my mind what was most characteristically English about it...was the part played in the difficult and dangerous embarkation—not by the warships, magnificent though they were—but by the little pleasure steamers...They seemed to belong to the same ridiculous holiday world as...automatic machines and crowded sweating

promenades. But they were called out of that world . . . Yes, these "Brighton Belles" and "Brighton Queens" left that innocent foolish world of theirs—to sail into the inferno, to defy bombs, shells, magnetic mines, torpedoes, machine-gun fire—to rescue our soldiers . . . the little holiday steamers made an excursion to hell and came back glorious.[11]

When he wrote this broadcast, Priestley cannot have known the fate of the *Brighton Belle* and the *Brighton Queen*. Both sailed to Dunkirk, but neither came back glorious. The *Brighton Belle*, as its captain told Mary Mulry, 'struck the wreck of a ship' as she was returning 'and slowly sank.' The *Brighton Queen* was shelled and sunk off Dunkirk on 1 June.

Although Churchill called the Dunkirk evacuation 'a miracle of deliverance' in his defiant 'we shall fight them on the beaches' speech to the House of Commons on 4 June, he also urged that this deliverance should not be assigned the attributes of a victory. Thankfulness for the escape of so many men, he said, 'must not blind us to the fact that what has happened in France and Belgium is a colossal military disaster'.[12] Priestley's celebration of Dunkirk as an English epic had no appeal for the French. From a French perspective, as historian Philip Bell comments, Dunkirk was 'a disaster on the road to further disasters'.[13]

Evacuations under Operations Dynamo, Aerial, and Cycle were more multinational than is usually remembered. They not only brought many European nationals to Britain, but also involved multinational ships and seamen. As the captain of the *Brighton Belle* told Mary Mulry, Belgian and French seamen were involved in Operation Dynamo. Belgian fishing boats were part of the 'ragged armada' of small craft—the *Lydie Suzanne*, the *Zwaluw*, the *Cor Jésu*, the *Jonge Jan*, and the *A5* evacuated a total of 941 people.[14] Belgian seamen were presented with decorations for the role they played and four Belgian fishing boats and two Belgian tugs were sunk by enemy action.[15] Belgian and Polish ships were also involved in Operations Aerial and Cycle. They included the Polish liners *Batory* and *Sobieski* and Polish colliers, coasters, and cargo vessels.[16] The expectation that Polish ships had a duty to evacuate Polish troops was evident later in 1940 when the Polish government-in-exile approached the British government to recommend British merchant seamen for Polish decorations to honour their role in evacuating Poles. In reply to a query about the award of decorations to honour the role of Polish seamen in the evacuations, the Ministry of Transport was told by the Polish authorities, 'Polish Masters would naturally be expected to help Polish troops and . . . the Polish Government would look for a higher standard before giving an award to a Polish Master than in the case of a foreign Master'.[17]

Arthur Mowbray, Head Postmaster of the Post Office in Dover, described people arriving from the evacuations as 'queerly clad, many wet through, tired to the point of exhaustion, dirty and wounded'. His diary also records that they were troops and civilians of many nationalities:

> In the Telegraph Room [at Dover Post Office]—special arrangements had to be made on the spot, as boats of every size imaginable were emptied of their human cargoes hundreds of telegrams were handed in... Needless to say, the counter was thronged from morning till night and the hours of business were extended to cope with the situation. Most of the pressure was due to evacuated troops, and refugees in their hundreds who accompanied the troops. People of British, French, Belgian, Dutch, Polish and unidentifiable nationalities turned the Public Office into a tower of Babel.[18]

Polish troops who made their way to Britain were under orders to do so. General Sikorski, Prime Minister of the Polish government-in-exile, broadcast on the BBC on 19 June—five days after German troops had entered Paris—instructing them to make for the French ports, where ships were standing by to take them to Britain.[19] In contrast, many Belgian airmen were under orders not to leave France. The King of Belgium surrendered to Germany in late May, but members of the Belgian government wanted to continue the fight. This caused some confusion. The Belgian Foreign Minister, Paul-Henri Spaak, approached the British government in mid-June asking for facilities to be given for the evacuation of Belgian troops from France.[20] At the same time, Belgian airmen who had withdrawn to the South of France after the German invasion of Belgium were ordered to stay there. A number of them disobeyed this order. Jean Offenberg, the Belgian pilot, sought his officer's blessing for his plan to take one of the Belgian air force's remaining aeroplanes—a Fiat—to escape. In his diary, he recorded what his officer told him. 'You're mad Offenberg. If you leave without orders you will be posted as a deserter. Don't make your case any worse by pinching a Fiat into the bargain... I forbid you to move from here'.[21] Offenberg disobeyed this order. Some of the Belgian pilots and pilot cadets who crossed the English Channel were tried *in absentia* for desertion in French courts.[22]

The exile and separation from family involved in the passage to Britain represented one further stage of a long journey into exile for many of those arriving. Czech and Slovak airmen who crossed the border into Poland or

Hungary in 1939 after the German invasion of Czechoslovakia began a series of journeys that took them across Yugoslavia, Greece, Italy, Turkey, and Syria to arrive in France or French North African colonies. One Czechoslovak airman wrote to a friend about his journey into exile, 'The outbreak of war and the French mobilisation found some of us in Africa, in the first regiment of the Foreign Legion stationed at Sidi-bel-Ades. We had been serving as infantry; now we were ordered to join the French Air Force... And we stand there on the railway station and wait for the train... No one has come to say goodbye to us. We are without homeland, parents, sweethearts'.[23]

Antoni Slonimski, a Polish poet and playwright who sailed from France to Britain, wrote of his feelings about his journey into further exile:

> We came here [Britain] disillusioned and embittered by defeat, fleeing for the second time. Crowded into little cargo-boats and colliers, we left France sadder than when we had left Poland to continue the struggle, because then we were leaving our own country with an unshakable faith in final victory, convinced of the transient nature of our exile. But, when the shores of France vanished from our sight a cloud of sorrow and despondency obscured our hope and our faith.[24]

Wladyslaw Struk, a young Polish airman who was evacuated from St-Jean-de-Luz harbour on the *Arandora Star*—one of the last ships sailing to Britain in Operation Aerial—also faced permanent exile. On a picture postcard written in Saint-Jean-de-Luz just before he embarked, and addressed to his family in Chodorow, he wrote, 'I am leaving France because this is my fate... I can't describe to you how I feel... but I am surprised how I manage to bear it. I am writing these words to you, I know that they will not reach your hands, but I will keep this memorable thought that one day God will allow me to read these words to you myself as evidence that I remembered you'. The postcard, found by his daughter among his papers after his death, was never posted.[25] Struk reached Liverpool on 27 June—two days after France formally surrendered. He never saw his family in Poland again, dying in Britain in 1999.

Poles, Czechs, and Slovaks in France who boarded ships for Britain not only faced further exile and separation from family, but also the possibility of life or death in a Nazi-occupied country. There was every reason to expect the imminent invasion of Britain after the fall of France. Opting for Britain in 1940 was not a decision to be taken lightly. People whose journey to Britain was motivated by their determination to continue the fight have left more records than those who did not share this determination. Many Czechs and Slovaks who had fought in France chose voluntary demobilization after France fell. Some accepted safe conduct back to the Protectorate, agreeing to spread defeatist propaganda.[26] When 27 Belgian officers petitioned for the establishment of a Belgian military unit in Britain, only a minority of the Belgian troops who had been evacuated chose to continue the fight.[27] Many French troops who arrived in Britain opted for repatriation to France rather than joining the British army or the Free French.[28]

Miroslav Liskutin, a Czech pilot who had been fighting in France, was one of those who determined to continue the fight and opted for Britain. As France was collapsing, he was in Merignac and hoped to fly out before the Germans arrived. His senior officer offered no orders or suggestions, but told Liskutin that he was hoping to reach England somehow as 'the only country still at war with Hitler, and likely to keep fighting'. Liskutin, sharing this hope, identified various aircraft that he could use for an escape, but found them all sabotaged. He decided that Bordeaux harbour was his best bet:

> On reaching the harbour we found that the remaining ships at the quayside were getting ready to leave. The first ship I tried was a Polish cargo vessel, evacuating their own nationals. Approaching the duty officer at the gangway, I explained in my best though inadequate Polish that we were Czechoslovak aviators. He was quick in urging us to step on board, his captain had already given approval to take other Allied servicemen too. The other important point was that their destination was England... this was one of the last ships to leave Bordeaux before the Germans arrived.[29]

Liskutin's account records his uncertainty about the future:

> The overall situation was rather frightening, but my emotions were numb with shock. This tragedy which had overtaken France had sunk in, creating a feeling of dismay, bordering on physical pain. My mind was filled with sad thoughts... What will happen to France? Is England still fighting? What may be the situation awaiting us in England?

On board, he picked up a few bits of news. The only welcome information was confirmation of a British refusal to capitulate. 'Our aim', he remembers, 'was only to get somehow to Britain. There we saw a hope of a new start and perhaps a better tomorrow'. It was not until his arrival in Falmouth that he was certain that he had come to a place where the fight could be continued: 'what a relief to learn that England was still at war, intending to go on fighting!'[30]

Other Czechs journeyed to Britain on their own initiative. Two Czech airmen chartered a French cargo ship at Bordeaux and sailed with 270 Czech soldiers and airmen, 126 Czech women, some civilian refugees, and a Polish artillery officers' school that had been established in France. While they were at sea, all French ships were ordered to return to home ports, but the passengers encouraged the captain and crew to join de Gaulle and the Free French in Britain and they continued their journey, sailing to Gibraltar before joining a British convoy.[31] Although the majority of troops arriving were men, some women members of the Polish forces were evacuated. Sailing to Britain from La Rochelle on the British collier *Aderpool*, they were ordered by the captain to move to the crew's quarters, where they had toilets, cooking facilities, and privacy.[32]

A number of European monarchs and governments also arrived in Britain in 1940. Queen Wilhelmina of the Netherlands travelled by ship to Harwich and was followed a day later by the Dutch government. Lesser-known monarchs arriving were King Zog of Albania, and King Haakon VII of Norway, who journeyed to London on the British cruiser *Devonshire* in June with the Norwegian government. The Polish government-in-exile, initially set up in Paris by General Sikorski, moved to London after the fall of France. The Czechoslovakian National Committee also moved from Paris to London and in July was provisionally recognized by the British as the Czechoslovakian government-in-exile. This provisional status became the object of ridicule from Jan Masaryk, the Czechoslovak Foreign Minister, who took to signing his letters 'provisionally yours', and to asking if Czech airmen killed in the Battle of Britain were 'provisionally dead'.[33]

King Leopold III of Belgium was absent from the list of European sovereigns taking up residence in Britain. The King was urged to leave by the Belgian government in May, when the British government notified him that two motor torpedo boats were ready at Ostend to evacuate him together with his ministers. But Leopold could not be dissuaded from a decision to stay with his army, and surrendered to Germany on 27 May.[34] Following Belgian surrender, the Belgian government was divided about whether to leave for London. This was a course favoured by the Prime Minister, Hubert Pierlot, and the Foreign Minister, Paul-Henri Spaak, but opposed by other ministers. Pierlot, wanting to keep his coalition government working together, acquiesced in the decision of the majority. He and

Spaak subsequently crossed the border from France into Spain, where they found themselves under virtual house arrest. After careful planning, they journeyed to Portugal in October, hidden in a secret compartment of a truck owned by the Belgian consulate in Barcelona and taking back roads to avoid attention from the police. From Lisbon they took a seaplane to London.[35]

The secret compartment of a truck was one of an extraordinary range of means of transport that people improvised, borrowed, or stole as they made their way to Britain. Many French refugees arrived in Britain with the bicycles they had used to get to the French coast. The Women's Voluntary Service recorded the large numbers of bicycles arriving in Britain with some alarm and exaggeration, 'practically everybody is bringing over a bicycle ... The number of bicycles coming into the country is, I am told, fantastic'.[36] Historian Nicholas Atkin records that Léon Wilson, one of the first French arrivals to enlist in the British army in 1940, had come across a deserted bicycle shop on his retreat to Dunkirk with colleagues. They appropriated the bicycles they found there to speed their journey. When Wilson revisited the area sixty years later, he discovered that the bicycle shop still existed and felt guilty about his act of theft.[37]

A New Zealander Squadron Leader in the RAF, patrolling the beaches at Dunkirk, was shot at by a German Dornier and forced to crash land about five miles from Ostend. His journey back to Britain was by foot, bus, car, motorcycle, and ship. He 'borrowed' several cars on his way. 'Plodding down the road', he wrote, 'I noticed lots of cars, with keys left in the ignition, parked in the ditches ... so I decided to commandeer one. In a few seconds I was roaring down the main road heading for Dunkirk. But alas, after a few miles the car ran out of petrol. So I "borrowed" another'.[38] He eventually arrived at the outskirts of Dunkirk on a motorcycle before boarding a destroyer to return to Britain.

Polish soldiers also travelled in a commandeered car and by foot and ship. Joseph Lipski began his journey with a group of fellow soldiers following General Sikorski's broadcast instructing the Polish army in France to make for French ports and 'in the hope of picking up transport to Great Britain'. The group 'carefully selected one of the many motor-cars abandoned in the Vosges'. At first, they joined a French administrative column, but suddenly the French column stopped:

> All French soldiers were ordered to leave the cars, and we then discovered that we had arrived at a prisoners of war camp, and were about to be marched off into it! That wasn't at all what we were looking for, so we broke away and

travelling at full speed we reached the head of the column. The German
sentries at the entrance of the prisoners' camp were apparently misled by our
effrontery and allowed us to pass without troubling to challenge us.

When the car ran out of petrol, the Polish soldiers began what Lipski calls
'our long and weary tramp across France', marching by night and hiding in
the woods by day. After six days they met people who gave them civilian
clothing. Dressed as respectable working men, they were able to move freely
through French towns, even when these were occupied by German troops.
On the seventeenth day they reached 'the blue waters of the Mediterranean',
and by the middle of September had 'set foot on English soil'. Lipski then
rejoined his unit in Scotland.[39]

Aeroplanes, as well as bicycles and cars, were appropriated for journeys
to Britain. Czech and Slovak airmen in France 'acquired' planes, some of
them from the French Air Force, which was not consulted on this. Other
'acquisitions' that they made in France included 'private and sporting aeroplanes', which were packed with many more people than they were designed
to hold and 'with spluttering engines and creaking airframes' flew to the
nearest seaport. One bomber that arrived in Britain in June held some fifty
Czechoslovak and French airmen. Some flights were made directly to Britain,
while others were via Egypt and the Cape of Good Hope, circumnavigating
Africa before arriving.[40]

The diversity of sea vessels used to get to Britain is even more evident than
the diversity of aeroplanes. In Operations Dynamo, Aerial, and Cycle, vessels
used included warships, minesweepers, destroyers, cruisers, fishing boats,
pleasure steamers, cargo ships, coasters, colliers, wherries, barges, drifters,
rowboats, punts, and cockle boats.[41] Some 150 daredevil Netherlanders—
named 'England-farers' in Holland—crossed the North Sea using canoes
and other boats.[42] A Belgian on a rowboat with friends was strafed by
German fighters, but rowed on to reach Britain.[43]

Belgian fishing boats participated in the evacuation of troops from Dunkirk
and increasingly began to journey to Britain on their own account. An article in *Message*, a Belgian review published in Britain, attributed their arrival
to an agreement with the population of a small fishing port, 'In May 1940,
by a pre-arranged plan, Belgian fishermen "invaded" and subsequently
"annexed" a small fishing port on England's Channel coast; the English
inhabitants of the tiny port say they "adopted" the Belgians for the duration.
The Belgian fisher folk came anyway, in scores of craft and brought their
wives and families with them'.[44] By June an Admiralty report estimated

that there were approximately 500 Belgian fishermen and 250 Belgian fishing boats in Britain—around half of the Belgian fishing fleet. The report described a range of Norwegian, Danish, and Dutch as well as Belgian small craft that had made their way to Britain, calculating that they totalled between 600 and 700.[45] This total did not include French fishing boats, which came mainly from Boulogne and the Breton coast to Cornwall, where many of them had fished before the war.[46]

The Admiralty report noted the arrival of Norwegian fishing boats in the Shetland Isles. In the winter of 1940, several Norwegian crews were asked to sail back to Norway, land a passenger and then return. At the end of the year, organization of a continuous traffic began. This was the beginning of 'the Shetland Bus' which sent personnel and weapons to train and equip the Norwegian resistance and to bring back refugees. The use of fishing boats provided crews with some cover. Once they reached the Norwegian coast, they behaved like ordinary fishermen to deceive passing German patrol boats and aircraft. The journeys were made in winter—the continual daylight in the summer so far north deprived crews of the cover of darkness that they needed to make secret landings in Norway. David Howarth, who assisted in organizing the operation, writes that the seas between Shetland and Norway in winter are among the stormiest in the world and 'it is possible that in all the history of man's seafaring no other series of journeys has been undertaken deliberately in such bad weather and in such small boats'.[47]

Journeys undertaken in 1940 were frequently dangerous and there was a heavy death toll. On 17 June, the passenger liner *Lancastria*, evacuating troops and refugees from St. Nazaire in Operation Aerial, was hit by a German dive-bomber. An estimated 4,000 people drowned—more than the combined losses of the *Titanic* and *Lusitania*—in what Jonathan Fenby describes as 'Britain's greatest maritime disaster'.[48] Reporting of the sinking was suppressed on Churchill's orders and survivors were told that it must be kept secret. Churchill recalled later: 'I had intended to release the news a few days later, but events crowded upon us so black and so quickly, that I forgot to lift the ban, and it was some time before the knowledge of this horror became public'.[49] In 1941, the War Office Casualty Branch, seeking information about men who had gone missing during the 1940 evacuations, compiled a list of ships that had been sunk and lost in Operations Dynamo, Aerial, and Cycle. The list, including 'motor boats and other small craft', named 175 vessels. Belgian and French ships involved in these operations were among those sunk, including destroyers, trawlers, minesweepers, tugs, coasters, cargo ships, and several Belgian fishing boats.[50]

Other major losses were on journeys from Britain. On 24 July, the merchant ship *Meknès*, sailing to France to repatriate French naval officers and men, was sunk by a German E-boat, with the loss of 400 lives.[51] On 17 September, the passenger liner *City of Benares*, evacuating ninety British children to Canada under the Children's Overseas Reception Board scheme, was attacked by a U-boat. Only thirteen children survived and 121 of the crew drowned—the majority of them Indian Lascars.[52] On 2 July, the *Arandora Star*, which had earlier evacuated Wladyslaw Struk and other Poles from Saint-Jean-de-Luz to Liverpool, was torpedoed by a German U-boat off the coast of Ireland; with the loss of over 700 lives.

The *Arandora Star* was en route to Canada when the torpedo hit. On board were Austrians, Germans, and Italians who had been interned by the British government and were being deported to Canada, and prisoners of war who were also being deported. Those who died when the ship went down included Austrian and German refugees—predominantly Jewish— who had escaped to Britain before the outbreak of war and Italians who had been rounded up and interned after Italy's declaration of war against Britain in June. The sinking of the *Arandora Star* marked a significant moment in the history of British responses to people of enemy nationality in Britain and to the government policy of interning them.

Fifth Columnists and Spies

The early months of 1940 saw a worsening climate for refugees in Britain who had arrived before the war—chiefly from Austria, Czechoslovakia, and Germany. The view that they were welcome as anti-Nazis was increasingly displaced by the view that they represented a danger to Britain as spies and fifth columnists. In April, Sir Norman Angell—a former Labour Member of Parliament who campaigned on behalf of refugees—wrote a lead story in the popular wartime magazine *Picture Post* condemning what he called 'a rampage against the refugee in Britain', carried out for months by some daily newspapers. The cover of *Picture Post*, advertising this story, asked 'Refugees—Allies, or Enemies'? The magazine's answer to this question was evident from its photo spread of Austrian and German refugees who had arrived before war was declared and worked in Britain as scientists, writers, musicians, and actors. The caption read, 'Only a Few from the Hundreds of Refugees whose work has enriched our science and our culture'.[53]

Over the next few weeks, *Picture Post* published a range of letters in support, demonstrating that not all public opinion was on the rampage against refugees. They included one from Eleanor Rathbone, an Independent MP who had strongly opposed appeasement of Germany and Italy in the 1930s, and who championed saving the Jews of Europe throughout the war. Rathbone wrote, 'Look at the title page and reflect what a loss it would have been if Stefan Lorant had still been "Hitler's prisoner"'.[54]

The title page of *Picture Post* bore Stefan Lorant's name because he was its editor. Lorant was born in Hungary but moved to Germany to make films and was imprisoned soon after Hitler came to power for his opposition to the Nazis. He was well known in Britain in 1940, not only through the success and popularity of *Picture Post*, but also because he was the author of *I Was Hitler's Prisoner*—a diary he had written in prison in 1933. First published in 1935, the diary came out as a Penguin Special in 1939. In June 1940, the BBC broadcast an adaptation of *I Was Hitler's Prisoner*, starring Emlyn Williams as Lorant and Peggy Ashcroft as his wife, Niura, who had campaigned for his release.[55] Lorant's work for *Picture Post* brought him to the attention of Winston Churchill, who invited him to lunch in October 1939. At the lunch, Churchill proposed that the magazine should run a special edition on America. Lorant recorded of their meeting: 'Sooner or later—so he [Churchill] said—they [America] would have to join England in the war. Thus it would be of some help if *Picture Post* would present a better image of our future fighting ally'.[56] When the special issue was produced, Lorant received congratulations from Joseph Kennedy, American ambassador to Britain.

Despite his considerable reputation and work for British propaganda, life was made very difficult for Lorant in 1940 by the British government. His bicycle was impounded and his car confiscated under a government order of 23 May that extended the restrictions imposed on enemy aliens to refugees in Britain. He was also required to report to the police weekly and refused naturalization as a British subject, even though his application for naturalization had a number of eminent champions.[57]

These champions were men in high places and all of them emphasized the value of Lorant's work. Kenneth Clark, Director of the Film Division at the Ministry of Information, wrote '*Picture Post* is anxious to do a great deal of our propaganda for us... we could almost count this great organisation as part of the Ministry'. Robert Boothby, then an under-secretary at the Ministry of Food, wrote to Lorant, 'I have followed your work very closely in recent months, and consider its propaganda value so great that we ought not to lose it'. Brendan Bracken, who became Churchill's private parliamentary secretary in 1939, wrote in similar vein, 'The very remarkable work you have done since coming to England, and your record in relation to Hitler, are obvious grounds for special consideration of your case'. Bracken also wrote to Duff Cooper, Minister of Information, urging that something should be done about Lorant's naturalization, 'He is one of the best propagandists in the land, and God knows we need such people'.[58] Despite these champions, the Home Office took the view that the dossier that had been compiled on Lorant was 'not a good one' and other Ministries went with this view. The refusal to grant him British nationality and the restrictions on his movements made working life difficult for Lorant. It is a measure of the worsening climate for aliens in Britain in 1940 that he departed for the United States on 20 July, his name disappearing from the title page of *Picture Post*.[59]

Under Lorant's editorship, *Picture Post* reported regularly on the press campaign against refugees in Britain, first noting its development in February, particularly in the *Sunday Express* and *Daily Telegraph*.[60] The Home Secretary, Sir John Anderson, was also concerned about the press campaign. He told his father on 2 March, 'The newspapers are working up feeling about aliens. I shall have to do something about it, or we may be stampeded into an unnecessarily oppressive policy. It is very easy in wartime to start a scare'.[61] As Home Secretary, Anderson had established tribunals in 1939 that divided Austrian and German refugees into three categories on the basis of their potential threat to national security. Those categorized as 'A' Class were deemed to be a high risk; 'B' was an intermediate class, where there was uncertainty about a possible risk. People who were judged to present no security risk as 'friendly' enemy aliens were categorized as 'C' Class. The tribunals put the vast majority of those who came before them in 'C' Class.

The extent to which Anderson was anxious to avoid an unnecessarily oppressive policy was evident in his written reply to a Parliamentary question on 1 March, which demonstrated that very few of those who had appeared before tribunals had been interned—only 569 of the total of 73,353 people dealt with. A further 6,782 had been exempted from internment but not from special restrictions applicable to enemy aliens. Anderson gave the number of Germans and Austrians in Britain who were known to be 'refugees from Nazi oppression' as 'no less than 55,457' and stated, 'in my view, there would be no justification for a policy under which all aliens of German and Austrian nationality were treated alike, without regard to the fact that the majority of them are refugees from Nazi oppression and are bitterly opposed to the present regime in Germany'.[62] The phrase 'refugees from Nazi oppression' recurred in Anderson's policy-making. Tribunals were asked to record whether those who appeared before them belonged to this category. Some 77 per cent met that condition and had their registration certificates stamped on the inside with the words 'refugee from Nazi oppression'.[63] German refugees in Britain sometimes adopted 'refugee from Nazi oppression' as a self-description.[64]

In April, Anderson's characteristic description of Austrian and German refugees in Britain was challenged by a very different label used in a mounting press campaign against them. This label—'fifth columnists'—identified them as enemies within who acted as subversive agents and agitators. Mass Observation reported:

> April has been marked by a campaign against 'the enemy in our midst', the sinister, invisible enemy; the Fifth Column. A Campaign against the Fifth Column, led with restraint by MPs, has been whipped up into something rather different in the Press; a campaign to intern all refugees. The Sunday Press has been particularly active on this subject; several papers have ignored the point made by MPs and the serious weeklies, namely that the Fifth Column may be mainly composed of persons in high positions, British born and bred.[65]

The idea that foreigners plotted against Britain as fifth columnists, spies, and saboteurs had a considerable twentieth-century history. The century began with the 'spy fever' and fears of possible German invasion expressed in an extensive body of Edwardian popular fiction.[66] The latter years of the 1930s saw a spate of British spy films, some of them based on Edwardian novels. The ideas paraded in the press in mid-1940 already had considerable currency in British culture.

In May and June, many British people lumped all foreigners in Britain together as potential spies and fifth columnists. Home Intelligence reported from London that shop assistants were 'becoming insolent to people with foreign accents'.[67] Both Mass Observation and Home Intelligence reported that many people wanted internment for all aliens, not just those of enemy nationality—as many as 55 per cent of those surveyed in four areas of

London in June by Mass Observation.[68] Although the government's exten-
sion of internment applied mainly to enemy aliens, their actions also suggest
mistrust of all refugees in Britain, particularly in the order of 23 May that
deprived Stefan Lorant of his bicycle and his car.

Speaking to the House of Commons in August, John Anderson described
the policy adopted before May 1940 that had distinguished refugees from
Nazi oppression from other categories of enemy aliens as one 'which gave
me personally the greatest satisfaction' and was 'in accordance with the best
traditions of the country'.[69] He went on to explain why he had abandoned
this policy on 12 May:

> It was a matter of military necessity. The departure [from the previous policy]
> was not made all at once but by stages... The first significant step was taken
> on 11th May, after Norway had been overrun and when the attack had already
> been launched on Holland and Belgium. The military authorities came to me,
> late one evening, and represented that, in view of the imminent risk of inva-
> sion, it was in their view of the utmost importance that every male enemy
> alien between 16 and 70 should be removed forthwith from the coastal strip
> which in their view was the part of the country likely, if invasion took
> place, to be affected. I listened to the representations of the military authorities
> and came to the conclusion that it was quite impossible to reject the case
> put before me. I accepted their suggestion and carried it into force within
> 24 hours... There was not a responsible newspaper on 13th May who did
> not applaud what had been done.[70]

Most men from the coastal strip were arrested and interned regardless of
whether they had been previously put in 'C' Class by tribunals as 'friendly'
enemy aliens posing no security risk. The initial round-up involved the
internment of around 2,000 men, but as Anderson's record acknowledged,
was only the first step in a reversal of his previous policy. A total of some
27,000 men and women classified as 'enemy aliens' were eventually interned.[71]

In the context of the German invasion of Norway, Belgium, and the
Netherlands, Anderson's policy had substantial support. Even liberal newspapers such as the *Manchester Guardian* and the *News Chronicle* saw internment
as a necessary, if regrettable policy. The *News Chronicle* acknowledged that
the government's policy 'may seem drastic when so many [Austrians and
Germans] are known to be friendly to the Allied cause' but went on to
argue that 'in the new circumstances that have arisen recently, it is a military
necessity, and the only question is whether it applies to a large enough area'.[72]
The *Manchester Guardian* took the view that the refugees were welcome in

Britain, 'because they look for Hitler's downfall...feel as we feel and are only anxious to assist us' —a welcome that can hardly have been evident to Austrians and Germans on the day after arrests and detentions. But the newspaper went on to suggest that fears about fifth columnists were justified, 'the news of what Hitler has accomplished by attacking so many countries from within is extremely serious...it would be folly not to assume that he will have tried hard to provide some help for his parachutists and troop-carriers should he send them'.[73]

Public opinion was also generally supportive of the policy of mass intern-ment. Two days after the round-up of Austrians and Germans in coastal districts, Mass Observation reported that stories of German parachutists being assisted by fifth columnists in Belgium and Holland meant that 'the always latent antagonism to the alien and foreigner began to flare up'. Its report traced a shift in feelings about aliens after the introduction of mass internment on 12 May. At the beginning of the month 'there was little feel-ing for interning aliens en masse' and 'it was still...the done thing to show a liberal sympathy for German aliens who had fled from Germany because of the Nazis'.[74] But by the middle of the month, '[T]he Dutch parachute news, and the news of their linking up with aliens already in Holland, had a deeper, immediate and "alarming" effect. Now the enemy in our midst is easily visualised...Nearly everyone as previous research has shown, is latently somewhat anti-Semitic and somewhat anti-alien. But ordinarily it is not the done thing to express such sentiments publicly. The news from Holland made it quite the done thing, all of a sudden'.[75]

The report noted that the new restrictions on aliens, corresponding with this feeling, were therefore widely welcomed. Three investigators working on the afternoon of the 13 May had found that by 3.00 p.m. there were still many people who were not aware that many Austrians and Germans had been rounded up. Even so, they wanted them interned or more strictly dealt with. A further Mass Observation report on 18 May on a small survey of 60 people found that 'opinion was definitely in favour of the internment of more people. In fact this view was expressed by nine times as many people as said: "No" and by five times as many as said they didn't know'. When asked who should be interned, the focus was entirely on aliens.[76] Tom Harrisson, one of the creators of the Mass Observation project, later summarized the shift of atmosphere in May, 'many people who a month before were inclined to be tolerant of aliens were now almost pogrom minded'.[77]

Mass Observation findings were based on small surveys, but they corresponded to findings from Home Intelligence. Almost all its daily reports in May and June contained references to feelings against aliens from places as diverse as Belfast, Bristol, Cardiff, Edinburgh, Leeds, London, Manchester, Nottingham, and Reading.[78] Demands for stronger action against aliens were reported from Cardiff, Edinburgh, Leeds, and Reading and there was strong approval for the action taken against fifth columnists from Reading.[79] By early June a Home Intelligence report called feelings about fifth columnists 'hysteria', and judged that this was 'reaching dangerous proportions in some towns and villages'.[80] Germans who were interned remember being marched through the streets of Liverpool and the spectators who lined the streets, sometimes sympathetic and sometimes curious, but often antagonistic. Anna Spiro remembers people spitting at them 'because we were bloody Germans'.[81] When they arrived on the Isle of Man, where there was a large internment camp, they were watched by a silent crowd.[82]

Italians became targets of hostility even before the Italian declaration of war—in May Home Intelligence regularly reported a build-up of hostility in the expectation of Italy's entry into the war.[83] When the declaration of war came on 10 June, there were attacks on Italian communities in many British towns and cities. On 11 June, Home Intelligence reported 'many windows broken in the South Wales valleys', 'some anti-Italian demonstrations in Belfast', 'Italian café smashed at Exeter', 'looting of Italian shops' in Edinburgh, and 'ice-cream shops wrecked at Ashington and Middlesbrough'.[84]

Italy's declaration of war transformed Italians in Britain into enemy aliens overnight and the policy of internment was immediately extended to them. Home Office policy was to intern Italians known to be members of the Italian Fascist party and all male Italians between the ages of 16 and 70 with fewer than twenty years' residence in Britain.[85] An observer working for Mass Observation on the night of the Italian declaration of war—when there were anti-Italian riots in Soho—provided a vivid account of comments she heard there on the round-up of Italians:

> As OBS [observer] stood about, a woman seized her by the hand. 'They're rounding them up' she said with excitement and an air of great satisfaction. She was eager to talk: a capable middle-aged working-class woman who knew her own mind. 'They've raided the Italian Club near St. Martin's Lane' she continued. 'Fifty police went in'. Another, slightly older working-class woman was with her. 'After they've cleared out the Italians, they'll clear out the Jews' she said. 'You'll see—and a good job too. I ask you, why should these foreigners be here'.[86]

According to many reports, Italy's declaration of war caused little anxiety because 'contempt for the Italian fighting qualities is very common'.[87] Mass Observation commented, 'In the past three days, there has been a big increase in scorn for Italy... especially a widespread and almost complete disregard for Italy as a military factor... The way people are talking at the moment... one might think that Italy was Andorra'.[88] A comment from a woman in a village in East Suffolk was critical of events in Soho, but echoed the common verdict on Italian fighting qualities:

> Such a pity they had to come into it. The Italians I mean. They've got a lot of good points. I've no time for these here people who went round smashing up Soho, as if things won't be damaged enough before long. Those London Italians don't mean no harm. It's nothing to do with them. They can't fight tho' that's one thing.[89]

A report on a Mass Observation directive in October 1940 provided a more complex version of this verdict on Italians—Italian unwarlikeness could be understood as a likeable quality, signalling 'a peace-loving people whose heart is not in the war against this country'. But the report also noted that 'an equal number interpret this peace-loving as cowardice, laziness, and general lack of guts'.[90]

In the aftermath of the anti-Italian riots, signs appeared in many shop and restaurant windows with Italian names, advertising the Britishness of their owners. Announcements also appeared in local newspapers, like one in Swansea from Virgie Cresci, who informed the public that he and his family were British subjects and that his brothers were serving in the Royal Welsh Fusiliers and the British mercantile marine.[91] The report by the observer of the round-up of Italians in Soho, recording hostility to Jews as well as Italians, suggests how far both groups continued to be regarded as foreigners, despite their histories of settlement in Britain. Hostility to Jews drew on pre-war anti-Semitism but acquired distinctive wartime resonances. Home Intelligence noted an increase in anti-Semitism in London and Leeds in June—'rumoured attempts of rich Jews to leave the country' and charges of 'wealthy Jews "panicking to the USA"'.[92] One man, interviewed by Mass Observation on 10 May, stated, 'I'm not a jew (*sic*) and you know what I think of them. Shouldn't be surprised if fifty per cent of them belonged to the Fifth Column'.[93]

In May and June, when anti-Italian feeling, mistrust of foreigners, and support for the mass internment of enemy aliens were at their height, any idea of Britain as a tolerant country was seriously challenged. *The First Days*—a British documentary film made in 1939 that recorded the early days of the Second World War in London—used an image of men and women queuing to register as aliens to demonstrate British tolerance. 'They are', the commentary stated, 'a part of London, part of its broad culture'.[94] The film-makers could not have predicted that many of the aliens they filmed in 1939 would be held behind British barbed wire in British internment camps by mid-1940, with no way of knowing if or when they would be released.

Popular support for the government policy of mass internment was about refugees already in Britain, but many more arrived in May and June. The government had anticipated in January that as many as 500,000 refugees might come to Britain from the Low Countries, but the speed of the German invasion and occupation of Belgium and Holland meant that in the event numbers were much lower.[95] How were they received?

Refugees Arrive

On 1 June 1940, during the evacuation from Dunkirk, George Orwell recorded in his diary the scenes he had witnessed at Waterloo and Victoria stations the previous night:

> Actually I saw very few British soldiers, i.e. from the B.E.F [British Expeditionary Force], but great numbers of Belgian or French refugees, a few Belgian or French soldiers, and some sailors, including a few naval men. The refugees seemed mostly middling people of the shop-keeper type, and were in quite good trim, with a certain amount of personal belongings. One family had a parrot in a huge cage. One refugee woman was crying, or nearly so, but most seemed only bewildered by the crowds and the general strangeness. A considerable crowd was watching at Victoria and had to be held back by the police to let refugees and others get to the street. The refugees were greeted in silence but all sailors of any description enthusiastically cheered.[96]

The nationality of the sailors who were cheered is not clear from this diary entry, but in the context of Dunkirk it is not difficult to understand why the crowd greeted all of them enthusiastically. Home Intelligence also reported an enthusiastic response to the arrival of French troops evacuated from Dunkirk, 'Southampton welcomed French troops enthusiastically' and 'French troops warmly welcomed on South Coast and French speakers generally in demand'.[97] This enthusiasm contrasts with the response that Orwell witnessed to the arrival of refugees—silence.

Accounts of an enthusiastic welcome for French troops also contrast with comments in the same reports on 'nervousness about aliens and Fifth Columnists', employers hesitating to take aliens on, and the dismissal of aliens from factories in Weybridge and Newbury 'on demand of fellow workers'.[98] Both Home Intelligence and Mass Observation regularly used the term 'alien' without clarification. There is no way of knowing whether these reports on 'nervousness' and discrimination were about particular national groups or all civilian foreigners. But refugees arriving in June 1940 were associated with fears about fifth columnists. A Home Intelligence report from Nottingham commented that Dutch and Belgian refugees were 'not popular as it is felt that they should work for their food, also unpopularity due to Fifth Column fears'. From Tunbridge Wells, Home Intelligence also reported 'some confusion as to our attitude towards French refugees. Hope that adequate precautions will be taken to ensure that these do not include Fifth Columnists'.[99] As late as September a Mass Observation observer overheard two women in the Fulham Road saying 'you can't tell me there's no spies among the refugees—they should send them back to their own countries'.[100]

A mixed reception for refugees also involved criticisms of young males of military age who were not in military uniform. Home Intelligence reported from London in June, 'Five hundred Belgian refugees kindly received in Southall Institute. Inhabitants have found them surprisingly nice, though families who have husbands or sons in the Army are critical of the young Belgian refugees of military age'. A further report from Chiswick in July noted a similar criticism, 'Two hundred Dutch and Belgian refugees resented by soldiers' wives as many are men of military age. Work should be given them as they are bored and appear ungrateful'. By August, Home Intelligence was recording from Peckham that 'an enthusiastic reception of 700 to 800 Belgian, French and Polish refugees' had changed to 'suspicion and resentment' caused by the 'number of able bodied men hanging about'.[101]

The mixed reception for refugees arriving in May and June is apparent throughout Home Intelligence and Mass Observation reports. In May, Home Intelligence noted advocacy of internment of Dutch refugees from Leeds, but two days later, also from Leeds, 'Many spontaneous offers to shelter refugees'.[102] There were offers of support as well as hostility. Mass Observation reported from Cricklewood at the end of May, 'On the whole the refugees still appeal to the pity of the public, a lot of people object, some have no room, but about half are quite ready to help in any way they can to relieve the sufferings of the Belgium (*sic*) and Dutch refugees'.[103] The Mayor of Wimbledon, extending a welcome to refugees from Belgium and Holland on 10 May, explicitly identified them as allies, not aliens, expressing confidence that 'the Burgesses of Wimbledon will... desire to do everything within their power to lighten the terrible blow which has fallen upon our friends and allies'.[104]

On the same day, a letter from the Minister of Health asking town councils to help with the reception of refugees was equally explicit in naming them as allies: 'I need not dwell on the claims that these refugees have on our help. They are now our Allies and I am sure that I can rely on your cooperation and that of your district in this war work'.[105] Historian Bill Williams records a warm welcome for Jewish refugees who arrived on the last transport to leave Holland. Their boat docked in Liverpool and they were immediately taken inland, away from the coastal 'protected area', by train to Wigan. On arrival at the station, they were greeted by a crowd cheering, clapping, and waving handkerchiefs. Local families invited them to their homes and accompanied them to local events. They were also given free tickets for performances at Wigan's Princes Cinema, where Hans Levy had his first experience of seeing a film. Since he was Jewish, Levy had been banned from cinemas in Germany. The film he saw in Wigan was *The Hunchback of Notre Dame*.[106]

Women were particularly involved in supporting refugees before and during the war. This support ranged from the cups of tea and clothes provided by members of the Women's Voluntary Service, through women's important contribution to the work of local refugee aid committees, to Eleanor Rathbone's campaigning activities on behalf of refugees and her opposition to internment. The Jewish community in Britain had offered a range of support to Jewish refugees arriving from 1933—from national initiatives by the Board of Deputies of British Jews to local initiatives to billet Jewish arrivals in the homes of Jewish volunteers.[107] Like their non-Jewish counterparts, Jewish women took prominent roles on local refugee aid committees. Women's activities on these committees ranged from running hostels to setting up clubs, finding jobs in domestic service for women, and arranging for refugees to stay in private homes.[108] Their work could attract opposition. Joan Strange, a member of the Worthing refugee committee, recorded in her diary in 1939, 'Awoke to find Alice, our maid, telling me that our front step, path, wall and pavement outside had been written in tar "Jews get out", "Britons before aliens"'.[109]

In 1940, there was much business for the Women's Voluntary Service, refugee committees, and campaigners to transact. The mass internment of Austrian and German nationals who had arrived before the war and the arrival of more refugees as Germany invaded and occupied much of Europe generated a heavy workload. Women on the refugee committee in Worthing corresponded with the commandant of Huyton internment camp, sent parcels and made visits to the camp, acted as advocates for refugees on a range of issues, and applied for some to be released. Their activities on behalf of recently arrived refugees included persuading a local barber to give complimentary haircuts, a local cobbler to mend shoes free of charge, and the local cinema to offer tickets on the house.[110] At the height of the fifth columnist scare, an observer for Mass Observation wrote about the work undertaken by the Women's Voluntary Service:

> The distribution centre for refugees is on the premises of a convent-school.... Middle-class, middle-aged ladies with WVS uniform, overalls or brassards, stand about or offer the refugees coffee, sweets or sandwiches. A small baby is carried about by a grey-haired WVS officer. Round the door stand members of ARP [Air Raid Precautions] stretcher parties, waiting to drive people to their billets.[111]

Eleanor Rathbone, the Independent MP, was one of the most prominent figures in campaigns for the release of refugees from internment. In December 1938, she set up the Parliamentary Committee on Refugees, which, by the outbreak of war, was backed by some 200 MPs. From July 1940 the Committee worked on building cases for release from internment, gathering references, and evidence that internees fell into categories of release, such as records of anti-Nazi activity. By September 1941, 1,693 cases for release had been submitted to the Home Office, of which 1,069 were successful.[112]

The mixed reception for refugees arriving in 1940 is apparent from the evidence of support and welcome, as well as resentment, mistrust, and hostility. The silence that met the arrival of Belgian and French refugees at Waterloo and Victoria stations recorded by George Orwell in his diary contrasts with the cheering and waving crowd greeting Jewish refugees arriving at Wigan Wallgate station. Historian Bill Williams, who traces the history of responses to refugees from Fascism in the city of Manchester, focuses on 'rescue' and the role of Manchester people and a wide range of Manchester organizations in facilitating the arrival of refugees and supporting them. But he also notes that the majority attitude was one of indifference.[113] Such indifference was in strong contrast to British attitudes to people who arrived in military uniform.

Troops Arrive

Antoni Slonimski, the Polish poet and journalist, wrote in 1941:

> We came to England as soldiers defeated and betrayed, as writers broken by disbelief and bitterness, bewildered and distrustful, yet still thirsting for further battle. Here on the soil of England we were received with cordial hospitality. On the first day of our arrival a dock labourer gave us a friendly smile as he offered us his bread. And wherever we went this English smile was before us...Our faces brightened before this trustful and friendly smile.[114]

One of the Warsaw Squadron pilots who disembarked from a Dutch coaster in Plymouth has similar memories. Everybody smiled at them and 'workmen threw their lunch-packs and packets of cigarettes in through the train windows to us, and spoke to us in what was for us a still incomprehensible language'. A Polish airman who marched through the streets of Liverpool after arrival remembers, 'We marched...in fours, and the British shouted "Long live Poland!" and held their thumbs up'. According to another Polish airman, when Britons saw the 'Poland' shoulder flashes on uniforms, 'they would walk up to airmen in the street and invite them home. Bus conductors refused their fares, waiters settled their restaurant bills for them and they only had to walk into a pub to be offered free drinks'.[115]

As these accounts suggest, when the presence of a foreigner in Britain was indicated by a shoulder flash on a military uniform, the response was far more likely to be welcoming and friendly than the response to foreign civilians. But some shoulder flashes on military uniforms were more welcome than others. The arrival of troops in May and June coincided with the fifth column scare, which had been strengthened by reports of fifth columnist activities in Holland. This may have shaped the response noted by Home Intelligence in July to the presence of the Dutch army in Pembrokeshire, which was 'viewed with some distrust, and many of the public doubt their efficiency, and in some cases even their loyalty'.[116]

A popular welcome for troops arriving was particularly evident for those coming from the British Empire. In the context of military disasters and the expectation of an imminent invasion, Home Intelligence noted on several occasions that their presence boosted confidence. From London it reported 'pleasure expressed at arrival of Australians and new confidence shown because of it' and from Tunbridge Wells 'arrival of empire troops cheering'. Reports at the end of the month told the same story, 'the presence of Dominions troops in London is having an excellent effect. Many observers report that the fact that these men are being seen is stimulating confidence'. In July, a further report from London noted that 'many people think Dominion troops should have had proper official welcome'.[117]

Enthusiasm for troops of different nationalities waxed and waned during the course of 1940. As the Battle of France continued after the Dunkirk evacuation, Home Intelligence reported 'increasingly warm feeling for French and demand that we are giving them all the help we can' and 'great anxiety that all possible aid shall be sent (even at the expense of our own home defences) to France'. As France fell, it reported from Cardiff 'no bitterness against French', but from London, 'anti-French feeling growing very strong since capitulation'. Mass Observation reported overhearing the comment 'Bleeding French'.[118] Later reports focused on the uncertainty that French surrender prompted. How should the French in Britain now be regarded? The presence of French troops in Glasgow was described as 'vaguely disturbing... people are uncertain about their attitude'. In other localities where there were French troops 'the public is uncertain of its attitude towards them' and 'the French troops themselves are confused and ignorant about the course of events'.[119]

General Charles de Gaulle arrived in Britain on 17 June—the day of Marshal Pétain's broadcast announcing the negotiation of an armistice with Germany. On the following day, he broadcast on the BBC to appeal to his compatriots to fight on, 'Whatever happens, the flame of French resistance must not and shall not die'.[120] Before his arrival in Britain, de Gaulle was a junior member of the French government—in early June, he had been appointed Under-Secretary for War by Reynaud. He was little known either in France or in Britain. Few French people heard the broadcast.[121] Pierre Lefranc, who came to Britain to join the Free French and later became one of de Gaulle's closest advisers, remembers, 'The population had been scattered by the war and radio reception was not easy. The basic message of the broadcast [by de Gaulle] was passed on by those few newspapers that were still appearing. The news that a member of the last legitimate government of the Third Republic had taken this initiative soon spread, but few people were stirred by it. France was in complete disarray and the prestige of Marshall Pétain was great'.[122]

Comparatively few of the French troops and civilians who arrived in Britain in 1940 responded to de Gaulle's call to continue the fight. Many of the French troops evacuated to Britain were quickly repatriated to France to continue the fight there, but the majority of French soldiers who remained in Britain after evacuation did not enlist in the Free French or British forces.[123] Instead, they chose repatriation, which at least promised reunion with their families. Life in Britain was often hard—most French troops were accommodated in makeshift camps where they lived under canvas, often with primitive washing and cooking facilities. Churchill observed that soldiers were also 'discouraged by some Officers from volunteering'.[124] Historian Nicholas Atkin records one case where French officers, visiting soldiers in hospital wards in July, claimed that 'any man who volunteered for the Free French would be under "penalty of death"'. In another case, it was a Gaullist officer, attempting to recruit men to the Free French, who reminded them that if they enlisted, 'they would be immediately under sentence of death'.[125] The message, wherever it came from, can hardly have been encouraging.

Olympia became briefly a Gaullist barracks, the headquarters of General de Gaulle and the Free French Volunteers. On 12 July, Churchill noted 'I found the conditions at Olympia very bad'.[126] On 14 July—Bastille Day— Mollie Panter-Downes wrote in her war diary that Olympia was 'normally associated in Londoners' minds with Christmas circuses and Ideal Home exhibitions'.[127] These associations may have contributed to a climate where the British public found it difficult to distinguish between Free French volunteers and French soldiers bent on repatriation.[128] By October, according to a report on a Mass Observation directive, attitudes to the Free French in Britain were mixed—42 per cent of respondents viewed them favourably, 32 per cent unfavourably, with the rest 'half and half' or 'vague'. A female student commented: 'Very little sympathy with them as I do not think they represent the French... The true Frenchman has stayed in France and suffered'. But the report also noted that 'more than a quarter of all people spontaneously consider them worthy of admiration for their courage, loyalty, idealism and patriotism'.[129]

The same Mass Observation directive found that Czechs were the most popular national group in Britain. In an analysis of replies from fifty men and fifty women, over half responded favourably to Czechs, with only 9 per cent unfavourable. A feeling of 'having let them down' through the Munich agreement was noted. A 19-year-old woman wrote 'I admire the Czechs exceedingly. After our government had betrayed them and democracy, it is marvellous the way they have rallied in this country to the cause'.[130] Mass Observation described the National Panel of Observers who responded to directives as 'biased in a middle-class direction, consisting of people of more than average intelligence and broadmindedness'.[131] But admiration for those continuing the fight from Britain was not confined to the middle classes. A Lieutenant Colonel in the Czechoslovakian Air Force recalled a 'pleasant memory' of an incident that occurred in 1940 after Czechoslovak airmen were involved in shooting down a German plane:

> There appeared at the squadron a man with a large envelope full of small change, which he handed with an embarrassed air to the Squadron Commander. The workmen who were at work on the aerodrome had got up a collection among themselves for the pilot who had shot down the German machine! The kindly hearts of these Englishmen had sought in this way to thank those who were fighting for their freedom; the Squadron Spitfire Fund duly profited to the tune of some 2 pounds sterling.[132]

The role of Polish and Czechoslovak airmen in the Battle of Britain received considerable publicity and may have informed the comments made in the October Mass Observation directive, where 26 per cent of respondents spontaneously mentioned Polish 'bravery'. During the Battle of Britain, a school in Ruislip had a whip-round and sent 450 cigarettes for 'the brave Polish fighters'. The Borough of Willesden, which had collected money to fund a Spitfire, stipulated that it should be flown by a Pole.[133]

A welcome for people who could assist the war effort was far less evident from the top brass of the British armed forces. In the RAF, there were serious doubts about Czechoslovakian and Polish airmen. In May, responding to a proposal from the Czechoslovak Air Attaché in London for the formation of a specialist Czech bomber unit in Britain, the British Director of Air Intelligence, Air Commodore Archibald Boyle wrote 'I doubt very much if this is worth pursuing. We don't know (1) if there are any pilots worthy of the name and if they are available; (2) their integrity (I am doubtful of many Czechs)'. Responding to a proposal for the formation of an independent Polish Air Force in Britain in July, Air Commodore Sir Charles Medhurst wrote 'The senior Polish Air officers, I have been reliably informed, are completely useless and are only out to line their pockets in filling cushy jobs'.[134] There were similar views at the Admiralty, where serious doubts were expressed about the reliability of Dutch and Norwegian sailors, based on reports of a 'defeatist spirit'.[135] However, there was also some awareness at the Admiralty of the potential value of Allied seamen to the war effort. A report in June noted:

> Under existing conditions, allied aliens are generally left in enforced idleness and are subject to irksome restrictions. The inference to them must be that we regard this war as *our* war, and not their war, and that we do not require their help; or, perhaps, they will believe that this country mistrusts them— which may be correct. The effect of this on the spirit of these men can hardly be exaggerated...By our own inaction, if it continues, we shall transform men, who might be of tremendous value, into useless or even dangerous characters.[136]

Churchill was a strong champion of Allied contingents in Britain, but was clearly aware that they were not receiving a whole-hearted welcome from the forces. In July, he wrote to General Ismay, asking him to bring government policy to the attention of the Chiefs of Staff:

> It is the settled policy of H.M. Government to make good strong French con- tingents for land, sea and Air service, to encourage these men to volunteer to fight on with us or with de Gaulle, to look after them well, to indulge their sentiments about the French flag, etc., and to have them as representatives of a France which is continuing the war. It is the duty of the Chiefs of Staff to carry this policy out cordially and effectively. The same principle also applies to Poles, Dutch, Czech, Norwegian and Belgian contingents in this country, as well as to the Foreign Legion of anti-Nazi Germans. Mere questions of administrative inconvenience must not be allowed to stand in the way of this policy of the State...I hope I may receive assurances that this policy is being whole-heartedly pursued.[137]

Two days after Churchill's instructions were issued, Charles Medhurst's publicly expressed views came into line with what Churchill had identified as the 'policy of the State', with no more talk of 'cushy jobs'. Medhurst stated at a conference that of the 4,800 Polish Air personnel who had arrived in the UK, there was 'a large number of trained flying and ground personnel' and of the 700 Czechoslovak Air Force personnel, 'a high percentage of skilled pilots and mechanics'.[138] There was an official welcome for Polish and Czechoslovak troops in July from Anthony Eden, Secretary of State for War.[139] In September, Winston Churchill wrote to welcome 'every Polish soldier, sailor or airman who has found his way over to help us fight and win the war'.[140]

After the fall of France, Churchill regarded the Free French, as well as the other European Allied contingents in Britain, as significant assets for propaganda purposes. In his memorandum to Chiefs of Staff instructing them to look after Allied contingents, he wrote, 'It is most necessary to give to the war which Great Britain is waging single-handed the broad, international character which will add greatly to our strength and prestige'.[141] The presence of armies-in-exile from continental Europe strengthened Britain's claims to be fighting in the cause of democracy and freedom. This presence could be used to demonstrate—particularly for an American audience—that Britain was not fighting simply to preserve and defend the British Empire. Stories about continental European armies and airmen continuing the fight as friends and allies were developed as part of a media vision of a multinational community in Britain united in a common cause against a common enemy—the 'allies' war'.

'Allies' War'

In 1940, after the fall of France, a cartoon in the *Evening Standard* by David Low showed a British soldier standing defiantly on a shore nearly engulfed by waves and shaking his fist at a sky full of Nazi planes. The caption was 'very well alone!'[142] The idea that Britain was alone after the French surrender did not disturb King George VI, who wrote to his mother, 'Personally I feel happier now that we have no allies to be polite to & to pamper'. A. P. Herbert told a story of a Thames tugboat captain shouting, 'no more bloody allies!'[143] But in the British media, a 'together' message was usually more prominent than the 'standing alone' message of the Low cartoon. Much publicity was given in 1940 to the imperial war effort and to the efforts of European Allies fighting on from Britain.

The 'together' message was prominent in a BBC series about the imperial war effort—*In It Together*. Publicity for the series in the *Radio Times* told readers, 'It is incorrect to imagine we are alone in the struggle against Nazi tyranny: Great Britain, Canada, Australia, South Africa, New Zealand, as well as India and the British colonial empire are all in it together.[144] The series included interviews with Australian and New Zealander troops in Britain and an Indian serving in the RAF. In July, a cartoon in *Punch* poked fun at the 'standing alone' message. It showed two soldiers on a shore looking out to sea. One says 'So our poor old empire is alone in the world'. The other replies: 'Aye, we are—the whole five hundred million of us'.[145]

Newsreels in January showed some of these 'five hundred million' arriving in Britain—Australian, Canadian, and New Zealand servicemen, and Newfoundland lumberjacks who had crossed the Atlantic to fell timber in Scotland for Britain's war needs.[146] Disparate stories were brought together at the beginning of the year in a newsreel on 'Defenders of the Empire'. Over shots of Australian airmen marching and parading in Britain the voice-over says, 'The Empire's New Year greeting to the Mother Country is to send its sons to join us in the fight'. Over shots of a troopship docking at Liverpool and Canadian troops disembarking, the message is, 'all the Empire stands together in the fight for freedom'.[147] Such concerted publicity for the imperial war effort may have shaped the response of one woman in May 1940 to the news that Belgium had surrendered: 'she did not see how England could lose with all the Australians and New Zealanders'.[148]

European Allies also received a good deal of attention in the British media, with France featuring prominently in the early months of the year. *Friends and Allies* was the title of a weekly BBC series of talks, relayed from France and made in collaboration with *Radiodiffusion Nationale de France*, that began in February. *Vive la France*—a fortnightly series on French national life and character—began in March. Enthusiasm for the French continued right up to June 1940. The last talk in the *Friends and Allies* series went out on 18 June—the day after Marshal Pétain's broadcast announcing the negotiation of an armistice with Germany. *Vive La France* went out for the last time on the same day. Like *Friends and Allies* it was then taken off.

A regular reminder from the BBC that Britain had European allies was the programme of their national anthems, played on Sunday night, before the nine o'clock news, and ending with 'God Save the King'. The programme began in the spring of 1940, with the anthems of France and Poland. After the German invasion of Norway in April, the Norwegian anthem was added, and the BBC acted swiftly to add the Belgian and Dutch anthems on 12 May, after the German invasion of Belgium and Holland two days earlier. Norway, Belgium, and Holland were all neutral countries before German invasion, but were now claimed by the BBC as allies of Britain. The Czech anthem was added in July, the Greek in October, and the Luxembourgois in December.[149] Listener research at the BBC at the end of 1940 reported that when listeners were asked whether they liked to hear the anthems of the Allies each Sunday, the response was 'emphatically affirmative'. Roughly two thirds of the Research Panel of Honorary Local Correspondents answered 'yes'.[150]

Churchill's memorandum to his Chiefs of Staff instructing them to welcome Allied contingents from the continent in Britain included a reference to a Free French event two days later. 'An opportunity of assisting the French', he wrote, 'would be to make a great success of their function of July 14, when they are going to lay a wreath on the Foch statue'. This function on Bastille Day was favourably reported in newspapers and newsreels, providing an early example of British propaganda that focused on European forces continuing the fight from Britain. Newsreels showed the ceremony at the Cenotaph where de Gaulle laid a wreath inscribed 'les Français libres' [the Free French]. Churchill's interest in the success of this event is demonstrated by the message he sent to de Gaulle for the occasion, spoken on newsreel, which began, 'I look forward with confidence to a time not far distant, when July 14th will once again be celebrated as a day of rejoicing by a free and victorious France'. His message ended, 'The spirit of France is not dead. In this hour of her adversity, there still lives the spirit of independence which for 150 years has been her proudest claim. France will rise again!'[151] In September, Basil Nicolls, the BBC's Controller (Programmes), reported to his department heads, 'The Prime Minister attaches special importance to the boosting of de Gaulle and the Free French movement... I gather that the mandate extends to boosting de Gaulle personally'.[152]

The story of Allied contingents in Britain continuing the fight that Churchill had identified as giving the war 'a broad international character' was told many times after July. A newsreel in August that showed Czech airmen 'flying in the cause of liberty' included the announcement, 'Every week brings us more pictures of the sons of other nations who stand in the fight beside Britain'.[153] By the autumn, there was increasing publicity for the records of Polish and Czech airmen in the Battle of Britain. A newsreel showing the King's visit to Polish and Canadian airmen stationed in South East England commented, 'This Polish Squadron brought down 80 German planes in one month'.[154] *The Manchester Guardian*, reporting that Czech pilots had brought down five enemy planes in the greatest raid yet seen on London, called them 'valuable allies'.[155] In September, the King spoke of 'the stirring feats of Polish aviators in the air battles now proceeding over England'.[156] His private secretary wrote, 'The King has heard about the excellence of the Polish forces now in this country... I believe that their pilots are absolute tigers, and have made a substantial score of German raiders. One cannot help feeling that if all our Allies had been Poles, the course of the war, up till now, would have been very different.'[157] A telegram sent to Polish airmen demonstrated a commitment to celebrating Allies in Britain at the highest levels of the BBC. It came from the Director General, who sent 'warm greetings to the famous 303 Polish Squadron with lively congratulations upon its magnificent record and all best wishes for its future. You use the Air for your gallant exploits and we for telling the world of them. Long live Poland!'[158]

The significance of the 'fighting on' theme is demonstrated by the BBC's autumn schedules, which devoted two feature series to Allied contingents continuing the fight from Britain. The first episode of *Fights On* told the story of the French forces who 'escaped from the clutches of Germany to continue . . . to fight for their country and for Europe'.[159] This was followed by *Czechoslovakia Fights On*, and *Vivat Polonia*. Another autumn series—*Comrades for Freedom*—chronicled 'life in Britain as seen by our allies, their views of what we are fighting for [and] stories of their adventures in reaching these shores'.[160] It began with a programme on 'our comrades in arms—the Poles' and went on to cover the other five Allied contingents identified by Churchill as giving the war 'a broad international character'—French, Czechs, Dutch, Norwegians, and Belgians. The emphasis on 'freedom' and 'Europe' in the description of these programmes fitted a view of a war fought to liberate occupied Europe—a common effort on the part of Europeans to resist Nazi tyranny.

The theme of continuing the fight was also in evidence on the BBC's European Services. A special fifteen-minute daily programme on the Dutch service, titled 'Radio Oranje', was placed at the disposal of the Dutch government-in-exile and opened on 28 July with a message from Queen Wilhelmina, who told her compatriots, 'our gallant men will continue the struggle'.[161] King Haakon of Norway told Norwegians in September, 'I and my Government have been obliged to carry on this fight outside the country . . . we who are away will do everything possible to ease the condition for you who are at home, we ask you all to feel sure that we will never give up the work to create a new, free and independent Norway'.[162]

The BBC's European services expanded rapidly in 1940 after small beginnings in 1938, when news in French, German, and Italian was broadcast during the Munich crisis to counter German and Italian propaganda.[163] By the end of 1940, news was broadcast in sixteen different European languages.[164] Expansion involved the recruitment of many refugees, émigrés, and exiles from the continent. As scriptwriters, speakers, linguists, translators, and actors, they made a significant contribution to British propaganda targeted at Europe. The French service was headed by Michel Saint-Denis, who adopted the pseudonym Jacques Duchesne after he was evacuated from Dunkirk. It broadcast for forty-five minutes after 1 July, but by September, this had been expanded to three and a half hours.[165] The German service also expanded in 1940, with a features section founded in the autumn, headed by Walter Rilla, who had come to England with his Jewish wife in the 1930s and, like many other German-speaking émigrés, acted in British films.[166]

Some émigrés and refugees also wrote scripts for Home Service programmes. They included Josef Schrich, a Czech refugee journalist, who scripted *Czechoslovakia Fights On*, in collaboration with a Manchester journalist, John Midgley. Their collaboration led to a BBC feature programme in August— *The Air is Our Sea*—which told the story of airmen arriving in Britain from the continent, 'Many people will have read in their newspapers of a British bomber which landed at an English aerodrome in the evening of June 18, during the hour of France's capitulation. Out of this one bomber climbed fifty pilots. A few were French; thirty-eight were Czechoslovaks who . . . had come here to continue their fight'.[167]

The idea that Britain stood alone in the year between the fall of France in June 1940 and the Soviet Union's declaration of war against Germany in June 1941 has featured strongly in post-war memories of 1940. But the regular references to European Allies continuing the fight from Britain, as well as publicity for the imperial war effort, suggest how far the British media projected an image of 'togetherness' at the time. A directive issued by Basil Nicolls to all BBC programme departments in June 1940, just before France fell, instructed them, 'Use "Allied" in preference to "British" wherever possible e.g. "Allied war effort"'.[168] This directive was for BBC programmes only, but all British media were involved in celebrating an allied effort. This vision of an allies' war fought by a multinational community was increasingly developed and expanded as the war continued.

Change of Climate

The celebration of a multinational community of allies in the media focused on men in military uniforms. Its most characteristic image was of men marching and parading. Mid-1940, Britain was not a good place to be non-British, for those not wearing uniforms. A Mass Observation report on 'feelings about aliens' in May noted, 'If you ask people what they think about "foreigners" you establish an immediately unfavourable attitude. And the word alien goes even further in this direction, having a close mental association with the adjective "enemy"'.[169]

The sinking of the *Arandora Star* when the ship was en route to Canada on 2 July was the starting point for a change of climate in British thinking about foreigners in their midst. It was a turning point in attitudes to internment, making clear how indiscriminate the round-up of Germans and Italians had been. Internees and prisoners of war who were being deported to Canada and drowned when the ship went down included not only Nazis and Fascists but also anti-Nazi German refugees, anti-Fascist Italians, and naturalized Britons. This was widely publicized in the press and in Parliamentary debates. On 6 July, Home Intelligence reported from Manchester, 'Indiscriminate internment of all aliens distresses more thought-ful people who regard it as evidence of panic action'.[170] On 10 July, a Parliamentary debate prompted by the *Arandora Star* revelations lasted for almost six hours. The government set up a judicial inquiry into the disaster, which reported in December.

In July and August, opposition to mass internment mounted. On 17 July, an article by journalist Michael Foot in the *Evening Standard* asked, 'Why not lock up General de Gaulle'? Foot argued that 'all who can give proof of their solid anti-Nazi and anti-Fascist resolution' should be 'welcomed by us as treasured allies'.[171] He wanted the words 'refugee' and 'alien' banished from the English language. Two days later, the *Evening Standard* featured a David Low cartoon which showed 'German and Italian enemies of Nazism and Fascism' on one side of a barbed wire fence. On the other side are strutting men and women, carrying messages announcing 'lock up all for-eigners', and 'suppress the press', who are labelled 'our own total-minded little Hitlers'. A little girl asks, 'Which are the dangerous ones we have to keep behind barbed-wire Uncle?'[172] Four days later, the *Evening Standard* followed this with an article, under the headline 'Shame', which identified refugees in Britain as friends, whose treatment by the English had disgraced the nation:

> Some stepped on our shores and drew a deep breath of freedom. They were ready to serve and work and fight for England, for England's cause they believed was the cause of free men the world over. What have we done with these our friends?...It is folly...It is worse than folly. It is sabotage against our war-effort. It is a damnable crime against the good name of England.[173]

In a July debate in the House of Commons, Viscount Wolmer echoed this view, asking that 'every one of these [internees'] cases should be properly investigated and dealt with on their merits' or 'we shall do harm to the good name of Great Britain'.[174] In August Viscount Cecil of Chelwood, speaking in the House of Lords, described mass internment as 'one of the most discreditable incidents in the whole history of this country'.[175] In August, Victor Cazalet, a Conservative Member of Parliament, described mass internment as 'this bespattered page of our history'.[176]

The idea that the policy of internment had disgraced the name of Britain was particularly apparent in charges that it resembled Nazi policy. Cazalet said in the House of Commons that the British government had unwittingly given material to German propaganda, since they had started 'to pursue the Nazi policy of interning every Jew in the country'.[177] Marjorie Redman, a subeditor of the *Listener* magazine, made a similar connection between British and Nazi policy, writing in her diary, 'Feel ashamed...because we consider ourselves better than the Nazis, but these are like their methods we despise'.[178] G. M. Trevelyan, the Cambridge historian and academic, wrote to *The Times*, 'One of my Italian anti-Fascist friends is at the bottom of the sea, having been sent in that ill-omened barque [the *Arandora Star*] in spite of clear proof lodged with the authorities of his friendship to England and his hostility to Mussolini...The Nazis keep their concentration camps for their enemies; we use them for our friends'.[179]

The mounting campaign against internment led to changes in government policy. The deportation of internees was abandoned. July saw the publication of a white paper which set out eighteen categories under which internees could be released. Release was slow at first but gathered pace, and by February 1941 had been authorized for more than 10,000 internees. By 1942, only a few hundred remained in internment camps.

The reversal of government thinking had its counterpart in popular opinion. On 3 August, Home Intelligence reported from Manchester 'disappointment that so little has been done to stop internment of anti-Hitler aliens' and on 24 August, also from Manchester, 'as details of internment camps become known, there is growing feeling about our treatment of anti-Nazi aliens.[180] In early August, a Mass Observation investigator recorded his impression of a small survey: 'Less than a quarter now think all should be interned, most think, some, those to be let out who could do useful work for us'.[181] One man interviewed for the survey remembered the David Low cartoon and supported the view it took, 'It's absurd to intern them wholesale.

Obviously some are all right (*sic*) and some are Gestapo. I agree with Low's cartoon about the men in the cage'. The more formal report on the Mass Observation survey put the number of people 'who now think that all aliens should be interned' as down to about a third of all those interviewed, although noting that the fifth column scare was 'still operative and uppermost in some people's minds'.[182]

Too much reliance should not be placed on such small surveys, but fears of fifth columnists and spies certainly receded. At the end of 1940, many Austrians, Germans, and Italians remained in internment camps. Even so, there had been a substantial shift in attitudes away from the intense hostility to foreigners in May and June and there was no wartime recurrence of the riots and violence of June. The change of climate is suggested by an absence of scaremongering about enemy aliens released from internment to join the British army and to do war work. In May and June, such recruitment would have caused an outcry about fifth columnist activity, but under the conditions given in the July white paper it became grounds for release from internment. Fifth columnist fears were occasionally revisited later in the war, but survived mainly as comedy in wartime films where comedians like Arthur Askey or Will Hay unmasked fifth columnists—often inadvertently.[183]

A shift in climate was certainly evident in Mollie Panter-Downes's 'Letter from London' for the *New Yorker*. On 19 May she toed the government line, describing 'the sudden announcement that all German and Austrian men between the ages of sixteen and sixty were to be interned' as 'a precaution which most Britons feel should have been taken long ago'. On 24 May, she made it clear that she thought the fifth columnist scare was justified, commenting, 'the Fifth Column menace is taken very seriously here, as well it might be'. On 12 August, her message was quite different:

> It's hoped by all sensible men here that something will soon be done to remedy the mistakes of the wholesale internment of refugees...The present unimaginative state of affairs seems to most Englishmen like an appalling waste of skilled manpower, time, and money, even if it doesn't show up in the still worse light of an insulting betrayal of men of good will.[184]

Figure 2.1 Susanne Medas (by kind permission of Susanne Medas).

2

Enemies and Neutrals

Susanne Medas (see Figure 2.1) arrived in Britain from Prague in June 1939. She was one of 10,000 children and teenagers who travelled on a scheme organized in 1938–9 with the aim of saving lives threatened by Nazi persecution in Austria, Germany, and Czechoslovakia—the *Kindertransport*. The scheme was for children only, involving separation from their parents.

Susanne Medas (originally Bernstein) was born into a Jewish family in Berlin, where she spent the first ten years of her life. She was ten years old when Hitler came to power in Germany in 1933 and her father's life was threatened. He was political editor of the Social Democrat newspaper *Vorwärts* (*Forward*), which was immediately banned by the Nazis. The Bernstein family escaped to Prague, where they had friends and where Medas joined *Die Rote Falken* (*The Red Falcon*). This was a socialist children's movement with a similar ethos to that of the Woodcraft Folk in Britain. In the summer of 1937 Medas travelled to Britain for the first time to attend an international camp in Brighton organized by the Woodcraft Folk.

On her second journey to Britain on the *Kindertransport*, Medas was with Red Falcon friends who were sponsored by the Woodcraft Folk in Britain. She remembers:

> I'd been to England in 1937 and I travelled [on the *Kindertransport*] with my Red Falcon friends...I'm sorry to say that I don't even remember whether my mother came to the railway station. I was nearly sixteen. I probably said to my mother, 'why do you have to come to the station? We're going—me and my friends—like we always do'. We go hiking in the winter, we went skiing or we went tobogganing, and in the summer we went to camp.[1]

Travelling from Czechoslovakia, the train passed through Germany and then crossed the border into Holland—a crossing that features in many accounts by *Kindertransport* children. Medas records of her journey from Prague:

> What happened was that the carriages were sealed to protect us because we had to travel through Germany...the whole train was just children with a few adults, so nobody got on or off in Germany...I remember that at one particular station which could have been Nuremberg, but I'm not sure, the Germans on the platform knew that these were Jewish children who were escaping and they were...shaking their fists at us...Then we got to a very small station called Venlo [in Holland]. That was the border crossing coming from Czechoslovakia...And at Venlo it was the total opposite because the doors were unlocked and the atmosphere was totally different. And women with big jugs of cocoa and bananas...they knew that this train was stopping at Venlo...and going on to England...They must have known from the station master when that train was arriving and how long it was stopping in Venlo— enough time for them to bring these goodies onto the platform.[2]

On Medas's first visit to England in 1937, a party from the Woodcraft Folk camp went on a coach trip to London, where they visited the Czechoslovakian Embassy and were received by Jan Masaryk, then Czechoslovakian ambassador to Britain. It was Masaryk who later ridiculed the British government's 'provisional' recognition of the Czechoslovakian government-in-exile by asking whether Czech pilots killed in the Battle of Britain were 'provisionally dead'. Medas remembers the reception laid on at the Czechoslovakian Embassy:

> There we were given something that I had never seen before—cucumber sandwiches with the crust cut off...and on some of the sandwiches was something that I described to my parents when I wrote to them as 'grass'. Of course it was mustard and cress...And for cereal [at the Woodcraft Folk camp] we had something which I now know is Shredded Wheat...So England was very fascinating and very different and little did I know that two years later I would come to live here for the rest of my life.[3]

Medas's brother Heinrich, who had preceded her to Britain, was arrested and interned in 1940 as an enemy alien and then deported to Australia on the *Dunera*—on a voyage that caused a scandal when information began to leak out about British soldiers guarding internees who had robbed and beaten them.[4] People who were interned in 1940 were predominantly Austrian, German, and Italian and predominantly men. In 1941, as more countries became enemy belligerents, internment was extended. After the Japanese attack on Pearl Harbor in December 1941, thirty-four Japanese arrived on the Isle of Man, where the bulk of the internment camps were based. They were mainly businessmen who had worked in London—some of them officials from the London branch of the Yokahama bank. December 1941 also saw the arrival of Finns, Hungarians, and Romanians. By February 1942, internment camps on the Isle of Man housed ninety Japanese and 340 Finns. Japanese who were interned included government officials, journalists, and seamen, as well as businessmen. Most of the Finns were merchant seamen.[5]

As the arrivals on the Isle of Man demonstrate, people of enemy nationality in wartime Britain were very disparate. The substantial pre-First World War German community in Britain collapsed as a result of wartime anti-German riots, internment, and deportations—from 53,324 in 1911 to only 14,981 in 1931, by which date it was outnumbered by the Italian-born community. But by the outbreak of the Second World War, the numbers of Germans in Britain exceeded their pre-First World War level as a result of the arrival of German refugees escaping Nazi persecution. The numbers of Italian refugees were smaller. Some 500 Italian Jews escaped to Britain, more than half migrating onward to the United States or Latin America.[6] But migration to Britain from Italy had a considerable history, which meant that there was a sizeable Italian community in Britain at the outbreak of war, numbering some 35,000.[7] In the later stages of the war, both the Italian and German presences were swollen by the arrival of prisoners of war. When the war ended, 381,632 Germans and 153,779 Italians were held as prisoners in Britain.[8]

People of neutral nationality in Britain were also very disparate, but by far the largest numbers were from Éire. The 1931 census had counted more than half a million Irish-born, and during the war there was brisk recruitment of war workers from Éire, when more than 100,000 travelled to Britain. Estimates of the numbers of volunteers for the British armed forces from Éire vary from 42,000 to 165,000.[9] In 1944 the *Manchester Guardian* put the figure as high as 300,000, while an American report, also in 1944, estimated 150,000 volunteers and 300,000 war workers.[10]

This chapter traces the shifting places that Austrians, Germans, and Italians occupied on the spectrum that had 'enemies' at one end and 'allies' at the other. The policy of mass internment in mid-1940 placed them unmistakably at the 'enemies' end of this spectrum. On release from internment, their contributions to the allied war effort as soldiers, war workers, and propagandists meant that their position moved closer to the 'allies' end. In the later stages of the war their place at the 'enemies' end was taken by other Austrians,

Germans, and Italians who arrived as prisoners of war and attracted considerable hostility.

'Neutral' was also a category with unstable and shifting meanings. Southern Ireland attracted far more attention in the British media than any other neutral nation. In the early stages of the war, ideas circulating in Britain about Southern Ireland were mixed. Sometimes Southern Ireland was portrayed as a brave little country threatened, like other small neutral states, by brutal Nazi aggression. 'Éire Menaced by Germany' was the title of one newsreel. Another, titled 'Éire Stands Guard on her Coasts', promised that 'Britain's Navy, Army and Air Force are ready to stand beside these cousins of ours in the Emerald Isle'.[11] But in November the Éire government's refusal to allow the use of its ports as British bases—a refusal that was seen as causing the deaths of British and Allied seamen in the Atlantic war—brought strong criticism in Parliament and the press. Such criticism was sanctioned by Churchill.[12]

In 1943, the Ministry of Information was anxious to 'prevent violent Press criticism of Éire's neutrality', regarding 'ill-considered criticism' as 'extremely harmful'.[13] Even so, Éire continued to be criticized for refusing to allow Britain the use of its ports. In 1944, the Éire government's refusal to expel German and Japanese legations in Dublin in the build-up to D-Day prompted further strong criticism for endangering Allied lives, risking secrets leaking across its land border with Northern Ireland, and 'playing Hitler's game'.[14] Both these refusals were widely viewed in both official and popular opinion as acts of hostility, rather than of neutrality, placing Éire somewhere at the 'enemy' end of the enemy–ally spectrum—a quasi-enemy. Mistrust spilled over into attitudes to the Irish in Britain, who were sometimes regarded as spies and fifth columnists. But Irish volunteers serving in the British forces were usually regarded very differently—as allies.

Brian Inglis—an Irishman who volunteered for the RAF—reflected on his wartime experience, 'People who have been brought up to be loyal to their country, with never the occasion for doubt which country it is, find it hard to appreciate the conflicts that disturb and, in some cases, destroy the individual who has a dual loyalty'.[15] Dual or multiple attachments and loyalties that crossed national boundaries were characteristic of many Italians, as well as Irish, but paradoxically, service in the British forces often strengthened a sense of Italian and Irish identity—for Irish from Northern Ireland as well as from Éire. Austrians and Germans were more likely to identify with the exile community of anti-Nazis than with their former compatriots.

Within disparate groups, people had many different reasons for their journeys to Britain and a wide range of experiences. Even so, there are common transnational themes in their histories—the journeys they made, the families they belonged to, the allegiances they held.[16] Falling outside national memories, these histories have been consigned to what Wendy Ugolini, writing about Italians, calls a 'commemorative no man's land'.[17]

Enemy Nationals in the British Army and as Prisoners of War

Ralph Fraser and his brother were German Jews who came to Britain as refugees before the war and were arrested in 1940. Like many other internees they were deported to the British Empire—in their case to Canada. They record their reaction when, on release from internment in 1942, they returned to Britain to join the British army, 'We came in as dangerous enemy aliens in the morning, and at four o'clock in the afternoon we walked out as members of His Majesty's forces... We laughed as we walked out of the camp'.[18] Their laughter may express relief that they have arrived at a better place than internment, one where they can walk out of a camp. But they tell the story to emphasize laughter at the absurdity of such a sudden switch in the meaning of their nationality—from enemies to soldiers in British uniform in less than twelve hours.

As Ralph Fraser's story demonstrates, questions about whether Germans in Britain were enemies or allies did not always receive clear-cut answers. They could be both—although not simultaneously—shifting from one category to another. The shift began in 1940 and was part of the change of climate following the mass arrests and internments of May and June. It was in the first week of June, only six weeks after he had announced the policy of mass internment, that Winston Churchill urged his Chief of Staff, General Hastings Ismay, to recruit enemy aliens to a foreign legion. He wrote, 'I see no question why enemy aliens, wishing to fight against Germany, should not be incorporated in a military body where the discipline is strict, where the penalties are severe, and where they can be under constant observation... We should aim at 5,000 to begin with'.[19]

In July, Ismay informed Churchill that there had been steady recruitment of enemy aliens to the Pioneer Corps before May. Recruitment had then been closed down by the 'general demand for internment', but had now been reopened.[20] Churchill personally oversaw this recruitment, asking for weekly returns of numbers and occasionally writing notes on these. At the end of August his note complained, 'This is very slow. Ask that the numbers should be at least doubled. These men are better and safer in units than in internment camps, provided they are anti-Nazis'.[21] A government White Paper in July listed eighteen categories under which internees could be released. Acceptance into the Pioneer Corps, a non-combatant unit of the British army, was one of these—Austrians and Germans were not allowed to serve in combatant units until 1942. Initially, release under the eighteen categories was for Austrian and German refugees, but two further White Papers in August and October 1940 added new categories and extended their application to Italians.[22]

Francois Lafitte, who worked for Political and Economic planning, criticized the release policy as 'narrowly utilitarian' in his 1940 study of the internment of aliens, published as a Penguin Special. Under the categories listed in the July White Paper, release was permitted not only for those accepted into the Pioneer Corps but also for those judged to possess skills that equipped them for a range of work 'of national importance'. Refugees, Lafitte argued, 'are not cattle or horses to be kept locked up in stables . . . and only taken out when their owner has some use for them'.[23] Rhys Davies, Labour Member of Parliament for Westhoughton, echoed this view, saying in a debate in the House of Commons: 'If these people on release can be of service to the national cause, we . . . will let them out. That smells a little too much of Hitlerism for me. These men should be let out of the internment camps because they are innocent and not because they are useful. That is the test'.[24]

Some internees took the utilitarian view. P. F. Wiener, who had been a modern language master at Rugby school before he was interned, drew attention to internees' wish to 'do our bit' in a letter to *The Times* in July 1940, written from an internment camp:

> [T]he greatest complaint of most, if not all of us, is the inactivity into which we are forced. Many of us have outstanding technical, scholarly, or industrial qualifications; others are young and healthy as myself, and very fit for military service or agricultural work. It is a most bitter disappointment to us that we have to sit quiet behind barbed wire, and are not allowed to do our bit in any

way whatsoever in this fight against our common mortal enemy, for our great common cause.[25]

Recruitment to the Pioneer Corps may have satisfied Weiner's plea that internees should be released to 'do our bit' for the common cause and eroded the idea that all Germans and Italians in Britain were enemies, but it positioned them in a lowly place at the 'ally' end of the 'enemy to ally' spectrum. In a wartime context, where martial masculinity was highly valued, they were 'permitted to take up not arms but scrubbing brushes and spades'.[26] Mark Lynton, like Ralph Fraser and his brother, was a Jewish German who had been interned in 1940, was then deported to Canada, and was subsequently released to join the Pioneer Corps. He wrote a comic description of his time there:

> There are few airports, roads, and probably not a single public toilet built in the west of England between 1941 and 1943 where I did not participate in the construction... We built various structures for the public weal: roads, runways, Nissen huts, and such. But our prime time and talent were devoted to latrines. We built them in Gloucestershire, Wiltshire, Shropshire, even in Hampshire, and well into Wales—a seat for every citizen, or almost.[27]

By no means all those recruited to the Pioneer Corps found a comic dimension to such manual labour. Peter Masters, a Jewish refugee from Vienna, found service in the Pioneer Corps 'a dreary existence' made up of 'dull, unchallenging work'.[28] Anton Walter Freud, the grandson of Sigmund Freud, had been arrested and interned on the Isle of Man and then deported to Australia on the *Dunera*. Freud was released in summer 1941 to return to Britain and join the Pioneer Corps and records that 'its cap badge showing a pick and shovel was not one that I was very proud of'.[29] George Clare also disliked the pick and shovel. When he was offered a commission by a War Office Selection Board, he turned it down, and writes, 'I was too much of a snob myself to want to be seen ever again, even as an officer, with that gravedigger's emblem on my uniform.[30] Clare was a Jewish German refugee who served in the Pioneer Corps until the summer of 1943, when he transferred to the Royal Artillery. He describes the Pioneer Corps as a 'miserable outfit' and a 'navvy unit'.

Postal Censorship found other complaints about the Pioneer Corps in letters from internees—objections to its unarmed status and to enforced recruitment. A report in October 1940 noted, 'The AMPC [Pioneer Corps] is not a popular service with German refugees. Many of them declare "the real Army or nothing". It is not possible to tell whether this is their sincere conviction, or whether they hope to escape service for "the real army", because they know that they will not be accepted'.[31] The same report recorded that another letter-writer 'declares that he has decided not to join the AMPC because he doubts the value of enlistment of those whose only alternative is continued internment'. It commented, 'This view of his is, incidentally, shared by many Internees, who resent the fact that they are more or less forced to enlist if they wish to be released'.[32] In a further letter intercepted by Postal Censorship, an internee wrote, 'It's not pleasant that they hold the revolver to our breasts, so to speak, in order to get out we must join the Pioneer Corps'.[33] Since most internees were aware that their letters were censored, these letter-writers may have wanted to bring their views on forced recruitment to the notice of the authorities.

Service in the Pioneer Corps involved downward mobility for many Austrian and German refugees who had no previous experience of manual labour. Mark Lynton—who had been studying at Cambridge University when he was arrested and interned—served in a Company of the Pioneer Corps made up of aliens of various nationalities, commanded by the British. At one time it included six Nobel Laureates:

> The Nobel laureate ingredient within the 251st Company, as well as the lofty level and range of conversation, did not measurably add to our digging competence or our building skills... Our [British] sergeants and officers dealt with us in an aura of helpless exasperation. We were reasonably able to cope with the jobs, but it was those pauses, when half the ditch leaned on their shovels to listen to someone propound a variant on Hegel's concept of objective logic, that drove them crazy.[34]

One Pioneer studied for an Honours Degree in English while serving in a Pioneer Company. When digging or unloading he carried little papers round his wrist, which were held by an elastic band and closely written with things to be memorized.[35]

Postal Censorship found discontent among members of the Pioneer Corps at official failures to recognize the skills they could contribute to the war effort. One letter-writer complained that Dr Weiss, the former camp doctor, had to break stones and do 'other unproductive work' and that qualified engineers, doctors, and dentists who were 'all damned to do the same unproductive work' were growing 'depressed and losing their confidence in victory'.[36] As with internees' criticisms of forced recruitment, this letter-writer may have wanted to bring his view to the notice of the authorities who censored his letter. The *Onchan Pioneer*, the newspaper produced by internees at Onchan camp on the Isle of Man, also seems likely to have been addressing the authorities when it produced a survey of internees in its November issues. This showed their wide range of skills—graduate engineers, merchants, skilled workers and craftsmen, and professionals including physicians, writers, lawyers, artists, and teachers. The anonymous writer asked 'Why not enlist our knowledge and abilities'?[37]

In the summer of 1942 enemy nationals in the Pioneer Corps were armed for the first time. In 1943, they could apply to join fighting units and many did. Others were recruited as Commandos, Paratroopers, and for work in the Special Operations Executive—a secret wartime organization operating in occupied Europe to aid resistance movements. Anton Freud volunteered for the Special Operations Executive and Peter Masters joined the Commandos. During the fifth columnist scare in mid-1940, enemy nationals had been seen as the enemy within. During their service in the Pioneer Corps they had occupied a lowly place in the hierarchy of allies. By 1942, earlier mistrust was succeeded not only by recruitment to the British army, but also by recruitment to work on missions that were often highly secret.

Language skills were particularly valued in the British forces. German-speakers in 101 Squadron RAF worked as special radio operators to jam German radio transmitting.[38] German-speakers in the Intelligence Service of the Tank Corps intercepted the enemy's radio and confused their radio operators. In the Women's Auxiliary Air Force, German-speakers and Italian-speakers transmitted false orders to the pilots of enemy aircraft.[39] In the later stages of the war and its aftermath, German-speakers worked in the denazi-fication project in prisoner-of-war camps in Britain. During the occupation of Germany when the war was over, Germans serving in the British forces were recruited to the Interpreters Corps and the Intelligence Corps, where they translated, interpreted, investigated, and interrogated. Their work included interrogation of war criminals and translation and interpreting during war crimes trials.[40] Italians in the British army were also involved in interpreting—in prisoner-of-war camps in Britain and Italy, and in liaison work with the local population during the Allied occupation of Italy.[41]

Through their war work and their service in the British army—at first as non-combatants and then in fighting units—men and women who had attracted intense hostility as enemy aliens in mid-1940 gradually moved

further to the ally end of the enemy–ally spectrum. But in the later stages of
the war, there was a resurgence of hostility towards enemy aliens in Britain,
now directed not at Germans and Italians who had been in Britain in 1940,
but at prisoners of war who had subsequently arrived.

Complaints about prisoners of war centred on the idea that they were
too well treated. In a context where oranges were very scarce and eggs were
rationed, Home Intelligence reported:

> [T]here is some indignant comment at the idea that 'oranges and milk are
> supplied to them [German prisoners of war] while our own people go short'.
> In Warrington it is rumoured that German prisoners at a local camp are
> allowed to walk about outside the camp sucking oranges; in the Chester-le-
> Street (Co Durham) neighbourhood, the rumour that wounded German
> prisoners in the local hospital are given a shell egg for breakfast every morning
> is causing indignation.[42]

Reporting and photographs of starved British prisoners in Germany in
April 1945 prompted renewed protests on the same theme—German
prisoners in Britain were too well treated, receiving the same rations,
under the Geneva Convention, as their soldier captors. Reporting focused
on the disparity between prisoners of war and British civilians working
together, where Germans ate better than their British fellow workers.[43]
Members of the Manchester Grocers' Association asked the government
to reduce prisoners' rations.[44] In the wake of the liberation of Belsen
concentration camp, an editorial in the *Sunday Express* entitled 'Feed the
Brutes' stated:

> When the brutal guards of the concentration camps are marched away into
> captivity what happens to them. If they are brought to this country they are
> well housed with twice the food ration of a British civilian. It does not make
> sense and the people of this country resent it deeply. Here and in the US we
> are keeping something like 2 million German soldiers in a fitter condition
> than any other people in Europe.[45]

The *Daily Mail* published a cartoon of two fat German prisoners of war,
sitting with their feet on the table, picking their teeth, after what was
evidently a satisfying meal. Outside British demonstrators bear placards:
'Help wanted on the land.Your food depends on it'. One German prisoner
tells the other:'Don't worry Heinrich, it doesn't mean us—we just eat it'.[46]

Italy's surrender to the Allies in 1943 and declaration of war on Germany
meant that Italians were officially assigned a particularly ambivalent classification

in the 'enemy to ally' spectrum—neither enemies nor fully-fledged allies, but 'co-belligerents'. Paradoxically it was when they ceased to be enemies that Italian prisoners of war attracted particular hostility. Their reclassification as 'co-belligerents' did not involve their release, but they were offered the option of becoming 'co-operators', who could talk to British civilians and accept invitations to their homes. Home Intelligence reported 'resentment…at the privileges and freedom allowed to Italian co-operators' and noted disapproval of 'the slackening of restrictions', the 'soft treatment' this involved, and 'the government's rooted determination to pamper these men'.[47]

Many Italian prisoners of war were brought to Britain (see Figure 2.2) to work in agriculture, where there was a serious shortage of labour. Their bicycles, provided by farmers or the Ministry of Agriculture for their journeys to work, were also the subject of complaints. 'People object also to their receiving bicycles when civilians have none'; 'people again complain of their amorous disposition, their insolence, their laziness and their bicycles'.[48] There were regular reports of criticism of their association with British women and girls and Home Intelligence also noted that 'uncertainty about Italy's status as a co-belligerent' led to a revisiting of fifth column suspicions, 'Some think they are still on Germany's side, and would make a good Fifth Column in the event of counter-invasion'.[49] Amid a stream of complaints in 1944 about Italian prisoners' privileges and bicycles, Home Intelligence also noted a complaint that suggests some diversity in attitudes. The complaint was about resentment of the 'friendliness and hospitality shown by some local people to Italian co-operators'.[50]

Writing about prisoners of war in Britain during the Second World War, historian Bob Moore argues that government policy turned them from liabilities into assets, working in essential industries where there were labour shortages.[51] In 1943, as these shortages increased, particularly in agriculture, Churchill looked forward to 'getting 100,000 more Italians into England for work purposes' and by 1944 the Ministry of Labour's estimate of the number of prisoners who could be usefully employed in Britain had risen to 250,000.[52] The government's wartime need for labour runs through the history of enemy nationals who were interned and subsequently released, as well as the history of enemy nationals held in Britain as prisoners of war. In both cases, government policy turned them into assets useful to the British war effort and fitted Lafitte's description—'narrowly utilitarian'.

Figure 2.2 Italian prisoners of war arriving at a British port, 26 April 1942, Liverpool (© Imperial War Museum, A 8469).

Irish Volunteers and War-workers

Winston Churchill took a personal interest not only in the recruitment of enemy aliens to the British forces, but also in the formation of an Irish Brigade. He supported a suggestion made by General Gough in a letter to *The Times* in 1941, which noted that 'very large numbers of Irishmen have joined HM Forces since the outbreak of war', and urged that 'existing Irish units should be regrouped as an Irish brigade or division'.[53] Following Gough's letter, Churchill wrote to the Secretary of State for War and the Secretary of State for Air enclosing a passage from Postal Censorship, which had reported, 'Many young Irishmen and women are serving with the Allied forces and writers complain that this fact is still not sufficiently recognised in England'. Churchill wrote, 'I think now the time is ripe to form an Irish Brigade also an Irish wing or Squadron of the RAF...the pilot Finucane might be a great figure'.[54]

Churchill suggested that the proposed RAF Squadron could be named 'Shamrock'—a symbol of Ireland and the emblem that decorated Finucane's aircraft. Brendan Finucane was popular in wartime Britain as a leading fighter ace, but perhaps a surprising figure to win Churchill's admiration— his father had fought with de Valera against the British in Dublin during the Easter uprising in 1916. Mary Mulry, the Irish nurse, had dinner with Finucane in Farnborough in the summer of 1940. Her diary does not record how she met him, but her father, like Finucane's, had fought against the British in the Easter uprising.[55] Churchill's enthusiasm for Irish volunteers, like Finucane, who were serving in the forces did not extend to Irish civilians in Britain. In 1941, he was not initially attracted by a proposal that Italian prisoners of war should be brought to Britain to work on British farms, but subsequently reflected: 'it might be better to use these docile Italian prisoners of war instead of bringing in disaffected Irish over whom we have nothing like the same control'.[56]

Home Intelligence reports in 1940 show that, like Churchill, popular opinion on Irish civilians in Britain saw them as 'disaffected', with persistent suspicions that they were fifth columnists and spies. In mid-1940 'great discontent' was reported from Cardiff about 1,000 Irishmen employed on building defence in Anglesey, who were seen as 'a useful Fifth Column nucleus'. In Scotland the passage of homing pigeons between Ireland and the West of Scotland caused anxiety as 'a potential method for Fifth Column Irish communication'.[57] Private employers began to discharge not only

people of enemy nationality but also Irish employees.[58] Suspicions of Irish
civilians were also reported in 1942—rumours that 'Irish labourers who
leave the country after 6 months to avoid income tax are...a particularly
dangerous source of information for the enemy. They are said to queue
outside the German Embassy in Dublin to lay information at £2 a time'.[59]

   In 1944, suspicions of the Irish reached a high point in the context of the
Éire government's refusal of the Anglo-American request that German and
Japanese legations in Dublin should be expelled. Home Intelligence
reported, 'Éire workers in this country, never popular and usually mistrusted,
are now bitterly resented' and that this resentment was about 'the potential
danger to our war effort of having them here'. A report from Scotland
stated, 'many of them are said to listen to Haw Haw nightly at 10.30 and to
nothing else'.[60] 'Lord Haw Haw' was the nickname given to William Joyce,
who broadcast propaganda from Germany to Britain and was sentenced to
death for treachery when the war was over.

   It is difficult to assess the significance of the persistent association of the
Irish with spying. Historian Enda Delaney comments that oral testimony
from Irish migrants to wartime Britain suggests that 'for the most part [they]
were not subject to any overt hostility' and that interviewees 'seem on the
whole to be positive about their experiences in Britain'. As he suggests, 'the
problem of interpreting isolated outward manifestations of prejudice or
hostility as indicative of a widespread attitude is obvious'.[61] Churchill's
view of the Irish as 'disaffected' was out of step with a report by Home
Intelligence in February 1941 that 'Southern Irish living in this country are
becoming more and more favourably disposed towards our cause. Though not
indifferent to Éire's situation, many of its subjects when writing home are
loud in their praises of England, and urge their friends to join us in the war'.[62]
Some letters from Ireland to Britain intercepted after this report was written
also support this view, including one from County Wicklow in December 1941:

> There is a lot of the fellows returned for Xmas that went over to England
> from here...All of them I might say went over starving and bitter enemies
> of England. Well, you never saw such a change. All speak so highly of the
> Englishman, all are going back, it is going to make a big change in this coun-
> try...To listen to Pallord would do you good, a complete change over from
> the I.R.A. to 'up England'.[63]

The same view is apparent in a letter from County Mayo in 1942, 'Hundreds
of men who have been on munition work in England are back on their
holidays. The atmosphere in general of all who return is entirely pro-British'.[64]

In contrast to the mistrust of Irish civilians in Britain, Irish volunteers in the British forces were honoured in the British media—particularly Brendan Finucane, who was invariably named 'Paddy'. Newsreels provided close-up shots and celebrated his distinctions. 'Squadron Leader Paddy Finucane with 2 DSOs and 3 DFCs, the RAF's fighter pilot ace from Ireland'.[65] When he was shot down in July 1942, 2,500 people attended his Requiem Mass at Westminster Cathedral. The *Daily Mirror*, reporting on the Paddy Finucane memorial fund, wrote that 'Paddy Finucane is dead, but he lives and is loved in the memory of people all over the world'.[66] A programme on the BBC European service was devoted to him:

> Fighter Pilot of the Royal Air Force! That was what Finucane was. One of the very best. There could be no prouder title . . . he was an Irishman, that is a citizen of a country which has declared itself neutral in this war but many, many thousands of whose citizens have refused to be impartial in a conflict between good and evil and are fighting today with us . . . We mourn him. We shall honour him. I hope you in Europe will, too. He died and fought for you as well as for us.[67]

A newsreel celebrating the twenty-fifth anniversary of the RAF in 1943 named Finucane as a hero.[68]

After Finucane's death no Irish figure emerged to match him in popularity, but from 1943 the Ministry of Information advocated paying 'generous recognition to the contribution of the volunteers from Éire serving in HM Forces' and compiled lists of those who had won distinctions which were regularly updated.[69] Newspaper and newsreel reports featuring Irish volunteers drew on these lists.[70] In 1943 the Ministry of Information also instructed that criticism of Éire should not be 'ill-judged' and 'violent', explaining that this 'not only inflames opinion in the United Kingdom against Éire, but also when repeated in Éire inflames Irish opinion against the United Kingdom'.[71]

Like the Ministry of Information, the Ministry of Labour was concerned about inflaming Irish opinion. Their concerns were about the opinions of Irish workers in Britain which, they warned, might be inflamed as a consequence of a proposed American letter reproaching Éire for its neutrality. Churchill's response to this view was scathing. He wrote, 'I do not understand why if the United States writes a letter of this kind to De Valera Irishmen working for good wages in England should be inflamed against us, and even if they are why we should not survive their rancour'.[72]

When an Anglo-American letter was eventually sent in 1944, requesting the closure of Japanese and German legations in Dublin, and the Irish government refused this request, Churchill's criticisms were accompanied by the praise of Irish volunteers that the Ministry of Information had advocated. Announcing the travel ban between Northern Ireland and Éire that followed Éire's refusal, Churchill stated in the House of Commons, 'I need scarcely say how painful it is to us to take such measures in view of the large numbers of Irishmen who are fighting so bravely in our armed forces and the many deeds of personal heroism by which they have kept alive the martial honour of the Irish race'.[73] Implicitly, Irishmen who, in conformity with the Irish policy of neutrality, are not in the British forces, bring dishonour on the Irish race.

In his Victory broadcast of 1945, Churchill returned to the theme of brave Irishmen—this time in the context of comment on the Éire government's refusal to allow the use of Irish ports as British bases:

> Owing to the action of Mr. de Valera, so much at variance with the temper and instinct of thousands of southern Irish men who hastened to the battle front to prove their ancient valour, the approaches which the Southern Irish ports and airfields could so easily have guarded were closed by the hostile aircraft and U-boats. This was indeed a deadly moment in our life... However, with a restraint and a poise to which, I say, history will find few parallels, His Majesty's Government never laid a violent hand upon them [the Irish]... and we left the de Valera government to frolic with the Germans and later with the Japanese representatives to their heart's content'.[74]

Churchill balanced this censure of the Irish government's 'frolic' with the Germans and the Japanese with a celebration of brave Irish volunteers, invoking names from the lists of those who had won distinctions compiled by the Ministry of Information, 'When I think of these days... I think of Lieutenant-Commander Esmond, V.C., of Lance-Corporal Kenneally, V.C., and Captain Fegen, V.C., and other Irish heroes that I could easily recite, and then I must confess that bitterness against the Irish race dies in my heart'.[75] Churchill makes an opposition between Irish government policy, which obstructs the British war effort and the actions of brave Irish soldiers, which assist it. The best of Irishmen are in British uniform supporting the British war effort. Brian Inglis, who was an Irish volunteer like those celebrated by Churchill, recorded that he was 'too indignant with Churchill for his sneers at de Valera in his Victory broadcast to be appeased by his references to the Irish volunteers who had won VCs'.[76]

Like Churchill's speeches, a 1944 feature film—*Halfway House*—combined criticism of Irish neutrality with celebration of Irish volunteers. The film

shows Irishman Terence (Pat McGrath) experiencing a change of heart
and mind, abandoning his plan to join the Irish legation in Berlin in favour
of joining the British forces. Terence is one of ten guests from diverse back-
grounds spending the night in a Welsh hotel. He is in Britain to see his
fiancée Margaret (Philippa Hiatt). They quarrel when he tells her about his
intention to join the Irish legation in Berlin—Margaret is English and in
military uniform.

At dinner, where all the guests gather, Terence defends Irish neutrality,
including the refusal of their ports, 'If England used our bases, Germany
would claim it as a breach of neutrality and she'd be justified. Germany has
as much right to a neutral base as England'. Opposition to his view is voiced
not by the British guests, but by a Frenchwoman, played by Françoise Rosay,
whose son has died at sea. In a set-piece speech, she tells the dinner guests
'Some of my countrymen also decided that anything's better than war. Now
they see what real Frenchmen have always known. That one doesn't get
peace by refusing to fight, because there is no peace for those who are dominated and despised. What's the use of living without freedom and dignity'?

It is when German planes bomb the hotel that the quarrel between
Terence and his fiancée Margaret is resolved. Going in search of Margaret,
Terence finds her frightened by the bombing and experiences a change of
heart, calling German bombers 'Swine! Filthy swine'! This is the moment
when he abandons his intention to join the Irish legation in Berlin in favour
of enlisting in the British forces—'I won't be the first Irishman to ask is this
a private fight or can anyone join in'? Terence's final words in the film conform to the Ministry of Information's guidance on propaganda about Irish
volunteers, celebrating the Irish contribution to the Allied effort, 'There
isn't a family in all Ireland that hasn't someone fighting in this war'.[77]

Enemy Nationals in the British Media

The Ministry of Information's instructions that Irish volunteers should be
given 'generous recognition' meant that they featured more prominently in
wartime British propaganda than Germans or Italians. Germans made a
substantial contribution to wartime propaganda as scriptwriters and speakers
on BBC programmes, through monitoring enemy propaganda at the BBC
monitoring service, and through their roles in British cinema, where they
were often cast as Nazis.[78] Italians also contributed to BBC programmes.

This work for British propaganda was rarely publicized. Germans and Italians serving in the British armed forces rarely featured in the media vision of an 'allies' war'.

German-speaking exiles played a key role at the BBC as early as 1940, through the development of satirical series on the German service. Historian Krista Meier comments that, when Britain was 'dealing with the threat of invasion...when Germany's propaganda machine was at full blast and the victory trumpets of German radio blew loudest, the BBC launched its attempt to fight Hitler with laughter'.[79] The first satirical series on the German service was *Frau Wernicke*—produced by the German-speaking émigré, Walter Rilla, who headed the features section of the German service from autumn 1940. Annemarie Hase—a Jewish German actress who had been banned from the German stage and arrived in Britain in 1936—played the Berlin housewife of the title.[80] In autumn and winter 1940, two more satirical series were added. *Adolf Hirnschal* was about a First World War veteran serving on the front line and his weekly letter to his wife. *Kurt und Willi* presented dialogues between an official who works in the German Ministry of Propaganda and a German schoolteacher. All these series had long runs and were scripted by Jewish émigrés—Bruno Adler and Robert Lucas. Lucas wrote about his use of satire, 'It seemed to me very important... in the battle for the souls of the German population—and that is what it was about in those years—to use the weapon of humour'.[81]

Also in 1940—on April Fool's Day—Martin Miller contributed to the effort to fight Hitler with laughter through impersonating him on the BBC's German service. Miller was an Austrian Jewish exile who came to London in 1939 and acted in British film and in émigré cabaret and theatre. The spoof Hitler speech that he spoke and scripted was frequently interrupted by recorded chants of 'Heil'. It included Hitler's claim that when Columbus discovered America he did so with the aid of German-made equipment and instruments and that this gave Germany territorial claims on America. The speech ended, 'Mr. Roosevelt should take note that it is my indomitable will finally to occupy the chair destined for me in the White House so that it finally becomes the Brown House one way or the other'! The impersonation successfully fooled CBS, the American broadcaster, which contacted the BBC to ask where it had picked up Hitler's speech.[82]

German-speaking exiles and émigrés also broadcast on the Home Service in a series entitled *Under Nazi Rule*, which included speakers who had been in Dachau, Buchenwald, and Sachsenhausen concentration camps. They contributed to discussions of conditions in Nazi Germany, including the administration of justice, the position of women, and conditions of life in Germany. Most of their contributions were anonymous since, as the *Radio Times* explained, 'Listeners will realise that it is not advisable for Germans in this country who still have relatives in Nazi Germany to broadcast under their own names'.[83]

Under Nazi Rule is a comparatively rare example of a wartime radio programme where Germans speak directly to a British audience. However, they played a significant role in scripting and producing Home Service programmes.[84] Walter Rilla and Karl Otten both worked in the Features Department of the German Service in 1940, but lost their posts when the service was reorganized in 1941. They continued to work on anti-Nazi propaganda for Home Service programmes. Broadcasts written and produced by Walter Rilla included *Diary of Chaos*, based on the diary of Yanina Monsior and telling the story of her escape from Warsaw to France and eventually to Britain. Among other programmes that he wrote and produced were 'Kaj Munk'—a portrait of the Danish priest and playwright who openly attacked the Nazis in his plays and sermons and was murdered in 1944—and *The Gestapo Over Europe*, a two-part programme on the German secret state police. Otten wrote episodes in a range of series, including *Black Gallery*, which dealt with the vicious habits of Nazi leaders. His contributions to *It Might Happen Here*—a series which imagined the Nazis coming to Britain—were an episode which imagined railway workers in a Britain under Nazi rule and another that transposed the oppression of Belgian miners under Nazi occupation onto a coalfield in South Wales.[85]

Italians working at the BBC, like Germans, scripted satire. Elio Nissim, an Italian Jewish refugee who had been a lawyer in Florence, wrote and spoke the satirical *Monologue of the Man in the Street* for the Italian service—a series which ran from May 1941 until April 1945.[86] Germans and Italians worked in 'black' radio as well as 'white', broadcasting from clandestine stations in Britain which aimed to sound as though they offered a German or Italian view transmitted from Germany or Italy.[87] Brigitte Eisner was a Jewish refugee who began working at a black radio station broadcasting to Germany in 1944. She was employed as a typist and told on her first day that broadcasts were all in 'proper German', not 'refugee German', so that they could not be traced back to refugees who had left Germany. Anti-Nazi German prisoners of war were employed to broadcast, and Reisner was 'totally taken aback' when she was told she would be working alongside them.[88]

In the later stages of the war, Austrian, German, and Italian prisoners of war also broadcast directly to their compatriots on the BBC. *Austrian News*, the organ of the free Austrian movement in Britain, reported in September 1944, 'Many Austrians, prisoners of war, volunteer for propaganda, among them a number of officers, and are admitted to the microphone to appeal to their compatriots, and to show them how best to serve the Allied cause. These radio talks by prisoners of war, freely given...give account of the prevailing anti-German spirit among them'.[89] Similar appeals to serve the Allied cause were made by German and Italian prisoners of war.

The idea that propaganda should make use of Germans who were 'supporting us' had been canvassed earlier in the war by Kenneth Clark in a debate at the Ministry of Information:

> If the Germans really are incorrigible, what can be the outcome of the war? Are we hoping to exterminate 80 million people or to keep them in continual subjection?...It would seem in our interests to stress the very great difference between the Germany of 1914–18 and today, by pointing out how in the last war all the best elements of science and culture were still in Germany and were supporting the German cause, whereas now they are outside Germany and are supporting us.[90]

Comparatively little propaganda along these lines was addressed to a British audience. German-speaking émigrés and refugees played a prominent role in anti-Nazi propaganda through their work in British cinema, but those working as actors were generally cast, not as Germans who were 'supporting us', but as Nazi enemies. They included Walter Rilla, who acted occasionally in wartime British cinema, in addition to his workload at the BBC, and played Nazi officers in both *The Adventures of Tartu* (1943) and *Mr Emmanuel* (1944).

One documentary film sponsored by the Ministry of Information did show Austrians and Germans 'supporting us'. *Lift Your Head, Comrade* featured 74 Company of the Pioneer Corps and took its title from a song that had been written by a young Austrian poet in Dachau concentration camp. The song was performed in the film by men of 74 Company and accompanied by their orchestra.[91]

> Pitiless the barbed wire
> All around us, charged with death
> Keep your step, Comrade,
> Lift your head, Comrade,
> And always think of the day Comrade,
> When the bells of freedom will ring.

The voice-over that tells the story of the Pioneer Corps Company is that of their British officer and establishes from the outset that they are 'supporting us'. Speaking to camera he states, 'Each man has been subjected to the racial and political persecution of their own countries. They have gone through the hardest trials a man can endure for his convictions, and their loyalty to our cause is absolute'. An emphasis on such persecution runs through the film. The British officer, introducing a member of the Corps as a mathematician, asks him for the total time men in 74 Company have 'served in gaols and behind barbed wire'. The reply is '125 years, 7 months and 6 days'. A review of the film in *Documentary Newsletter* expressed confidence that, with a script by Arthur Koestler, 'one takes it for granted that the subject is treated as a refugee would wish'.[92] But although Koestler had taken service in the Pioneer Corps as his own route out of internment, the barbed wire of British internment camps is not mentioned anywhere in the film.

Austrians and Germans serving in the Pioneer Corps were predominantly Jewish, but *Lift Your Head, Comrade* makes only one reference to the persecution of Jews. It comes in a reply by Bobby Spooner to a question about what had happened to him, 'I was in Vienna when Hitler took over. I was arrested with many other Jews and sent to Dachau'. Spooner's story is then elaborated—he had been amateur bantamweight champion of Europe, but had both his hands broken in Dachau and never boxed again. A radio drama broadcast in 1942—*The Fingers of Private Spiegel*—which told the story of a German refugee serving in the Pioneer Corps, was equally guarded in its reference to Jewishness. Private Spiegel has secured British naturalization before the war after abandoning a career as a violinist in Nazi Germany because of his opposition to the Nazi regime. There is one reference to Nazi anti-Semitism as part of what he opposes, 'Too much marching, too much shouting…and they talk of banning the works of Jewish composers…it's absurd. Why are we to give poor old Mendelssohn the cold shoulder?' But this radio drama does not identify Spiegel as Jewish.[93] Such limited references to Jewishness were the result of concerns at the Ministry of Information that publicity for Jews would stimulate anti-Semitism in Britain.[94]

Italians serving in the British forces received even less attention than Austrians and Germans. Unlike the Irish, viewed by Churchill as a people of 'ancient valour', Italians were seen as 'unwarlike', a term used in the joint American-British Plan for Psychological Warfare in Italy in 1942, which described them as 'temperamentally unwarlike' and reported that they 'instinctively hate killing, maiming, hurting' and 'tend to be passive or feminine (*sic*)'.[95] This view of Italians was deeply embedded in both official and popular British thinking. In 1943, Mass Observation reported, 'The Italians are mostly pictured as a peace-loving, lazy sort of people, dragged into the war by Germany. Those whose feelings are mixed... often look on the Italians as incompetent fighters though pleasant enough socially'.[96]

The Times, reporting the posthumous award of a Victoria Cross to Dennis Donnini, reversed this common stereotype, speaking of his 'superb gallantry and self-sacrifice' and his 'magnificent courage', and noted that 'his father is an Italian who came to England 46 years ago'.[97] Donnini died at the age of nineteen, rescuing a wounded companion in Holland. He was claimed as 'Our first VC' by The National Union of General and Municipal Workers.[98]

A *Daily Express* front-page story made much of Donnini's Italian descent. Under the headline 'Ice-cream Man's son Wins VC', it reported that Donnini's roots went back to 'the terraces of Tuscany' and that his father, Alfredo, was 'Italian by race and by law', having 'never applied for naturalization'. The story featured two pictures of the Donninis—the only pictures on its front page that day. One was of Dennis and the other of Alfredo. The caption to the picture of Alfredo—'My family has served England well'—was taken from an interview in which he also said, 'I love this country'. The story provided details of his family's service. Three sons and two daughters had been in the British Army. It ended with the words of the citation to Dennis Donnini, which commended his 'superb gallantry' and 'magnificent courage'.[99]

The theme of a brave and loyal Italian who served Britain was echoed in tributes to Fortunato Picchi in the British media. Arriving in Britain in the 1920s, Picchi worked as head waiter at the Savoy hotel. He was interned in 1940, took a route out of internment through the Pioneer Corps, and subsequently volunteered to serve in the Special Operations Executive in Italy, where he was captured, tried as a spy, and executed in April 1941. Headlines in the popular press emphasized his courage and loyalty—'A Brave Italian'; 'Italian dies for Britain's sake'; 'Savoy's Picchi dies for us'.[100] The *Times* obituary, published under the headline 'Life Sacrificed for Freedom', concluded with the words of one of Picchi's friends, who had heard news of his death on Italian radio: 'If the report is true, in a very real sense he died for both Italy and Britain'.[101]

Tributes in the British media to Italians and Germans were sparse and, in the case of Italians, confined to individuals like Donnini and Picchi. They featured men serving in British forces, excluding women in the forces and both male and female civilians. Even so, they suggest a change of climate from the intense anti-alienism and fifth columnist scare of mid-1940, claiming Germans and Italians in the British forces as loyal allies.

Identities

During the war, many Austrians and Germans in the British forces anglicized their names, not out of a desire to assimilate and avoid hostility in Britain, but on the instructions of the War Office. Name changes were intended to afford them some protection in the event of capture by the enemy, preventing charges of treachery and enhancing their performances as British soldiers. Zobel, a Private in 229 Company of the Pioneer Corps, who was always last in the queue in pay parade, took the opportunity to change his name to Abingdon.[102] Some Germans were reluctant to change their names. Flight Sergeant Gerhard Heilig, who arrived on a *Kindertransport* in 1938 and volunteered for the RAF in 1943, recorded, 'First, they would have to shoot me down... second, I would have to survive... and third, they would have to catch me.... I decided to follow my father's example when arrested by the Nazis... and bear my name with honour and trust to providence'.[103]

If anglicized names, along with British uniform, provided some cover for Germans in the event of capture, Irish volunteers had to divest themselves of British uniforms when on leave in Éire. The government of Éire did nothing to stop them volunteering but, with the cooperation of the British government, provided dumps of civilian clothes at Holyhead so that they could change out of uniform before their arrival in Éire. The bizarre Holyhead changing-room was intended to ensure that non-neutral Irish serving in the British forces were invisible on the streets of neutral Éire.[104] These contrasting disguises and performances—German soldiers with British names and Irish soldiers in civilian clothes—draw attention to the complex questions of identity involved when enemy and neutral nationals contributed to the British war effort. All those enlisting in the British forces swore an oath of allegiance to King George VI, but many retained a range of transnational ties and attachments—to their own countries, communities, or families.

The invisibility of Irish volunteers in the British forces was increased by strict censorship of Irish media, which banned references to them. Robert ('Bertie') Smyllie, editor of the *Irish Times*, resented this ban and got round it with coded stories. Most famously, he reported the survival of a former Irish colleague—John Robinson—who had volunteered for the Royal Navy and was serving on HMS *Prince Of Wales* when the ship was attacked and sunk by the Japanese off Malaya. Addressing the 'many friends of Mr. John A. Robinson who was involved in a recent boating accident', Smyllie's report continued, 'he is a particularly good swimmer and it is possible that he owes his life to this accomplishment'.[105] Brian Inglis, who had been working as film critic for the *Irish Times* before leaving to join the RAF, records another coded story by Smyllie in the paper—his own farewell message. Smyllie wrote, 'Mr. Inglis [will] be absent from Ireland for an indefinite period. He has always been interested in flying but had few opportunities in Ireland to follow his bent. I shall be surprised if he has any further cause for complaint in this regard'.[106]

The motivations of Irish volunteers in the British army were varied, including a search for adventure, anti-Nazi convictions, and relatively high pay by comparison with wages in Éire or for service in the Irish army. Irish women could enlist in the British forces but not the Irish forces.[107] Mixing across divides between Northern and Southern Irish was common to war workers and volunteers. Flann Campbell helped to organize Irish working on airfield construction sites into trade unions. At a conference of the Connolly Association, which campaigned for Irish workers in Britain, he stated, 'The border too is forgotten here. Belfastmen and Dubliner work side by side and neither have any time for Fascist propaganda'.[108]

Such mixing could produce an Irish identity that crossed political and religious divides—between Northern Protestants and Catholics as well as Southern and Northern Irish. When Denis Murnane—a warrant officer in Bomber Command from Éire—was threatened in a London pub by two men who accused him of being 'one of those bastards who refused to give us the ports', two men from Northern Ireland came to his rescue. One was a Catholic from the Falls Road in Belfast and the other a Protestant from the Shankill Road. A similar assertion of a common Irish identity that crossed divides between Catholics and Protestants from Belfast was evident in a wartime celebration of St. Patrick's Day, when Sam McAughtry, who had joined the RAF and was stationed in Cheshire, walked down a local street with Paddy Johnston. Both wore sprigs of shamrock in their caps. McAughtry had grown up in the Protestant Tiger's Bay area. Johnston was a Catholic from the Falls Road.[109]

Sam McAughtry remembers wartime as a period of 'warm discovery of my Irishness', when he would 'corner the owner of every Irish accent, North or South...find out where in Ireland he came from and...pull out the fags or buy beer and talk about home'.[110] Fighting with the British could also strengthen a sense of Irish identity for volunteers from Éire. A volunteer from a pro-British Dublin background who enlisted in the Royal Engineers sewed a 'Southern Ireland' label on his shoulder flash.[111] Brian Inglis, whose departure to join the RAF prompted Smyllie to write the coded message in the *Irish Times*, was born in Dublin but educated in England and records, 'by the time the war ended I was more Irish—in the sense of thinking of myself as Irish—than when it began'.[112]

Many volunteers supported both the British war effort and Éire's policy of neutrality. Fergus Duffy from Bantry, who served in the RAF, told a newspaper that he had 'no problems with Irish neutrality' and that in the RAF he met many people who could see the reasons for it.[113] Brian Inglis disliked criticism of Irish neutrality and defended 'the right of the Irish to go their own way'. Inglis made an agreement with a fellow Anglo-Irish officer that if Britain violated Irish neutrality, they would resign their commissions, refuse to fight, and face the consequences.[114] Bernard Kelly's work, drawing on oral testimony from Irish veterans who served in the British forces, concludes, 'Irish people could have multiple loyalties—to the Allies, to London, to their regiments, to their associations, to their comrades—and still be loyal Irish citizens.[115]

Support for Irish neutrality was also evident among Irish war workers in Britain. Home Intelligence reported in 1942 that a British newsreel criticizing Éire's refusal to allow the use of its ports as British bases provoked 'considerable agitation' when screened in an area where Irish workers lived. A disturbance was planned, but 'owing...to its brief showing no trouble arose'.[116] In 1944, when the American letter requesting the expulsion of German and Japanese embassies from Dublin was sent, a report noted that the opinion of Éire workers in Scotland was out of step with the general indignation and disgust at Éire's refusal to comply. They expressed 'sympathy with Mr. De Valera's point of view "usually raking up past history as justification"'.[117] In 1943, Home Intelligence had reported another issue where workers from Éire supported de Valera—his appeal to save Rome from Allied bombing. This contrasted with their reports of considerable British criticism of the appeal—'de Valera's wail about saving Rome has just about put the lid on everything'.[118]

'Irishness' could have different meanings in different contexts. In 1941 Romie Lambkin, a Dubliner, joined the Auxiliary Territorial Service—the women's branch of the British army. She was posted to a base in Northern Ireland (Drum House) where she worked as a driver. In 1942, she wrote in her diary: 'Coming back to Drum is beginning to feel more like coming home than going to Dublin these days'. The place that felt more like home than Dublin was Hut 12 in an army camp which she shared with, among others, an Englishwoman and five Danes in exile. This army hut, shared with other women who were at war, contrasted with neutral Ireland. So did London. On a visit there, travelling by tube, Lambkin saw families settling down on station platforms to take shelter from night-time air raids and wrote, 'They are marvellous people, these Londoners. It's such an entirely different world from the placid one Ireland lives in that I feel ashamed'.[119]

On this visit to London, Lambkin also found diversity in wartime Britain exciting. She wrote in her diary that she donned a new frock for a party with an Australian RAF bomber crew and then went on to the Overseas Club to dance. Her diary describes the people assembled there as 'an exciting forces mixture...ranging from the Free French to Poles, Belgians, Yanks, Australians, New Zealanders, not to mention plenty from the good old Emerald Isle'.[120] A similar identification with a multinational community of allies is apparent in an earlier entry in Lambkin's diary about an American forces concert, 'The band struck up the US National Anthem and then "God Save the King"—it is a good feeling, incidentally, being part of a whole uniformed audience standing to attention in wartime'.[121] Lambkin's identification with a community of men and women on active service gives Irishness a meaning that contrasts with Ireland as the placid neutral place that makes her feel ashamed. Irishness is also 'plenty from the good old Emerald Isle'—the community of other Irish volunteers at war.[122]

Italians, like Irish, mixed with fellow nationals across a range of divides. Italians in the British army who encountered Italian internees, Italian prisoners of war, or local Italian communities in Britain, often formed friendships and networks based on a sense of common Italianness. The same was true of their encounters with the local population during the Allied occupation of Italy.[123] There was also a range of encounters between local Italian communities and Italian prisoners of war in Britain, often through attendance at Sunday mass. Camp authorities sometimes approached local Italian families to suggest they invite prisoners of war to their homes.[124] As in the case of Irish mixing, Italian mixing could express and strengthen national identification. Historian Wendy Ugolini demonstrates that this was particularly the case for Italians who served in 270 Company of the Pioneer Corps, which was based in Slough from 1941 to 1946, enabling them to travel to Soho at weekends and socialize with the Italian community there.[125]

Regional identity was also significant for Italians. Prisoners of war sometimes chose not to become cooperators because they did not want to be separated from fellow prisoners who came from the same region. One cooperator took pleasure in mixing with local Italian families because, among other things, this meant he could hear his dialect spoken. He wrote:

> The co-operators look forward with excitement to Sundays, because on that day numerous families of fellow citizens residing in Britain arrive at the camps... cheerful bursts of women's laughter can be heard, together with the gracious and familiar intonation of our dialects—and all this reminds us of Italy... In this way the co-operators gradually come back to life.[126]

A number of Fascist Italians who were interned in 1940 did not mix across divides. They took the view that loyalty was indivisible, regarding service in the British army as treachery to Italy, and chose to remain in internment rather than joining the Pioneer Corps. There were also a few instances where second-generation men of Italian descent and British nationality went to prison because of their refusal to serve in the British forces. Such refusal was rare and there were families, like the Donninis, where the whole second generation was involved in the British war effort, with sons serving in the forces and daughters in the Auxiliary Territorial Service, Women's Auxiliary Air Force, Women's Land Army, or munitions factories. Wendy Ugolini's work, drawing on oral testimony from Scottish-Italian veterans in the British army, reaches similar conclusions to those of Bernard Kelly's work on Irish veterans—many had complex loyalties and identities. Their stories, she argues, articulate 'a dual identification with both Britain and Italy, illustrating the extent to which they appeared to inhabit "two worlds"'.[127]

German Jewish refugees in Britain had little control over changes of identity, which came thick and fast from the 1930s. Peter Masters describes joining the Pioneer Corps as 'the fourth metamorphosis' they experienced.[128] In the early 1930s, most were respectable German citizens and

many were highly educated middle-class professionals. Nazi policies pro-
gressively stripped them of these identities—depriving them of German
citizenship, dismissing them from jobs, banning them from professions,
universities, state schools, cinemas and public places, looting their shops,
burning down their houses and synagogues, sending them to concentration
camps. Those who escaped to Britain acquired the new identity of refugee,
often 'refugee from Nazi oppression'. In 1940 British government policy in
its turn stripped them of this identity, transforming many into internees
held behind barbed wire in Britain, and some to deportees held behind
barbed wire in Australia or Canada.

Despite the increasingly ruthless and relentless persecution of Jews in
Germany, refugees did not always abandon all attachment to a German
identity. Some German-speakers identified with a community of exiles
bound together by common language and ethnicity. Harry Rossney (formerly Helmut Rosettenstein) recorded feeling 'shattered and alone' when
he was transferred away from 93 Company of the Pioneer Corps, which had
been an 'oasis of fellow Jewish-German and Austrian refugees who understood and felt the same, had the same outlook, accents and humour'.[129]

Many Germans who joined the British forces valued the opportunity to
wage war against their former compatriots in Nazi Germany. Patriotism for
Peter Block—who was released from internment to join the Pioneer
Corps—meant allegiance to Britain against Nazi Germany. He records that
he joined the British army because 'we wanted our freedom...we were
super patriotic and wanted to get at the Germans'.[130] Block later transferred
to the Parachute Regiment.

The value of fighting for the anti-Nazi cause is a main theme of Peter
Masters's memoir of life in 3 Troop, No. 10 Commando, which he entitles
Striking Back. The memoir traces years of frustration after his arrival in
Britain before he is handed Commando shoulder flashes. Initially there is
the frustration and injustice of internment, 'We who had hoped to fight the
common enemy were held prisoners by our own side, probably for the
duration of the war—our war!' Subsequently there is the frustration of service in the Pioneer Corps, 'The war was going on before our very eyes.
How were we supposed to satisfy our immense motivation to fight the
Nazis by unloading freight cars?' But finally he is able to join what he
describes as 'an argumentative bunch of mostly young Jewish refugees who
volunteered for special and hazardous duty' in the Commandos. The significance of this move as one which gives Masters some agency, even if this

is only the agency to choose how to die, is evident in his description of fellow refugees in the Commando unit, '[T]he antithesis of "lambs to the slaughter", we fought and many of us died ... Those who died preferred their fate to being gassed and cremated by the Nazi brute'.[131]

At the end of the war, Walter Wurzburger reflected on what the opportunity to fight Nazi Germany had meant. Wurzburger was from a Jewish family in Germany and left for Paris in 1933. He was a musician who played the saxophone. In 1939, he accepted an invitation to join a band in Singapore because 'further away is safer'. After the declaration of war he was arrested by the British, interned, initially in Singapore, and then deported to Australia.[132] In a letter to *The Herald*—a Melbourne newspaper—written when the war was over, he wrote:

> I had volunteered for army service...but [was] not accepted for the AIF [Australian Imperial Force]. My two brothers, just as alien as I, were accepted by the British Army and had the chance of fighting their way back to Germany to help to bring justice to the inventors of the gas chambers through which my parents and another brother had to pass.[133]

Germans in the British forces who fought their way back re-entered Germany as victors. They were now the forces of occupation—in a position of considerable power and authority over their former persecutors. As Wurzburger stated, many were involved in bringing justice to the inventors of the gas chambers through their work in interrogating suspected war criminals, investigating war crimes, and acting as interpreters in war crimes trials.

Germans in the British army who re-entered Germany as victors exhibited varied responses to their power and authority over former persecutors, and to post-war Germany. In 1945, Eric Walters-Kohn escorted SS and Gestapo prisoners on a train journey from Normandy to Ostend. Kohn had spent time in Dachau and Buchenwald concentration camps before his arrival in Britain in 1939. When the train was held up for half an hour in Bruges, Flemish workers gathered on the platform and threatened the prisoners. Kohn intervened to protect his former persecutors.[134] Mark Lynton (formerly Max-Otto Ludwig Loewenstein, and the ex-Pioneer who wrote a comic description of his time there) records, 'Despite being a German Jew, and thus only providentially having escaped the Holocaust, I have never equated all Germans with being Nazis, and I therefore did not feel uncomfortable among Germans in 1945, or since.[135] Lieutenant Alberti, another ex-Pioneer who had been in Dachau concentration camp before he arrived in Britain and who served in the Royal Army Service Corps during the occupation of Germany 'got a kick' when a German officer stood smartly to attention before him. The officer was Major-General von Blaskowitz, who later committed suicide while awaiting trial at Nuremberg.[136]

Few Austrians and Germans who ended the war in their countries of origin wanted to return there after they were demobbed. Unlike many Irish and Italians, service in the British army did not strengthen their national identities, as Germans or Austrians. Walter Richards, who came to Britain on a *Kindertransport* and was an interpreter during the Allied occupation of Germany, records, 'Words cannot describe how I felt at that time towards the German people. Yes, I was trying to be polite as a young man, but I hated them'.[137] Max Dickson (formerly Max Dobriner), who also came to Britain on a *Kindertransport* and did interrogation work at the end of the war, records, 'One day, one of our Jewish boys was interrogating a Gestapo man who had sent his parents to their deaths. We had to restrain him physically'.[138] Most of those who continued to identify as Germans or Austrians did so as anti-Nazis, identifying with other German-speaking exiles, not their compatriots in post-war Germany.

German Jews had been stripped of their German citizenship in 1935 and were stateless on arrival in Britain. Most remained stateless at the end of the war—they did not fulfil the five-year residence requirement for British naturalization before the outbreak of war when, with occasional exceptions, naturalization was suspended for the duration. Rudi Friedlaender, the son of a Jewish lawyer from Munich, had volunteered for enlistment in the Pioneer Corps in April 1940, before the introduction of mass internment, and later volunteered for 'hazardous service' and was selected for the Special Air Service. In 1944, he ended a long letter to his father:

> I am happy to be able to fight for my principles and for Britain, the nation which now champions these principles and has become a second home to me. If I survive there will be only one ambition left: to be able to continue to fight for freedom and peace as a British citizen.[139]

This ambition was never fulfilled. Friedlaender was stateless when he died in 1944, giving his life for the anti-Nazi cause.

Family Loyalties

The dual or multiple allegiances of people of enemy and neutral nationality in wartime Britain were often made more complex by family loyalties.

Emilio Scala was an Italian, interned on the Isle of Man, whose son put loyalty to his father before all other allegiances. His son wrote to him, commenting on a cutting from the *Daily Sketch*:

> It [the press cutting] gave a good account of how things stand in our family— it reads how after living here 40 years and serving in the British Army in the last war you were interned with one son already fighting and the other preparing to go, that's me! I was preparing to go, I won't say much but I know this much I am not going in the army till you are home, come what may, that's final. I know you would not wish me to do this but I'm afraid it's the only way. If I am asked to fight so that men may be free, I shall do so, but my own war aims come first.

The letter continued:

> What does it profit a man if he frees all enslaved men and suffers the loss of his own father? . . . Arturo from Battersea has had his calling up papers . . . so I guess mine are due almost any day now. When they come it means either you come home or I come up to the Isle of Man for the duration. It is hardly possible that I will be interned, but the fact remains—I am not going in the army till you are home.[140]

Graham White, Member of Parliament for Birkenhead, read out a letter similar to Scala's in a House of Commons debate on internment in July 1940. This letter was also written by the son of an Italian who had fought with the Allies in the First World War, but was interned after the Italian declaration of war against Britain in 1940. The son wrote:

> My mother and I are British born and my sentiments are all with this country. My father, an Italian, came to this country as a young man, and fought for the Allies in the last war, when he was badly wounded in the head. He had no political ideas and he did not belong to any association. He lived for his work and home. My parents had never been apart a single day during the whole of their married life. On 11th June he was taken away to be interned. On hearing of the *Arandora Star* being torpedoed we were rather worried. We found that he was on the *Arandora Star* and posted as missing. I am an only son and will soon be 20. I applied to join the L.D.V. [Local Defence Volunteers] but was turned down because my father was Italian. I managed to join the A.F.S. [Auxiliary Fire Service].

White added that a more personal note had been appended to the letter: 'says that he will be called up for Army service in a month or two, and asks whether his experience can help him to fight for this country'.[141]

Nationality played a significant role in shaping the different fates of members of the same families in Britain. It was not only British-born

Italians of British or dual British-Italian nationality, like these letter-writers, who were subject to call-up to the British forces, while their fathers were arrested and interned. Members of Italian families who had successfully applied for British naturalization before the war were also subject to call-up. This meant that when Italy declared war in June 1940 and the government policy of mass internment of enemy aliens was extended to Italians, Italian families in Britain could be split across different categories and different camps, with some family members going to British army camps and others to internment camps. Silvestro d'Ambrosio, a confectioner from Hamilton who had lived in Scotland for forty-two years, had sons in the British and Canadian armies. His application for naturalization, made only weeks before Italy entered the war, did not go through in time to prevent his internment as an enemy alien. He was deported on the *Arandora Star* and drowned when the ship went down.[142]

The Pieri family was also split across different camps and categories because of decisions over British naturalization. Joe Pieri, whose parents had migrated to Glasgow after the First World War, when he was two, did not apply:

> Despite my almost purely Scottish lifestyle, I just did not feel British. Almost daily I was reminded of the fact that I was Italian . . . Italy's invasion of Abyssinia and Mussolini's intervention in the Spanish Civil War had created a wave of ill feeling against Italy in the general population. The childhood taunts of 'dirty wee Tally' had given way to . . . 'Tally bastard'.[143]

The consequence of Pieri's decision against applying for naturalization was his internment and deportation to Canada. His brother, who had opted to apply for naturalization, served in the British army.

The call-up to serve a country that had labelled their parents 'enemy' and in many cases interned them was one reason for ambivalence or opposition on the part of some second-generation Italian men and women towards fighting for Britain. Another was the prospect of killing family members. Joe Pieri writes that an important reason why he decided not to apply for British naturalization before the war was that this would mean military service for the British, 'It was clear that if the war did come Italy would be on the side of Germany against Britain, and I had no desire to be placed in the position of possibly having to fight against cousins and relations already serving in the Italian army . . . I agonised, vacillated, rationalised and remained as I was'.[144]

Romeo Ugolini, who was serving in the Black Watch at the time of the North African campaign, refused to go abroad because he did not want to fight his uncles. He was transferred to the Pioneer Corps.[145] The fear of killing family members could also deter Italians from doing war work. In a letter intercepted by Postal Censorship, Ugo Bragoni wrote to Mrs F. Bragoni from an Isle of Man internment camp, 'Since I have not the slightest intention of working in munitions to kill my dear ones in Italy, I advise you to ask no more for my release; I do not wish to compromise myself with the Italian Government'.[146]

For Irish volunteers from Éire who enlisted in the British forces, family loyalties could also be significant. Some were following a family tradition— particularly those from Anglo-Irish families, where it was not uncommon for the British forces to be regarded as services where Anglo-Irish served Britain as 'our country'. John Jermyn joined the British army in 1939, when he was 21 years old, and recalls, 'My mother's only brother was killed at Gallipoli in World War One, he was a second lieutenant in the Royal Munsters and was 19, and in some foolish way I felt that perhaps I should take his place'.[147]

Volunteers for the British armed forces from republican families could encounter family opposition to enlistment. Mothers who tried to negotiate their sons' release from the British army with the Éire government's Department of Foreign Affairs included one who wrote of her son, 'I hope you will leave no stone unturned to secure his release as I do not wish a child of mine to take any part in Britain's war'.[148] Stephen Kennedy's uncle, a Republican, told him, 'I like a good Irishman and I like a good Englishman, but I don't like an Irishman who fights for England'.[149] Kennedy's family took no pride in his service in the British army, despite the Military Medal that he won in the North African campaign. In 1944, Mary Mulry's father opposed her decision to join the British Army's nursing branch after she had finished training as a nurse. Her marriage to a British Army officer in 1946 also brought opposition from her father. She wrote in her diary, 'His Ireland versus England bitterness still goes on... My father will never change now. He will want to fight the British until the day of his death, and all because of his dream of a United Ireland.[150]

Unlike Italians, most Austrians and Germans in the British forces did not face the prospect of killing family members. The majority were Jewish, their families more likely to be in German concentration camps than in the German forces. But in the early stages of the war, some decided against volunteering for the Pioneer Corps because they feared reprisals against family members who had remained in Austria and Germany.[151] Like Italians, German families were often split across different camps and categories. Volunteers who enlisted before the introduction of mass internment were generally exempted from internment and were in British army camps, while their fathers and brothers, and more rarely their mothers and sisters, were sent to internment camps.[152]

Germans who had not applied for British naturalization were also sent to internment camps, while their British-born sons and daughters were called up to serve in the British forces. Peter Masters—the Jewish refugee from Vienna who was interned in 1940—records meeting a man in his internment camp who had arrived in Britain from Germany as a boy and was interned because he had never applied for British naturalization. Masters records that 'he wore a rainbow of British World War I medal ribbons' and 'would proudly show off photos of his sons in the British Navy and the RAF'.[153] Less common was a case where family members were split between different camps and categories because of the internment of a woman. George Strauss, a Labour Member of Parliament, who criticized the government's policy on internment in a House of Commons debate in July 1940, quoted a case of a family of refugees where the son had volunteered for the Pioneer Corps and was serving in the British army, while his mother, despite her Class 'C' classification—'friendly' enemy alien posing no security risk—had been interned.[154]

Government policy played a considerable role in splitting up Austrian and German families, even before the war. A Ministry of Labour scheme permitted Austrian and German women to enter Britain, but only on condition that they worked as domestic servants. For many of the 20,000 women—predominantly Jewish—who arrived under this scheme between 1933 and 1939, this involved separation from their families. Like their male compatriots in the Pioneer Corps, who were digging and shovelling, women who came as domestic servants were often experiencing manual labour for the first time. Many came from households in Austria and Germany that had employed servants, but on arrival in Britain had to don a cap and apron to scrub floors. Married couples advertised in newspapers like *The Times* for employment together, working as cook-housekeeper and butler or driver/gardener.[155] Bronka Schneider and her husband Joseph managed to get employment together, both working as domestic servants in a remote castle in Scotland, for a British couple who had recently returned from India.[156] But many women on domestic service visas came alone.

The mass internment policy and its implementation split up families in many different ways. Among internees, men outnumbered women, so that husbands and wives were separated, with men going to internment camps and their wives often subject to relocation outside protected areas. British-born daughters in Italian families who were too young to be con- scripted sometimes continued the running of family businesses in their mothers' absence, experiencing isolation and anti-Italian hostility.[157] When husbands and wives were both interned, they were initially placed in separ- ate camps. In August 1940, wives who were in camps in Port Erin and Port St Mary on the Isle of Man were allowed to visit husbands in camps in Douglas—a few miles away—for the first time. The *Isle of Man Times* reported that men had picked hydrangeas and fuchsias in the gardens of camp houses to present to their wives.[158] Many of these separations ended in May 1941, when a camp for married couples was opened on the Isle of Man. Postal Censorship reported on letters from internees, 'The new mixed camp for married couples...appears to be a complete success, and has earned genuine gratitude. It is described variously as "a wonderful dream", "a real miracle"'.[159]

Letters intercepted by Postal Censorship demonstrate some of the con- sequences of family separations. One German Jew, who had volunteered to join the British army before his internment and was ultimately released to join the Pioneer Corps, complained: 'I eventually got out but as a final culminating "stroke" we were sent direct to our Training Centre without being allowed to go home for even 24 hours, with the result that I only saw my mother during my leave a few weeks ago, almost eight months after I left her last July; during that time she had been bombed twice out of her house.'[160] Another letter-writer protested:

> The internments grew to some cruelty, for instance, the brother of Mr. Jaray...was dying and asked to see his father who was interned. But the red tape couldn't permit it and so the young man died without having seen his father again, and you may imagine the feelings of his poor father. Both father and son went to England with full permission of the English government, vic- tims of Nazism and hoping for the English hospitality.[161]

Family loyalties meant that people who successfully escaped to Britain often felt responsible after arrival for getting their relatives out. Gertrude Winik, a

Jewish refugee who had been dismissed from her job as a kindergarten teacher in Vienna in 1934, records:

> I came in February [1939] and war broke out in September. I tried. I didn't know anybody in the whole of Great Britain so I couldn't get anybody out and that's what happened, you see. And that makes you feel guilty for the rest of your life. It never stops. You have it with you day and night... Either I should have stayed with them or they all should have come with me.[162]

Walter Wurzburger, the saxophonist, was unable to convince his parents to leave Germany early as he had—they considered themselves too old to start life over again. When he arrived in Singapore in 1939, he tried to get visas for them but was unsuccessful.[163]

The weight of responsibility for getting family out fell heavily on children. Lore Groszmann, the daughter of a Jewish accountant in Vienna, came to Britain on a *Kindertransport* when she was only ten years old. On the last evening before her departure:

> All the cousins and all the aunts came to say goodbye. And there was one aunt who had twins who was extremely angry with my parents for getting me onto this transport and for not having managed to get her twins onto the transport. There was grief and panic and fury in that room. And there was a moment that my father took me between his knees and he said 'now when you get to England you have to talk to all the English people you meet, and you have to ask them to get your mother and me out and your grandparents'. And because this aunt was there and had been so unhappy and so angry, he said 'and aunt so and so's twins'. Before long I had a list of people whom I at ten years old had promised to save from Hitler.[164]

Groszmann successfully negotiated work permits for her parents with the Domestic Bureau in London: 'From Dovercourt camp I wrote a couple of letters to the Refugee Committee in London. And I think they must have been moved by a letter from a child asking to get her parents out of Vienna. And they did get my parents a domestic service visa. And my parents appeared... in Liverpool on my eleventh birthday. And I remember feeling that some terrific weight that I had been carrying and had known I had been carrying was taken off my back'. This domestic visa brought Groszmann's parents jobs as cook and butler to a family in Kent, although her father was subsequently interned on the Isle of Man, splitting the family again.[165]

The weight of responsibility felt by children could be increased by letters from parents asking for help to get them out. Ruth Schneier, who had grown up in a working-class district of Vienna, came to Manchester to live with relatives when she was twelve years old. In February 1939 she received a letter from her father which urged her to 'keep on trying' to find ways of getting her parents out. Enclosed with the letter was another, from Ruth's teenage friend in Vienna, which also asked for help. There was a further call for Ruth's help in the last letter she received from her parents, asking her to contact an uncle to 'get us out of here'. By then, her parents had fled to Croatia. After the war, Ruth was informed by the International Red Cross that they had been killed by the pro-Nazi Utasha regime in Croatia in 1941.

Helmut Beck was fifteen when he came to Britain from Breslau with his brother Walter in 1938. He made attempts to bring his parents over by making contact with a group in Stockport attached to the parish church, but nothing came of this. At the end of August, his mother, Hildegard, wrote to Walter: 'Keep on trying to do something for us. Write to Helmut and talk to him about it. But don't accuse him of not going fast enough'. Later she wrote to Walter that her 'most terrible thought' was that she might never see her children again. Hildegard and her husband Rudolph were eventually deported from Breslau and murdered by the Nazis. Historian Bill Williams, who records these cases, concludes, 'Helmut Beck lived the rest of his life . . . with the consequences not only of separation from his parents, but of his "failure" to rescue his mother and father'.[166]

Kindertransport children were separated from their parents through a scheme that was for children only. Although a few of them boarded aeroplanes to get to Britain, most journeys were by train and boat—partings from their parents took place on stations. Vera Gissing, who was ten years old when she set out for Britain, remembers, 'It was a very big moment and we clutched each other's hands as the train left the station and all we could see were the faces of our dearest parents who at that moment could not mask the anxiety and the fear'.[167] Emmy Mogilensky, who was fourteen, records:

> I know my father kissed me and blessed me and told me to be a good girl no matter where I am and to mind my manners and all that, and always saying it won't be long, we will all be together again soon. I was all torn up inside. I couldn't believe that I was saying goodbye and it was really only when I looked out of the window of the train and saw my father standing there totally frozen that it hit me that I might never see him again. But by that time it was too late to get back out of the train and the doors started to get closed.[168]

John Grenville, who was ten, remembers 'very vividly the moment of parting, which must have been terrible for my mother who simultaneously saw her three boys leave and was extremely uncertain whether she would ever see them again. And that made a very deep impression, I am certain, on all the children who left... to some degree overshadow[ing] the rest of their childhood and, I believe, their lives'.[169]

Some children, like Lore Groszmann, were reunited with parents who followed them to Britain. Others were reunited after the war with parents who had survived the Holocaust. Many never saw their parents again. Max Dickson was one of these. He had arrived in Britain on a *Kindertransport* in 1939, when he was thirteen years old:

> It was not an easy journey. We had to look after one another. A train load of children with only a handful of grownups. Each one of us had a label around our neck. Some of the children were only three years old. On arrival at the Dutch-German border, the SS came through the train. We were all scared they might send us back again. We were permitted to carry on. What a relief! As soon as we arrived in Holland we were made welcome. Some of the helpers gave us a big hug and then sent us on our way. Although I did not realise it then, I would never see my parents again. I often thought that they sacrificed their lives to make sure we had a chance.[170]

After the outbreak of war all letters from his parents stopped, but he continued to communicate with them with messages confined to twenty-five words, written on postcards, in a service provided by the Red Cross, and received similar postcards in reply. These at least provided him with reassurance that his parents were still alive, but in early 1943 even the postcards stopped, 'It was a sad time. From then on I learned to live on Faith and Hope'.[171] Dickson later volunteered for 3 Troop, No. 10 Commando, and ended the war in Germany where, like many other German-born members of the British army, he was given leave to search for relatives. 'Each search ended the same way. Last known in Buchenwald or Dachau or Oranienburg, then transported to Auschwitz, which always meant the same: "Gas chambers"'. Later he received a Red Cross letter telling him that his brother was alive.[172] When he heard of Bergen-Belsen, he went there in the hope of finding someone from his family who had survived. Dickson writes, 'The sight that greeted me was so horrendous I nearly lost my mind that day. So many experiences crowding in on me it was almost impossible to cope with the emotional strain. By then I was 19 years old'.[173]

Susanne Medas was another *Kindertransport* traveller who never saw her parents again. Before setting out on her journey, she took family photographs from the family album (Figure 2.3 shows a photograph of her parents taken in 1912):

Richard + Gisela Bernstein
Holland — newly married
1912

Figure 2.3 A photograph that Susanne Medas took out of the family album and brought to Britain with her shows her newly married parents, who were later murdered in Auschwitz (by kind permission of Susanne Medas).

We didn't know that there was going to be a war, we didn't know anything. And so, one thing which is significant for me personally is that—you know every family have a photo album. And we had a photo album, and in it of course there were photographs of my mother's family and so on. And my parents were hoping that we would meet again either in England or in Norway... So I said to my mother when it was time for me to leave for England, 'You know what'—I was a very bossy child—'I can't take this big album with me so I'll take out the photographs and later when we are together again we'll put them back in the album'. And because of that, I've got a whole lot of photographs... But many children... they don't have anything of their parents... And I felt sorry because my parents didn't have the photographs. But then my parents ended up in Auschwitz, so the photographs would have been lost anyway.[174]

Figure 3.1 Zulfiqar Bokhari (second from right) in the BBC Home Guard (© Imperial War Museum, D 4558).

3

The Empire Comes to Britain

Rudolph Dunbar is a little-remembered figure, but had a remarkable wartime career as a musician, journalist, and broadcaster. He was from British Guiana (now Guyana), but in the early 1920s he lived in New York, where he studied composition, clarinet, and piano at the Institute of Musical Art (later the Juilliard) and was also involved in the Harlem jazz scene.

In 1925 Dunbar moved to Paris, where he continued to study music, and then moved on to Britain in 1931, establishing a school of clarinet playing and publishing a treatise on the subject. In London, he continued to be involved in jazz and led two jazz groups.[1] One of these—'Rudolph Dunbar and his Coloured Orchestra'—broadcast on BBC variety programmes and was the first all-British black band to be heard over the air.[2] Dunbar also worked from 1932 as the London correspondent of the Associated Negro Press—a news agency that supplied news releases to nearly all the major black newspapers in the United States.

Dunbar's career reached a high point in wartime. One respondent to a Mass Observation directive on 'attitudes towards people of colour' named him as a black achiever, alongside the celebrated African-American Paul Robeson, who had been voted most popular singer by BBC radio listeners in 1937. The respondent wrote, 'I believe that, given the proper education, surroundings etc. etc. that all coloured peoples can compete with white in the intellectual field: Robeson, Dunbar, and many other names spring to my mind in this connection'.[3] Given the publicity that surrounded many of Dunbar's wartime activities, it is not hard to understand why his name was among those that sprang to this respondent's mind. Dunbar was the first black man to conduct the London Philharmonic Orchestra, to considerable acclaim. In 1942–3, he conducted this orchestra several times, as well as the London Symphony, Liverpool Philharmonic, and National Philharmonic orchestras—and he played the clarinet in performances at the Wigmore Hall in London.[4]

Dunbar continued to work at the Associated Negro Press throughout the war and also worked at the Ministry of Information, as West Indian Press Officer. Through these activities, he made connections in high places. In 1942, after he conducted a concert at the Royal Albert Hall, the Under-Secretary of State for the Colonies, Harold Macmillan, gave a lunch in his honour.[5] Bernard Bracken, Minister of Information, wrote a piece for the *Sunday Express* in 1942, entitled 'Colour Bar Must Go', that began, 'Mr. Rudolph Dunbar has asked me to write an article about the Colour Bar'.[6] In 1944, Dunbar took part in the Normandy landings, conducted an orchestra in liberated Paris, and went on to become the first black man to conduct the Berlin Philharmonic Orchestra during the Allied occupation of Germany.[7]

In 1942, Noel Sabine—who headed publicity at the Colonial Office— wrote to the BBC suggesting that Dunbar should be invited to be guest conductor for a broadcast with the BBC orchestra. He offered a reminder that Dunbar had 'scored a considerable success' conducting at the Albert Hall, followed by further successes at the Bournemouth Musical Festival:.

> We have taken a considerable interest in Mr. Rudolph Dunbar's activities and he is in a measure representative of many of the coloured peoples from our Colonies now taking their place in the war effort and in the social life of this country. For this reason we should welcome such an invitation being extended to him. As in the case of the Albert Hall concerts such a performance would, we believe, create a good impression among the West Indians and many people of African descent throughout the Colonial Empire; but please do not take this other than a suggestion which I put forward for you to consider.[8]

Sabine had earlier suggested a talk by Dunbar in the BBC's Home Service *Postscript* series.[9] He had good reason to think that Dunbar might 'create a good impression' in the colonial empire not only through his conducting but also through BBC talks and journalism. An early press release Dunbar wrote for the Associated Negro Press was titled 'Men and Women of Color Continue Rapid Rise to Prominence in England'. It claimed, 'there is a real effort being made on the part of the heads of government departments to abolish color prejudice and to employ West Indians and Africans in positions worthy of their intellectual attainments and capacities'.[10] The Colonial Office itself was a source of information for pieces like this. An official there wrote to the BBC about Dunbar, 'we see a good deal of him ... and have supplied him in one way and another with information of which he has made good use in the Negro press of America'.[11]

The Colonial Office's missive suggesting that Dunbar should be invited to broadcast a talk on the BBC Home Service expressed confidence that he would not include in his talk 'any material which would be controversial or undesirable to make public'.[12] A draft script by Dunbar appeared to justify this confidence. It described Britain as 'the last bastion of democracy in Europe', provided a catalogue of evidence for the contribution of people of colour to the British war effort and, like his earlier piece for the Associated Negro Press, claimed that the government was acting against racial prejudice. Even so, the Colonial Office noted that they would want to see the script if the BBC went ahead with the broadcast.

A vision of a progressive British Empire with a tolerant, liberal Britain at its centre acting against racial prejudice was exactly what the Colonial Office wanted to project to the world and particularly to America. Dunbar's identity as a black British subject from the colonial empire and war correspondent for the Associated Negro Press put him in a particularly good position to project this vision. When Sabine suggested that Dunbar should broadcast in the BBC Home Service *Postscript* series, he imagined 'quite a good and beneficial talk being given by Dunbar, whom I regard as really very reliable'. But he had some misgivings, 'One or two of the things he says he has seen on his travels would not make particularly good publicity, particularly in wartime...we should certainly see the script. We do not want to hide any abuses there may be but in wartime we simply cannot afford to let anybody broadcast matters which would give ammunition to enemy propaganda'.[13] Dunbar's services were required only if he stuck to a censored script and proved himself 'reliable' by saying nothing that might undermine the official vision of Britain and its empire, approved by the Colonial Office.

Dunbar rarely broadcast on the Home Services, but spoke on a number of programmes on the BBC's Overseas Services on topics where there was little danger that what he said would create the wrong impression. He made three programmes on 'West Africa's Musical Heritage' for the *Calling West Africa* series. His contributions to *Calling the West Indies* including programmes on African-American spirituals and choirs. From 1944, listeners in the Caribbean to *Calling the West Indies* and *West Indian Diary* could follow his movements as he took part in the Normandy landings, entering Paris and then Berlin. His contributions to these series reported on his varied experiences—'France From Within', 'Revisiting Paris after the occupation', 'Christmas with an American Negro Unit on the Western Front','Dodging Germans', and 'The Next morning in Berlin'.[14]

In 1945, *Picture Post* featured a photograph of Dunbar conducting the Berlin Philharmonic orchestra and commented 'the end of Nazi race laws summed up in one picture'.[15] When the war was over, Dunbar continued to travel the world and extended the reach of his international career, conducting in America, Cuba, Haiti, Jamaica, Poland, and Russia. But he rarely conducted in Britain.[16] The BBC had turned down Sabine's suggestion that he should be invited as a guest conductor of the BBC orchestra in 1942. In an interview shortly before his death, Dunbar 'spoke about the particular vindictiveness of a director of music at the BBC who derailed his musical career in Europe' when the war was over.[17] After an interview with Dunbar in August 1945, the BBC Director of Music wrote 'partly, I believe, through the insistence of the Ministry of Information his musical talents have been praised by the press on political grounds out of proportion to his actual achievements, and this has given him an inflated idea of his own abilities'.[18] The Deputy Director of Music was equally disparaging, writing to *Radiodiffusion Française* in 1946:

> He is from the West Indies and a British subject, and the reason why he got so much encouragement and support during the war was that he represented the West Indies in our Ministry of Information. Recently he seems to have devoted his programmes to American music—hence, I presume the similar support from the American press. It is a pity that he cannot conduct, because he must have done harm rather than good to the cause of the coloured people. He was a clarinet player—but again not quite good enough to play the interesting pieces he offered—and I think that really he was always more at home with a band than an orchestra.[19]

Dunbar had been celebrated in wartime Britain as a distinguished conductor of classical orchestras and courted in high places as a journalist who could disseminate the idea of a progressive British Empire in America. When the war was over, his services were no longer required. He died in Britain in obscurity in 1988.

The Colonial Office's concern to 'create a good impression' in the colonial empire was continuous throughout the war. It therefore sought to avoid policies that were discriminatory against non-white people from the colonies who came to Britain, while other government departments sometimes advocated discriminatory policies. Such policies potentially undermined wartime propaganda portraying an empire and an imperial war effort where people were united across differences of race and ethnicity. Wartime propaganda was also potentially undermined by evidence of the practice of colour bars—in the empire and in Britain—as well as by evidence of tensions and antagonisms between imperial allies. But disruption of a publicly disseminated vision of a united empire was kept to a minimum. When government departments advocated discrimination, they did so in private, confidential documents which were not made public and which made clear that discrimination was to be covert, not open. Colour bars in the empire and at home and antagonism between imperial allies—especially when this involved violence—went under-reported.

The British Empire at the BBC

Rudolph Dunbar was one of many men and women from the British Empire who made wartime programmes at the BBC. A photospread in *Picture Post* in 1943 showed people in the BBC canteen 'soaking up coffee... blowing out cigarette smoke and eating hasty tray meals' and described them as 'the most colourful and cosmopolitan crowd anywhere in the world today'. Pictures of Colin Wills and Gerry Wilmot were accompanied by text explaining that they came from Australia and Canada to report the war. A picture of Una Marson—the first black woman to make programmes at the BBC—was captioned: 'The Girl Who Looks After the West Indian Service. Miss Una Marson, a Jamaican journalist and author, came over here specially to take over the programmes relayed to the native population in the West Indies'.[20]

A community of imperial allies at the BBC's Eastern Service is particularly evident in a photograph taken in 1942 of a recording session for its poetry magazine series. This shows Una Marson from Jamaica with Venu Chitale, Narayana Menon and Mulk Raj Anand, all from India, Meary Tambimuttu from Ceylon (now Sri Lanka), and William Empson, Nancy Parratt, George Orwell, and Christopher Pemberton, all from Britain. The poet, T. S. Eliot—born in America, but a British citizen by the date of the photograph—is also a member of the group.

The canteen was one of a range of places where BBC staff mixed. During the Blitz these included underground shelters where they slept. Robert McCall, who was seconded to London from the Australian Broadcasting Corporation and flew to Britain in October 1940, wrote to an Australian colleague about an encounter there, 'I was pulling my pyjama trousers on when another man came in and began to change. To break the ice I ventured

"How do you do, I'm McCall!"; "Well, well, glad to see you" he replied, "I'm Ogilvie"—And so I met the Director General'.[21] George Smith, a producer also seconded to London from the Australian Broadcasting Corporation recorded:

> When we work here at night we sleep in underground shelters. There you meet people from all parts of the service, Home and Overseas, Empire and manual staff, defence, Home Guards. You meet Indians, South Africans, and men who broadcast in other languages ... It is all such valuable experience ... I am learning every day from London life and from broadcasting here.[22]

Zulfiqar Bokhari (see Figure 3.1), who arrived in Britain in 1940, may have been among those that Smith met. He became an organizer of the Indian section of the BBC's Eastern Service and served in the BBC Home Guard. When the war was over, he was appointed as the first director of Radio Pakistan.

By no means all those who broadcast to the Empire in non-English languages were men. Venu Chitale joined the BBC in 1940, began by assisting George Orwell—talks producer in the Indian service from 1941 to 1943—and later devoted her time to programmes in her mother tongue, Marathi. Her broadcasts to India included several programmes of recipes. She wrote to Eileen Blair, George Orwell's wife, thanking her for some recipes she had sent:

> I am sure this is the sort of thing we want to use for India, and I know that anything which has to do with Pancakes or fritters will of course be most welcome. Scones and biscuit things made on top of the heat sound simply ideal. Any recipes in that line are just the sort of thing an Indian housewife would like to try out, so will you choose the ones you think useful to our purpose, and send them to me at your leisure.[23]

Another woman who broadcast on the Indian service was Princess Indira of Kapurthala, who came to Britain from India in 1935, when she was twenty-three, hoping to become a film star. She drove an ambulance during the Blitz and worked at the wartime BBC, where she was known as 'the radio princess'. She hosted a half-hour radio programme in Hindustani for Indian forces stationed in the Middle East and the Mediterranean, and broadcast a weekly report to India on the proceedings in the House of Commons, where she was the only woman in the Press Gallery.[24] She also acted as a compère in a programme in which 'Bevin trainees' sent messages home to India.[25] 'Bevin trainees' were young Indian men selected for technical training in Britain in engineering and industry and named after Ernest

Bevin, the Minister of Labour, who organized the scheme. Their work was publicized in newsreels and newspapers, which showed them learning the skills of aeroplane rigging and tool-making and receiving a visit from the King and Queen.[26] They were perhaps better known in India than in Britain. A popular programme broadcast in Hindi on the BBC Indian service was a series for children about the adventures of Salamo—an Indian mouse who had arrived in Britain in the suitcase of an Indian Bevin trainee.[27]

The BBC was highly conscientious about producing programmes that promoted the idea of imperial unity. The *In It Together* series in 1940 aimed to 'illustrate the unity in diversity which is the surest token of the Empire's ultimate victory', with programmes featuring interviews with members of the Dominions Forces in Britain and with 'visitors from various parts of the colonial empire'.[28] The BBC also made considerable efforts to reach popular domestic audiences through a variety programme on empire called *Travellers' Tales* and a quiz programme called *Brush Up Your Empire*.[29]

Media historian Sian Nicholas comments on the problems encountered in reaching this popular audience. Programmes about the British Empire, she argues, had limited appeal to a British audience and the BBC had difficulties in persuading this audience that the empire was relevant to them.[30] But Listener Research at the BBC on the Sunday night *Postscript* series suggests that messages about the Empire—increasingly renamed the Commonwealth—had considerable appeal when they were conveyed by a speaker from the Dominions. The Sunday night *Postscript* series was highly prestigious, attracting a large audience that stayed tuned in at the end of the 9 o'clock news. The *Daily Express* called the series 'a British institution' and 'a serious rival to ITMA'—Tommy Handley's highly popular wartime comedy show.[31]

Speakers from the Dominions were well represented on the series. The Dominions Office pressed for this and approval was given, by both the government and the BBC Board of Governors, to the principle of employ-ing Dominions speakers.[32] Robert McCall, from the Australian Broadcasting Corporation, who had been pulling on his pyjama trousers when he met the Director General in 1940, gave a Sunday *Postscript* before he returned to Australia in 1941.[33] A manufacturer in Kirkcaldy commented: 'an intensely interesting account of an Australian's visit to Britain well told. It demonstrates once more how we are all banded together in the British Commonwealth'.[34]

Enthusiasm for the idea of a Commonwealth banded together in a common cause recurred in Listener Research on a range of *Postscripts* by speakers from the Dominions. The report on a *Postscript* by Eric Baume, the New Zealander journalist, commented, 'this frank talk on the unity of the British Empire in these critical days and the comradeship of the British and Australians and New Zealanders in the Near East was well received'.[35] The report on a *Postscript* by Major Piet Jooste—made just before his return to South Africa—noted that 'most speakers from the Dominions are assured of a very sympathetic audience'. A warehouse clerk commented on the broadcast: 'People feel that with a few more speakers like Major Jooste an even stronger feeling of fellowship will develop amongst the British Empire'. A housewife in Halifax commented, 'Such talks are conducive to the drawing together of our Empire and making all feel not only a sense of deep responsibility, but also of friendship between each other'.[36] There were similar comments on a *Postscript* by Leonard Brockington, former Chairman of the Canadian Broadcasting Corporation. Listener Research reported, 'As a speaker from the Dominions he was heard by an audience already predisposed in his favour, and his subject—the solidarity of the Empire and the strength of the united war effort—was congenial to most listeners'. A miner from Whitehaven liked Brockington's broadcast 'because he is only one of the millions in our vast Empire, who is heart and soul in this war and to whom we owe so much'.[37]

Despite the substantial black presence in wartime Britain, there were no black speakers—from America, from the British Empire, or from Britain—in the Sunday night *Postscript* series. Sabine's suggestion that Dunbar might broadcast a *Postscript* specified that this would not be in the Sunday series, but on a weekday.[38] A talk by Learie Constantine was originally intended for the popular and prestigious Sunday slot, but was rejected on the grounds that it was 'too controversial'. Constantine was from Trinidad and well known in Britain before the war as a first-class cricketer. In wartime, he was the first black man to serve as a Welfare Officer in the Ministry of Labour's Welfare department—he was also a member of the League of Coloured Peoples. In his *Postscript*, he talked of his experience of racism in Britain. This did not go down well with George Barnes, Director of Radio Talks, who wrote, 'With a British audience I should have thought far more sympathy would be obtained if the speaker identified himself with his audience by describing…some of the joy of first class cricket'. However, Barnes saw no reason why the script should not be accepted for a weekday, if

Constantine's own Ministry and the Colonial Office would pass it, and the programme went out in September 1943 on the Home Service. Rejecting the script for a Sunday *Postscript*, Barnes minuted, 'You will remember that the object of that series is to stress unity rather than diversity'.[39]

Creating a Good Impression: the People's Empire

The British wartime media often projected the British Empire as a multi-racial community—a 'people's empire'—where men pulled together across differences of race and ethnicity, united in a common cause.[40] Although white 'sons of empire' were always more prominent in imagery than those from Asian, African, or Caribbean colonies, this was an empire where all marched together. The poster designed to advertise the imperial war effort presented a community of men marching, and its slogan was 'Together'. It showed troops from Canada, Australia, Britain, South Africa, New Zealand, India, and Africa united under the fluttering Union Jack of Britishness. Their togetherness is nevertheless arranged in a racial hierarchy, where the Indian and African figures march at the back behind those from Australia, Britain, Canada, New Zealand, and South Africa. Empire propaganda also offered some coverage of women in the forces and as war workers, but this was limited.

The focus on men in military uniform was particularly apparent in the celebration of the sons of empire and their martial masculinity. 'Martial race theory', used in British recruitment to the imperial forces in the nineteenth century privileged ethnic groups that were considered to be 'martial races', identified the qualities that made good soldiers—naturally warlike, courageous, loyal, disciplined (when well led), and of considerable physical prowess—and made being warlike synonymous with manliness.[41] Newsreels about imperial troops in Britain often celebrated these qualities. One that showed the King inspecting Indian troops in Britain called them 'these magnificent soldiers from India... renowned for their fine physique, stately bearing and intense loyalty to the Crown'. Another, that showed the King inspecting Australian troops in Britain, called them 'sturdy Aussies' and commented on their 'toughness' and their 'sun-tanned brawn'. A 1945 story of former Indian prisoners of war from Germany, visited by royalty in a camp in Norfolk, acclaimed their contribution to the war effort as 'warriors of India', and spoke of them receiving a royal tribute for their 'heroic contribution to the Allied victory', having fought with distinction 'in the honoured tradition of fighting India'.[42]

Publicity for the contributions of black and Asian troops to the imperial war effort usually showed them on the fighting front in theatres of war that were far away from Britain. But the documentary *Africa's Fighting Men* (1943), which showed African troops in Ceylon (now Sri Lanka) and in Africa, also celebrated Emanuel Peter Thomas, who sailed to Britain from Nigeria in 1941. Thomas was the first West African to come to Britain as a volunteer for the RAF and the first to qualify as a pilot and be commissioned. He was killed in a flying accident in bad weather in January 1945. *Africa's Fighting Men* was made by the Colonial Film Unit, sponsored by the Ministry of Information, and intended for an African audience. The film ends with commentary celebrating a 'people's empire' over shots of Thomas shaking hands with a white officer, 'The colonial people...from the beginning have shown that they are able and ready to take their place side by side with all the peoples of the empire in the battle for freedom'.[43]

Another documentary sponsored by the Ministry of Information that celebrated a 'people's empire' was based on one of the BBC wartime programmes to which Dunbar contributed—*Calling the West Indies*—but reversed its title and the direction of its messages. The film was made in two versions—one, for a West Indies audience, entitled *Hello! West Indies*, and a shorter version, with an added introduction for a British audience, entitled *West Indies Calling*.[44] In reversing the title of the radio programme, the British version of the film also reversed the direction of the messages. A narrative voice, absent from the West Indies version, was inserted at the outset to explain that: 'Each week some of them [West Indians] broadcast messages home...But this evening, they are broadcasting to Britain'.

The radio programme in which West Indians in Britain broadcast messages home was generally organized as a party, sometimes held in London, sometimes in Glasgow and Edinburgh, with music and West Indian guests.[45] Its compère was Una Marson, who was also a key figure in its production. She wrote scripts for the broadcast and recruited men and women to speak on it. A considerable amount of research effort went into tracing West Indians in Britain and letters were sent out regularly from the BBC to commanding officers to request their release for a day so that they could appear on the programme.

Marson also acted as compère in the film *West Indies Calling*, introducing Learie Constantine, Carlton Fairweather from the British Honduran

Forestry Unit, and Flying Officer Ulric Cross—a bomber navigator from Trinidad who joined the RAF in 1941 and was a Squadron leader by the end of the war, and the highest ranking West Indian serviceman in the RAF. These speakers provide the narrative voices for shots of Caribbean men employed in munitions factories in Britain, some of the 10,000 West Indian male and female volunteers in the armed forces in Britain, and volunteers from British Honduras working as foresters in Scotland. The film emphasizes a multi-ethnic Caribbean identity, with friendly mixing between African Caribbeans, Indo-Caribbeans and white Caribbeans. A 'people's empire', where a community of imperial allies unites across differences of ethnicity, is very evident in shots of a West Indian pilot, Jimmy Hyde, chatting with members of his squadron. The commentary explains, 'In Hyde's squadron, there are pilots from New Zealand, Poland, Britain and Canada. Friendships are being made between people who before the war knew little or nothing about each other, and we find it impossible to believe that these friendships will just fade out when the war is won'. The film shows Hyde as part of this friendly group, but its message clashes with Hyde's own sense of isolation—'no friend, no girl, no one in all England. I am alone'.[46]

The public celebration of a 'people's empire' in *Africa's Fighting Men* and *West Indies Calling* conflicted with the private views expressed by the government in confidential documents. In 1942, the War Cabinet noted 'the serious social consequences which might arise from the demobilisation in this country of any appreciable numbers of certain classes of coloured men who are serving in His Majesty's Forces'. It also noted that those from British colonies could not be deported if they proved to be 'undesirable', since they were British subjects with a right of settlement, and that overt discrimination, in the form of a colour bar, could not be accepted. In this context, covert discrimination was recommended:

> The only course open to us is to recommend very strongly that service departments should do all they possibly can by administrative action to reduce to a minimum the opportunities these men might have of being demobilised in this country. The concentration of these men in separate units, the restriction of their service to theatres of war overseas, and the repatriation of men in complete units would do much to prevent a serious social problem arising.[47]

The discrepancy between what government policy-makers record here privately and the public messages sponsored by the Ministry of Information could scarcely have been wider.

The British government's repression of the Indian nationalist movement
was particularly damaging to the government's message about a 'people's
empire' and to any claim by Britain to be fighting for the cause of freedom
and democracy. Mulk Raj Anand—the Indian writer and novelist who came
to Britain in the 1920s to study for a doctorate—declined an offer of work
at the BBC in 1941, explaining:

> Briefly, as you know... the position of Indians in this war has become very
> invidious. Particularly is this so with regard to the Indians resident in England
> at the moment. Because even those who have the most distant affiliations with
> the Congress [Indian National Congress], are bound to feel a certain sense of
> national humiliation if, with full awareness of the internment of hundreds of
> their compatriots and the savage sentence on Pandit Nehru, they do anything
> to help the war effort.[48]

At the same time, recognizing that 'fascism would destroy all I stand
for' Anand wrote that he was 'torn between conflicting loyalties'.[49] Although
Anand eventually agreed to work for the BBC, he continued to be torn.
In an autobiographical piece drafted during the war, he wrote, 'there can
be no dignity in the... relations of British and Indian intellectuals unless
British writers realise that the freedom of speech... they take for granted is
denied... their Indian friends, and unless they see... that intellectuals everywhere enjoy equal rights of citizenship'.[50]

   In 1942, when the Quit India movement told the British to 'purify themselves by surrendering power in India' and nationalist leaders, including
Mahatma Gandhi and Jawaharlal Nehru, were arrested and imprisoned,
there was violent repression by the British of Quit India demonstrations,
with the RAF brought in to machine-gun demonstrators from the air.[51]
In this context, Anand refused to participate in a BBC programme that he
considered opposed the interest of India's independence movement.[52]

   Noor Inayat Khan (see Figure 3.2), similarly, had to negotiate between
her anti-fascist convictions and support for Indian independence. Khan was
a young Muslim woman of mixed American and Indian parentage, who
arrived in Britain from France in 1940. She volunteered for the Women's
Auxiliary Air Force, where she trained as a wireless operator. Later she was
recruited to the Special Operations Executive to work in France, where she
was captured, imprisoned, and tortured. Finally, she was taken to Dachau
concentration camp and murdered. During her recruitment to the Special
Operations Executive she had said, 'my first loyalty is to India. If I had to
choose between Britain and India I would choose India'.[53]

Figure 3.2 Noor Inayat Khan (© Imperial War Museum, HU 74868).

The conflicting loyalties and tensions between anti-imperialism and anti-fascism experienced by Anand and Khan potentially disrupted the vision of a united empire of togetherness portrayed in the British media. But damage to this vision was kept to a minimum through under-reporting. The practice of colour bars throughout much of the British Empire, notably South Africa, received little media attention and Britain was shown as tolerant in contrast to the racism of others, particularly Nazi Germany. Practices at home, as well as in the empire, conflicted with the image of empire co-operation and unity. In particular, evidence of colour bars in Britain threatened to undermine the aim of Colonial Office publicity—creating a good impression.

Colour Bars in Britain

In 1944, Arnold Watson—chief of the Ministry of Labour's Welfare department in the North-west region—wrote a report on discrimination against West Indian technicians and trainees in Britain, which recorded several instances of British dance halls that had refused them entry. In one case, the manager had imposed a colour bar when white American soldiers stated that they would 'boycott' and perhaps even do 'something worse' to the dance hall if black soldiers were permitted entry. Watson wrote:

> It is to be noted that one of the stable features in all 'incidents' which have come to our notice many of which have not been reported—is the general toning down of such happenings. Something like a verbal eiderdown blankets every such occurrence. The reason for this is the widely accepted view that great caution should be exercised, that the less said the better, that the aggrieved should be soothed into a more 'reasonable' mood etc. etc. All because of the—possibly quite erroneous—view that to bring the question out in the open would affront our good friends and Allies. On the other hand, the Americans should not be blamed unjustifiably.[54]

Watson's image of a 'verbal eiderdown' smothering the incidents he reported may refer to official neglect and failure to take action on them, but also the failure of the British media to bring them to public notice. It is also clear that he believed that evidence of incidents involving white Americans was toned down by the British government, to keep their US ally sweet.

At least one of the cases noted by Watson was reported in the press. George Roberts—a West Indian trainee from the Leeward Islands—was refused entry to the Grafton dance hall in Liverpool when dressed as a civilian, but subsequently returned in his Home Guard uniform, and was once again refused. Later, he informed his Home Guard commander that his uniform had been 'insulted' and that in future he was not prepared to attend Home Guard duties.[55] Roberts was fined £5 by Liverpool Police Court for failing to attend these duties but on appeal, this fine was reduced to a farthing [one quarter of a penny]. The court hearing attracted some press interest, which focused on the Liverpool Recorder's judgement:

> When people come over here to risk their lives on behalf of what they proudly call the Mother Country…I cannot understand that there can be any colour bar. It is impertinence for any country to accept the aid of coloured people and then to say, 'Our laws don't enable us to deal with you on terms of complete equality'. If you accept aid from coloured people…they should be the first to receive justice at your hands, and if they do not receive it it is a shameful business.[56]

The *Daily Mail* reported the story under the headline 'Colour Bar is Shameful'.[57]

The case of George Roberts prompted Harold Moody—founder and president of the League of Coloured Peoples—to write a letter to *The Times* in which he commented that English people were disinclined to bring the question of the colour bar into the open.[58] A Colonial Office report on 'Colour Discrimination in the UK' made a similar comment, noting that in hotels, boarding houses, and public houses, 'colour discrimination . . . is very frequent but only the more outstanding cases are brought to public notice such as the cases of Sir H. Gour, an Indian, and of Mr. Learie Constantine, the West Indian cricketer at the Imperial Hotel, London'.[59] Sir Hari Gour was a distinguished Indian lawyer and social reformer who, like Constantine, was refused rooms in a London hotel.

In a letter to the *Manchester Guardian*, Kenneth Little—a pioneer of the study of race relations in Britain—also noted that the practice of colour bars in hotels and other accommodation was widespread but under-reported. He wrote, 'Absence of comment on the colour bar in this country may give the impression that the experience suffered by Mr Constantine is a rare phenomenon. In point of fact, it is still something of a byword amongst coloured visitors from the colonial countries who look for lodgings in London and other large cities.[60] Little had found in a pre-war study that around 60 per cent of establishments in England offering accommodation operated a colour bar.

There was some limited press coverage of the case of Sir Hari Gour. Hotel staff had told him that they did not accommodate foreigners, and when Gour replied that he was a British subject, they told him that the hotel only accepted English people.[61] Constantine's reputation as a first-class cricketer regularly in the news made his case a far more prominent story than Gour's, but it was not until Constantine decided to take legal action—more than a month after the refusal of rooms—that the publicity began. Reports of his intention to sue the hotel appeared in the press on the same day that he broadcast his *Postscript* on the BBC. Home Intelligence noted that this broadcast 'was appreciated, and is said to have been very sympathetically received' and that there was 'strong indignation' about the treatment meted out to him at the hotel. The report continued, 'Discrimination against any coloured men . . . is deplored "If they are good enough to fight for us, they are good enough to live with us". In the Southern Region, people are said to feel that the matter cannot be left where it is, and in Scotland "a number suggest that Mr Constantine should be invited to lunch with the Royal Family at Buckingham Palace"'.[62] In the following two weeks, there were continued reports of appreciation for Constantine's broadcast and condemnation of the hotel's action as ' "Hitlerism" that exists in this land of ours and must be rooted up'.[63]

Publicity about Constantine's case coincided with reporting of a refusal of farm work to a British-born woman of Caribbean descent—Amelia King. The Women's Land Army was charged with operating a colour bar. The *Daily Mirror* reported: 'She is British born, her father is a merchant seaman, her brother is in the Navy, but she has been refused work on the land BECAUSE SHE'S COLOURED'.[64] A Mass Observation poll found that 'even those who do not entirely believe in colour equality were against this particular case of colour prejudice which was regarded as detrimental to the war effort'.[65]

According to Mass Observation, publicity about Learie Constantine and Amelia King, 'focussed public attention of the Colour Bar—a problem which has been creating increasing interest ever since the arrival of the American coloured troops'. This interest contrasted with the findings of a short Mass Observation survey at the beginning of the year, which found 'a fairly high percentage of indifference' to questions on 'colour prejudice':

> The fact that both these cases occurred within one week, and that Constantine's name is familiar to most people interested in sport, accounts for the vehemence and strength of public opinion. Both the cases were front-page news in the daily papers, which seized the opportunity to air the whole question of the colour bar and thus roused yet more interest.[66]

A 'snap survey taken in the London streets' by Mass Observation found that public opinion was 'very vigorously' on the side of Constantine and King and that 'it was very generally felt that the colour bar could hardly be reconciled to the claim to be fighting for democracy'. Mass Observation reported, 'There were many comments on the part which coloured men are playing in the war and [people] who felt that this fact alone entitled them to claim equality'. There were also many comments on the contradictions between opposing Nazism and practising a colour bar—'racial persecution is one of the things we are supposed to be fighting against and...in admitting a colour bar, we are...giving away our own side'. One man said, 'it is regretted that we should want to imitate Hitler'.[67]

There was renewed press interest in Constantine's case when it came to trial. Some reporting highlighted the issue of an American colour bar, not a British one. According to the manageress, Constantine had been refused rooms because of the presence of white American soldiers in the hotel, who would object to a black fellow guest. A witness told the court that Constantine had 'stated the fact that he was a British subject, and that he saw no reason why Americans, who were aliens, should have any preference at the hotel over a British subject'.[68] Arnold Watson, who gave evidence at the trial, later wrote of the hotel manageress as the 'lying witness of Imperial London Hotels', who had foisted 'her own strong racial opinions on to some unnamed Americans, not one of whom could be produced or identified'.[69] The judge at the trial found that the manageress 'used the word nigger and was very offensive'.[70] When cases of colour bars in Britain came to light, they were often blamed on white Americans. As the report on 'Colour Discrimination in the UK' noted, many did not come to light. Constantine's case and the judge's findings about the hotel manageress supported Watson's view that 'the Americans should not be blamed unjustifiably'.

The piece Bernard Bracken wrote in the *Sunday Express* at the request of Rudolph Dunbar acknowledged that 'everyone has read occasional stories of Negroes being turned out of doors by landladies and hotel managers simply on account of their colour'. The piece went on, 'I should like to say at once that the British Government is in favour of putting an end to this prejudice as quickly as possible'.[71] The government's record on action against colour bars included lifting the bar that restricted recruitment to the British armed forces to people of 'pure European descent' soon after war was declared. But although the Colonial Office put pressure on other ministries to recruit non-white people from the colonies for war work and service in the armed forces, a range of government departments expressed reservations. In 1942, a Foreign Office official—after discussion with other departments— noted that 'the recruitment to the United Kingdom of coloured British subjects, whose remaining in the United Kingdom after the war might create a social problem, was not considered desirable'.[72] It was in the same year that covert discrimination was recommended by the War Cabinet to reduce their opportunities to stay on in Britain when the war was over.

At the RAF, there was also some advocacy of covert discrimination in discussions about whether the colour bar should be reinstated when the war was over. One participant in this discussion recommended an 'unwritten rule' through which non-white applicants would be rejected:

> I felt we certainly cannot tell candidates to their faces that their colour is a bar to a normal career...Politically, ethically and religiously it is expedient that we should not shut the door to coloured colonials but we all know that to have a coloured officer in command of whites just does <u>not</u> work—certainly not where Dominion troops are concerned. Therefore on paper coloured troops will be eligible for entry to the Services, but the process of selection will eliminate them. The applications of this unwritten rule will require great tact and diplomacy.[73]

Even so, when the war was over, some black West Indians signed on for a further term of duty.[74] Others, who were demobbed back to the Caribbean, returned to Britain and rejoined the RAF.

The conflict between the image of a united empire of friendship and equality projected in the media and the practice of colour bars in Britain was generally smothered by the 'verbal eiderdown' that Watson reported. The refusal of rooms to Learie Constantine was one of the rare occasions when a colour bar was given wide publicity. David Low—a New Zealander who arrived in Britain in 1919—took the opportunity to point up the gulf between image and practices in a cartoon. Low was the creator of Colonel Blimp, whose name became a byword for reactionary imperialism and warmongering. His cartoon shows a hotel labelled 'British Empire Hotel, Colonel Blimp, Manager', with signs announcing 'no dogs or natives' and 'Hitler race theories, please take one'. A hotel manager with the walrus moustache of Colonel Blimp is ejecting a black man carrying a cricket bat from the building. He is saying 'Gad, sir, we can't have a coloured man here. It would take the minds of resident stinkers off their struggle for the ideals of the British family of free and equal peoples'.[75]

The range of attitudes to colour bars in wartime Britain is too diverse to admit a single evaluation. The condemnation of the hotel's treatment of Constantine in the press and in popular opinion—as reported by Home Intelligence and Mass Observation—contrasts with the evidence that colour bars were widely practised. There was also divergent opinion within different government departments. Policy-makers at the Colonial Office encouraged the recruitment of non-white people from the colonies, aiming to strengthen their ties to Britain and the empire through their accounts of positive experiences in Britain when they returned.[76] The Colonial Office therefore sought to avoid policies that were discriminatory, in contrast to other government departments where covert discrimination was advocated.

In the wake of the publicity about Constantine, however, even the Colonial Office proposed covert discrimination. John Keith at the Colonial Office wrote, 'I am afraid that incited by the Constantine case, a lot of well meaning people are now going to rake up colour bar instances'.[77] The case brought demands that there should be legislation to make all racial discrim-ination illegal.[78] The Colonial Office supported the idea of limited legisla-tion to make discrimination by innkeepers and hotels illegal, but mainly to create a good impression. Keith saw the legislation as 'declaratory' only—a measure that would 'satisfy Colonial opinion'. Discrimination could still take place, so long as innkeepers and hotel managers did not create the wrong impression by making reference to colour. Even this toothless legislation was not pursued.[79] It was not until twenty years after Constantine was refused hotel rooms that the first Race Relations Act came on the statute book, and not until the second Race Relations Act of 1968 that racial discrimination was finally made illegal in the areas of housing, employment, and public services.

Friendships and Frictions

The practice of colour bars in Britain produced considerable friction within the imperial community of allies and was one of many causes of tension and conflict. Relationships made by arrivals with British women were a major cause of violence (see Chapter 6). Other tensions included those arising from the subordinate colonial status to which arrivals from the empire were consigned by some British people, who called them 'colonials' and regarded them as less civilized and less developed than the British. It seems likely that, like colour bars, conflicts between imperial allies went under-reported. In the forces, there were many close friendships—this being particularly evident in the RAF, where crews depended on each other for their lives. Good relationships were also frequently promoted by mixing in domestic contexts—when troops from the empire were billeted in British homes or invited as guests.

Before the war, stories about the British Empire in films, novels, and children's literature developed racial imagery which showed non-white people as primitive, childlike and irrational, or savage and violent. Many respondents to a Mass Observation directive on race in 1939 which asked, 'how do you feel about Negroes', thought of them as 'simple' and intellectually inferior, although others strongly asserted that they were equal.[80] But a directive in 1943 that aimed 'to discover current trends of feelings to members of different coloured races' and asked respondents to comment on their 'own personal attitudes to coloured members of different continents', found evidence that mixing with arrivals from America and from the empire led to changes of attitude. A quarter of observers recorded that they were more 'pro-colour' because of personal contacts. One respondent wrote, 'Yes certainly wartime events have considerably changed my attitude towards coloured people. There are many coloured soldiers round here. Their "cause is our cause"".[81] Even so, this directive found that 'out of every ten observers', one had a strong anti-colour bias, while one in fifteen felt coloured people to be inferior to white races'.

According to a further Mass Observation directive on 'Feelings about Australians', white men from the empire were also seen by some respondents as at a different stage of development from the British—not so much childlike as adolescent. One respondent wrote about Australians, 'Just growing up but a fine boy. Had some psychological troubles, due to early life, and plenty of "growing pains". Should prove a good citizen'. Another echoed this view, 'The Australians always seem to me like rowdy adolescents, with all the symptoms of the pains of growing up...I think they will be a fine people in time'. Most of the comments collected made the assumption that Australians were men—there were no comments on Australian women. Men were seen as 'tough he-man fighters' and 'good blokes though a bit too cocky. We must stick by them whatever happens'. Australian men were admired for their fighting qualities but with reservations. One respondent called them 'crude and uneducated on our standards'. Another observed, 'The splendid physique of the Australians is my chief impression, but their bearing and manners are uncouth and brutally frank if judged by British standards'.[82] The report concluded:

> Most people think the Australians are a fine virile people, particularly good fighters. But as a race a considerable proportion think of them as less developed than the British, and as individuals some consider them rather 'crude'... Thus, though there is a good deal of criticism of the Australians there is also a great deal of sympathy and a great deal of admiration'.[83]

The view that they were 'less developed than the British' was not lost on Australian men, especially when they encountered this view in their British commanding officers. At Penrhos Advanced Flying Unit, Errol Crapp, an Australian navigator in Bomber Command, wrote in his diary:

> For being late on parade owing to very-late serving of breakfast at the mess, we N.Z, [New Zealander] Canadian and Australian pilot-officers were severely reprimanded by an RAF "wingless wonder" Flight Lieut who said that so far he has had decent officers under him. I mention this as this R.A.F. attitude of being a step above the "Colonials" is apparent wherever you go'.[84]

A similar complaint came from a Canadian at the radio school at RAF Cranwell, who wrote home, 'We're not liked here makes us wonder why the hell we ever came...our w o [Warrant Officer] here gave us a lecture first morn called us a bunch of rotten Colonials'.[85] An Irishwoman who arrived in Britain at the end of the war to work in a specialist unit for burns victims that mainly treated pilots from the RAF recorded, 'I loved seeing the interaction between the English and the New Zealanders and the Australians. They called them colonials'.[86]

Sometimes tensions spilled over into violence. There were many violent confrontations between black volunteers from the empire and white Americans, British, and Canadians. Sometimes fights were caused by offensive remarks made to black volunteers.[87] Many were caused by their relationships with white women. Robert Murray from British Guiana, who volunteered for the RAF in 1944, comments, 'The Westindians were disliked for one major reason—always women, always girls, always the white men not wanting their women to fraternize with those blacks. It was this singular thing that caused fights'.[88] There is also evidence of fights between British and Canadian troops, which were attributed by Canadian censors to the 'general inaction' by troops who were 'spoiling for a fight' but 'would probably prefer to expend their energies on the enemy'.[89] Many of the Canadian troops who began arriving in Britain in 1939 saw no action until the D-Day landings in 1944. Home Intelligence reported, 'From one region where a very large number of Canadian troops is stationed come "disturbing stories of their bitterness at being barred from all theatres of war". They are said to be "heartily sick of comparative inactivity" '.[90]

If inactivity could breed conflict between imperial allies, action often gave rise to good relationships. These were evident in the army overseas, where Postal Censorship reports quoted from letters that showed appreciation of an imperial community of allies by the British. In the Mediterranean theatre, a British soldier wrote, 'We had a pleasant surprise last week...the King inspected us and congratulated our Division. We have Canadians with us and we are proud to have them. They are good lads and terrific fighters'. Another British soldier wrote of Indians, 'No doubt you have seen in the papers what grand work the Indians are doing here...They are grand fellows and I'm proud to be serving in the Div with them'. New Zealanders prompted particular admiration. One British letter-writer expressed the view that 'admirable New Zealanders...are the greatest soldiers in the world, in addition they are modest and retiring by nature'. Another wrote, 'The Kiwis and Maori from New Zealand stand out as being grand chaps, they share everything they've got and their good will is enormous'. A third wrote, 'We are fighting next to the Kiwis—God they are fine blokes, always there where the stiffest fighting is on'.[91]

Action in the RAF also promoted good relationships, which is particularly apparent in the term 'band of brothers', used by Bob Kellow to describe the crew in which he served in Bomber Command. Kellow was an Australian member of this crew, which comprised two Australians, three English, and two Canadians.[92] Although the Canadian and Australian governments wanted their airmen in national squadrons, this involved breaking up existing mixed-nationality crews which were functioning successfully, risking loss of life.[93] Many crews therefore remained mixed.

Cy Grant, who, like Robert Murray, was a volunteer for the RAF from British Guiana, arrived in Britain in 1941. He made a close relationship with his French-Canadian pilot, Alton Langille. Grant spent much of the war as a prisoner of Germany after bailing out over Holland, and was described in a German newspaper as 'a member of the RAF of indeterminate race'—a description he uses as the title of his war memoirs. In these memoirs he describes his 'happiness and joy' when Langille arrived at the prison camp. 'To have him with me in the same camp was the best thing that had happened to me since I had been shot down'.[94] George Hawes, an Australian in Bomber Command, also formed a close friendship with a Canadian—Bob Weatherell—and asked him to look after his possessions in the event of his death. When Hawes was killed, Weatherell kept Hawes's diary, so that he could post it to his family in Australia from Canada and avoid censorship. When Weatherell was killed in his turn, it fell to an Englishwoman who had been host to these men to ensure that the diary reached Hawes's family.[95]

Many airmen, like Weatherell and Hawes, mixed with the British in domestic settings. Paddy Rowling—an Australian airman—made close relationships with families near his airfield and, if he stayed overnight, was treated in the morning to poached eggs for breakfast in bed. He instructed that, in the event of his death, his Hercules bicycle should go to Len Nettleborough, 'for the many kindnesses he and his wife have shown me'.[96] In some cases, arrivals in Britain, who were treated as members of the family, were literally family members. Doris Carter, a Canadian nurse working at a hospital in Marston Green—a small village in between Coventry and Birmingham—lived near enough to her aunt and cousin to visit them.[97] Leonard Peake—another Australian airman—had no close relatives in Britain, but his contact with distant relatives took him on visits to different branches of the family in places as far afield as

Harrogate and Oakworth (both in Yorkshire), Purley (South London), and Thetford (Norfolk). When he stayed in Purley, he was always given breakfast in bed.[98] White people from the empire who visited relatives in Britain were sometimes meeting aunts, uncles, or grandparents for the first time.[99] Black troops and war workers were less likely to have relatives in Britain. Robert Murray writes 'a predominant number of Westindians suffered the disadvantage of lacking a customary, or even temporary place of refuge in off-duty periods'.[100]

In the case of Canadians, the good relationships that followed mixing in domestic settings first emerged in 1940, when they were billeted in British homes in Northamptonshire during and immediately after the evacuation from Dunkirk. Home Intelligence reported from Kettering on 3 June, 'good effect on local morale from Canadian troops billeted there. Their toughness and efficiency awaken feelings of true Empire cooperation'.[101] Howard Clegg, one of the Canadian billetees, wrote in his diary, 'We are supposed only to sleep in our billets, between our own blankets. But the good people insist on supplying all bedding, sheets, pillow-slips etc., and on feeding us as often as we will surrender to their insistence. Some of the fellows have been virtually adopted by their host families'.[102] In a later diary entry, Clegg commented that 'the hospitality has been overwhelming'. The Canadian verdict was 'The English are tops'![103]

This pattern was repeated in 1941–2, when Canadians settled in Sussex and became part of local communities. The Diary of the Canadian Black Watch Regiment noted on 11 August 1941, 'People in Eastbourne seem genuinely sorry to see us go. We are beginning to feel very much at home and there's no doubt that the stay here has been the most pleasant time we've been having in England, as yet'. In July 1942, when they were informed that they would be returning to Eastbourne, the Black Watch Diary noted, 'This is very good news as this battalion feels that they belong to Eastbourne and Eastbourne belongs to them. Since our first visit there, many men have married Eastbourne girls'.[104] Canadian censors concluded from their reading of Canadian soldiers' letters that when men moved into billets and came into more direct daily contact with British civilians, friendship followed, as well as invitations to British homes. This hospitality, censors reported, was 'greatly appreciated by the troops, who make frequent reference to it in their letters'. One Canadian soldier wrote in a letter home, 'The Canadian Army...have eventually settled down to fraternize with the people, marry their daughters, return their hospitality and settle down to tea-drinking with gusto. We ... now speak easily and unashamed of fags—blokes—darts—mild & bitter—wireless sets and winkles. It has become part of our daily system'.[105]

The complex and varied relationships involved when imperial allies mixed and mingled is particularly evident in the case of Canadians. Those who had been so warmly received in Kettering in May and June 1940 were unpopular when they moved to Oxford in mid-June. In Oxford, they lived under canvas with little chance to meet local people—their unpopularity due to a drunken minority harassing women and careering around the streets in military vehicles.[106] Canadians may also have been among the Dominions men who felt that the British were slow to offer hospitality:

> Reports that "they are having a dreary time" in this country come from Dominions men now serving here with the RAF. The gist of their complaint is that they are not being entertained as their families and friends would entertain men from the Home country, if these were serving in the Dominions.[107]

In contrast, the war diary entry of one Canadian regiment for 31 August 1944, written during fierce fighting in France, paid glowing tribute to the friendship they had found in Britain, 'We who have spent so many years in England think and speak constantly of England and of our friends there ... even to the point of appearing disloyal to Canada. The thought of returning there on leave sometime soon alone makes life supportable at times'.[108]

Nila Kantan's memories offer a different vision of imperial allies mixing and mingling. Kantan grew up in a small village in Andra Pradesh, before volunteering for the Indian Army in the Second World War. He served with the Eighth Army in the North African campaign and then in the Allied advance up the Italian peninsula. Kantan remembers his experience of Monte Cassino:

> I still can't forget the Cassino ruins. There was nothing but rubble. The bodies were still trapped, stinking—I had to cover my nose as I passed through. I saw legs there, blown off the stomach. I have never seen such a number of dead bodies in any battle. I counted more than 800—then I gave it up. They were just there in the rubble, covered with a blanket. I felt very sorry. I didn't know where they were born, how they came there, whether they were enemy or our own troops—they were all mingled together. So many New Zealanders, British, Germans, Indians ... Seeing that, I felt there should never be a war again. I abhor war. I hate war.[109]

Figure 4.1 Zbigniew Siemaszko (right) and his older brother Zdzisław, Trafalgar Square, London, 23 September 1945 (by kind permission of Zbigniew Siemaszko).

4

Allies

After the German invasion of the Soviet Union in June 1941—an invasion that forced the Soviet Union to enter the war on the Allied side—the Polish forces in Britain received additional Polish troops. The connection between these two events was the Soviet invasion of Eastern Poland in 1939 and the subsequent deportation of many Poles to the Soviet Union. After the Soviet declaration of war, approximately 100,000 of the Poles who had been deported came out of the Soviet Union under a Polish–Soviet treaty sponsored by the British government. The treaty agreed to the formation of a Polish army in the Soviet Union and to a so-called 'amnesty' for 'all Polish citizens now detained on Soviet territory'.[1] Many Poles who came out of the Soviet Union under this 'amnesty' did army training in Iraq and Palestine and went on to fight in the Italian campaign. Zbigniew Siemaszko who had been deported to Kazakhstan by the Soviet Union, was one of those who joined the Polish forces in Britain (see Figure 4.1).

Siemaszko had grown up in Eastern Poland before the war. He was sixteen in September 1939 and attending a Jesuit school in Vilnius when Poland was invaded from the West by Germany and from the East by the Soviet Union:

> The Red Army came in on 17 September and this changed my life. My father was arrested soon afterwards, most probably he was shot in the spring of 1940, but we never obtained any definite information on that. The remainder of the family—my mother, my elder brother...and the sister who was six years younger than me—we were taken in April to Kazakhstan.[2]

Siemaszko was away from home when his family was rounded up for deportation. Riding back the following day on horseback, he was told the news. Intent on escape, he went to the station, where he was approached by Soviet police, who asked him what he was doing and where he was going.

He told the police that his family had been deported on the previous day and he was at the station to board a train for Kazakhstan to join them. The Soviet police took him away—first to the local police station and then to a camp, with others who should have been deported. Eventually they put him on a train to Kazakhstan.

There are various estimates of the numbers of Poles who were deported from Eastern Poland to different parts of the Soviet Union between the Soviet invasion of Eastern Poland in September 1939 and the German attack on the Soviet Union in June 1941. These range from 1,000,000 to 2,000,000.[3] When Siemaszko arrived in Kazakhstan, he remembers, 'There fortunately we were not in a collective farm but in a little town...Conditions were very primitive and very tough...I worked there mainly physically most of the time. That lasted for two years. Most of the time I was hungry, there was always something to eat but there wasn't enough'.[4]

When he first heard about the 'amnesty', Siemaszko says that 'for myself, I saw it as a great opportunity to get out of the Soviet Union, but the problem was that my mother and sister stayed behind...luckily enough they survived'. He describes his journey with his brother to the camp in Lugowoy where the Polish army was forming at 'quite a long distance'—an understatement.[5] It took them more than three weeks to cover this distance, which was almost 2,000 miles. To reach the local station they started out on sleighs—Zbigniew's drawn by two horses and Zdzisław's by a camel. Then they boarded a train and travelled with a group of forty-three men, initially in sub-zero temperatures—minus 25 to minus 30 degrees. Siemaszko describes his feelings on first seeing the Polish army camp:

> Before we reached Lugowoy...I saw on the plains, some distance from the railway line, against a background of hills on the horizon, the first camp of the Polish Army in the Soviet Union. It was early, before reveille, and the camp was still asleep. You could see the straight lines of tents and flying above them, on a high mast, the Polish flag. For a moment I felt as if a hand squeezed my heart.[6]

Arriving at the camp, conditions were 'pretty awful, food was very scarce and the tents were overcrowded'. On his first night there, Siemaszko felt ill and had a temperature. He went to the recruiting sergeant's office and asked for medical attention. The recruiting sergeant told him, 'Lad, as a sick civilian you will die miserably. No-one will send you to sick bay, you'll get no medicine, no-one will even bring you water to drink. You'll lie somewhere under a fence. First you must become a soldier, then you can allow yourself to be sick. I'll take you to the front of the queue, but when you stand before the commission, say nothing about a temperature. You feel quite well, completely normal. Understand'?[7]

Siemaszko was feeling better on the following day and had been assigned with his brother to the 28th Infantry Regiment. That evening they were issued with uniforms and equipment supplied by the British, 'In those conditions, the British army equipment seemed magnificent—shining knives and forks, fluffy towels, the soft fabric of the army greatcoat, wonderful warm underwear! The only items missing were scarves. We also got a rucksack, knapsack, two blankets, a helmet and a leather belt'.[8]

Siemaszko did not stay long in the army camp. Like many Poles who came out of the Soviet Union under the 'amnesty', he was only at the beginning of an epic journey. He travelled from the camp across the Caspian Sea to Iran—one of 31,189 Polish soldiers and 12,408 civilians who were evacuated to Iran in March and April 1942.[9] From there he went on to Palestine, where he was trained in signals, including Morse code. Then he was transferred to Iraq. His journey to Britain was via South Africa, where he eventually boarded the Queen Mary, arriving in Scotland in the early spring of 1943.

Journeys south to get out of the Soviet Union were often as traumatic as the earlier deportations. Bolek Turowicz was deported to Siberia at the age of eight with his parents and younger brother. On his journey south, he remembers, 'the train was packed with Poles all wanting to leave Russia. Conditions were terrible, starvation and disease were rife and many people lost their lives, including my younger brother Bogdan'.[10] Danuta Przełęska was deported to Siberia at the age of five with her father and mother and two brothers. Her older brother died in Siberia and her younger brother died on the journey south.[11]

Families with children often travelled together until men joined the Polish army. Many women with children then went on to spend the war in refugee camps in Iran, India, Palestine, and East Africa. Other women joined the women's branch of the Polish army—the Women's Auxiliary Service. Like Siemaszko, Zdzisława Kawencka was issued with a British uniform, but she had less reason to be pleased with it—it was a men's winter uniform, with trousers that came up to her armpits and were held up by a belt that went round her waist twice.[12]

By the time that Siemaszko arrived in Scotland in 1943, Polish and other Allied soldiers were already a familiar sight in many parts of Britain.

Their uniforms attracted a good deal of attention. In January 1943, a few months before Siemaszko's arrival, Edward Raczynski—formerly the Polish Ambassador in Britain and later Minister of Foreign Affairs in the Polish government-in-exile—wrote a description of wartime London. 'The streets are full of foreign uniforms, especially Polish ones distinguished by the shoulder badge and four-cornered cap. Lately I have seen a good many French, who, like the Poles, are easily distinguished by their headgear. A large proportion of the British of both sexes are in uniform, which is a novelty as far as the women are concerned'.[13]

The novelist Rose Macaulay, writing about the 'consolations of war' in January 1941, also noticed Polish and other Allied uniforms:

> The pageant of life is enormously enriched by the presence of so many foreigners in our midst... the uniforms of Polish soldiers mingle with those of Czechs, Norwegians, Dutch and Free French... And not only foreigners. Driving in the country, you are continually hailed by the rich accents of young men in battle-dress from Alberta or Montreal, who seldom know where they are and always want to go somewhere else. They are, as a rule, enormously charming.[14]

Mollie Panter-Downes, in her regular 'Letter from London' for the *New Yorker*, in June 1942, produced a similar description of the transformation of British street scenes and soundscapes after American GIs began to arrive, 'Londoners are beginning to get accustomed to the uniforms of American troops, who are now seen in ever-increasing numbers in the streets. Middle West and Southern accents are heard in the crowds as frequently as the French, Czech, Polish and Norwegian which make a blackout saunter down Piccadilly a nostalgic Cook's tour'.[15]

William Sansom, who was a full-time firefighter in London during the Blitz, noticed 'many uniforms from all over the world'. In his description of wartime London street scenes, they provide vivid colour and smartness in an otherwise drab, war-torn landscape: 'French sailors with their red pom-poms and striped shirts, Dutch police in black uniforms and grey-silver braid, the dragoon-like mortar boards of Polish officers, the smart grey of nursing units from Canada... the scarlet lining of our own nurses' cloaks, the vivid electric blue of Dominion air forces... a few greenish-tinted Russian uniforms and the suave black and gold of the Chinese navy. The town moved smartly against its boarded and tattered and charred facade'.[16]

Military uniforms continued to mark people out as fighting with or alongside the British and therefore welcome, but the British sometimes had reservations about the military prowess of those who wore them—particularly white Americans. Even the uniforms Americans wore did not always find favour. Home Intelligence reported that American troops were seen by some Britons as 'too smart and flashy', and 'overdressed for real war'.[17] White Americans were not always welcome and attracted more varied criticism from the British than any other group from overseas—they were 'unsoldierly', over-confident, and arrogant, they threw their weight about, they mistreated their black compatriots, they were given too much publicity in reporting of the D-Day landings. There were also many complaints about their relationships with British women (see Chapter 6).

William Sansom took a different view, writing about the arrival of Americans in London, 'So the town went gum-chewing and in many restaurants an American way of life was set. Baseball was played in the parks. Jokes were made about the Yanks. But never before was an invasion so welcome'.[18] This American 'invasion' very considerably extended the multinational community in Britain. From 1941, the image of an 'allies' war' in the British media expanded to include many new allies and emphasized inter-allied friendship and solidarity with occasional conflict—often due to misunderstandings—that was easily resolved. Outside the world of propaganda, mixing in Britain produced many close transnational friendships, camaraderie, and mutual respect—in the wider community of allies, as well as the imperial community. But mixing did not always bring people together. There was also considerable inter-allied antagonism and violence.

Fighting Men

In a newsreel on Polish airmen training in Britain in 1940, the voice-over accompanying shots of physical jerks and boxing commends them, 'On the physical side these men of Poland leave no complaints. They're fit, and they're longing to hit back at the aggressor'.[19] But over shots that show them marching, the voice-over shifts to criticism—'that march is a little too much like the goose-step'.

Warlike qualities—highly valued in martial race theory—became problematic in a Second World War context through their association with goose-stepping German troops, whose discipline and martial prowess were widely regarded as over-regimented, excessively warlike, and aggressively hyper-masculine. Historian Sonya Rose argues that a restrained version of exemplary masculinity, representing a home-loving, quiet reticence—what she calls 'the temperate hero'—became the wartime British ideal, in opposition to jack-booted Nazis.[20] Given the widespread British contempt for Italian fighting qualities, this ideal could be regarded as positioning British troops somewhere between German warlikeness and Italian unwarlikeness.

Martial prowess nevertheless remained highly valued in the British and their allies and was significant in responses to the arrival in Britain of troops from overseas. When Allied troops enjoyed popular approval, it was commonly for their toughness, virility, and bravery—qualities assigned by a range of Mass Observation interviewees not only to Australians, but also to Czechs, Free French, and Poles. Polish airmen were sometimes singled out for particular admiration.[21] But praise for the martial qualities of American troops was rare. The most common criticism of Americans reported by both Home Intelligence and Mass Observation—that they were boastful, brash and over-confident—suggested how far they were regarded as falling short of any 'temperate' masculine ideal.

The contrast between American and British masculinity is initially very evident in the 1945 film *The Way to the Stars*. When Americans arrive at an RAF bomber base in Britain, there are pleasant and friendly exchanges between British Peter Penrose (John Mills) and American Johnny Hollis (Douglass Montgomery), but then Friselli (Bonar Colleano) arrives—the archetypal brash American. Friselli's opening words mimic the English— 'Hallo my jolly old fellow'. He stops briefly in his tracks when he is introduced to Penrose and then proceeds to boast in a loud voice about the merits of American bombers, dismissing bombers used by the British as 'all right for reconnaissance'. In contrast, Penrose is reticent, politely answering questions. Penrose is much shorter than any of the Americans in the room and, as he attempts to pack, needs to keep ducking in and out of Friselli's expansive hand gestures and wagging fingers as Friselli explains that 'our bombs are going right where they're meant, right on that little old target, Zonk, Zonk, Zonk, every time'. Friselli is scarcely aware of Penrose, particularly after Penrose says he is Controller and not a flyer. The film has established that before the arrival of Americans, Penrose has successfully completed forty-three missions. His flying credentials are not in doubt. Friselli has only just arrived and has completed none.

The film cuts to a game of baseball with much enthusiastic American shouting, prompting the British officers to retire to the mess, where the theme of British-American difference is extended in ways that complicate the contrast between Friselli and Penrose. American ignorance of tea-making does not go down well with the British. When the British officers in the mess ask for milk, Americans bring hot milk and neglect to warm the pot. The British express disapproval of Friselli's coming into the mess in flying clothes. Their fussing over their tea ceremony and their formality, set against the loud enthusiasm of Americans for the baseball game, casts British masculinity in a potentially unattractive—even an unmanly—light. But British–American tensions are resolved through increasing cooperation and friendship between them as the film develops. Friselli, initially brash and boastful, becomes more temperate and thoughtful. Johnny Hollis is a more fully developed character and the film's American hero. When offered the chance to go home, he decides to stay on in Britain because 'if a guy didn't get here until the middle of things, maybe he should stick around until the end'. Hollis is neither brash nor boastful, and ends by sacrificing his life to prevent his plane crashing into the village near the base. British–American tensions give way to mutual respect sealed by his death.[22]

British–American tensions off-screen were not always so easy to resolve. Friselli's initial boastfulness and over-confidence in *The Way to the Stars* exemplifies a theme running through many British criticisms of Americans. A letter from London to America intercepted by Postal Censorship demonstrated anger at American claims that they were winning the war, 'It makes me seethe when the American troops over here say to our fellows who have been through hell, "It's about time you had us over to win this war for you. You should have sent for us long ago"... Friendship between the two countries would be such a great thing but you can't expect our fellows to like them when they throw their weight about so'.[23]

Another letter from London to America intercepted by Postal Censorship also criticized Americans for throwing their weight about, both before and after they entered the war:

> I have met a few of the American officers who came over here several months ago as observers and trainers. They were most outspoken in their criticism of the way the English were running what was at that time their war. One of them was so loud and so condemnatory at the Dorchester Hotel dining room one evening that he nearly had a quarrel on his hands. The English feel that their mistakes are their own mistakes and don't thank the Americans for all their too-free advice when they had nothing at stake. Now they resent the way in which some Americans take it for granted that they are now going to

win the war for England in short order, one, two, three, and that England should be everlastingly grateful for being shown how to do it. They also dislike so much American talk about how they [Americans] are going to settle the peace and run the world after the war.[24]

In February 1943, in the context of American reversals in their first battle with German forces at Kasserine Pass, Home Intelligence reported that 'the most marked reaction...has been satisfaction, going as far as jubilation in some cases, at "the American set-back"...it is felt that "getting a few knocks will have done the Americans good by teaching them some salutary lessons"..."It will take them down a peg: they shouted so much about the help they would give"'.[25]

The low esteem in which the British held American martial masculinity was demonstrated by a Gallup Poll in 1943. This asked who was winning the war and offered respondents a choice of four countries—America, Britain, China, and Russia. The publication of the Poll's findings in the *News Chronicle* prompted Winston Churchill to write to Sir Walter Layton, Chairman of the *News Chronicle*, 'Nothing will more arm hostile elements in the US against us than this most mischievous publication and the publicity it is bound to attain...This is one of the worst things that has happened in the newspaper world since the war began'.[26]

Churchill's strong protest against this 'mischievous publication' was due to the Poll's findings, which showed 50 per cent of British respondents opting for Russia as the country that was 'winning the war' and a further 42 per cent for Britain, leaving China and the United States in single figures. The United States was at the bottom of the poll, below China, with only 3 per cent. A report on the same poll taken in America showed that American public opinion was almost as unenthusiastic about British claims to be winning the war as the British were about American claims. American respondents put Britain in third place, with 9 per cent; Russia came second, with 32 per cent; and China last, with 4 per cent. Americans' confidence in their own claims to be winning the war was apparent from their position at the top of the poll on 55 per cent.[27]

The poll's findings on British opinion's high esteem for Russia as the country most likely to win the war and low esteem for America as the country least likely to win chime with the findings of Home Intelligence and Postal Censorship in 1942–4. In contrast to occasional jubilation at American setbacks, there was delight at Soviet successes and 'sincere admiration and gratitude' for the Soviet war effort. Calls for more support for the Soviet people were fuelled by awareness of their sacrifices and suffering as they bore the brunt of the fighting, and contrasted with attitudes to America, 'While the public are prepared to make any sacrifices necessary to help Russia... they have no such disposition towards America'.[28] In 1943, there was 'a revival of feeling that "Russia is making all the big sacrifices", and the desire that "her offensives should be supported by a supreme effort on the part of the other Allies"'.[29]

The Poll's findings also chime with the evidence of widespread admiration in Britain for Russian military prowess. In late 1941, during the Siege of Leningrad, Postal Censorship found that more than 75 per cent of over 2,000 intercepted letters that commented on the Russian campaign expressed 'wholehearted admiration and sympathy for our Allies, and confidence in their ability to resist'. A letter-writer from Manchester to Canada went so far as to claim that 'Russians' sacrifices and magnificent fight has aroused the admiration of the entire British people and no one grudges any sacrifice on their behalf'.[30] Home Intelligence reported in 1943, 'Enthusiasm for Russia is higher than ever, and admiration for the Red Army is now described as boundless'.[31]

Soviet citizens visiting Britain received a warm welcome. A Youth Delegation was mobbed in the factories in Manchester, while in the Midland region the workers gave them a 'rousing reception by banging on the benches'. The manager of an aircraft factory in this region said 'the workers have got so blasé over distinguished visitors that even the King wouldn't raise a cheer—but the Russians did'.[32] Admiration extended to Russian women. Home Intelligence reported from Scotland that 'country women are constantly referring to the example of Russian women, and are anxious to take an active part in the event of invasion. It is pointed out that "a basket of hand grenades is no heavier than a basket of turnips"'.[33] There was particular admiration for Lyudmila Pavlichenko, the Russian sniper who was reputed to have shot over 300 Germans on the Eastern Front and was enthusiastically received when she visited Britain in 1942.[34]

In contrast to the admiration for Russia's 'magnificent fight', there were regular reports from Home Intelligence of criticism of white American martial masculinity as 'unsoldierly'—'carry themselves badly', 'doesn't look like a soldier', 'wants a hair cut', 'overbearing and arrogant manner', 'boastfulness and throwing their weight about', 'slovenliness and lack of discipline', 'too "cocky" and full of themselves, and too keen to "shoot a line"'.[35] The 'slovenly appearance or bearing of American troops', Home Intelligence reported, 'makes a very great many doubt whether the American soldier will ever be the equal of the British'.[36] A letter from Northern Ireland to Liverpool expressed the hope that 'our next Army will be British as they are quite different to the Americans who are not at all a disciplined Army'.[37] Criticism was predominantly of white Americans. Black American troops were referred to as a 'fine lot of men' and were also seen as 'better behaved and less sloppy than whites'.[38]

Criticism of white American soldiers continued even after most of them had departed from Britain. In December 1944, Home Intelligence reported, 'Some still think the Americans unsoldierly and lacking in discipline; and that they are too casual, and boisterous in attitude and manners'.[39] But reports in September, following the D-Day invasion, also suggested increasing respect for Americans as fighting men, 'There are a number of references to the Americans becoming increasingly popular, mainly because of the fine job they are doing in Normandy, which has changed people's opinions of their fighting qualities'.[40] Letters by British soldiers quoted in Postal Censorship reports offered a similar verdict. One wrote, 'The Yankees are fighting very well over here now. In times gone by some of us doubted their soldierlike qualities, but by heaven they can fight'. Another wrote, 'There is no doubt about it, since landing in Normandy the Yanks have accomplished a lot, I take my hat off to them ... I have made many happy contacts with Yanks over here, and found them a fine lot'.[41]

Despite this increasing respect, there were complaints that, in reporting of the D-Day landings and subsequent fighting, Americans were given the lion's share of attention, 'Too little publicity given to the British and Canadians in France, and too much to the Americans ... Press and newsreels are particularly blamed ... "Have we no army in France?" Forces' wives are specially bitter. Some people fear the "capture of the limelight by the Americans" is a very bad augury for post-war relations'.[42] A report from Scotland on the screening of a newsreel of the invasion stated that cinema patrons in Falkirk were said to have called out 'Where is the British Army?'[43] There were even some criticisms of all Allied vehicles being marked with a white star, 'since this is generally regarded as an American marking, it is thought it will make it look as if there are no British troops in the Western offensive'.[44] But reports of complaints about Americans getting all the publicity noted, 'at the same time there is no wish to minimise the wonderful achievements of the US troops'.[45]

Criticism of Americans was certainly common, but as Mass Observation cautioned in 1943 in a report on 'Mutual Anglo-American feelings':

Spontaneous remarks about the American soldiers are for the most part unfavourable—often strongly unfavourable; but this must not be taken as the general opinion about them for the simple reason that those with grumbles are always much more ready to say things of their own accord than are those who have no complaints. In reply to a direct question, it was found that the majority of the general public said that they liked the American Troops.[46]

The yearly percentage of people responding favourably to the question, 'How do you feel about Americans', increased from 45 per cent in 1941 to 58 per cent in 1945.[47]

Whatever the criticisms of American soldiers, their masculinity was rarely questioned, but Jews were seen as an unmanly people—ostentatious and cowardly.[48] Charges of cowardice in 1940 were associated with allegations that Jews were getting out of London to avoid the Blitz. An observer working for Mass Observation reported a conversation s/he had overheard between a man and woman getting into a train near Cambridge. The man said, 'There'll be a lot of Jews getting into the train lower down'. The woman replied, 'O no they won't, not going towards London'.[49] A letter-writer from Oxford commented, 'The Jews are well up in the front of the evacuees as usual'.[50] Home Intelligence reported from Merseyside in 1941, 'Anti-Jewish feeling is said to be growing. Jews are supposed to be cowards who have fled to the best billets in safe areas and who avoid fire-watching duties'.[51] There were similar charges, when the flying bomb raids started in 1944, of Jews being 'first out'.[52]

Charges of cowardice were particularly apparent in March 1943, in the wake of the Bethnal Green tube shelter disaster when more than 170 people died in a crush as air-raid warnings sounded and crowds tried to enter the station and go underground to shelter from bombs. The disaster was widely blamed on Jews—a charge officially repudiated in the government report on the incident. Mass Observation reported that 'some of the talk and rumours overheard were violently anti-Semitic in tone'. Conversations that observers overheard included, 'All they think of is saving their skins'; 'Stinking lot of cowards they're (sic) are'. A woman was overheard commenting, 'They're all saying it was all the fault of the Jews. They lost their nerve. You know, like they did in the blitz. They haven't got steadiness like what we have. We may be slow but we are sure. But the Jews are different, they're like foreigners; in fact you might say they are foreigners'.[53]

Contributions to the war effort were rarely attributed to Jews, who were accused variously of evading military service and war work, engaging in black-market activities, evacuating to safer areas, and indulging in ostentatious spending.[54] A woman interviewed by Mass Observation in 1943 stated, 'They injure themselves to get out of the army. They pay £200 a time to get faked certificates, but our poor boys have to go'.[55] In 1943, Home Intelligence reported 'talk is "cropping up again" of Jews being thought "to contribute nothing to the war effort: they dodge the call up, wangle out of the Army, and you never see any in factories or working as labourers"'.[56] The accusations levelled against them placed Jews well outside any vision of a united allied community and the idea that they were cowards, as Sonya Rose argues, made them 'other' to the heroic manly British nation at war.[57]

This idea of a manly British nation at war meant that comparisons between Allied and British soldiers rarely favoured Allies over British—but there were occasional exceptions. In the Huddersfield area, black GIs were viewed as 'better behaved than the British troops'.[58] Home Intelligence reported of Polish troops in the East Riding of Yorkshire, '[they] have made a very good impression as being quiet and well-behaved, contrary to first expectations. People in the area generally have taken them to their hearts, and compare them very favourably with our own troops who had been stationed previously in the district. There is genuine regret at the departure of Polish troops from the area'.[59] One letter-writer from Northern Ireland commented, 'We have had the Yanks over here... they gave us a marvellous time and quite frankly the British who have again taken over, seem very dull'.[60] But Allied troops were seldom approved without reserve. Unreserved approval belonged mainly to the British.

Multinational Communities of Allies

In 1940, the pilots of the First Czechoslovak Fighter Squadron in Britain (see Figure 4.2) wrote a statement addressed to an English comrade, John Boulton, who had been their flying instructor:

> Today, alas! we can do no more than remember you... We never knew how you went. We came back out of that roaring whirl of aircraft, machine-gun fire, smoke and shell-bursts one by one. We waited for you all that evening— September 9th. And the next—and the next. You never came back. We will avenge you... We remember how you yourself avenged the death of the first of our comrades to fall in Great Britain; we saw you, in your first air battle, shoot to pieces a Heinkel 111 'in payment for Jarda'. The six Germans that we shot down in the fight in which you fell are the first instalment of the price

Figure 4.2 Airmen in 310 Squadron RAF which was made up of Czech pilots and fought in the Battle of Britain. John Boulton, whose death they vowed to avenge, is seated in the middle of the picture, wearing a lifejacket (© Imperial War Museum, CH 1299).

we shall exact for your young life. You gave it for those same ideals which are graven on our own hearts in letters of burning flame.[61]

The tribute paid by Czech airmen to their English flying instructor was reciprocated by Flight-Sergeant Crocker, in an English tribute to the Czechoslovak Fighter Squadron, 'I'm proud to be able to work with these men who are fighting so pluckily at the side of our own pilots...The whole world ought to know how you went into the fight, met and shot down the enemy, and how you all got your machines home, some of you with wounds which you deliberately concealed, omitting to report them lest the medical officer might certify you as unfit to fly the next day'.[62]

The comradeship and friendship evident in these tributes were often characteristic of the wider community of allies as well as the imperial community. Mixing in the forces, in workplaces, and in British homes frequently led to good relationships. There were also many tensions and conflicts, which were under-reported and rarely portrayed in the media. Notable among these were tensions between white Americans and white British, which had many causes, but included conflict over mixing. When white British mixed with black GIs, clashes with white Americans often resulted and were particularly evident when white British women mixed with black men, whether from America, Britain, or the British Empire (see Chapter 6).

The RAF was the setting for many inter-allied friendships. *The Times* reported in 1941 that the experiment of having Allied and British air squadrons on the same stations, sharing the same mess, had led to 'unstrained friendliness and mutual respect'.[63] There was also mixing on visits to stations. A Polish pilot officer recorded in his diary in 1941:

> Returning from a bombing raid a Czech crew landed near our aerodrome. As our leaders in London have decided that from now onwards we and the Czechs are one, we resolved to receive the kindred tribe with great solemnities...We played them our Polish tunes on a mouth organ, they then sang their Czech songs, and in the intervals we mutually confessed our past sins. We talked a lot about the new life awaiting us, and we reinforced our arguments with numerous rounds of drinks. It took a long time to work out the perfect Polish-Czech union, but in the end we all gave it up and passed out completely.[64]

Miroslav Liskutin, the Czechoslovakian pilot who served in 145 Squadron RAF, remembered the community there providing a sense of belonging, 'The squadron pilots were a real mixture of all Allied nationalities who impressed me as a genuinely friendly bunch. It came as no surprise that in this stimulating friendly and helpful setting I felt quickly at home'.[65]

Willy Hirschfeld speaks of a similar sense of belonging, fostered by mixing in the British army. Hirschfeld was a German Jewish refugee, who had been interned by the British in 1940 and then deported to Australia. He returned to Britain in 1941 to join the Pioneer Corps and transferred in 1943 to the Royal Armoured Corps, where he worked as a tank driver with a British crew. His tank suffered a direct hit in September 1944 and he was the only survivor. He records of his crew, 'You sleep together, you work together, you eat together, it's like a family...right up to that moment we were always one team'.[66] Postal Censorship reported that comments on relations between Polish soldiers, English, and Americans serving overseas were 'always highly favourable', with particularly good relations between Polish and English soldiers, marred only by what they ate for breakfast, 'Englishman (sic) being attached to Polish units feel very well, having only many troubles with food, because Poles have "cheese for breakfast and no milk in tea"'.[67] Kenneth, an Irish volunteer who joined the Royal Artillery in 1942, felt that his outlook on life was changed by the sheer number of different nationalities he encountered there, 'I served with Mohammedans, Muslims, you name it, every kind of race out there, Jews, we had quite a number of Jews... Canadians, Norwegians, Danes, Poles, Czechs'.[68]

Good relationships could be found in domestic settings as well as in the forces. When Willie Van Lierde, a Belgian pilot, was invited to a local home for Christmas, he was deeply impressed when, after listening to a broadcast by King George VI, everybody stood at attention for national anthems—the British God Save the King and the Belgian Brabançonne. After receiving a surprise gift from a British friend, Van Lierde wrote in his diary, 'There's no denying it; the British are a kind people. All the marks of friendship extended to me from the start have been a great comfort to me, and made my exile a little easier. I shall never forget their kindness and, more than ever, I am glad I came here'.[69]

Free French who spent time in British homes also reported good relationships. In February 1941, when the Free French army in Britain was given seven days' leave, virtually all the men were placed with British families. Georges Le Poittievin records that when he stayed for a week at Wembley, the British family treated him as though he was their own son.[70] Pierre Lefranc has similar memories, 'We spent our leave in the homes of families where the men were serving in the forces far away and were made to feel like sons of the house. Surrounded with affectionate thoughts for our comfort, we tasted for a few days at a time the joys of home life'.[71]

American troops were rarely billeted in British homes before 1943. When some billeting proved necessary as numbers of Americans in Britain mounted, it was regarded initially as a 'dangerous experiment'. According to a War Office report, it proved an unexpected success, 'excellent relations had prevailed throughout between hosts and guests, and the system had evidently led to a much friendlier attitude on both sides than had previously existed'. A census showed that complaints had been received from only one out of every thousand men billeted.[72] Billeting in Bury in Lancashire in 1943 produced 'exceptionally good relations', according to Home Intelligence:

> There is little or none of the usual resentment of Americans, on the ground of bragging, high pay, drunkenness or loose morals... Now hostesses are sorry to see the Americans leave, and want more of them next time—rather than British officers or Poles. Men write to Bury townsfolk after they have left, and many homes display photographs of their American friends. Some Bury people would now like to go to America, and are forming friendships with the parents of the billetees, who have sent over parcels.[73]

These good relations were attributed to the fact that this transatlantic encounter was between people of the British and American middle classes. There had been 'careful selection of billets... mainly of middle-class people' and the men billeted were 'not the ordinary doughboy'. The people of Bury 'found them "quiet, studious and well-mannered", and attributed this to the fact that they came from the "officer class"'.[74]

Black GIs were also invited into British homes. One wrote that British people were 'exceptionally good to us' and that most knew 'no color line or discrimination'. Another, who had been a guest in several homes, including one where they baked a cake for his birthday, wrote to a friend in March 1944, 'You know the more I see of the English, the more disgusted I become with Americans. After the war, with the eager and enthusiastic support of every negro who will have served in Europe, I shall start a movement to send white Americans back to England and bring the English to America'.[75] A survey in 1943 found that black GIs were more likely to have a favourable view of the British than their white compatriots.[76] In their turn, many British had a more favourable view of black GIs than of white Americans. Their courtesy and considerate behaviour drew much favourable comment.[77] George Orwell wrote, 'The general consensus of opinion seems to be that the only American soldiers with decent manners are the Negroes'.[78]

Walter White, leader of the National Association of the Advancement of Colored People—the American civil rights organisation—visited Britain in 1944 and heard contemptuous references by white Americans to 'British people who ignored the color line and invited Negroes to their homes'.[79] He considered that a main reason for friendly relations between black GIs and white British was that black GIs, unlike their white compatriots, did not consider the British backward, having in common with them an absence of 'mechanical gadgets' in their homes. Black GIs were therefore less prone to make derogatory comments on British living than their white fellow Americans, and their better manners in any case meant that they would not want to cause offence. As a result he concluded, 'the British developed respect and friendship for Negro soldiers which they, in turn, cherished. For many of the Negroes it was their first experience in being treated as normal human beings and friends by white people'.[80]

The derogatory comments by white American soldiers on British backwardness reported by Walter White were about 'the absence of telephones and radios, electric refrigerators and vacuum cleaners'. For some of them, White suggested, this 'denoted an inferior civilisation' and they made no attempt to conceal their contempt for towns and people that did not possess them. White concluded, 'When such opinions were loudly and frequently expressed within earshot of the British, they made no contribution to Anglo-American amity'.

A Special Report commissioned by Home Intelligence supported the view that white American soldiers found British people backward. The report was compiled by a civilian American who 'struck up conversations with American soldiers...at all hours of the day and evening', but at no time told them that an investigation on their attitudes to British people was in progress. His conversations were exclusively with white American soldiers and he concluded from them:

> [The American soldier] thinks the country is inexcusably old-fashioned. He concedes there is something to be said for tradition, but he will not admit that you can say enough in this direction to counterbalance the agonizingly leisurely shopkeepers, the uncomfortable hotels, the outmoded lavatory equipment, the funny trains, the cut of the women's clothes, the style of men's haircuts, the left hand drive, the slovenly business offices, and the dozens

of other things that visiting Americans have, with a singular lack of either originality or effect, been mentioning for years.[81]

Frictions between British and Americans were part of a wider picture of inter-allied antagonism that sometimes involved violence. Confrontations included British–American street brawls and British–Polish fights that were caused by drinking or by Polish men's relationships with British women.[82] The Office of the Inspector General of the US Army, reporting on racial incidents, wrote of what he variously described as fights, assaults, and 'riots' between black and white GIs.[83] Attacks by white Americans on West Indian technicians in Britain were also reported. The Colonial Office provided a catalogue of cases, including one where 'single technicians have been assaulted by groups of American soldiers' and another where 'a West Indian technician... was waiting in a queue for admission to a cinema when some white Americans came and told him that he had no right to go into the cinema. They attacked him and he was badly handled but some English people came to his rescue'.[84] Learie Constantine, providing information about further attacks, including two in Birkenhead, where technicians had been 'clubbed by American soldiers', wrote, 'I cannot lay sufficient emphasis on the bitterness being created amongst the Technicians by these attacks on coloured British subjects by white Americans'.[85]

The segregation of the American armed forces and white Americans' treatment of black GIs was a regular cause of British–American friction. According to BBC listener research, 'The attitude of white American troops to their coloured compatriots was mentioned only to be condemned and used as evidence against the reality of American democracy'.[86] There were many clashes over British fraternization with black GIs. From the North Midlands Region, Home Intelligence noted that 'the kindness meted out to coloured Americans by their British hosts is said to be resented and misunderstood by the white Americans who do not mix with them'.[87] In an incident reported from the Eastern Region, 'British soldiers were taken to task by those from America for fraternising with the Negroes. The British replied that as both black and white troops had come 3,000 miles to help us win the war they saw no reason to draw distinctions between one type of American and another'.[88]

Objections to the way black GIs were treated sometimes involved direct confrontations. The American military supplied the British government with a report on a number of incidents where 'British personnel... interfered in disputes between white and coloured US troops', siding with black GIs against white American authorities. In one case where American military police were arresting a black soldier, 'a group of civilians gathered and were heard to make such remarks as "They don't like the blacks", "Why don't they leave the blacks alone" and so on, until the civilians were moved on by the civil police'.[89] In another case, 'British civilians interfered between American white officers and a negro driver. They took the part of the driver both verbally and by laying hands on the American officers to get them away from the driver'.[90]

British criticism of white American attitudes to black GIs boosted an image of British tolerance against the racism attributed to white Americans, but was made in a context where racial discrimination was very frequently practised in British hotels, pubs, and boarding houses. The British government played no part in such criticism. Privately, some government departments wanted to make British civilian attitudes conform more closely to the segregationist attitudes they attributed to white Americans.[91] Policy-makers vacillated between the desire to keep their American ally sweet and the desire to avoid fomenting disaffection with British colonial rule by policies that were openly discriminatory. But their view of the overriding necessity of keeping America sweet meant that the British government refrained from all criticism of the segregation of the American armed forces, throughout the war.

Allies in the Media

The image of the 'allies' war' in the British media, like the image of an imperial community, emphasized unity, not conflict. It was developed by a multinational community working in British cinema and at the BBC and honoured Britain's allies in what I call here a wartime 'culture of tribute'. As the war developed, the list of nations to be honoured grew ever longer. From 1941, tributes extended to powerful new allies—the Soviet Union, the United States, and occasionally China. The 'culture of tribute' was firmly embedded at the BBC—its *Salute to* series, broadcast on radio in 1942, found a very wide range of anti-Nazi groups and nations to salute. The series duly saluted the Soviet Union and the United States, but salutes to European allies were also prominent. Sometimes doubts were raised about the appropriateness of a particular tribute. The BBC reported that the Foreign Office was not keen on saluting Mexico—'their point is that Mexico is doing nothing much in the war'—but the programme went out all the same.[92] Even so, tributes to some groups in wartime Britain, including non-white and Jewish servicemen and servicewomen, were limited.

Honouring the Soviet Union was not straightforward. Immediately after the German invasion in 1941, Mollie Panter-Downes commented, 'The press still seemed a bit shy of the word "ally" but enthusiastically discovered "partner", emphasizing that the new line up was to be strictly a business arrangement, with Britain tactfully closing an eye to the Hammer and Sickle and the Soviet Union presumably doing ditto to the Cope and Crown'.[93] She was right about attitudes to Soviet Communism. The Ministry of Information's policy was to praise the virtues of the Russian people, but references to Communism were avoided.[94] The omission of the Internationale from three BBC programmes of Allied national anthems that went out after the Soviet Union entered the war prompted much criticism. Churchill had banned it—a ban that was not lifted until January 1942—which put the Internationale on a par with the anthems of enemy nations, also banned by the BBC.[95] The BBC responded to Churchill's ban by taking off the programme of rousing Allied national anthems, such as the Marseillaise, and replacing it with a series of programmes of Allied national airs. These included a programme on Russian national airs, to which Churchill evidently had no objection.

The Internationale became part of pro-Soviet propaganda after Churchill's ban on it was lifted. A vast programme celebrating the twenty-fifth anniversary of the Red Army in 1943 culminated in a pageant at the Royal Albert Hall, which was broadcast by the BBC as *Salute to the Red Army*. It ended with a storming performance of the Internationale by military bands, the London Philharmonic Orchestra, the BBC Symphony Orchestra, and the choir of the Royal Choral Society. The *Daily Mail* described the anniversary programme as 'the greatest celebration to honour another country ever held in Britain'.[96] The 1944 film *Tawny Pippit* shows Olga Bocolova receiving a hugely enthusiastic welcome in the small town of Lipton Lea, which involves a choir of schoolchildren singing the Internationale, to applause from the crowd. Bocolova, who is based on Lyudmila Pavlichenko, the Russian sniper, tells the crowd, 'I myself have shot over a hundred Hitlerites and I am looking forward to shooting many more', to cheers and applause. When she finishes speaking, the schoolchildren's rendition of 'Land of Hope and Glory' is drowned out by more cheering. Performances of the

Internationale may have tacitly acknowledged that the Allied community included Communists, but explicit references were rare. They were avoided in coverage not only of the Soviet Union but also of European resistance to Nazi occupiers, despite the prominence of Communists in resistance movements after the Soviet Union entered the war.

It was a broadcast on the BBC European service that provided resisters in occupied Europe and the 'allies' war' with an enduring symbol. In April 1941, Victor de Laveleye—formerly Belgian Minister of Justice and from September 1940, head of the Belgian section of the BBC—made a broadcast from London to Belgium, proposing the letter V as the Belgian rallying sign, choosing the letter because it stood for 'Victoire' in French and 'Vrijheid' in Flemish:

> Why? All Belgian patriots should have a special sign, and that sign should be shown wherever possible so that, seeing it on all sides, you will realise what a multitude you are... The letter V is the perfect symbol of Anglo-Belgian unity... easily and rapidly drawn... your Vs can cover the walls in our towns... you can scratch your V on the paintwork of Boche cars. But watch your step. The idea is to infuriate them and never to be caught. And when a great forest of Vs springs up all over Belgium, what a striking proof this will be of your confidence and patriotism.[97]

De Laveleye also provided detailed instructions for signing a V with fingers, 'Just lift the right hand, or the left hand if you are left-handed, to shoulder height, palm turned inwards and fingers pointing up. Separate the index and middle fingers, lower the thumb and the other fingers, and there is your V'.[98] De Laveleye was evidently unaware that in British culture the V-sign made with the palm turned inward is a highly offensive gesture. Most Britons who took up the V-sign were careful to turn their palm outward, although Winston Churchill—who adopted the V-sign with enthusiasm—did not always do so. In September 1941, John Colville—Churchill's private secretary—wrote in his diary, 'The PM *will* give the V-sign with two fingers in spite of representations repeatedly made to him that this gesture has quite another significance'.[99]

De Laveleye was a member of a multinational, multilingual community that was very evident in the BBC's European Services, where émigrés, exiles, and refugees from occupied Europe, as well as enemy nationals, worked as scriptwriters, announcers, translators, speakers, singers, actors, and producers. Most of the literature on European émigrés and exiles at the wartime BBC focuses on their work for the European Services—the French service has attracted particular attention.[100] But many were also involved in broadcasts on the Home Services, addressed to a British audience. De Laveleye was one of these, scripting a broadcast on Louvain for the *They Shall Rise Again* series, which paid tribute to famous cities now under Nazi occupation.[101] Josef Schrich, the Czech journalist and Viktor Fischl, a Jewish Czechoslovakian who worked for the Czechoslovakian government-in-exile, both wrote a range of programmes on Czechoslovakia. Louis de Jong, a Jewish Dutch journalist in exile, wrote an episode of *Escape to Freedom*—a series which told 'true stories of how patriots from occupied countries have come to Britain'.[102] Albert Rasmussen, a Norwegian sailor and shantyman who became the BBC's Mediterranean Naval Correspondent, broadcast about Norway.[103] French speakers who broadcast on both the Home and European Services included Pierre Lefèvre, Jean Oberlin, and Françoise Rosay, the French actress. Tahu Hole, Overseas Talks Manager, wrote to Rosay, telling her that her broadcast on Bastille Day 1944 had a script that was 'movingly written' and that it succeeded 'in giving one a feeling of the true and noble spirit of France'. Rosay refused payment for all her BBC broadcasts, calling them 'a gift to France'.[104]

One of the broadcasts for which Rosay refused payment was a *Postscript* in the prestigious BBC Sunday night Home Service series. Listener Research at the BBC reported an appreciation score of 81: 'Interest in the subject of M. Rosay's talk was heightened by the fact that she was speaking from personal experience. By the apparent sincerity of her emotions and the intensity of her appeal, she brought home very vividly to listeners the agony of Occupied France'.[105] Rosay also worked in British wartime cinema. In two films for Ealing Studios—*Halfway House* (1944) and *Johnny Frenchman* (1945)—she plays a patriotic anti-Nazi Frenchwoman. *Johnny Frenchman* begins with inter-Allied conflict, showing rivalry between Cornish and Breton fishermen, but this is transformed by the end of the film into Cornish–Breton cooperation and friendship in common opposition to the Nazi enemy. While Rosay was filming, news of the liberation of France arrived, which prompted a transnational celebration. Michael Balcon, who produced the film, records, 'Somebody produced champagne (pretty rare then) and we toasted Françoise who was much moved. Then we all sang the Marseillaise'.[106]

Cumulatively, the Sunday night *Postscript* programmes offered their audience a way of imagining a community of allies speaking over the airwaves. Responses to them suggest that many audience members identified not only with an imperial community of allies, but also with a wider allied community. A Sunday *Postscript* by Theodor Broch, former Mayor of Narvik in Norway, was 'widely praised' and described as 'one of the most memorable postscripts given'. Listener Research reported that 'the majority of listeners were impressed' and that it had been described as 'deeply sincere and moving'. Like Françoise Rosay's *Postscript*, it scored 81 on the BBC listener appreciation index.[107] A *Postscript* by a Dutch officer about resistance in occupied Holland—including a national strike when more than twelve hundred Dutch were shot—earned a similar score, of 80. Listener Research reported 'listeners...noted the authenticity of the Postscript coming, as it did, from one who had personal experience of living under Nazi occupation'.[108] When a Polish officer spoke of friendship in the Polish underground movement between people prepared to die for each other, Listener Research reported:

> Postscripts by speakers from occupied countries are usually popular and this one was no exception. Listeners found this Postscript moving and interesting, and its first-hand story gripped the imagination and claimed the sympathy of its hearers. There was evidence of a small current of reaction against stories of the underground movement, which listeners feel are perhaps being exploited to a point where the law of diminishing returns in emotion is beginning to operate.[109]

American speakers in the Sunday-night slot were popular even before America entered the war. This was particularly the case with Quentin Reynolds's *Postscript* in 1941, which addressed Goebbels with a report on Britain and told him there were 44,000,000 people on Churchill's island and that he would have to kill all of them before he could make peace on his terms. Reynolds was London correspondent of the American magazine *Collier's Weekly*. Listener Research reported 'a landslide...this *Postscript* outclassed all others for which comparable reports are available. Not only was the quality but also the degree of enthusiasm for this *Postscript* remarkable'.[110] The BBC promptly commissioned Reynolds to give another *Postscript*. This time he addressed Mr Schicklgruber—widely believed to have been Hitler's original name—in what the *Daily Mail* described as 'the straightest talk ever delivered to the dictator of the new order'.[111] Listener Research reported that this second broadcast 'had a bigger audience than any Sunday night *Postscript* so far—50.1 per cent...it is significant that nearly nine out of ten people who heard the News continued to listen in order to hear Mr Quentin Reynolds.[112] After American entry into the war,

a *Postscript* by the American journalist Ed Murrow was also well received—
'spontaneous praise for Mr. Edward Murrow's Sunday night postscript
which was appreciated for its straightforwardness, and frank handling of our
relations with Americans'.[113]

The idea of a multinational community of allies was promoted on film
as well as radio. Émigrés and exiles from occupied Europe who worked
in British cinema made a number of documentaries that showed their
compatriots continuing the fight from Britain. Poles and Czechs formed
their own film units in Britain. Jiri Weiss—a Czechoslovakian Jewish
film-maker who had fled from Prague in 1938—directed *Night and Day*
(1945), produced by the Czechoslovakian Film Unit, which showed members
of the Czechoslovakian 311 squadron working for Coastal Command. They
successfully complete a mission, attacking a U-boat and blasting it out of the
sea. The film's commentary identified a transnational team, 'The skipper
comes from Prague, the gunners from Budĕjovice, Brno, Hana, the navigator,
once a lecturer at the University of Prague, is British'.[114]

The Polish Film Unit produced documentaries on a Polish bomber
squadron in the RAF, on Polish soldiers training as paratroopers in Britain,
and on the story of Poles who came to Scotland, trained to fight, learnt to
know Scottish men and women, and ceased to be strangers.[115] Eugeniusz
Cekalski, the Polish film-maker, scripted and directed *Diary of a Polish
Airman* (1942), which shows a British–Polish effort of mutual respect and
sacrifice. It traces the Polish airman's wartime life through his diary entries,
before he is killed in action. As the Germans surround Warsaw, he fights on,
initially from France and then from Britain. After his arrival in Britain, he
records, 'Here at last we have found a real ally and real strength. The RAF is
ready to meet the Germans and we Poles do our best in defeating them'.
The diary entry for 10 September 1940 honours all Polish airmen, who
had already shot down over 200 German planes, and the film ends with the
Polish airman's death and the statement that 'others will finish this diary'.[116]
A survey of 36 viewers found that 19 of them 'strongly approved' of the
film, which was thought to show 'the courage and patriotism of Poles
and their faith in victory' as well as their 'hatred for the Germans and desire
for revenge'.[117]

Mass Observation surveys often recorded admiration for Polish airmen,
but if films played a role in fostering this, it was the intense romanticism of
Dangerous Moonlight (1941)—a feature film with much wider distribution
than *Diary of a Polish Airman*—that made a greater popular impact.[118] The

Warsaw Concerto was composed for the film by Richard Addinsell, its impassioned lyricism first heard against the roar of German planes and the brutality of the German bombardment of Warsaw. The Concerto was particularly popular with the Royal Air Force and Women's Auxiliary Air Force.[119] Within the film, its composition is attributed to the Polish hero, Stefan Radetsky (Anton Walbrook), an airman, composer, and concert pianist. He begins the composition in Warsaw and completes it in neutral America, but subsequently abandons his musical career to join the RAF and continue the fight from Britain.

The main focus of all these films was on fighting men. British women serving in the forces and doing war work received a good deal of attention in the British media which also featured a range of stories about women's contribution to the war effort in America, Australia, Canada, Russia, and South Africa. But Allied women in Britain were thin on the ground in images of the 'allies' war'. *The Gentle Sex* (1943), which focused on women in the Auxiliary Territorial Service, was exceptional in portraying a Czechoslovakian exile serving in the women's branch of the British army. Erna Debruski (Lilli Palmer) is initially introduced by the narrator of the film as 'this foreign-looking one whose face is so lost and yet so angry' and her anger features strongly in how she is portrayed.[120] An earlier documentary—*Fighting Allies* (1941)—made for the Ministry of Information also showed Czechoslovakian women. They are doing war work—making pit props and working on the land. Vera, Vlasta, and Anna—now land girls in Britain—were secretaries in Czechoslovakia. The film also shows Czechoslovakian men working on farms and as lumberjacks, but begins and ends with shots of men in military uniforms marching.[121]

Jews were rarely shown as fighting men and women and their visibility in the 'culture of tribute' to allies was very limited. The Ministry of Information's concerns about an increasingly anti-Semitic climate in Britain in 1942 and 1943 were shared by the Board of Deputies of British Jews, which sent a deputation to the BBC in April 1942 led by its Chair, Professor Selig Brodetsky. A BBC official recorded:

> They said the reports of growing anti-Semitic feeling in the country had been passed on to them by the Ministry of Information... They began by saying that they were opposed to any direct campaign against anti-Semitism for the obvious reason that it would produce the least wished for effect. But, they suggested, broadcasting by indirect methods could help to make it better known that not all Jews were dirty dogs, most of them being in fact good law-abiding

citizens, proud of their democratic citizenship and anxious to play their full part in the war effort. The achievements of Jewish pilots should be mentioned from time to time, likewise instances of Jewish civilian gallantry...the active role of Jews as the arch-enemies of Nazism...and so on.[122]

In 1942 broadcasts paid considerable attention to mass killings of Jews by the Nazi regime. In June, the BBC reported the findings of the Bund, a Jewish labour organization in Poland, on both its Home and European Services—700,000 Jews had been murdered by the Nazis in the previous year. A programme in the series of talks by 'Everyman', that were broadcast anonymously on the European Service by Noel Newsome, the Director of European broadcasts, stated:

> These Jews so foully done to death were our brothers and sisters...If I single them out it is because their special suffering earns for them a special honour. For ten long years they have endured the humiliation and tortures to which all the Nazis' victims have been more recently subjected. And still their cup of suffering is filled with more overflowing measure than that of any other section of martyred humanity.[123]

In December 1942, the BBC also gave substantial coverage to the United Nations declaration which condemned 'in the strongest possible terms this bestial policy of cold-blooded extermination [of Jews]' and to Anthony Eden's speech in Parliament, where he read out this declaration. Eden's speech was followed by a one-minute silence in Parliament for the victims.[124] A directive to the European Service said:

> The issue today of the joint declaration about the massacre of the Jews, simultaneously in London, Moscow and Washington, is a story of historic importance... The scene in the House of Commons today when all members stood in silence in tribute to the murdered Jews, gives this story a solemnity and picturesque interest which entitles us on all counts to make this great international protest our lead story for the day. I think it would create a tremendous impression in Europe, if we lead all our bulletins, for the next few hours, with this story.[125]

There was a marked shift in attitudes to reporting on Jews in 1943. The BBC's thinking was shaped by a Home Intelligence report in January 1943, which found that while atrocities against Jews 'continue to be regarded with horror', one result of publicity for them was that 'people are more conscious of the Jews they do not like here'.[126] The BBC received a range of letters in 1943 that requested more coverage of anti-Semitism and atrocities against Jews, and when rejecting these requests, regularly quoted its record of what the delegation from the Board of Deputies of British Jews had said, to justify the view it took.[127] From April 1943 BBC policy stated, 'the present time is not opportune for dealing with the Jewish problem in our programmes'.[128] In November 1943, the BBC refined this policy: 'Jewish references in programmes should be accepted simply on their news (or entertainment) value'.[129]

This policy meant that from 1943, coverage of Jewish contributions to the war effort was mainly confined to occasional 'favourable notices of Jews' in news bulletins, along the lines that the Board of Deputies of British Jews had suggested. An announcement of the death of Brigadier F. H. Kirsch on the 9 o'clock news in April 1943, for example, referred to his 'distinguished career in the last war' and identified him as the 'Chairman of the Palestine Zionist Executive', while an item on a British anti-tank detachment in May 1943 noted that it was 'commanded by a Jewish officer'.[130] As late as 1947, the BBC policy on Jews was reaffirmed in the context of anti-Jewish riots in a number of British cities, following the hanging of two British sergeants in Palestine by the Irgun group.[131]

Non-white people contributing to the war effort in Britain also had limited visibility in the 'culture of tribute'. Although there were films that celebrated their contributions, sponsored by the Ministry of Information or made by the Colonial Film Unit, these usually had limited or no distribution in Britain. Films about seamen serving in the merchant navy showed them as white, even though the service was particularly diverse by ethnicity and nationality, including African, Arab, Caribbean, Chinese, and Indian seamen.[132] A Ministry of Information documentary—*The Chinese in Wartime Britain* (1944)—showed Chinese seamen in the merchant navy, but the film was designed for distribution in China, not for a British audience. The commentary was written by Hsiao Ch'ien, who had arrived in Britain in 1939 to teach Chinese at the School of Oriental and African Studies, and paid tribute to Poon Lim, who was serving as a steward on a British merchant ship when it was torpedoed by German submarines in 1942. Ch'ien stated that Poon Lim became 'the holder of a world record of endurance'. He had survived for 331 days on a raft, and received the British Empire medal, which brought him some publicity in the press. The *London Gazette* reported that Poon Lim 'displayed exceptional courage, fortitude and resource in overcoming the tremendous difficulties with which he was faced during the long and dangerous voyage on the raft'.[133]

Ch'ien's tribute to Poon Lim in *The Chinese in Wartime Britain* was part of a wider tribute to Chinese serving in the wartime merchant navy:

> China fights not only on the land in the East, engaging huge Japanese forces, but in the West her men fight on the merchant navy front shoulder to shoulder in the greatest battle of naval history alongside their British seamen comrades. They too brave the torpedoes, bombs, and mines...making history under fire. Here in Britain, the Chinese seaman is not only doing a splendid job of work. He is getting an insight into those better conditions of labour that are a commonplace in modern Britain.[134]

Views expressed confidentially by the government offer a different view of Chinese seamen and their conditions of labour. During the war, the government had assisted the ship-owners Alfred Holt and Company to force Chinese seamen to join the *Sarpedon*, despite the government's own view of this vessel: 'to describe it as a "hell-ship" from a crew point of view would be an under-statement'.[135] In strong contrast to the tributes offered to Chinese seamen in the film, the British government made plans to repatriate and deport Chinese seamen when the war was over.[136]

Messages sponsored by the government, like *The Chinese in Wartime Britain*, were rarely undermined by public knowledge of the government's private thinking and practices. The main message of a harmonious and united multinational community was rarely disrupted. Occasionally inter-allied friction was shown—as in *The Way to the Stars*—but it was resolved in imagery of growing friendship, cooperation, and tolerance. The image of the 'allies' war' offered an expansive view of Britain as a member of a diverse community that was fighting with or alongside it, inviting British audiences to imagine themselves as members of this community and to identify with it. The evidence that this image was often favourably received suggests that there were Britons who identified with a diverse community making a common effort in a common cause.

Some allies were more visible than others. Men in uniform were highly visible and fighting men also enjoyed much popular approval—although with many reservations in the case of white Americans. Allied women in Britain were largely invisible. Accusations levelled against Jews placed them outside the idea of an allied community making a common effort and Jews were also increasingly excluded from the media's vision of an allied community, after 1942. Even when the BBC directive to the European Services in December 1942 instructed that the Allied declaration about the extermination of Jews should be the lead story for the day, it was the 'international protest' and the silent tribute in the House of Commons that were seen as 'a story of historic importance', not the genocide of Jews. Despite some images and voices telling of people pulling together in wartime across differences of race and ethnicity, the main focus of the media vision of an 'allies' war' and of the 'culture of tribute' was on white men.

Figure 5.1 Alfred Kerr, portrait by Erich Salomon, *c.* 1930 (by kind permission of the Berlinische Galerie, Landesmuseum für Moderne Kunst, Fotografie und Architektur).

5

Language, Speech, and Sound

Alfred Kerr (see Figure 5.1) was a prominent Jewish German writer and broadcaster who escaped from Germany in February 1933 after receiving a phone call from a police officer. The caller did not give his name, but warned Kerr that the police planned to confiscate his passport on the following day.[1] Kerr moved first to Switzerland, then France, and finally Britain. In July 1933, he and his wife were deprived of their German nationality. Alfred Kerr was declared a public enemy of the Reich.[2]

Kerr's son, Michael, tells a story about a visit Alfred made to England in 1896. 'When he went into a tobacconist to buy a pipe, he said that they had failed to understand him when he said perfectly clearly: "Goodbye, have you a whistle?"'[3] English remained difficult for him at the time of his arrival in Britain in 1935. Alfred's daughter, Judith Kerr, talks about her father's 'halting English'.[4] Kerr himself described the English he spoke in wartime as 'pidgin'.[5]

Both Judith and her brother grew up as German-speakers, but became fluent in French during their time as refugees in France, and learnt English quickly on arrival in Britain. Alfred was also a fluent French-speaker. Judith Kerr describes conversations with her father in *Bombs on Aunt Dainty*—an autobiographical account of her life in wartime, written in the third person:

> There was an initial difficulty to overcome in that she did not know the words for what she wanted to say in German, and Papa did not know them in English. She had to speak in each language in turn, with a bit of French thrown in for good measure, until her meaning came across—more she sometimes felt, by telepathy than anything else. But then Papa understood completely.[6]

Alfred Kerr continued to write throughout the war but—like many other Austrian and German writers in exile—he could no longer command an audience. He was virtually unknown in the English-speaking world and the chances of published translations of his writing were small. Between the wars, with the exception of one or two small publishing houses, British publishers focused on work written in English, with translations comprising only 2 to 3 per cent of their output.[7] In the German-speaking world, Kerr's work had commanded huge audiences before the rise of Hitler. It was then banned. No German-language publisher or newspaper editor was likely to take on new work. A one-sided correspondence between Kerr and Berthold Viertel—the Austrian director then working for the film company Gaumont-British—demonstrates Kerr's awareness of his fading reputation. Before his arrival in Britain, Kerr approached Viertel with a film script dealing with a life of Napoleon's mother. When Viertel did not reply, Kerr added as a postscript to a further letter, 'What I find intriguing in all this (perhaps you do also) is the question: whether you would have left a letter from me unanswered ten or twelve years ago'.[8]

When Kerr sent the script on the life of Napoleon's mother to Alexander Korda—the Hungarian-born film director working in Britain—he was paid £1,000 for it. Like Kerr's other film scripts, it was never made into a film, but the payment financed his family's journey to Britain. Kerr published two books while he was in France and in the year of his arrival in Britain he published a volume of anti-Nazi poetry—*Melodien*. But this was his last published book. His exile robbed him of what had been a towering reputation in Germany and plunged him into poverty. *Ich kam nach England* (I Came to England), written in Britain during the war, was eventually published posthumously in Germany in 1979. Like his other work, it has never been translated into English.

In contrast to the frustrations experienced by her father, Judith Kerr later became well-known as the author of children's books including *The Tiger Who Came to Tea* and a series about Mog, the cat. In *Bombs on Aunt Dainty*, she records the outline of her family's story and her father's frustrations as she heard it told by her mother and 'explained so many times that she almost knew it by heart':

> Six months in Switzerland...two years in France...the Depression...the film script on the strength of which they had come to England...No, the film had never been made...No, it didn't seem to matter then that Papa didn't speak English because the script had been translated, but now of course...A writer without a language.[9]

Speech, as well as writing, had been significant in Kerr's work in Germany in the 1920s and early 1930s. He broadcast frequently on Radio Berlin, his output including anti-Nazi broadcasts. Radio Berlin clearly recognized the dangers that such broadcasts involved. A police escort was provided to take Kerr to and from the studio. Six months before Kerr left Germany, the broadcasts were stopped.[10] In Britain, Kerr hoped that he could make a significant contribution to the BBC's German Service, but most of his proposals were rejected. Michael Kerr records:

> My father could not get any paid work, although he was constantly writing. Among other possibilities he was besieging the World Service of the BBC to write for them and to broadcast to Germany. But this was never permitted. He was not popular with the small clique of refugees who ran that side of broadcasting. Their official excuse was that he was too well known, too implacable in his views, and that he would alienate listeners in Germany.[11]

In 1941, the BBC paid Kerr for several satirical songs that he wrote for the German service. After that he had little BBC work until 1944–5, when he scripted programmes for the Latin-American service. It seems likely that an old feud between Kerr and a fellow Jewish German writer, Kaul Kraus, contributed to the regular BBC rejections sent out to Kerr. Although Kraus had died in 1936, his close friend and literary executor, Heinrich Fischer, worked in the cultural section of the German service.[12]

In the later years of his exile, Kerr referred to Germany as his 'Sprachland'— the land of his language.[13] Michael Kerr wrote of his father's loss of language through exile, 'So it gradually became clear that my father would no longer be able to earn his living in the German-speaking world, and that he would lose the thing he valued most and which had been his whole working life, the German language. It was to be like a pianist losing most of his fingers'.[14]

The German language which was Kerr's whole working life was not valued in Britain, where propaganda in both twentieth-century world wars associated it with barbarism. Winston Churchill also made this association when he sent a telegram to Bernard Bracken at the Ministry of Information in 1944 about how the capture of Aix la Chapelle/Aachen should be announced, saying, 'Please try to introduce Aix la Chapelle instead of Aachen, which is pure Hun, into your BBC statement'. Bracken's reply assured him that when the announcement was made, the BBC would make use of the 'more civilized term'.[15]

Churchill's instruction on how to name Aix la Chapelle/Aachen suggests a hierarchy of language with German, in a wartime context, at the bottom. Although the sounds of the European Allies were portrayed in the media as civilized—particularly in contrast with the barbarism ascribed to German sound—it was English sound and language that was generally regarded as occupying the apex of this hierarchy. A view of English as civilized above other languages, particularly those heard as 'mumbo-jumbo' with its associations of the primitive, had a considerable history. But there remained a further hierarchy within the range of English-speaking allies. Who sounded most civilized? This was a question on which there was no agreement.

Learning English

Like Alfred Kerr, many people arriving in Britain spoke little or no English. Their own languages were unlikely to be understood by British people they encountered—knowledge of non-English languages was thin on the ground in Britain. As late as 1968, Gallup Polls showed that only 18 per cent of respondents in Britain said they could speak another language sufficiently to make sense of a newspaper written in that language. Fifteen years later, the proportion remained virtually unchanged at 19 per cent.[16] Many arrivals learned English (see Figure 5.2), but few British people learned to speak non-English languages in wartime—although at RAF Northolt, where large numbers of Poles were stationed, some British people spoke pidgin Polish.[17] Language differences were often the source of considerable anxiety and could cause misunderstandings, irritation, and hostility.

Fears that the sound of the German language would arouse hostility in Britain were evident in advice from the German Jewish Aid Committee to refugees who arrived in Britain after Hitler's rise to power in 1933: 'Spend your spare time immediately in learning the English language and its correct pronunciation. Refrain from speaking German in the streets and in public conveyances and in public places such as restaurants. Talk halting English rather than fluent German—and *do not talk in a loud voice*. Do not read German newspapers in public'.[18] This advice may have shaped the practices of one refugee from Vienna who worked at a small hairdresser's near Piccadilly. An observer working for Mass Observation reported their conversation:

Figure 5.2 Leading Aircraftwoman Halina Door, a 23-year old Pole who served in the Women's Auxiliary Air Force, studying a Polish-English dictionary somewhere in north-west Britain, 9 May 1944. Like Zbigniew Siemaszko, Halina Door was deported to the Soviet Union and came out under the so-called 'amnesty' (© Imperial War Museum, HU 12813I).

REFUGEE: I try always to speak English in the street.

OBSERVER: Very wise of you. If the war developed, you might find there was irritation directed against things German.

REFUGEE: Yes. We <u>couldn't</u> be enemies, but I'd understand how they felt about the German language.[19]

The advice of the German Jewish Aid Committee may also have shaped the fears recorded by some German refugees—that as enemy aliens with German accents, they would be treated badly or even physically attacked.[20]

Germans' fears that their accents would identify them as German probably overestimated the ability of British people to distinguish between different foreign accents. Speech and language received a good deal of attention in responses to questions about attitudes to foreigners and a number of those questioned identified all foreign accents that they heard in the streets as a common alien sound—'jabbering'. 'I'm a bit sick of the foreign jabber everywhere', said one woman, 'but I don't mean the soldiers'.[21] A common view that foreign accents were comic informed other comments by women. 'It's amusing to hear them jabbering away when you pass them', said one. 'Yes, I've noticed them about and it makes me laugh to hear them talking in their funny lingo', said another.[22] Speech was a main criterion used by one advocate of the mass internment of foreigners, who was interviewed for a Mass Observation survey in mid-1940 and defined those who should be interned as 'all what don't talk plain English'.[23] But not all comment was unfavourable. Mass Observation collected two contrasting views of the way in which foreign speech impacted on the London soundscape. One was, 'I can't fancy the streets all full of foreigners, and all jabbering away the way they do—makes you feel it isn't old London, sometimes, it sounds like some foreign place'. Another, 'It makes the streets of London more interesting to see strange uniforms and hear foreign voices'.[24]

German-speaking émigrés and exiles who worked in British cinema as actors generally had little choice but to follow the advice of the German Jewish Aid Committee and talk halting English rather than fluent German—at least in working hours. They were never cast as Britons, but frequently cast as Germans or other continental Europeans, who spoke for the most part in English. Learning English was therefore a requirement for acting in British cinema, whatever the role. German-speaking actors recorded a range of responses to this requirement. Peter Lorre's reputation had been established by his appearance as a serial killer preying on young girls in the

German film *M* (1931) before his departure from Germany. On his arrival in Britain, he could scarcely speak any English, but his appearances as a professional killer in Hitchcock thrillers—*The Man who Knew Too Much* (1934) and *Secret Agent* (1936)—made him widely known to British audiences. He claimed that he was cast by Hitchcock in *The Man Who Knew Too Much* by pretending to know English, 'Hitchy likes to tell stories, so I used to watch him like a hawk and whenever I thought the end of a story was coming... I used to roar with laughter and somehow he got the impression that I spoke English and I got the part'.[25]

Lorre also claimed that he learned English in two or three months after his arrival with the aid of a tutor. But Lucie Mannheim—who, like Lorre, was a Jewish German-speaking émigré—continued to be anxious about speaking English long after her arrival. She spoke German in broadcasts on the BBC European services, but for broadcasts on the Home Service as well as wartime roles in British cinema, she had to speak English. Requesting a copy of the script of a programme on Liszt, broadcast in October 1944, she expressed her anxieties about the need to speak English, 'I am so utterly lost when I have to read the part on the first rehearsal without having looked at it before. English is still a difficult language for me'.[26]

Some groups who came to Britain learned particular versions of English. The Air Ministry assigned the task of teaching English to non-English-speaking Allied aircrew to the British Council, which suggested that phrases like 'it lies plumb on your route' might be confusing. The Air Ministry responded that Allied pilots would hear such phrases all the time and needed to get used to them.[27] The Air Ministry also required the teaching of what they called 'technical and operational English'. This included RAF and other slang, such as PBI (Poor Bloody Infantry), 'in the drink' (in the water (of a ditched plane)), 'out for a duck' (roughly translatable as crashing or being captured having had no success against the enemy), and NBG (no bloody good).[28]

Jocelyn Green records the versions of English learned by Italian prisoners of war. As a teenager, she lived near a prisoner-of-war camp and records of one prisoner, 'Naturally, the first English taught to him by his workmates consisted largely of swear words. So then he would say: 'You bl...y lovely girl', or—'I love you, you b...r'.[29] She records of another prisoner, 'Amletto (*sic*) carried an English Phrase book around with him and, as we approached, would look up suitable things to say. He had a terrific crush on our friend Irene, who was six feet tall. Little Amletto was a very serious Italian, and as

he gazed passionately into Irene's kneecaps, would say—via his phrase
book: "It is fatty (fate) that we meet like this". He was completely aston-
ished when we shrieked and rolled around with laughter'.[30] Other Italian
prisoners were issued with phrase books through which they could learn
'pidgin English'.[31]

There were many misunderstandings caused by language differences.
After arrival in Britain in 1940, Joe Kobak, with other Polish soldiers, travelled to Scotland to join the Polish army-in-exile. He records:

> We were marched in column to railway station and as we walked along
> platform we noticed this writing on windows of train: SMOKING and NO
> SMOKING. And of course since 'smoking' in Polish means dinner jacket, we
> were surprised that one has to wear dinner jacket to get into train, so we all
> looked for windows where there was no smoking—and promptly lit up our
> cigarettes.[32]

Gino Caprara, an Italian prisoner of war on the Orkney Islands, records that
when Italian prisoners played football against a team of British soldiers, an
Italian objected to the behaviour of one of the opposing team by shouting
'ora basta'—'that's enough'. The soldier thought that he had been called a
bastard—a misunderstanding that prompted violence between Italians and
British.[33] There was a further misunderstanding when Thomas Cook—
appointed as a welfare officer to tour Allied army and air camps—liaised
with the Women's Voluntary Service, which ran a wide range of fund-raising
events to provide home comforts for the Allied contingents. Cook clearly
had organizations like the Women's Voluntary Service in mind when, after a
visit to 310 Czech Squadron at Duxford, he wrote about women's bodies,
'The men's immediate needs are being well catered for by voluntary women's
bodies in Cambridge'. This sentence evidently puzzled a Czech officer
reading Cook's report, who pencilled in the margin 'Please explain'.[34]

The different languages spoken within Britain came as a surprise to Jean
Offenberg—the Belgian airman—who travelled by train to Wales, noticed
Welsh place names, and found them unpronounceable. He recorded:

> As soon as we arrived on the Welsh border, the names of the villages we passed
> through, with their strange and improbably Celtic syllables which none of us
> Belgians could pronounce, formed a good subject of conversation....
>   'What about that one?'
>   'Wait. I'll spell it out to you. Take it down. S-k-y-d-i-r F-a-w-r. Are you
> certain we're still in England?'

'And that one?'

'Llanishen. There's no question about it. It's a beautiful language.'[35]

Leonard Peake—an Australian airman—also encountered Welsh place names, on a train journey to Wales when he was posted to Penrhos, but he reacted very differently, calling the Welsh language 'jabber'. He recorded in his diary that on the journey 'all the stations, and we stopped at every one, had an unpronounceable name'. Historian Diane Collins observes that white Australians often labelled Aboriginal speech 'noisy jabbering' and 'dreadful shrieks', portraying Aboriginal Australians as 'aural primitives'.[36] Peake heard the Welsh language in the same way during his posting in Penrhos, 'The batsmen [sic] (civilians) are funny, they jabber away in Welsh, like a party of abos.' He made a similar comment in his diary about French airmen, 'There are a lot of Free French about, the Mess is full of their jabbering'![37]

The identification of non-English speech as 'jabbering', made here by an Australian, resembles the British comments on foreign languages heard in the streets recorded by Mass Observation. Such comments suggest that many English-speaking people regarded English as more civilized than other languages and lumped all other languages together—including the non-English languages of Britain—hearing them as unintelligible and alien jabber. But wartime propaganda took a different view of foreign sound. Soundtracks in British wartime cinema differentiated sharply between the German enemy and European Allies. They gave Germans the sounds of barbarism while the sounds of civilization belonged to Europeans living under Nazi occupation.

German and Other Continental European Sound

Night Train to Munich (1940) offers an early example of the repertoire of sound developed in wartime British cinema to portray Germans and associate them with barbarism. The film begins with what increasingly became a characteristic idea of the language that Alfred Kerr valued so highly. The opening sequence shows Hitler ranting and thumping his fist repeatedly on a map of Austria, followed by the sound of marching troops and the chant of *Sieg Heil* at a Nazi rally. Hitler's loud and raging voice continues to speak in German as it resounds over other maps—first of Sudetenland, then of Prague—also followed by the sound of marching feet. As Hitler rants, his voice becomes increasingly disembodied, to comic as well as threatening effect. Most of his body disappears, leaving only a close-up of his fist thumping Prague on the map.[38]

Originally titled *Report on a Fugitive*, after the novel by Gordon Wellesley, *Night Train to Munich* was one of the first films to express criticism of Nazi Germany but get past the British Board of Film Censors successfully. Before war was declared, in the context of the official policy of appeasing Nazi Germany, 'no suggestion of politics' was the watchword of the British Board of Film Censors. This meant that film-makers had to avoid not only criticism of Germany, but also any plot-lines that could easily be identified with contemporary events in mid-Europe, including persecution and refugee movements. The censors passed one scenario that showed persecution in 1938 because it did not name Germany and the reason for persecution was not stated, 'I do not think any exception can be taken to this story providing the producers carry out their intention of not making the country identifiable in any way, and I suggest the exiles themselves are not made to look unmistakable Jews'.[39] Other scenarios were rejected as 'anti-Nazi propaganda'.[40] Several attempted to get past the censors by giving countries fictitious names—*The Lady Vanishes* (1938) opens in the fictional central European country of Bandrika.

Night Train to Munich was in many ways a remake of *The Lady Vanishes* as a comedy thriller, starring the comic bachelor duo of Charters and Caldicott (Basil Radford and Naunton Wayne), who had made their debut in *The Lady Vanishes*. Both films had the same scriptwriters—Frank Launder and Sidney Gilliat. Both show Charters and Caldicott inadvertently caught up in continental European adventures and displaying surprising skills in a shoot-out. But *Night Train to Munich* demonstrates the change in censorship policy once war was declared—Charters and Caldicott are shooting at characters identified as Germans and the German-speaking actor Paul Von Hernreid is cast as a Nazi. The censors called the scenario a 'good spy melodrama' and commented, 'This is a present-day spy story, mentioning Goering by name and with obvious references to Hitler. I presume the Film Censorship previous ban on this type of story, is now lifted, and consider it suitable for production as a film. I would be grateful to know any new wartime rulings'.[41]

Media historian Tobias Hochscherf argues that in the spate of pre-war spy films made at a time when criticism of Nazi Germany was banned by censors, the use of German-speaking actors to play spies who threaten

Britain hints at connections between the threat they pose and Germany.[42]
The Lady Vanishes was unusual in offering visual information that associates
its sinister characters with Germany—information that would not have
been apparent from the scenario passed by the censors. They wear the black
leather coats that were favoured by the Gestapo. Once war was declared,
Germans could be explicitly identified. It was the fate of many anti-Nazi
German-speaking émigré actors in Britain to be cast as Nazis, including
Gerard Heinz, Oscar Homolka, Carl Jaffé (see Figure 5.3), Albert Lieven,

Figure 5.3 Portrait of Carl Jaffé by Hans Casparius. Jaffé acted on stage and screen
and worked in the BBC German Service (by kind permission of Michael Jaffé and
Deutsche Kinemathek).

Lucie Mannheim, Martin Miller, and Walter Rilla. Many, like Carl Jaffé, continued to be cast as Nazis when the war was over. Paul Von Hernreid, who plays a Nazi in *Night Train to Munich*, fared better when he on-migrated to America and changed his name to Paul Henreid. Hollywood cast him as Victor Laszlo, the Czech resistance leader, in *Casablanca* (1942) and as Paul Lavallier, a Free French pilot in the RAF, in *Joan of Paris* (1942).

It seems unlikely that accents were picked up by many audience members as aural clues about nationality. The assumption that British people heard foreign accents and what was called 'broken English' as a generic foreignness to which no particular nationality was attached is evident in casting practices in British cinema, which resembled the Hollywood practices through which Paul Henreid was cast as Czech and French. British cinema never cast German-speaking émigrés as Britons, but they played continental Europeans of a range of nationalities in films made before and during the war. Walter Rilla played a Frenchman in *The Scarlet Pimpernel* (1934). Conrad Veidt played a Danish sea captain in *Contraband* (1940)—his last role in a British film before he left for Hollywood. In *The Gentle Sex* (1943), Lilli Palmer played a Czechoslovakian refugee in Britain who joins the Auxiliary Territorial Service. In a training film made for the army—*The New Lot* (1943)—Albert Lieven played a Czech soldier.[43]

Film historian Andrew Moor notes that Anton Walbrook 'downplays his voice's harsher registers' for his performance as the Polish hero of *Dangerous Moonlight* (1941), but he brings a Viennese accent to his role.[44] There were few British objections to these casting practices, which may have passed largely unnoticed, but there was an eloquent objection from a Polish journalist in 1949. He wrote to Caroline Lejeune, film critic of *The Observer*, about a British film—*The Lost People*—in which a German-speaking actor played a Polish professor:

> I wish to point out a few appalling mistakes, which you, not being Polish, will probably have missed. The 'Polish Professor' speaks with one of the strongest German accents I have ever heard, and the Polish accent in English differs from the German accent about as much as the French... At the 'wedding'... there is singing in Polish (with an atrocious accent) but the song is a Christmas carol, which to Poles sounds about as absurd as the tune of Lili Marlene would be to English ears at an Anglican service.[45]

The letter suggests the extent to which film-makers relied on the limited aural perceptions of British audiences and their use of accents that sounded 'foreign' for continental Europeans, regardless of nationality. Daniel le Roy du Vivier—a Belgian pilot serving in the RAF—was shot down in flames near London in 1942, parachuted into a girls' school, and probably made an accurate assessment of British auditory perceptions when he acted dead, afraid that his Brussels accent would be mistaken for German.[46]

Even if British audiences may rarely have recognized German accents, they could not have missed the qualities assigned to Germans through the use of sound in British wartime films and broadcasting. The repertoire of sound used for Germans included not only Hitler's ranting voice, chants of 'Sieg Heil', and the sound of marching feet, but also the roar of German planes and bombardment, the clamour of martial music, and the sound of machine-gun fire. German-speaking émigrés who were cast as Nazi Germans in British film spoke in particular tones and registers—guttural and aggressive, shouting, ranting, and threatening. Scriptwriters spilt a good deal of ink on exclamation marks, for Nazis issued a great many commands.

Crook's Tour (1941) was a six-part radio series, as well as a film, which starred the comic duo of Charters and Caldicott. It makes comedy from the German language when Caldicott confesses that he knows three words of German, 'Heil!', 'Swastika', and 'Ersatz'.[47] These were words that were also familiar to many members of British wartime audiences. A 1939–40 BBC radio series was titled *In the Shadow of the Swastika*. 'Heil Hitler!'s, accompanied by much heel-clicking, abounded on film. In *The Secret Mission* (1942), British agents, masquerading as German civilians on a visit to German headquarters in occupied France, perform the 'Heil Hitler!' salute six times and worry afterwards that they have indulged themselves: 'Do you think we overdid the Heils?'[48] In *Night Train to Munich*, even Charters and Caldicott manage one subdued 'Heil Hitler!' as they masquerade as German soldiers to help a Czech scientist to escape from Germany. Caldicott's German lexicon reduces the language that had been Alfred Kerr's whole working life to three words. Charters's comment on this three-word lexicon is comic, but captures the extent to which the association of the German language with barbarism was established by 1941—'That's practically all they know themselves old man'.

In contrast to German sound, the sound of European Allies was harmonious, patriotic, and Christian. This contrast is particularly apparent in *One of Our Aircraft is Missing* (1942), directed by Michael Powell and Emeric Pressburger—a film about downed British airmen in occupied Holland.[49] The film opens with drum rolls, followed by commands for execution in German as the camera pans down a government document listing the names of Dutch citizens who have been executed for their roles in assisting the British airmen to escape. The sound of firing follows.

The gentle tinkling of bells is the soundtrack to the first stage of the downed airmen's journey out of Holland by bicycle. Dutch resisters disguise them as Dutch civilians and take them to church en route to the sea to facilitate their escape to England. When they arrive at a crossroads, the need to halt for the German military is announced by the aggressive clamour of klaxons. Further blaring klaxons and a long series of barked orders herald the arrival of Germans at the church. As a German soldier enters, the sound inside is the murmur of prayers. Will the German soldier discover the British airmen in the congregation? The tension is heightened when the Dutch organist, in an act of defiance, plays a melody described by Pressburger as 'improbably high and improbably faint, yet still clear and distinct'. A Dutch resister helpfully whispers in English to one of the downed airmen, identifying this melody for him, as well as for the cinema audience, as the Dutch national anthem. When the German soldier leaves the church, the tension eases. There are more barked orders from unseen Germans outside the church, while inside 'the full volume of the anthem roll[s] out' and the congregation sings the Dutch anthem in affirmation of their national community.[50]

Emeric Pressburger, who wrote the script for *One of Our Aircraft*, co-directed a range of wartime films with Michael Powell. Pressburger was a Hungarian exile whose own linguistic range extended to Romanian, German, and French, as well as Hungarian and English. He found English difficult, spoke it with a heavy accent, and had difficulties in adjusting to Britain and its language.[51] In the script for *I Know Where I'm Going* (1945), set in the Scottish islands, he explores an experience akin to that of many émigrés, but transposed onto the story of an Englishwoman's journey to these islands, where she feels a stranger because she cannot understand Gaelic.[52]

In 1946, the Hungarian, George Mikes, poked fun at British film, writing that 'a little foreign blood is very advantageous, almost essential, to become a really great British film producer'. It seems likely that he had in mind the many Hungarians working in British cinema, including Pressburger. Mikes came to Britain as a journalist to cover the Munich crisis, stayed on, and became a friend of Pressburger's—both were Jewish Hungarians. In *How to be an Alien* (1946), he poked gentle fun at British attitudes to language. 'The knowledge of foreign languages is very un-English', he wrote. 'A little French is permissible, but only with an atrocious accent'.[53] In his script for

One of Our Aircraft Is Missing, Pressburger's comedy resembles Mikes's comedy in *How to be an Alien*. The first encounter that the film shows between the downed British airmen in occupied Holland and Dutch people involves children. One of the British airmen, feeling the need to address the children in a foreign language, mixes a few French words with English, speaking the French words with an 'atrocious accent'. The children are unlikely to understand his French or English, however spoken, since they are Dutch.

Although Nazi Germans dominated the portrayal of Germans in British wartime cinema, anti-Nazi Germans appeared not only in the documentary *Lift Your Head Comrade*, but also in two feature films directed by Michael Powell and Emeric Pressburger—*49th Parallel* (1941) and *The Life and Death of Colonel Blimp* (1943).[54] Anton Walbrook—one of the few German-speaking émigré actors in British cinema to escape the fate of playing Nazis—is cast as an anti-Nazi German in both films. In *49th Parallel*, he plays a German Canadian in a Huttite community who denounces Nazis in an eloquent set-piece speech, delivered in English. In *The Life and Death of Colonel Blimp*, he plays a military officer who has served in the First World War and is committed to chivalry, but abandons this commitment during the Second World War, eloquently urging the uselessness of gentlemanly codes against the Nazis. Pressburger recorded later, 'I who lived for quite a while in Germany and had German friends, I wanted to express this feeling of mine that though my mother had died in the concentration camp and I was pre-conditioned about the whole thing, I always believed . . . that there were also good Germans'.[55]

Good Germans are less evident in *One of Our Aircraft*, which takes up the use of disembodied sound for Germans, apparent earlier in the war in *Night Train to Munich*. The German soldier who enters the church where the Dutch congregation is concealing the downed British airmen is one of the few Germans actually seen—the film registers their presence in Holland mainly on the soundtrack. Michael Powell later attributed to Emeric Pressburger the decision to 'hear Germans everywhere, but only to see them in the distance, if at all'.[56]

A similar decision to register the presence of Germans mainly through sound was taken during production of *The Silent Village* (1943)—a documentary film about the German massacre of Czechoslovakians in the village of Lidice. Humphrey Jennings, who directed the film, explained in a BBC broadcast, 'We proposed not to show any Germans . . . the main feeling of oppression, the existence of the invisible Germans is carried in the film by a German speaker, sometimes he's speaking on a loudspeaker, sometimes on radio sets, and so on—one voice'.[57]

The Silent Village was inspired by Viktor Fischl, a Jewish Czechoslovakian exile in Britain who worked for the Czechoslovakian government in exile. Fischl wrote to the Crown Film Unit, sending a synopsis for a film about events in the Czechoslovakian village of Lidice in June 1942. The village had been destroyed because its population stood accused of involvement in the assassination of Reinhard Heydrich—second-in-command of the S.S. All the men of the village had been shot, the women and children deported, and the village razed. Fischl's synopsis began, 'This is the small village of Lidice somewhere in Czechoslovakia. And this is the village of X in Wales. It is not so long ago since these two villages were exactly like one another'. At the Crown Film Unit, Jennings thought this 'one of the most brilliant ideas for a film that we'd ever come across.'[58]

The Silent Village shares with *One of Our Aircraft* the contrast between harsh German sound and the harmonious, patriotic, and Christian sound of Czechoslovakians before and during Nazi occupation. Taking up Fischl's suggestion, the film transposes the life of the mining village of Lidice in Czechoslovakia onto the Welsh mining village of Cwmgiedd. Its portrait, in the opening section, of a close village community is conveyed as much by sound as imagery—hymn-singing in the chapel in Welsh, male voice choirs on the sound-track also singing in Welsh, schoolchildren reciting lessons in Welsh, laughter in the cinema. The 'coming of Fascism' through the German occupation of Czechoslovakia, first announced in an intertitle, is registered in the film by jarring sound—martial music blaring from a loudspeaker van, followed by a German order, 'Achtung! Achtung!'

In the second section of the film, sound and image come together to portray resistance against the German occupier. Music from a Welsh harp plays over images of guerrilla fighters meeting at the castle. A male-voice choir sings the traditional Welsh folk song 'All Through the Night' over images of men setting explosives in the mine. There is prolonged silence on the soundtrack after the radio pronouncement of a death sentence on the villagers over images of their vigil through the night. As the camera shows dawn breaking, the silence is broken by the sound of men singing the Welsh national anthem in a final act of defiance as they await execution in front of the chapel and its cemetery. They continue to sing as they watch the women and children of the village being marched away and the commands for execution are given. Their singing ceases only with the sound of German gunfire.

The *Daily News*, reviewing *The Silent Village*, commented on the disembodied sound used for Germans, 'In all the magnificent drama we never see a German face to face. Several guards are shown but only their backs. And the announcements to the villagers come over a loudspeaker from a car that is driven through the streets'.[59] German sound remains disembodied in the sequences that show the final fate of Lidice. As the men of the village line up to await execution, the commands are given in German. During production of the film, a request went out for translation to establish the correct German terms for 'Halt! Attention! Present arms! Lower arms! Load! Take aim! Fire!', explaining that 'our actual intention in the film is to have the orders spoken in German and accompanied by the sound, only, of what each order would involve'.[60] Following the massacre, the radio announcement of the destruction of the village is in German, accompanied by Wagner, over shots of the ruins of Lidice, still burning. German is the language not only of commands to massacre the men of Lidice but also of the destruction of their village.

In December 1940, a group of anti-Nazi German refugees reclaimed the idea of the German language as the language of literature, not barbarism, redefining Germanness as the community of emigrants and exiles who had escaped from persecution. In Australia, where they had been deported by the British government, they wrote, 'We Germans are regarded as a people of poets and thinkers. Even though the works of poets and thinkers have been burned and banned by those who wrongly call themselves Germans, these works remain alive in us, the German emigrants . . . by embracing literature, we are proving that German and Nazism are not one and the same.'[61] British cinema increasingly abandoned such a distinction between German and Nazism. With some exceptions, particularly films by Powell and Pressburger, the sound of Germans—devoid of poetry, literature, or eloquence—conveyed brutality. German sound placed Germans outside any European family of nations. In contrast, the patriotic, Christian, and harmonious sound of Europeans who were living under Nazi occupation transformed them from alien foreigners into members of the family of allies.

Language, Sound, and the 'Allies' War'

In *How to Be an Alien*, George Mikes not only described the knowledge of foreign languages as 'very un-English', but also advised aliens to behave like the English and speak English with their compatriots—denying that they knew any foreign language. During the war, Mikes failed to follow his own advice, taking up employment in the BBC's Hungarian language service from 1941. Speaking a foreign language was an asset for people seeking employment in the BBC external services. Unlike actors in British cinema, many BBC wartime employees were required to speak non-English languages during working hours. The voices of presenters who were addressing their compatriots in their mother tongue were particularly valued, because they were considered to inspire more confidence in overseas audiences than would have been possible through a voice that signalled 'British spokesperson'.[62]

The rapid expansion of BBC services, which broadcast in seven foreign languages at the outbreak of war but forty-five by its end, involved the recruitment of people of a wide range of nationalities and ethnicities.[63] Chester Wilmot's airmails to his wife demonstrate some of the varied languages and language skills of BBC contributors. Wilmot came to Britain from Australia in 1944 to join the BBC team reporting the D-Day landings and wrote regularly to his wife back home. In one air mail, he told her 'Van Stewie who's been with the BBC's Dutch service throughout the war... [is] a remarkable bloke for he is bi-national. He speaks English with a perfect public school accent and if you didn't know it you'd think he was pure English... but to a Dutchman he seems one of them.[64] In another airmail, he wrote about Pierre Lefèvre, born in New York to French parents, who had spent most of the war broadcasting in French on the French service. Wilmot knew Lefèvre as a fellow correspondent in the BBC team reporting the D-Day landings and wrote to his wife:

> [He] is a delightful Frenchman, born in New York, educated as much in England as in France, and completely bi-lingual. There is no trace of an accent in his English and you'd never know he wasn't an Englishman—especially as he has an amazing mastery of English dialect, speaks Cockney, Lancashire etc almost as well as a native. This is the last thing in language mastery. In 39-40 he was in the French army, and escaped after Dunkirk. Since then he's been working in the BBC's European service, and is the chief French cpt [correspondent] in the BBC's [D-Day landings] team.[65]

Lefèvre's versatility as a speaker is also shown by the diverse programmes that he made. He broadcast talks on the BBC's Home Service in English and talks on the BBC's French service in French. On the French service, he also voiced 'Musso'—a dog representing Mussolini—in a series for adults and Babar the Elephant in a children's series.[66]

Wilmot was one of many white English-speakers who dominated sound portraits of an 'allies war' broadcast to audiences in Britain. Listeners became accustomed to hearing a wide range of English-speaking accents—American, Australian, Canadian, New Zealand, South African. The voice of Quentin Reynolds became familiar to British wartime audiences not only through his popular *Postscript* broadcasts but also through his appearance on two documentaries made before America entered the war—*London Can Take It* (1940) and *Christmas Under Fire* (1941). In both films, Reynolds deploys a type of ventriloquism to address American audiences as part of a British propaganda campaign against American neutrality. Through his narrative voice, films from the British Ministry of Information are made to sound like American messages, especially since Reynolds calls them 'film dispatches' that he is sending to America and emphasizes that he is no propagandist, but a 'neutral reporter'.[67] The impression of an American message was reinforced by the credits of *London Can Take It* for its American release, which named Quentin Reynolds but made no mention of the film's British directors—Humphrey Jennings and Harry Watt—nor of the Ministry of Information.[68]

In these documentaries, there are no British voices to disrupt the impression of an American message. Reynolds's voice offers unstinting praise for the courage and resilience of Britons. In *London Can Take It!* he tells the story of a night of the Blitz, celebrating the heroes of the night who are 'members of the greatest civilian army ever to be assembled', and the 'determination, confidence and high courage among the people of Churchill's island'. In *Christmas Under Fire*—described by its director, Harry Watt, as 'an obvious tear-jerker'—England is shown besieged but undaunted and courageous, celebrating Christmas underground. 'Today England stands unbeaten, unconquered, unafraid'.[69] This Anglocentric commentary survived for the British distribution of the film, but *London Can Take It!* was retitled *Britain Can Take It!* for British distribution and Reynolds added extra commentary to point out that the film's portrayal of the Blitz in London was representative of what was happening in every other British city and town.[70] As German planes bomb London, he assures his audience, 'These are not Hollywood sound effects. This is the music they play every night in London—the symphony of war'.[71]

White English-speakers dominated portrayals of the 'allies' war', but the incorporation of some black English-speakers into British film and broadcasting disassociated them from the sound often attributed to them in 1930s empire films—'mumbo-jumbo'. In feature films, the African-American

Paul Robeson, who had starred in a number of British films in the 1930s, made a final star appearance in *The Proud Valley* (1940), before he returned to America. He played David, a stoker off the ships seeking work in coalmines, who is incorporated into the life and work of Blaendy—a Welsh mining village—and into its male voice choir. He lodges with the Parry family and forms a close friendship with Dick, the father of the family, who is a miner and the choirmaster. When Dick is killed in a pit accident, David sings the spiritual, 'Deep River', at an Eisteddfod in tribute to him. Paul Robeson's popularity may have shaped the decision to give the film its premiere on radio rather than in cinema—a sixty-minute version of the film's soundtrack was broadcast on the Home Service in February 1940.[72]

On the BBC Home Service, Una Marson spoke about poetry to a British audience:

> You know that's the way thousands of West Indians get their glimpse of your country—through your poetry and history and indeed through those same books that you used in your childhood. Of course the best in your literature has survived and has come to us. That's why we always come here with beautiful mental pictures and great expectations... A common language, a common tradition and even blood relationships are real enough bonds.[73]

Her talk ended with a comment on how the bonds of a common language were one-sided, enjoying little recognition in Britain, 'We children learnt these poems and loved them without any thought that they came from a land where people thought us a very different race'.

Despite the substantial number of black GIs in wartime Britain, Americans who spoke in British film and radio were invariably white. The most prominent black voices in wartime British media were those of singers. Programmes of Robeson's songs continued to be popular in wartime after he had departed for America. The BBC reported in 1941, 'The popularity of Paul Robeson is again illustrated by the fact that 15.3% listened to a half-hour programme of records of him on...the Home Service. Listeners to this programme were three times as numerous as the audience to the Orchestral Half-hour in the Forces Programme at the same time'.[74] Elisabeth Welch, an African-American who came to Britain in the 1930s to work in British cinema, had starred in two pre-war films alongside Paul Robeson—*Song of Freedom* (1936) and *Big Fella* (1937)—and continued to work in British cinema in wartime. But like Robeson she was known mainly as a singer and gave 'singer of popular songs' as a self-description. She sang for the first time on the BBC in 1933, the year of her arrival in Britain.[75] In wartime, she joined

the first concert party to entertain servicemen and servicewomen and subsequently worked for the Entertainments National Service Association—an
organization set up in 1939 to entertain the troops.

Other prominent black singing voices on the wartime BBC included
those of Adelaide Hall—an African-American who, like Welch, stayed on
in Britain during the war—and Edric Connor, who came to Britain from
Trinidad in 1944. Discrimination against black artists was reported by
the Welfare Department of the Colonial Office in May 1946: 'The Royal
Academy of Dramatic Art has a rigid colour bar, and has, for example,
refused to admit Mr. Edric Conner [sic], the well-known West Indian
singer. A number of other coloured Colonial people have also applied
unsuccessfully for admission into this Institution. The Bar is against males
only'.[76] When the Programme Contracts Director at the BBC reported
that Adelaide Hall and her husband had gained the 'unfortunate impression
that there is some colour bar so far as "Starlight" [a variety show] is concerned', the programme's producers made a conscious move to give her
an appearance.[77]

The popularity of African-American singing voices, evident in the repu-
tations of Robeson, Welch, and Hall, was also apparent in the reception of a
concert by a black GI choir in the Albert Hall in London, which was widely
praised and publicized. A photospread in *Picture Post* highlighted Roland
Hayes, the African-American singer, who was widely known in Britain. In
a concert programme devoted mainly to spirituals, Hayes sang 'I Know that
My Redeemer Liveth', from Handel's *Messiah*.[78] The *Picture Post* piece produced a familiar stereotype of black singers: 'The coloured U.S. troops in
this country are true modern Americans. They wear slick American uniforms and speak the latest American slang. But they have not lost their great
traditional talent—the gift of singing. Music—simple, rhythmic music—seems
inborn in the Negro race'.[79] The head of the American War Department's
Negro Press Section wanted less reporting on singing and jazz bands and
more that showed 'the Negro performing his duties as a soldier', to combat
this stereotype.[80] But it was a stereotype that found support in Britain at the
highest levels. When the Colonial Secretary, Viscount Cranborne, urged in a
Cabinet meeting in 1942 that the United States Army must be asked to
respect the rights of black Britons, he cited a case where American officers
were responsible for barring a black official at the Colonial Office from a
restaurant in London. Winston Churchill responded, 'That's all right. If he
takes a banjo with him they'll think he's one of the band'.[81]

Black English-speaking voices were absent from the BBC team that reported the D-Day landings, where white people from the Commonwealth were strongly represented. The team included two Australian correspondents (Chester Wilmot and Colin Wills) and two Canadians (Stewart Macpherson and Stanley Maxted).[82] A. P. Ryan, News Controller at the BBC, instructed that interviewees as well as reporters should represent a range of nationalities, strengthening the sound portrait of an 'allies' war'. Voices, he said, would find an 'easier market' than sound effects. He wanted 'the voices of our home men, of Canadians and Americans, and of French and other liberated citizens. I hope that before the summer is out you will have been able to give us several nationalities saying in their own language "Thank God the Boche has gone". Such voices will be given in the Home and Overseas as well as in the European service'.[83]

Ryan reminded reporters that 'we have a world audience and we mean to give it the most accurate, the fullest and the most vivid and alive account of coming operations that we can'. Reaching this world audience excited Chester Wilmot, who wrote to his wife:

> The Traffic people tell us that most of our despatches are put out half a dozen times or more—in addition to being quoted in the news and translated for the foreign services. It's quite fantastic i.e. when you think of it—I sit dn somewhere in Holland and belt off a despatch—put it over fr Brussels—and in the next 24 hrs that despatch is heard or quoted—if it's a good despatch—in 30 or 40 countries—in a dozen languages—by anything up to 100 million people. I'm a little over-awed by it all.[84]

The wartime documentary *Listen to Britain* (1942) showed the BBC reaching the world audience that excited Chester Wilmot. The film offered sound-portraits of everyday life, paying tribute to the British war effort through what the Canadian, Leonard Brockington, introducing the film, describes as 'blended together in one great symphony, the music of Britain at war'.[85] A brief sequence shows the work of the BBC overseas services. Beginning with the chimes of Big Ben and the call sign 'This is London Calling', against shots of night-time London, there are voices on the soundtrack over shots of sound technology. They speak a range of languages, evoking the power of this technology in extensive communication with the world. They are heard speaking simultaneously, one drowning out another, bearing some resemblance to the idea of non-English languages as a common alien sound, which was expressed in the 'jabbering' verdict delivered

by some Britons. In 1940 this sound had identified people as deeply distrusted foreigners, as in the description by the advocate of mass internment
in 1940 for those s/he wanted interned—'all what don't talk plain English'.[86]
But as the brief sequence in *Listen to Britain* demonstrates, it was the presence of broadcasters who did not speak plain English that gave British wartime propaganda its global reach.

Sounding Civilized

The association of the German language with barbarism was not clear to
the BBC at the outset of the war, when there was considerable confidence
about the way that German was spoken on the BBC German service. A
1940 BBC Report contrasted this BBC sound with what it identified as 'the
abusive and vulgar methods sometimes used by the Germans', described the
BBC style as 'matter-of-fact', and commented that this style was well-suited
to the news, and might help to bring home to German listeners 'the contrast between realities and their own tendencious [*sic*] service'. The BBC
voice and presentation, the report argued, could stimulate the traditional
respect of the German for the English through its 'firmness, dignity and
Kaltblütigkeit [self-possession]'.[87]

A further BBC Report displayed considerable enthusiasm about a letter
received from a German listener which appeared to support the BBC's view
of what would gain respect from German listeners. The letter was regarded
as authentic. The German listener wrote that British officers and other soldiers who broadcast in German from London had 'charm' and were 'dis-
creet, polite, thoroughly distinguished and yet really properly manly. And
real straight manliness, without artificial emphases and over-expressiveness,
is among the finest things one can find on earth'.[88]

Responses to voices that broadcast in English on the BBC were often
much less flattering than the letter from the German listener. The problem
was not the use of English, but the accent in which it was spoken—often
referred to as 'BBC' or 'Oxford'. This accent was criticized in the English-
speaking world—by Americans, Australians, Britons, and Canadians—and
in contrast to the German listener's view, sometimes labelled 'effeminate'. In
1938, the film critic of the *Daily Telegraph*, Campbell Dixon, in an article
about 'effeminate accents spoiling British pictures', fulminated:

If we want to sell Americans our films, and we do, then we must avoid the vocal qualities they detest...What maddens Americans is the thin, high-pitched, petulant bleat that a certain type of young person associates with culture and a great many others with effeminacy. It would be a shock to a number of actors and actresses to know how many people in this country heartily agree with America.[89]

Similar views were held by young men in Australia before the war, according to the *Sydney Morning Herald*. At a time when British speech was often held up as a model to be emulated, it reported that Australian boys—especially early adolescents—appeared to have a contempt for 'correctly modelled speech', which they regarded as 'effeminate'.[90]

In 1942, Postal Censorship of the traffic of letters between the United States and Britain intercepted a number of criticisms of the 'Oxford' accent. 'I do wish they would get announcers without an Oxford affected accent to broadcast', one Briton wrote home from America. 'The Americans just laugh at him and won't listen'. Another Briton writing home reported the view of a Washington friend that 'the BBC or Oxford accent is a bad handi-cap'. The Washington friend was commenting on British speakers sent out to America and recommended 'more working men and more Welshmen, Scotsmen, Ulstermen, Yorkshiremen etc.—in fact anyone who seems to speak with a tongue with individuality in it'.[91] There was also criticism of the Oxford accent from the Canadian Broadcasting Corporation, which described it as 'affected' with 'unconscious overtones of superiority' and argued that this voice, even from BBC announcers, was never welcome and that Canadian listeners would protest if 'definitely southern English voices' were included among its own announcers.[92]

The Washington friend who equated 'BBC' with 'Oxford' would have had more difficulty in doing so as the war progressed. In 1939, newsreaders and announcers spoke 'BBC English' in the formal context in which they operated—one where, before 1939, they were required to wear dinner-jackets in the evening, even though their audience could not see them. The imperatives of presenting a 'people's war' pushed the BBC in new directions, incorporating more regional and working-class accents. The appointment of Wilfred Pickles as a newsreader in 1941 marked a decisive break with pre-war conventions. J. B. Priestley had prepared the way for Pickles in 1940 in his highly popular *Postscript* broadcasts, in which he spoke about serious matters of national importance with a regional accent. The

voices of both men fell well outside the narrow range of 'BBC English'—
they were born in Yorkshire, in the north of England, and spoke with
Yorkshire accents.

It was not only American and Canadian listeners who found fault with
'Oxford English' and 'BBC English'. In Scotland, there were complaints
about 'emasculated BBC voices'.[93] Postal Censorship intercepted a letter
from Oxford to London which recommended, 'Sack all BBC announcers
with grave, soft voices; put on men with a virile timbre, and some "rough"
speakers with a downright manner and stop everyone broadcasting pep
talks, not excepting Cabinet Ministers'.[94] A respondent to a Mass Observation
survey wrote, 'The announcers are bloody, why the stupid policy of picking
people with characterless voices as announcers, and perfect standard English
pronunciation. Let's realise that we are the United Kingdom of England,
Scotland, Wales and Ireland, with brogues, burrs, etc; and not the land of
standard English'.[95] Home Intelligence reported criticism of the 'Everything-
in-the-garden-is-lovely voices of the BBC announcers', which were compared unfavourably with the 'deep, powerful and convincing tones of
American news announcers'.[96]

British listeners who favoured the tones of American news announcers
may well have been among those who were impressed by the voice of
Quentin Reynolds, the American journalist and broadcaster, as heard in his
Postscript broadcasts. Listener Research reported on his first *Postscript*:

> There was pugnacity and aggressiveness in Reynolds' material, as well as in his
> delivery. 'Hard Hitting', 'Plain spoken', 'No Frills' were expressions frequently
> used to emphasise the appeal made by Reynolds' Postscript. And to contrast it,
> entirely to its favour, with the more gentlemanly and soft spoken Postscripts
> which, it is said, have sometimes been heard on Sunday evenings.[97]

Similar comments were reported on his second *Postscript*, 'It has been noted
in previous reports on Postscripts that any speaker who puts what he has to
say into vigorous, even pugnacious form, has considerable advantages over
those who pitch their talk in a quieter vein. Several Correspondents compared this postscript, entirely to its advantage, with others which they
described as 'Sunshine stories' and 'Sunday school talks'.[98] Despite this praise
for Reynolds, American speech did not always find favour in Britain. A 1943
Mass Observation report found that American language and accent came in
for unfavourable comment from one in twelve.[99]

In Australia, 'BBC English' had at least one ardent fan. Three days after
Australia declared war on Germany, Kathleen Hunt wrote from Harbord,
New South Wales to Robert Menzies, Prime Minister of Australia:

> There is an unfortunate tendency on the part of the ABC's [Australian
> Broadcasting Corporation's] announcers to obtrude their sometimes fatuous
> remarks into the perfectly delivered announcements of the BBC. We had a
> perfectly jarring example this morning when, during the London announcer's
> reading of the Empire programme for the day, the Melbourne announcer
> broke in with the inane remark, "Oh, if he's going on like that we'll have a
> Peter Dawson record"! This was insulting to the calm dignity and restraint
> which is typical of BBC announcers.[100]

Hunt followed this up with a further letter which referred to the 'perfect
diction' of BBC announcers, their 'authoritative pronunciation of difficult
foreign names and their smooth rhythmical reading which is so easy to
follow'.[101] In their turn, the British could respond favourably to Australian
speech. Chester Wilmot's voice was liked by a listener in Birmingham, who
wrote to him, 'I must tell you that until I heard yours I didn't much care for
Australian voices but now listen to you entranced. I think you must be
awfully brave too judging by all the sticky places you seem to get into'.[102]

Kathleen Hunt's view of BBC voices as a model for the English-speaking
world drew on pre-war views in Australia where the advent of talkies
brought particular objections to a 'filthy American twang'. Cultural historian,
Joy Damousi, comments: 'The American "twang" caused great offence,
while what was identified as the eloquence of the British voice was to be
promoted and emulated'. Between the wars, the British voice was used in
many public Australian contexts including theatre, radio, and public speeches.
At the same time, there were champions of a distinctive Australian speech.[103]
Debates continued during the Second World War. Should the policy of the
Australian Broadcasting Corporation on announcers using British voices be
changed? Supporters argued that Australian speech was 'as *good English* as
any speech to be heard anywhere in the English-speaking commonwealth'.
Opponents argued that change would 'degrade the cultural level of ABC
announcers'.[104]

Harry Watt, a British film director, was sent to Australia in 1943 at the
request of the Australian government, who were concerned that Australia's
contribution to the war effort was not being sufficiently recognized. Watt
reported that his Australian friends thought English film audiences would
object to what they called 'our expressionless drawl'. His own view of what

he called 'the Australian language' was that it 'often lacks the crispness of English speech'.[105] The outcome of this visit was a film celebrating an epic 1,500-mile journey by Australians, driving cattle across country during the Second World War to escape a potential Japanese invasion—*The Overlanders*.[106] An article in the *Sydney Morning Herald* predicted that Watt's film would exaggerate the extent to which Australians spoke an 'Australian language' by choosing Australians to appear in it who had the accent in preference to those who did not. By 'selecting men who speak as people overseas will expect them to speak', the article argued, 'the story that all Australians speak the Australian accent [will] gain fresh believers'.[107] *The Overlanders* was not released until 1946, when the newspaper's predictions were shown to be correct.

The idea that particular forms of English-speaking were superior to others was increasingly out of step with the presentation of an 'allies' war' in British media as one of 'United Nations'. Had Harry Watt been working at the BBC, his comment that Australian speech lacked English crispness would have violated instructions given by the Empire Talks Manager, 'In no circumstances assume a superiority of thought and action, and hold up England or the English as an example of something'. It would also have violated a further instruction that suggested concerns not to offend Australians on questions of speech, 'Don't refer to the Australian accent, other than to say "I knew by his voice that he was Australian"'.[108]

The BBC received a number of letters protesting about speech and language in their programmes. They engaged in lengthy correspondence with Rudolph Dunbar, who wrote to protest at their use of the term 'nigger'. An internal BBC memorandum about a letter he wrote in 1941 conceded, 'As there are, I believe, West Indian troops in the country, the point he made is, you will agree an important one'.[109] By 1943, awareness of the presence of black troops in Britain was reinforced by the arrival of black GIs. Producers were reminded that jokes about 'darkies', and references to 'a black man as a scare to white children' would be found offensive in a context where 'there are a lot of coloured people in the country now—Africans, West Indians and Americans, and there is therefore particularly good reason to be careful not to say anything which might be interpreted as showing colour prejudice'.[110]

Sidney Salomon—Press Officer at the Board of Deputies of British Jews—was another campaigner who engaged in prolific wartime correspondence with the BBC. His letters protested against the sound portraits of Jews in BBC drama, including children's programmes. His main objection concerned: 'a tendency on the part of certain producers to make people who are presumably, at least judging by their names, Jewish, speak with a ridiculous foreign accent'. He went on to explain, 'The average Jew, certainly the one who has been born and lives in this country, does not talk with a perceptible "Jewish accent" at all, but almost invariably with the accent of the people among whom he lives'.[111]

The BBC took note of objections from Salomon on other matters, but rarely made concessions about speech. In 1941, following his complaint about a production of Ivanhoe in which the character of Isaac of York had spoken 'like a caricature of the stage Jew', an internal memorandum conceded a change for the last instalment, but only in the context of insisting on 'the vocal peculiarities of the Jewish way of speaking', which the last instalment would make 'a little less peculiar'.[112] Other BBC responses to Salomon's protests variously argued that what had been spoken was a 'foreign' accent, or that of a 'stage villain', with no intention of suggesting Jewish intonation or imitation.[113] In 1950, an internal memorandum reverted to the view that Jewish speech had 'vocal peculiarities'. 'We cannot omit altogether from programmes the "Jewish dialect" accepted in show business and certainly based on fact for a great many years... I feel that Mr. Salomon and his friends are being unduly touchy'.[114]

In contrast to the BBC's dusty answers to Salomon, propagandists went out of their way to avoid offending Americans. Negative American responses to British voices became a preoccupation of the British wartime government when concerns about American reception of films and broadcasts outstripped concerns about their reception in any other nation. Evidence collected during the war was not encouraging. The British Information Services in New York identified a range of British speech in documentary film as unsuitable for American audiences—prosy, verbose, over-poetic, lacking vigour.[115] Before America entered the war, Foreign Office reports on voices broadcast on the BBC showed that Americans found the BBC voice 'too self-conscious' but also used a homophobic term of abuse to describe it—'Pansy'.[116] There was discussion about replacing the Oxford accent with a Canadian or Scottish accent in broadcasts to America.[117]

There was also criticism of English speech from American soldiers in Britain. The civilian American in Britain who was commissioned to compile a Special Home Intelligence report on American soldiers' attitudes to

English people found a distinction between their views on English language and their views on English speech. England to the American soldier was 'the traditional ally, the homeland of the mother tongue'. Opinions were less favourable on the English language as spoken by the English:

> The Englishman's precision of speech, the clarity of his enunciation, embarrass the American soldier in England. The fact that even an English waiter seems to talk 'better' than he does makes the American soldier in England feel uncouth. This manner of talking is associated, erroneously but firmly, in his mind with the upper classes. He thinks of it as a sort of national Harvard accent, put on deliberately by an entire nation instead of a small snobbish group in his own country, to make the outlander feel inferior, to 'ritz' him.[118]

The association of 'BBC English' and 'Oxford English' with the upper and upper-middle classes and what the Canadian Broadcasting Corporation called 'unconscious overtones of superiority' was also a problem for Harry Watt, when he directed the wartime documentary *Target for Tonight* in 1941. He remembers:

> I chose my players for the crew, but the CO [Commanding Officer] of a station is the CO and I couldn't make the Sergeant Major the CO. And the COs very often had the most appallingly over-posh accents, laid on to make them appear gentlemen, overlaid over their ordinary accents. And in point of fact several of our films had to be dubbed in America...because they couldn't stand this dreadfully British super-super accent, particularly from the senior officers...It was dubbed in America by Hitchcock...taking away some of the more extreme British accents.[119]

American complaints about British speech did not only target over-posh accents. There were also complaints about the unintelligibility of English when spoken by working people. Two letters intercepted by Postal Censorship about a BBC series titled 'Britain to America' criticized the programme for its use of what one letter-writer called 'workpeople's talk in dialect' and for its incorporation of Cockney, 'To the American ear, the straight King's English is tough enough to catch; Cockney on short wave is almost unintelligible'.[120] American complaints that British speech was incomprehensible were not reciprocated. When 'talkies' were first screened in Britain, the voices of American actors were sometimes heard as comic, but Hollywood producers had little need to concern themselves with this response—the dominance of Hollywood at box offices in Britain and throughout the English-speaking world quickly familiarized audiences with

Hollywood versions of American English.[121] In the wartime British film
This Happy Breed (1944), there are shots of a British audience viewing the
Hollywood musical *Broadway Melody*, and one British audience member
comments, 'I don't understand a word they say'. But this sequence is set in
the past, in 1929, the year that *Broadway Melody* was released.

Complaints from Americans about the way the English spoke English,
debates in Australia, the BBC's dusty answers to Salomon—all demonstrate
the range of verdicts on a hierarchy of English-speaking. The vocabulary
used for auditory perceptions suggests the range of responses. 'Emasculated'
and 'effeminate' were terms used to deny the manliness of voices. 'Vigorous'
and 'pugnacious' affirmed manliness. 'Drawl' contrasted with 'crispness'.
Oxford accents could be heard as conveying 'calm dignity and restraint' or
as 'affected' and 'snobbish'. Assessments of speech often involved moral
judgements about individual and national probity, but there was little agreement either within or between nations about which kinds of English speech
were more civilized than other kinds. Verdicts on who sounded civilized
were complex and contested. One letter-writer from America, commenting
on what s/he called 'the smooth, well-bred English voice', suggested that it
'conveys artificiality, insincerity' and went on to call it 'over-civilised'.[122]

In 1943, Churchill told the Cabinet, 'Propagate our language all over [the]
world... Fraternal association with U.S.—this would let them in too.
Harmonises with my ideas for future of the world. This will be the English-
speaking century'.[123] Churchill championed the English language throughout the war, conducting a wartime campaign for the use of anglicized names
in government correspondence—for cities and for countries—rather than
what he called their 'foreign names'.[124] In 1942, he instructed that 'the words
"Siam" and "Siamese" should invariably be used in future... in place of
"Thailand" and "Thai"'.[125] The BBC issued exactly opposite instructions,
'always use Thai and Thailand, never Siam or Siamese'.[126]

It is possible that Churchill had little objection to American influence
on British-English—he was an ardent supporter of the British–American
alliance (his mother was American). In 1942, he recommended the use of
'aircraft' and 'airfields' rather than 'aeroplanes' and 'aerodromes' not only as
'better English', but also as 'more in accord with American practice'.[127] But
wartime complaints about British speech from Americans—effeminate, verbose, over-poetic, lacking vigour, unintelligible—foreshadowed an increasing erosion of the status of British English. After 1945, as decolonization

gathered pace, there was further erosion—the names of countless rivers, mountains, countries, and places in the British Empire that had been anglicized under British rule were increasingly de-anglicized. 'English' remained the name of the language. The term 'anglicize' retained currency. But wartime reports anticipated wider post-war cultural, political, economic, and technological developments through which most versions of English, both written and spoken—including those written and spoken in Britain—became subordinate to American English.

Figure 6.1 Jack and Doreen Stang (by kind permission of Jack and Doreen Stang).

6

Sexual Patriotism

Sergeant Arthur Walrond was a Barbadian who came to Britain to serve in the Royal Air Force Volunteer Reserve as a wireless operator/air gunner. In June 1943, when he was based at RAF Mildenhall in Suffolk, Walrond went to a dance in the town hall at Bury St. Edmunds. In a letter to the Colonial Office, he told officials what happened there:

> I approached a young woman and requested a dance with her and a Sergt.—an American soldier—promptly ordered her not to dance. Despite this, obviously intending to ignore the instruction, she moved towards the dance floor when the same Sergt. attacked me with both fists followed by further assaults from his friend. I had said nothing to him and the attack was made quite suddenly and without provocation. The two soldiers concerned were perfectly sober and there can be no excuse for such an unprovoked assault.[1]

The letter requested that 'the incident referred to be thoroughly investigated and taken up by the Colonial Office and the people concerned punished'.

Walrond's specific complaint was about an unprovoked attack by an American soldier. He did not feel it necessary to identify the American soldier as white, but the theme of his letter is his experience of racism in Britain and he is clear that this racism—in the RAF and elsewhere—came from British people as well as Americans. 'In normal life', he wrote, 'both in this country and out of it, I undergo enough distress and suffer enough embarrassment by the silent, subtle, social and obviously racial prejudice and an indecent display of superiority by people of British nationality both in and out of the service (the former most unfortunately true)'. The letter cited a previous assault on him in Preston, Lancashire—in this case by a British officer. Speaking of the 'ugly evils of discrimination and prejudice', Walrond called them a 'horror of civilisation (supposed civilisation to me)'. The letter concluded, 'I came to this country as volunteer for air crew duties under the protection of the British government, and I demand as far as is humanly possible that I get that protection and its corresponding consideration. Is it fair, is it just, to ask me to risk my life nightly over enemy territory when, behind me, I have left something as treacherous to humanity as any "ISM"?'[2] Walrond wrote this letter on 29 June 1943. On the same night, he died on a bombing raid when his plane was shot down over Belgium by a German night-fighter.

In September 1943, Miss P. G. Palmer wrote to the Colonial Office from Wood Green in London, to ask what had been done about Walrond's case. She did not say how she knew Walrond, but it may be that she was the young woman that Walrond had asked to dance. Her letter referred to the 'Four Freedoms' that Franklin Roosevelt had set out in a speech in 1941—freedom of speech and worship and freedom from want and fear:

> [T]hese young men have come over half way across the world to fight in a cause which professes to stand for the Four Freedoms for all mankind, irrespective of race, colour, and creed. And yet, in our very midst, we find individuals who claim these Freedoms for themselves, whilst denying them to the Coloured peoples of the earth, who are contributing a most valuable part to this greatest struggle in all history.[3]

Miss Palmer wrote that Walrond's letter to the Colonial Office had been forwarded by the officer commanding No. 15 Squadron, but she was 'not aware that any steps have yet been taken in this most serious matter which concerns not only Sgt. Walrond, but all those who suffer in a similar way'. The Colonial Office had taken no steps because it never received Walrond's letter. John Keith, writing from the Colonial Office Welfare Department, discovered this when he put Miss Palmer's question to the Air Ministry. What action had been taken on Walrond's case? The Air Ministry in its reply apologized for failing to forward Walrond's letter and reported, 'as this airman failed to return from operations on the night of 28/29th July, no action was taken in the matter'.[4] John Keith subsequently received a similar response from the War Office, 'Considering the length of time since the incident occurred, and in view of the fact that Serjeant (sic) Walrond himself is now unfortunately missing... there is nothing that the War Office can do in the matter'.[5] Nothing was done.

Many white Britons would not have recognized Walrond's description of Britain as a place of 'silent, subtle, social and obviously racial prejudice'. The regular criticism of the racial segregation of the American armed forces in Britain suggests the extent to which British people thought of themselves as tolerant, in contrast to Americans. Within diverse popular attitudes, interracial mixing—including mixing between white British women and black men—was not only accepted, but also championed by a significant strand of popular opinion.[6] At the same time, popular opinion was invariably ambivalent or wary about interracial sex and marriage, and often hostile.

Relationships between white women and black men were among the main causes of inter-allied tension in Britain and dance halls were frequently the locations of conflict. When black men like Arthur Walrond asked white women to dance, violence often followed. The Home Office commented on an incident in Huyton, near Liverpool, where both white and black Americans were arrested after a street fight outside a pub, 'The cause of the trouble appears to have been due to the U.S. white troops resenting the Coloured troops associating with local females at local dance halls and in local public houses'.[7] Both white and non-white British men and women, as well as black GIs and black soldiers and war workers from the British Empire, often defended mixed dancing. A distinctive view of interracial encounters taken by many white British managed to combine the defence or championship of mixing with hostility to interracial sex and marriage—such encounters should be friendly but brief, with physical contact strictly confined to the dance floor. Much popular and official opinion converged on the 'friendly but brief' view, which persisted in the aftermath of war.

Uneasiness and hostility about British women's wartime relationships when they went beyond 'friendly but brief' encounters were by no means confined to those they made with black men. In 1944, Home Intelligence reported criticism of the behaviour of 'young women and girls with servicemen of every available nationality and colour'.[8] Some of this criticism was about young girls, including underage girls, and about married women's infidelities, but there was also wider resentment of British women who mixed with non-British men. I have coined the term 'sexual patriotism' to describe what much popular opinion demanded through its censure of British women's relationships with men of both enemy and allied nationalities. Sexual patriotism was also demanded by the British government, through its ban on fraternization with German and Italian prisoners of war. But the sexual patriotism demanded by public opinion was often more far-reaching, expressing uneasiness or hostility about British women's sexual relationships with all men who were not native-born Britons.

The unprecedented diversity of the population in wartime Britain threw an intense light on the requirements of sexual patriotism, which demonstrated a double standard—they rarely applied to British men. Women's responses to these requirements were diverse. Women were certainly among those policing sexual behaviour—monitoring, scrutinizing, and condemning other women's choice of sexual partners. But many women flouted the rules. Threading through this history is their desire for men who were not native-born Britons.

'Our Men' and 'Our Sweethearts'

In 1944, a British soldier serving in Italy wrote in a letter, 'It's coming to something when the "Hull Mail" put in an advert of Odol toothpaste with a photo of a Yankee soldier and an English girl. We boys here have decided to let our teeth rot rather than buy a tube of Odol'.[9]

The idea that British women belonged to British men was a key theme in anxieties about British women's non-patriotic relationships. This idea was also central to the message of *The Gentle Sex* (1943), a feature film about women's service in the women's branch of the British army—the Auxiliary Territorial Service. Leslie Howard, who directed the film, also spoke the voice-over. These were among his final words to British audiences, in the last film he made before his death, and were likely to be taken seriously. Howard was a well-known figure in wartime Britain—an actor and broadcaster as well as a film director. According to *Kinematograph Weekly*, British audiences voted him their most popular star in 1941 and 1942. When he was shot down in 1943, travelling in a plane that was bringing him back to Britain from a lecture tour of Portugal, Home Intelligence reported that this was 'the news of the week' for many people and had 'caused much comment and many expressions of regret'. He was considered 'not only a fine actor but a worthy representative of the British people, and many seem to feel his death as a personal loss'.[10]

Howard's pronouncements at the end of the *The Gentle Sex* deliver a verdict on what the film's portrait of female military service has shown about what he calls 'the women', but goes on to describe as 'our sweethearts, sisters, mothers, daughters'. His verdict is 'let's give in at last and admit that we're really proud of you'. Whether the 'we' he identifies here is the cinema audience watching the film or a wider collective of the British nation, it is defined as male when his voice-over continues, 'Pray silence, gentlemen. I give you a toast. The gentle sex!' Women, even when they are engaged in military service, are defined through their relationships, not to the nation, but to British men—'our sweethearts', 'our mothers'.[11] Men belong to the nation. Women, as 'our sweethearts' and 'our mothers', belong to the nation's men.

'Our men'—a phrase that was widely used in wartime—was very rarely used to mean 'our sweethearts' or 'our fathers'. The King's speech on Empire Day in 1940 referred to 'our fighting men' and their 'mothers, wives and sweethearts at home'.[12] An advertisement in 1941 acknowledged that women's place in wartime might not be at home. It urged women to join the Auxiliary Territorial Service, but its appeal—'Women!... Help our men to crush this evil Nazi menace quickly'—also made clear the different roles of men and women.[13] In wartime, 'our men' was used mainly to refer to British troops. It was elaborated to suit particular contexts—'our men fought on tenaciously', 'our men came home' (from Dunkirk), 'our men in the Middle East', 'our men in great heart', 'our men in Burma'.[14] Men displayed their patriotism through 'national service'—a term that officially encompassed civilian as well as military contributions to the war effort, but was often understood as military service. 'Our men' were those who risked their lives in the service of their country. Their willingness to fight and die was widely understood as a sign of their national allegiance. They remained 'our men' regardless of their sexual relationships, so long as these were heterosexual.

Many British men's relationships outside the national and ethnic collective were conducted overseas—part of a long history of such relationships in the context of war and empire. In the Second World War these sexual encounters overseas continued, but attracted little attention at home. The numbers involved will never be known—much of the British army was stationed at home before the cross-Channel invasion of June 1944.[15] Increases in venereal disease in the army caused considerable official concern and some criticism of British soldiers. But criticism did not focus on the fact that most soldiers' sexual encounters overseas were with non-British women.[16] Sexuality was not a significant element in definitions of male citizenship, belonging, or service to the nation.

The case was very different with British women. Like men, they were recruited into the armed services in wartime, but their military activities did not extend to combat—they were not 'our fighting women'. With the exception of female agents of a range of nationalities recruited to the Special Operations Executive and trained to kill, the only offensive weapons British women wielded were anti-aircraft guns. Although they did all the calculations

involved in aiming these guns accurately, they could not fire them. As
The Gentle Sex suggested, those recruited to the military remained defined
by their private roles—wives, mothers, sweethearts. The extent to which
women's belonging to the nation was mediated through British men is
particularly apparent in a double standard in the law about marriages to
aliens. British women who married foreigners lost their British nationality
on marriage and the rights of citizenship that went with it, including the
right to vote. Non-patriotic sexuality and marriage therefore placed them
outside the category of 'our women'. In contrast, British men who married
foreign women could bestow their British nationality on their wives and
children. Even after reform of the law in 1948, which meant that women
who married aliens could retain their British nationality, they could not pass
this British nationality on to their children until 1981.

Anxieties about British women's relationships with non-British men
peaked in 1943-4 with the build-up of American troops in Britain for
D-Day and of Italian prisoners of war to work on British farms. In these
years overseas service in the British army also peaked, with campaigns in
Burma and Italy as well as the cross-Channel invasion. Public reactions to
these campaigns featured regularly in Home Intelligence reports, including
complaints about publicity, 'American troops are accorded too much...often
at our men's expense'.[17] The phrase 'our men' recurred in such complaints,
which suggests strong investment in ideals of martial masculinity—pride
in the military prowess of 'our men', the conviction that this enhanced the
reputation of the nation, concern that it did not get the recognition it
deserved. Male soldiers' sexual relationships overseas featured nowhere.

In contrast, women's sexual relationships at home featured regularly in
Home Intelligence reports—virtually every week. In 1943-4, most of its
reports mentioned criticism and anxiety about such relationships, focusing
particularly on those with American GIs—both white and black—and
with Italian prisoners of war. Such criticisms continued after D-Day as
numbers of American troops in Britain dwindled. Italian prisoners of war
became a particular focus of attention in 1944, when those who opted to be
'co-operators' could talk to British civilians and accept invitations to their
homes. In this context, the government ban on all fraternization with prisoners of war in Britain became unworkable.[18] As late as December 1944,
Home Intelligence was still reporting, 'the association of young girls and
young married women with Italian prisoners of war and American troops
is particularly deplored. People expect "murder when our men get back"'.[19]

As the war was ending, there were increasing anxieties about the return of British husbands. One report expressed concerns about 'the increase in moral laxity—particularly of married women, whose husbands are abroad', with Dominion and US troops. It went on to quote an anonymous comment that had been reported or overheard, 'There will be mass murder unless the Government gets them out of the country before our men come back'.[20] In 1945, a British colonel echoed this prediction of mass murder, 'All the [British] men are thinking about is coming ashore with a Sten gun and moving through the countryside shooting all the Poles and Czechs and the Americans who've been sleeping with their wives and girls'.[21] Married women suspected of adultery came under scrutiny from welfare workers enlisted by the Army Welfare Service at the request of husbands serving overseas or of their commanding officers and padres.[22] There was no comparable scrutiny of men's behaviour—at home or overseas.

Criticisms of non-patriotic relationships did not target only British women. Home Intelligence reported of American troops in August 1944, 'their behaviour with young married women and with girls excites most censure', and of Italian prisoners of war in November 1944, 'people complain of their laziness, arrogant behaviour, and association with young women and girls'.[23] Sometimes these criticisms were elaborated. American soldiers were 'variously blamed for accosting, making love in public, having intercourse in telephone booths, leaving contraceptives about, and for "indiscriminate" choice of women'.[24] But reports strongly emphasized the censure of British women. Home Intelligence noted of Italian prisoners of war, 'The attitudes of some girls and married women towards these men has aroused disgust', that while Italians were criticized for their behaviour, 'the girls are equally blamed' and that there was 'indignation at the way girls and young women flirt and walk about arm-in-arm with them'.[25] Of American GIs, Home Intelligence reported, 'The women and girls concerned...in many cases are said to make most of the running. Blame of the girls is more widespread, and sometimes stronger, than of the men. Their predatoriness is particularly censured; some girls are said to be dunning as many as three or four US soldiers to provide for their coming child'.[26] Home Intelligence also reported the view that 'bad white women' were responsible for 'the colour question becoming a problem'.[27]

Comments in Home Intelligence reports were always anonymous, but there is some evidence that women were particularly likely to criticize men's behaviour. Occasionally Home Intelligence reported a distinct female view, 'Among women there is some fear of being molested by American troops in the black-out'.[28] Historian Leanne McCormick's work on American troops stationed in Northern Ireland demonstrates similar fears expressed by women in private correspondence. One member of the Women's Royal Navy wrote, 'It's not safe for us to be out unless we go together. I'd hate to be out in Derry alone after dusk believe me. These Yanks are positive fiends for women and should all be in homes (mental ones)'. Another woman wrote, '[N]ow at nights... if you go down the street at all there is a Yank after you all the time and as soon as we get shot of one lot another lot is at our elbow—it doesn't make any difference to them whether you say you are married and don't want them or not'.[29]

Interviews conducted by Mass Observation also demonstrate female criticism of Poles. In 1942, Mass Observation respondents—especially female respondents—were reporting the popularity of Polish servicemen among British women. One eighteen-year-old said, 'I don't care too much for any of them, [foreigners] except the Poles that is. I like them all right (Giggles). I think most of the girls like them, if you ask me'. Another, 'I've got a niece up in Scotland, and she's just mad about the Poles'. Another respondent said, 'when I was evacuated to Cheltenham... the place was full of Polish airmen—my, were they popular'! Some comments were critical. For example, one woman said, 'I don't fancy these Poles. Too keen on women and you don't know where you're up to with 'em'.[30] A second woman commented, 'I'm not keen on Poles. They've got a very bad name. They're marrying these English girls and a lot have wives in Poland'.[31] A third said, 'Some were nice, the ones I met seemed so. But we heard all sorts of talk of the way they went on with the girls where they were stationed, very young girls. The Scotch people did not like it'.[32] These views were out of step with the dominant discourse censuring British women. More obviously out of step were women who made relationships outside the national collective.

The numbers of such women were substantial. There were 4,000 British-Polish marriages by the end of the war, but this number was dwarfed by those of British-US marriages and British-Canadian marriages. The departure of British women to the United States is relatively well known and was given substantial publicity in the British media, where they were known as 'GI brides'. British-Canadian marriages, although lesser-known, were just as numerous. The first marriage between a British woman and a Canadian soldier took place in January 1940. It was followed by many more, with a total of 44,886 marriages of Canadian personnel in Britain by the end of 1946—the vast majority between Canadian men and British women. David Reynolds estimates the numbers of British-US marriages at a similar figure—between 40,000 and 45,000.[33]

When the war was over, many British wives of Americans and Canadians travelled thousands of miles to join their demobbed husbands, or to await their demob. But in wartime, women who made relationships outside the national collective risked being identified not as sweethearts or wives, but as 'good-time girls'—women with loose morals, who put their own pleasure above service to the war effort and 'threw themselves at men'.[34] They were sometimes shown doing so in wartime propaganda. In *Millions Like Us* (1943)—a film about women working in an aircraft factory—there is a brief sequence of Phyllis—a British woman—cuddling a Polish soldier. Phyllis is shown as a 'good-time girl', in contrast to her sister, who is shy and innocent and marries a Scottish airman who is killed on a mission.[35] There was also anxiety that 'good-time girls' damaged the national reputation. 'Some people are very concerned at what the Americans are going to say about British girls when they return home', Home Intelligence reported.[36] A letter intercepted by Postal Censorship commented on women who were 'all after the Yanks for a good time...it would make you feel ashamed of Northern Ireland'.[37] 'Our men' evoked national pride, regardless of their sexual relationships. In these comments, women who flout the requirements of sexual patriotism lose any claim to be regarded as 'our women' or 'our sweethearts'. Defined by their sexuality, they disgrace the nation.

'Friendly, but Brief'

In *Welcome to Britain* (1943)—a film made for screening to GIs on their arrival in Britain—there is a brief sequence of a white British woman leaning out of a railway carriage to shake the hands of two American GIs as they get out. One of them is Burgess Meredith, a white GI, who provides the narrative voice for the film. The other, Corporal Collier, is black. The woman leaning out of the railway carriage and saying her farewell to Collier comments on how odd it is that he should come from Birmingham too, and tells him that if he ever comes to 'my Birmingham', he must come and have a cup of tea with her. Meredith turns to camera to address the GI audience, as he does repeatedly throughout the film. His confidential aside

addresses them as a white group, even though many GIs stationed in Britain
were black:

> Now look men, you've heard that conversation, that's not unusual here, it's
> the sort of thing that happens quite a lot. Now let's be frank about it. There
> are coloured soldiers as well as white here, and there are less social restrictions
> in this country. An English woman asking a coloured boy to tea... Now
> look that might not happen at home. But the point is we're not at home.
> And the point is that if we bring a lot of prejudice here, what are we going
> to do about that?[38]

Welcome to Britain not only shows the encounter between Corporal Collier
and the white woman as 'friendly but brief' but also empties this encounter
of sexual meaning by making the woman elderly and motherly or grand-
motherly. Images in British propaganda addressed to an American audience
were generally targeted at white Americans, and care was taken that they
should not cause offence. American officials did not share the 'friendly but
brief' view of encounters between white women and black men. When
photographs of black men dancing with white women in London night
clubs were published in the American *Life* magazine, the American War
Department introduced a regulation prohibiting the passing for any purposes
of amateur photographs that showed 'negro soldiers in poses of intimacy
with white women or conveying "boy friend-girl friend" implications'.[39]
This was later toned down by General Eisenhower to allow black GIs to
post photographs home, so long as they were stamped 'For personal use
only—not for publication'.[40]

The British media took a different view. *Picture Post*, the nearest British
counterpart to *Life* magazine, published a photo spread on 'London's
Coloured Clubs' in 1943. Several pictures show black men dancing with
white women. The text celebrates the sights and sounds of interracial
mixing, 'At the Bouillabaisse you see the light-skinned Americans and
the black Nigerian. You hear the accent of Chicago mixing with Cockney
and Cardiff. Soldiers, Red Cross workers, students, factory workers, actors
and swing fans... they all mix in an international stream'.[41] The text has an
overt message, going on to highlight London clubs as places where 'the
continents meet' and where 'there is no colour bar'. But it is also notable
that in a *Picture Post* special edition on the Swansea valley in 1944, interracial dancing partners pass without comment. A photo spread on 'What
the Chapel Means' shows chapel activities including 'The Girls' Club,
'The Amateur Dramatics', 'The Lecture', and 'The Dance'. The caption to

the photo of 'The Dance' which shows a white woman with a black GI says nothing about this interracial dancing, but highlights its location—a Welsh chapel. The caption reads, 'Even Dancing is Allowed when it is a US Forces Club'.[42]

British cinema addressed to a British audience also offers occasional images of black men's encounters with white women. In *The Proud Valley* David (Paul Robeson)—the black stoker off the ships who works in a Welsh coalmine—forms a close attachment to local miner Dick Parry (Edward Chapman). When Dick dies in a mining accident, David goes on to form a close attachment to his son, Emlyn (Simon Lack). David has no comparable attachments to the white women of the village. The film shows only one encounter between David and a young white woman—an encounter which is 'friendly but brief'. This encounter is with Emlyn's fiancée, Gwen (Janet Johnson), and comes after a quarrel between Emlyn and Gwen. Its purpose is to bring them together again—bringing white couples together became a characteristic role of black men in post-war films.[43]

During filming of *The Proud Valley*, Britain declared war against Germany, and the script was revised to introduce a war theme. An explosion in the mine leads to its closure, causing unemployment and hardship in the village, and mine-owners initially reject the community campaign to reopen it. After the declaration of war, they agree to a reopening, to aid the war effort. It is during their work to reopen the mine that miners are trapped underground and David once more brings together Emlyn and Gwen. He sacrifices his life, detonating a blast that frees his fellow miners but kills him. His death ensures that Emlyn is saved and reunited with Gwen.[44]

West Indies Calling also offers images of 'friendly but brief' encounters. After showing the work of West Indians in Britain in forestry, munitions factories, and the RAF, the film ends with a long sequence of interracial dancing. This shows white Caribbeans, Indo-Caribbeans, and African Caribbeans mixing as dancing partners. The British Board of Film Censors operated a double standard, banning representations of sex between black men and white women, although not between white men and black women.[45] But as *West Indies Calling* demonstrates, there was no ban on images of social interaction, including physical contact. If the American War Department considered that such imagery conveyed 'intimacy' and '"boy friend–girl friend" implications', the sequence on interracial dancing in *West Indies Calling* was intended to convey friendship between peoples united against a common enemy in an empire that was increasingly renamed 'Commonwealth'.

Like the *Picture Post* photo-spread on London clubs, the film celebrates mixing and no colour bar.

Despite the message of *West Indies Calling*, black West Indian technicians and trainees in the north-west of England were increasingly refused entry to dance halls. An investigation by the Ministry of Labour found that many dance-hall managers attributed their introduction of colour bars to fear of loss of takings—some alleged that white Americans had threatened to boycott their halls unless they acted. Others attributed their colour bars to clashes between white and black Americans that were a result of white American objections to black GIs dancing with white women. These were bad for business—customers wanted a good night out, not a pitched battle. Officials concluded that 'the colour-bar difficulties have been stirred up by the Americans'.[46] In 1943, the Ministry of Labour reported that the Grafton dance hall in Liverpool 'has become increasingly the rendezvous of coloured people, and in recent times has degenerated on occasion into a racial fighting ground between coloured British subjects and white Americans'. In December, the dance hall imposed a colour bar.[47]

However convenient it may have been to blame white Americans for the introduction of colour bars, there seems little doubt of their role in the closure of the Casino dance hall in Warrington when Nat Bookbinder—its manager—refused to comply with an American request that it should bar black men. Bookbinder had opened the dance hall in 1938, and he held regular Harlem nights there, and paid tribute to black musicians. The *Daily Dispatch* recorded his refusal to bar a West Indian technician in December 1943, 'A young West Indian travelled 3,000 miles to do war work in Britain but when he attended a dancehall a group of soldiers asked that he be ejected. The manager refused and now the US military authorities have declared the hall "out of bounds"'.[48]

A Ministry of Labour report in 1943 described Herbert Greaves—the young West Indian referred to in the *Daily Dispatch* report—as 'a decent and self-respecting citizen, who attends regularly to his work: Mr. Bedford (Local Welfare Officer, Manchester) speaks of him as a very quiet diffident fellow'.[49] The dance hall had been declared 'out of bounds' to American troops, following a letter from Captain A. G. Laing of the US Army, who wrote: 'It is not our intention to dictate the policies of privately-owned establishments, but in the interest of eliminating trouble in which our troops may be involved, we will appreciate your co-operation in prohibiting Negroes from attending the dances'.[50]

Bookbinder did not cooperate. He refused to eject Greaves and told him that 'as long as he paid his admission money and behaved with his usual good manners the doors would be open to him and he would be welcome'. The heavy price Bookbinder paid for this non-cooperation was evident from the Ministry of Labour report, 'The Manager now finds that what he describes as his "idealistic" stand and his slogan "Fit to fight, fit to mix"... has already cost the hall over £3,000, the proceeds having dropped from round about £50 a week to less than £5 a week'.[51]

A letter to the editor of the *Warrington Examiner* stated, 'With the right of the American authorities to decide what is best for their own I am not prepared to argue; but when the British powers-that-be take a similar step, I think a great deal should be said... [The Casino manager] is entitled to stand up for the rights of coloured people without having to be persecuted... He will be assured the hearty support of every true Briton and anti-Fascist'.[52] But the Casino manager was not assured of support from the British government. In the correspondence and reports generated by the Colonial Office and the Ministry of Labour over dance hall colour bars, there was some advocacy of a pronouncement by the British government that 'American nationals should accept as normal in the UK the presence of coloured British subjects in hotels, dance-halls and pubs'.[53] But this came in July 1944, after substantial reduction in the number of American troops in Britain. The idea of challenging American objections to interracial mixing in places of leisure was entirely untypical of British official policy before D-Day.

'Fit to fight, fit to mix'—the slogan that Nat Bookbinder came to see as 'idealistic'—remained a widely held popular view. A difference of opinion between two respondents to a Mass Observation survey identified the role that such a slogan assigned to dancing partners. A male respondent stated, 'I'm against a colour bar. There should be equality—except that I wouldn't allow Negroes to marry white'. A female respondent disagreed, 'That's ridiculous. If they mix freely and have equality one or two are bound to fall for each other and on what grounds are you going to stop them marrying? Pollute the race? That's Nazism!'[54] Mixing was fine—both respondents could agree on this. But reports on public opinion suggest that many British people sided with the male respondent. Mixing was only fine if it was 'friendly but brief' and did not carry the implications that the female respondent identified—falling for each other. When the dance was over, both the black man and the white woman were meant to keep their distance.

The British Way?

In the summer and autumn of 1942, policy-makers in the British government were busy thinking through their response to the presence of American forces and the questions this raised about potential encounters and relationships between black troops and white women. One proposal from the Foreign Secretary was to reduce the numbers of black troops arriving.[55] The Cabinet also urged that America should 'reduce as far as possible the number of coloured troops... sent to this country' and the Foreign Secretary explained to the American Ambassador that British weather was 'badly suited to negroes'.[56] At the War Office, James Grigg—the Secretary of State for War—took the view that of all the problems he associated with the presence of black GIs, 'the question of the association of British women with coloured troops was regarded as the most difficult of solution'. Its importance, he wrote, lay in its possible repercussions on American opinion about Britain and on the morale of the British army. His priority was to handle matters 'in a way that will not arouse resentment in the United States'.[57] Given his subsequent efforts to prevent encounters and relationships between white women and black GIs, it is clear that he thought of the United States as a white nation.

The government's early responses to the question that Grigg thought so difficult included an interdepartmental government meeting in August 1942 that discussed the possibility of a 'whispering campaign', to discourage white British women from associating with black GIs. Another proposal was 'an open statement on the dangers of venereal disease'. Home Intelligence reported a rumour that 'the WVS [Women's Voluntary Service] have been told that on no account should American coloured troops be entertained in private homes owing to the prevalence among them of venereal disease'. In September, it reported that 'strong views have been expressed at "certain leaders of women's opinion" who are alleged to have been organising a whispering campaign in favour of the colour bar'.[58] At the Colonial Office, John Keith wrote:

> I understand that a certain amount of action has been taken by the Army authorities i.e. the ATS [Auxiliary Territorial Service] have been warned not to walk out with coloured soldiers, and that there has been a considerable whispering campaign emanating to some extent from Lady Reading's organisation of the Women's Volunteer Service against the association of white

women with coloured men. (Mr. Parker and Mr. Huxley of the Ministry of Information told me this).[59]

Action taken by the Army to warn white women against mixing with black GIs included a draft of confidential instructions to senior Army officers, which advised, 'White women should not associate with coloured men. It follows then, they should not walk out, dance or drink with them. Do not think such action hard or unsociable. They do not expect your companionship and such relations would in the end only result in strife'.[60]

If the government's thinking in 1942 was designed to bring British practices more closely into line with those it attributed to Americans, there were different views on what these were. The Foreign Office opposed a statement on the dangers of venereal disease, arguing that this would be regarded by 'progressive elements in the United States' as a 'slander on the American Negro'. Opposition to such a statement also drew on the idea of distinctive British attitudes. At the Colonial Office, John Keith wrote 'we should not allow any nonsense about rape, VD etc., to deter us from sticking to our principles and resisting the so-called Southern American attitude towards Negroes'.[61]

The *Sunday Pictorial* strongly censured those who warned of the dangers of white women mixing with black GIs, condemning the advice given by a British vicar's wife which included instructions to women to move if seated next to black GIs in a cinema, to cross the road to avoid meeting them, and on no account to invite coloured troops into their homes. The paper represented such advice as un-British, 'Any coloured soldier who reads this may rest assured that there is no colour bar in this country and that he is as welcome as any other Allied soldier. He will find that the vast majority of people here have nothing but repugnance for the narrow-minded, uninformed prejudices expressed by the vicar's wife. There is—and will be no persecution of coloured people in Britain'.[62]

There was some later modification of government thinking. The draft advice to women in the army was toned down to concede that 'friendly but brief' encounters were acceptable:

For a white woman to go about in the company of a Negro American is likely to lead to controversy and ill-feeling, it may also be misunderstood by the Negro troops themselves. This does not mean that friendly hospitality in the home or in social gatherings need be ruled out, though in such cases care should be taken not to invite white and coloured American troops at the same time.[63]

There was also some approval of mixing between black men and white women at the Ministry of Labour, which reported in 1943, 'In the last year or so the Anglo-Negro Fellowship have ... been most helpful in arranging for our [West Indian] technicians and trainees to visit the homes of English people, to arrange small informal dances at the houses of well-wishers, and to make arrangements for ladies interested in the Colonial problem to accompany the coloured men to theatres and dances'.[64]

Despite the view taken by the Ministry of Labour, most government thinking was out of step with government-sponsored public messages like *West Indies Calling*, with its sequence of interracial dancing. Another wartime documentary sponsored by the Ministry of Information—*Timbermen from Honduras* (1943)—uses the same shots of British Hondurans felling trees in Scotland as does *West Indies Calling*, with commentary expressing the gratitude of the mother country for their expert contribution to the war effort and their 'unfailing cheerfulness'.[65] But this was another case of conflict between the public message and the government's private thinking—the Ministry of Supply wanted to disband the Forestry Unit and deport its members. The chief complaint against the men was 'their bad behaviour generally, particularly their association with white women in the Camps'.[66] By 1943, there had been four marriages between white British women and black British Honduran men. With the exception of a case 'where a coloured Assistant Camp Manager married a local girl with the consent of the parents and the blessing of the Roman Catholic Priest', British women were warned that these marriages were 'undesirable'. Nevertheless, they went ahead.[67]

Concerns about the birth of mixed-race children in Britain were apparent early on in government discussions about black GIs in Britain. The Conservative MP Maurice Petherick wrote to the Foreign Secretary, Anthony Eden, that black troops 'will quite obviously consort with white girls and there will be a number of half-caste babies about when they have gone—a bad thing for any country'.[68] This was also the view of the Home Secretary, Herbert Morrison, who wrote, 'I am fully conscious that a difficult sex problem might be created if there were a substantial number of cases of sex relations between white women and coloured troops and the procreation of half-caste children'.[69] Winston Churchill was also concerned about mixed-race children. In October 1943, he asked for information on US coloured troops that included 'number of cases of mutiny, violence, illegitimate children etc.'. On this typed list, Churchill wrote an addition—'rape'.[70]

Churchill's request was prompted by information from his cousin, the Duke of Marlborough, who worked as liaison officer in the British army with the American armed forces in Britain. Initially, Marlborough delivered this information by telephone and added more in a letter, where he wrote that 'only ten cases of coloured babies being born are known in this country at the present time', but that he knew of many others that were on the way. He also listed a range of 'serious offences committed by coloured troops' including 'a number of cases of attempted rape . . . in which the unknown persons have escaped being apprehended by the police'. The letter went on to explain, 'there are many assaults of this kind which take place in the hours of darkness and with the limited number of civilian and military police, and on dark nights the assailants are able to get away scot free'.[71]

The British government had no jurisdiction over American soldiers charged with rape. Under the Visiting Forces Act of 1942, the United States military authorities had complete legal jurisdiction over their own troops.[72] Rape did not carry the death penalty in Britain, but Leroy Henry was condemned to death by American court martial, for his alleged rape of a British woman in 1944. The case caused much protest. A petition started by a local baker collected 33,000 signatures. The League of Coloured Peoples intervened with General Eisenhower on Henry's behalf. There were questions in the House of Commons.[73] The British woman who was allegedly raped was regarded locally as a 'good-time girl'. It seems likely that any associations of black men with rape were eclipsed by the associations of the 'good-time girl' with loose morals, which excluded the possibility of rape.

The *Daily Mirror* reported receiving large numbers of letters which 'reveal a widespread feeling of uneasiness at this man having to pay the extreme penalty'. In a leading article on the case, entitled 'Clemency', it set out what it saw as the British way:

> We are confident that we interpret the feeling of everyone in this country in expressing gratitude for the manner in which America has insisted on a high standard of conduct for her troops, and for her obvious determination to protect our womenfolk. Nevertheless, popular sentiment would be much appeased if justice could, in suitable cases, be tempered with mercy, and not least in cases where coloured men are the offenders. In America, which has a colour problem peculiar to herself, clemency might not be possible. Here, we venture to hope, it may not be impossible as an act of grace, to take a different view.[74]

When General Eisenhower commuted Leroy Henry's death sentence, Home Intelligence reported 'great relief'.[75]

Siding with black GIs accused of rape drew on the idea that death sentences for black GIs convicted of rape were un-British not only because rape did not carry the death penalty in Britain, but also because they smacked of discrimination, which was un-British. When two black GIs—Eliga Brinson of Tallahassee, Florida and Willie Smith of Birmingham, Alabama—were found guilty of rape and sentenced to death, Hugh Lawson, Member of Parliament for Skipton, asked the Foreign Secretary if he would inform the American government 'that the carrying out of such a sentence would be interpreted by many people in this country as racial persecution and therefore likely to cause bad feeling between the two countries'.[76] Home Intelligence reported that this case 'aroused strong local protests on grounds of colour discrimination'.[77] Both men were hanged—their sentences having been reviewed and confirmed by General Eisenhower.[78]

A British way of doing things, articulated in these rape cases in contrast to American practices and attitudes, rarely extended to the question of interracial sex and marriage. Interracial marriage was legal in Britain, unlike the majority of American states, but it was widely censured and sometimes regarded with visceral loathing. A 1939 Mass Observation directive on race included many unsolicited and disapproving comments, including one by a young Yorkshire salesman. He wrote, 'I feel that [Negroes'] association with white women is revolting', and added 'I have nothing against them as a class and I have every sympathy with them as regards the treatment which is meted out to them by the Americans'.[79]

In 1943, another Mass Observation directive on race, which asked no specific questions about mixed marriages, drew similar responses. One person in seven spontaneously mentioned them, and always disapprovingly. The report on the directive noted that 'many thought the question of children of mixed marriages insurmountable, believing it to be unfair on the children'. It also noted that 'many men admitted to an almost completely irrational feeling of disgust at the sight of a white woman accompanied by a coloured man', but that 'the case of white men and coloured women was hardly ever mentioned and aroused no strong feeling'. In support, it quoted a reply from a chemist, aged twenty-seven: 'I realise it is irrational, but whilst the sight of a coloured man with a white woman maked (sic) me feel sick, the sight of a white man with a coloured girl leaves me indifferent'.[80] Another Mass Observation respondent was particularly explicit about his own double standard, 'I could cheerfully clout coloured men I see with white women—but must confess to a definite desire to give careful investigation to some of the very bedworthy specimens of the other sex but the same colour that I have seen'.[81]

Wartime Home Intelligence reports on British attitudes supported these findings. Favourable comments on black GIs and strong criticism of the segregation of the American army were mixed in with anxieties about relationships between black GIs and white women—often in the same reports. A characteristic report in 1942 recorded the regular finding of 'considerable indignation . . . against any discrimination by white Americans against their coloured troops' as well as 'outspoken expressions of opinion' at 'the turning away of some negroes from a dance at Eye in Suffolk'. But the report also recorded 'apprehension' about relationships 'between white women and coloured troops'.[82]

The idea of a distinctive British way was prized by those who claimed there was no colour bar in Britain, or thought of America as a country with 'a colour problem peculiar to herself', or protested against bans on black GIs at British dance halls. There were many areas where British practices differed from American, including the legality of interracial marriage throughout the United Kingdom, the publication of photographs of interracial dancing, and considerable public support for 'friendly but brief' encounters between black men and white women. But on interracial sex and marriage and the birth of mixed-race children, the views of the American authorities, those of the British government, and much of British public opinion converged—they were beyond the pale.

When the War Was Over

In 1945, on the cusp of the end of war in Europe, as the allies entered Germany, six women in the British army expressed their hostility to British men's relationships with German women. In a letter to the *Sunday Express*, they wrote, 'If the men we are fighting with prefer the daughters of the enemy we would rather have our ticket now, for what *are* we fighting for?' On the same day, in another letter in the *Sunday Express*, the mother of a British prisoner of war in Germany wrote, 'Our boy has been a POW in Germany since May 28 1940, but if the price of his life and safety is to marry a German girl then I hope he never returns'.[83] These letters are a striking exception to most expressions of hostility to transnational and transethnic relationships, which were usually about those made by British women, not British men. Whatever British women's private wartime views on their male compatriots, their moment of public hostility to men's transnational sex and marriage awaited the war's end and was confined to their relationships with German women.

The women who wrote to the *Sunday Express* were part of a wider campaign against British soldiers fraternizing with German women in the context of the Allied occupation of Germany. The campaign was conducted mainly by British women. Historian Alan Allport calls this the 'fratting [fraternization] scandal' and shows that it generated a range of articles and much correspondence in national newspapers in 1945. Some took the view that German women were 'contaminating our soldiers'. Other blamed the soldiers, making it apparent that their sexual behaviour cast doubt on their credentials as 'our men'. In the *News Chronicle*, one female reader claimed that disgust with the behaviour of British soldiers was a feeling common to 'the girls of England'.[84]

For a brief period, official policy-makers shared the views of these campaigners. They banned all fraternization between British soldiers and German people, male and female, in occupied Germany. Echoing the view that German women were contaminating British troops, Field Marshal Montgomery accused them of 'carrying out an organised strip-tease campaign to break down the will of the British soldiers'.[85] But the numerous violations of the fraternization ban made the policy unworkable, and it was lifted in 1946. Between 1947 and 1950, 10,000 German war brides arrived in Britain.

The anger generated against British soldiers during the 'fratting scandal' demonstrates that their sexual relationships overseas were not always overlooked by people at home or exempted from charges of non-patriotic sex. Criticism of men was all the more remarkable in a year when women elsewhere who had flouted the rules of sexual patriotism were a focus of attention. As the liberation of occupied Europe progressed, many women were accused of what the French called 'horizontal collaboration' with German men and were punished by having their heads shaved. This punitive action was taken in Belgium, Denmark, France, the Netherlands, and Norway. Fabrice Virgili calculates that as many as 20,000 French women had their hair shorn.[86]

In 1944, Home Intelligence reported that although British opinion was divided on this shearing, 'a definite majority disliked the practice'. Images of shorn women in newsreels and in the press were reported to have particularly shocked people.[87] In correspondence in the *Loughborough Echo* about Italian prisoners of war, Bill Fairley, a British soldier, suggested that British women who had associated with enemy men should receive the same treatment he had seen meted out to Belgian women—'they were publicly paraded and deprived of their hair'.[88] Fairley was unlikely to have been aware of the shearing of British women that took place in Jersey in the Channel Islands, after he had written this letter. Women in Jersey who were accused of 'horizontal collaboration' with German occupiers were sometimes shorn and sometimes tarred and feathered, but this punitive action was given little publicity in the British media.[89]

There was no equivalent in mainland Britain to 'horizontal collaboration' with German occupiers, but marriage between British women and German prisoners remained illegal until 1947—a year after marriage between British men and German women was permitted in occupied Germany. Despite the continued ban on fraternization in Britain, British women and German prisoners managed to go out together. Jack Stang was taken prisoner in France and brought to Britain in the hold of a tank landing craft, spending several weeks in Scotland before being taken to a prisoner-of-war camp in Brayton, Yorkshire. He volunteered to work on a farm and got on well with the family there. When Doreen, the niece of the family, came to visit, they fell in love. (See Figure 6.1.) Doreen Stang remembers: 'We used to go all over, up and down the country by train. We flouted the law. No fraternising'.[90] Jack borrowed civilian clothes for these trips and married Doreen as soon as marriage was permitted, in 1947.

Fritz Zimmermann, who was taken prisoner at the Battle of El Alamein in 1942, was held initially in Africa and then in Canada, arriving in Britain in 1946. He worked on a farm where Lilian Hall, a member of the Women's Land Army, was also working. He records, 'After a while I fell in love with Lilian. On weekends when we were not working, we went together for bicycle rides in the country and into the town. For this I had to borrow civilian clothing because by law we were not allowed to go out together. British girls were not allowed to fraternise with aliens. Then Mr Roberts asked me if I would like to live in'. When the meetings between Lilian Hall and Fritz Zimmermann were discovered, Zimmermann was ordered back to camp and given twenty-eight days detention by the camp commandant:

> As a punishment I had to dig a hole and fill it in again. But I did not have to do my full term. During this time Lilian came to visit me every day, and our

love for each other grew stronger. When Lilian got to know about my detention, she was very cross as neither of us felt we had done anything wrong. So . . . off she went to London to see somebody at the War Office. When she got there she demanded to see someone high up and had a meeting with him. The following day, the law about fraternisation was changed. Lilian always said this was due to her![91]

Lillian asked Fritz to marry her and their wedding took place in September 1947, after the ban on British women marrying German prisoners of war was lifted.

Living together after marriage could be more problematic for German-British couples than going out together before marriage. June Fellbrich recalls that her future husband, Heinz, 'had to tunnel his way in and out of camp to meet me'. On their wedding day, Heinz had to return to the prisoner-of-war camp where he was held, and kissed June goodnight over the camp fence.[92] Peter Sinclair, who came to Britain on a *Kindertransport* and volunteered for the Royal Fusiliers in 1943, records his witnessing of similar wedding night arrangements. Sinclair was posted to a German prisoner-of-war camp in Essex in 1945. He remembers:

> I was told that we were getting a POW who had just been released from prison. He'd been given 96 days. After further inquiries I found out that he had worked on a British aerodrome somewhere in the UK and there was a WAAF [Women's Auxiliary Air Force] who had a relationship with him. She became pregnant. He ended up in prison, and she was discharged from the forces and sent to her parents. She was given permission to marry. So one fine day my driver and I took the German POW . . . and we met his girlfriend, the WAAF with the baby. The baby we looked after and they married at the registry office at Highbury. When they came back I took the fellow back to my camp, the girl went back to her parents.[93]

A total of 796 German prisoners married British women while they were still held in prisoner-of-war camps.[94]

Living together was also problematic for women who travelled to America, when the war was over, to marry black GIs, in states where interracial marriage was illegal. When Margaret Goosey, a shoe worker from Wellingborough in Northamptonshire, went to Virginia to marry Thomas Johnson—a black GI she had met in Britain during the war—her marriage had the support of her family, but was in defiance of Virginian law. For their attempt to flout this law, Johnson was sent to the State's Industrial Farm and Goosey was sentenced to six months in prison and then deported.[95]

Most white British women who had wartime relationships with black GIs did not marry them. Those who gave birth to mixed-race babies during and after the war were often unmarried mothers. Although interracial marriage was not illegal in Britain, difficulties placed in the way of marriages between black GIs and white British women in wartime had made for a more or less effective ban. In 1946, an article in *Ebony*—an American magazine addressed to an African-American audience—commented on the mixed-race babies born to black GIs and white British women:

> Permission to marry was denied hundreds of Negro GIs who wanted to accept the obligations of fatherhood and who applied in conformity with Army requirements... It is impossible to estimate how many of the illegitimate colored babies would be legitimate were it not for the stubborn refusal of white commanders to sanction the marriage of a Negro soldier and a white woman.

When the British woman was pregnant, the black American soldier involved was often transferred by the American army, while the British woman was counselled against marriage by British welfare organizations.[96]

The article in *Ebony* presented Britain as a liberal country, 'From the start, most Britishers, free from racism... greeted Negro soldiers warmly. Many publicly expressed a preference for "the blacks" whose courtesy and restrained behaviour contrasted with the swagger and bumptiousness of some white Yanks'.[97] At the same time, the article was clear that British liberalism had limitations. It reported that the British 'had demonstrated their freedom from prejudice and accepted Negro GIs as equals' but that 'the soaring illegitimacy rate strained British notions of equalitarianism and fair play'.

The limitations to British liberalism reported by *Ebony* were apparent in attitudes to mixed-race babies born to British women and black GIs during and after the war. Mothers who kept their babies could face hostility. In 1946, *Time* magazine reported one mother's experience, 'I am shunned by the whole village. The inspector for the National Society for the Prevention of Cruelty to Children has told my friend to keep her children away from my house... as didn't she know that I had two illegitimate coloured children? Is there anywhere I can go where my children will not get pushed around?'[98] Many mothers put their children into care. As the *Time* article stated, 'adoption is all but impossible'. A Ministry of Health official made the same observation in discussions of the mixed-race children born to British women and black GIs, 'a black child is almost impossible to get

adopted, nearly as difficult to board out and therefore is pretty sure to be
brought up in some type of Children's Home in this country, if separated
from the mother'.[99]

The view that mixed-race children were 'unadoptable' was taken by
many adoption agencies and meant that they did not accept responsibility
for finding suitable adopters or foster parents.[100] Difficulties in placing
mixed-race or black children for adoption were therefore caused more by
the attitudes of adoption agencies than by those of potential adoptive parents. Children who were fostered sometimes found loving homes. Tony
Martin, put into care by his unmarried mother, spent the first five years of
his life in a Barnardo's children's home, but was then fostered by a family
in Balsham, a village in Cambridgeshire. Martin describes his family. 'My
father was very quiet...My mother was always there for me...we were
treated all the same, my brothers and sisters, it was a happy place. It was a
very happy place'.[101]

Among mixed-race children who grew up in children's homes, many
knew nothing of their birth fathers. Denise Burt knew that her father was a
black GI, but 'presumed he had been a one-night stand who knew nothing
about me'. It was not until she applied for her file in 1997 that she discovered
her father's name was Turner Powell. She also found that her father did not
abandon her, as she had thought, but had written a number of letters to the
children's home. He had offered to support her, asked for photographs of
her, and enquired how old she would have to be before she could travel to
America without an escort. Turner Powell wrote to the children's home
for seven years, from 1945 to 1951, but never received a reply.[102] He died
without seeing Denise.

The limitations to British liberalism, apparent in the treatment of
mixed-race children, were also evident in post-war attitudes to transnational
and interracial relationships. The diversity of the wartime British population
was not for the duration only—the Second World War generated a range
of migrant and refugee movements to Britain, particularly in the context of
the acute post-war labour shortage. Both British men and British women
intermarried with a range of national and ethnic groups. Women who
married Polish men might be told to 'go and live in Poland', while Polish
men acquired a derogatory label—'Casanova'.[103] A woman who signed
herself 'Annoyed' wrote to the *Lancashire Daily Post* in 1946, complaining
that women who showed courtesy towards Polish soldiers were 'subject to
much unpleasant gossip'.[104]

Hostility to interracial sex continued, and the persistence of a double standard was evident in a question that was recurrent in the media in the 1950s, 'Would you let your daughter marry a Negro?'[105] Such a question was never asked of sons. An article in *Picture Post* in 1954 found that seven out of ten British men questioned agreed with a father whose daughter was dating a West Indian immigrant—'Rather than see her married to a nigger, I'd watch her die having a kid'.[106] The *Daily Telegraph* suggested in 1958, 'what most of us instinctively recoil from is miscegenation'.[107] In the same year, a Gallup poll found that 71 per cent of its respondents opposed interracial marriages.[108] Although the British Board of Film Censors' ban on representing sex between black men and white women did not apply to television, the BBC nevertheless showed considerable nervousness about representing interracial relationships. In 1950, after complaints about a programme where a black man sang a love song to a white woman, the Controller of Television noted, 'We must be extremely careful in the matter of employment of white and coloured artists on the same show. In particular, love songs between white and coloured artists must be very scrupulously considered'.[109]

Walter White, the leader of the National Association of the Advancement of Colored People, heard a story before he visited Britain in 1944 which presented Britain as more progressive than America. A British family had invited a group of American soldiers to their home for dinner and dancing. 'Everything moved smoothly during the meal, but when one of the Negro soldiers danced with one of the English women, he had been assaulted by a Southern white soldier. A free-for-all followed in which the British took the side of the negroes'.[110] This story of a progressive Britain, in contrast to racist America, was told a good deal in wartime Britain. It was also told by a number of black Americans in the aftermath of war. Historian Clive Webb argues that many African-Americans idealized Britain and that such idealization was 'informed by the experience of black servicemen stationed in [Britain] during the Second World War, including sexual encounters with white women that would have been unimaginable back home'.[111]

Idealization of Britain was particularly apparent in the pages of *Jet* magazine, targeted at African-American readers. After the war, *Jet* regularly ran stories reporting interracial marriages in Britain, including stories of interracial couples who had flown across the Atlantic from the United States in order to get married. These stories represented interracial marriage as an accepted

British social custom.[112] It was not. Whatever the differences between white British and Americans, they were at one on this. 'Fit to fight, fit to mix' may have enjoyed popular support in wartime Britain, when black men were often accepted as allies in a common struggle and valued as members of the allied community. But in the aftermath of war, as well as in wartime, they were rarely accepted as sexual partners or husbands of white women.

Figure 7.1 Chinese seamen learning how to handle an Oerlikon gun at the Gunnery school for inter-allied seamen, Liverpool, April 1942 (© Imperial War Museum, A 8200).

7

Aftermath

Miroslav Liskutin, the Czechoslovakian pilot introduced in Chapter 1, who served in the wartime RAF, arrived in Britain in June 1940 on a Polish cargo vessel evacuating Polish nationals from France, docking at Falmouth. Liskutin did not return to Czechoslovakia until his country was free from German occupation more than five years later, when he flew back from Manston in Kent in a formation of Spitfires:

> The final departure from England was quite professional. Prompt forming up was followed by a fly-past over Manston before setting course for home. This final departure from the British Isles was an extraordinary experience of a deeply emotional nature. I remember my last look across to Dover, Ramsgate, Margate and...goodbye England! It was difficult to suppress a tear in my eye.[1]

The journey was delayed by bad weather, involving a stop in Germany, where Liskutin stayed in a former Luftwaffe mess. After ten days, he finally reached Prague, where he describes the welcome as 'fantastic'. *The Return of our Airmen from England*, a film made by the RAF Film Unit and the *Ceskoslovenska Filmova Kronika*, shows a Prague welcome. Czechoslovakian airmen are still in RAF uniform. Women dressed in traditional costumes hand them flowers, crowds cheer and wave, families are reunited.[2] Liskutin writes, 'For us, the returning warriors, this was an emotional experience of great magnitude'.[3]

Likskutin had a further grand welcome when he arrived in Jirikovice, the village where he was born and where his parents still lived:

> There is no doubt that it was the largest festivity ever organised by my fellow citizens in the locality. Everybody seems to have turned up. Even a Red Army regiment was among the welcoming crowds and well wishers...And my family and friends were really kind to me. I will never forget it. Those few days at home will remain for ever in my mind. These were the best memories of my post-war life in Czechoslovakia.[4]

Until 1948, Liskutin's post-war life in Czechoslovakia appeared to go well. His British wife and first British-born son joined him in Prague, where his second son was born in 1946. He served with the Czechoslovakian Air Force in Brno, where he was appointed to a Permanent Commission in January 1946. But there was an undertow of anxiety in his realization that there was prejudice against 'aviators from abroad'—aviators who, like him, had served in the West:

> The nation was now orientated towards the East and the aviators from abroad did not fit into this new situation. The aviators brought from abroad an infection of foreign ideology... endangering the progressive development of the nation. The 'aviators from abroad' had a competing claim with the Red Army for the liberation. This was intolerable.[5]

These anxieties came to a head in 1948, after the Communist putsch in Czechoslovakia. On the same day that his wife and sons returned to Britain, Liskutin was dismissed from service in the Czechoslovak Air Force and instructed to find a job in one of the 'approved' sectors of civilian employment—agriculture, forestry, or coal mining. Warned by old friends that his name was on a list of 'Western aviators' who were about to be arrested, he made departure plans for a second journey into exile in Britain. His movements were being watched by the police but he managed to elude them, wading across a river to cross the border into the Russian zone of Austria and then taking a train to Vienna, where he made contact with the RAF and stayed at their barracks in Schönbrunn Palace. Through this journey, Liskutin escaped the fate of other Czechoslovaks who had served in the RAF and then returned to Czechoslovakia. Under the Communist regime, many were arrested and imprisoned or sent to labour camps. In August 1948, three years after his emotional farewell to Dover, Ramsgate, and Margate and his return to Prague, Liskutin was reunited with his family in Britain.

Miroslav Liskutin was not the only Czechoslovak airman who went back to Prague in 1946 and then returned to Britain. The dramatic story of a journey by eight of his compatriots appeared on the front pages of many newspapers in May 1948. As in 1940, they had taken planes for their journey to Britain without the formality of asking, but this time the 'loan' was not from the French, but—as they told the *Daily Express*—'we borrowed the plane from the Czech Air Line but in our hurry we forgot to sign for it'.[6]

The five pilots among them had all served in wartime Britain in the RAF. Of the other three, two were mechanics in the Czechoslovakian Air Force and the third a worker in the Czech Air Line, from which the plane had been 'borrowed'. They landed at Manston, which was just as well known to the five pilots as it was to Miroslav Liskutin. All of them had been stationed there in wartime. They had made various attempts to get out of the country, before 'borrowing' the aircraft.

In interviews, the newly arrived Czechoslovaks told reporters that they were trying to keep their identities secret and withheld information on their names, ranks, and home regions. The only photograph of their arrival, widely used by the British press, was a back view, which did not show their faces. Their luggage, according to the *Daily Mirror*, was 'a toothbrush apiece'.[7] They told *The Times* that they needed to conceal their identities because, if these were known, their parents, living in Czechoslovakia, who had been imprisoned during the German occupation, would be imprisoned again. One of them said in an interview, 'the principles of free living were taken from us in our native land—the principles for which we fought for six years on the battlefields of Europe. Soon there came what I called a persecution. Those Czechs who had English-born wives were dismissed from the services and even from civilian posts'.[8] On the same day that the Czechoslovak airmen flew to exile in Britain, the Czechoslovakian government announced that the police had arrested a number of people accused of assisting their escape.[9] There was a further escape in 1950 by Jan Kaucky, Josef Rechka, and Edvard Prchal, who had all fought in the Battle of Britain. They also 'borrowed' a plane and flew with their families to Manston.

Most departures from Britain after Allied victory in 1945 were less ceremonial than Liskutin's flypast over Manston, but there were many of them. Military forces were demobbed back home. Many refugees and exiles returned to countries no longer under German occupation. Not all departures were permanent. Czechoslovak airmen like Liskutin returned to Britain because of the threat of arrest, but people of diverse nationalities returned for other reasons—attracted back by employment opportunities in post-war Britain, as well as by attachments made in wartime.

Messages left or received by those who were departing suggest something of the diversity of people's experience in Britain. Victor de Laveleye—whose broadcast to Belgium had initiated the V-sign—returned to Belgium after

the liberation of Brussels and became Minister of Education in the Belgian
Government. In his farewell speech to Britain and the BBC, he said:

> Is it because you have a genius for friendship that you English show such a
> remarkable aptitude for living in the midst of your Allies, for understanding
> them, for making them work together, and for making them feel at home
> among you? Is it by natural inclination or by supreme political skill that you
> are so admirably tolerant, so understanding, and so generous...? However it
> may be, we have lived, worked, and talked in London during the war in an
> atmosphere of absolute independence.[10]

A letter from a British friend to an Italian prisoner of war on the eve of his
repatriation to Italy suggests a very different experience:

> When you see the coast of Britain disappearing in the distance don't—or
> at least try not to—feel bitter about all the stupid, cruel and degrading
> experience you have had here...We all miss you very much, Big Lug:
> I can't get accustomed to working without you...Towards the end of
> your letter you thank me for what I did for you: I should be the one to be
> grateful to you for your companionship, for the understanding which never
> failed all the time we were together. Who knows, some day we may meet in
> Italy...In any event all my wishes go to you...be happy, and may God
> bless you.[11]

Despite the many departures, the population of Britain in the aftermath of
war remained more diverse than it had been before 1939. Government
schemes generated many post-war arrivals through the recruitment of
workers, mainly from Europe, in the context of the acute post-war labour
shortage in Britain. Such recruitment was generally into jobs with conditions and pay that made them unattractive to home-grown labour. Under
other government schemes, people who had arrived in wartime stayed on.
The Polish Resettlement scheme meant that Poles who did not want to
emigrate elsewhere or return to Poland could settle in Britain. Many
decided to do so. Italian and German prisoners of war also stayed on under
government schemes.

Many of those who stayed on or returned remember a change of climate
in the aftermath of war—one which was more hostile and in which their
wartime contributions were forgotten. Such forgetting is also apparent in
cultural memories disseminated in British cinema and other media. The
celebration of an 'allies' war' was for the duration only—the images and
sounds of allies which had been so prominent in wartime Britain faded

rapidly when the war was over. In public memories, many groups who contributed to the Allied war effort were forgotten, not only in Britain but also
in their own countries.

Post-war Immigration Policy

In the aftermath of war, government policy on immigration was continuous
with wartime in the efforts made to restrict the numbers of non-white people
arriving from the colonies. Government efforts to turn refugees and prisoners of war into assets were also continuous with wartime. In the late
1940s, when the war was over, refugees from continental Europe recruited to
the British labour market, as well as prisoners of war, were directed into what
were called 'essential industries'—chiefly agriculture, mining, and textiles.

All the government's recruitment schemes to bring in workers favoured
Europeans. The Royal Commission on Population, reporting in 1949, took
a similar view to the government's. It welcomed the possibility of migration
from Europe, but dismissed the possibility of migration of non-white people
from the British Empire, in one sentence. This sentence was, 'Immigration
on a large scale into a fully established society like ours could only be welcomed without reserve if the immigrants were of good human stock and
were not prevented by their religion or race from intermarrying with the
host population and becoming merged in it'.[12]

The Royal Commission noted in 1949 that 'the main source of immigrants under the present schemes are the European Volunteer Workers'.[13]
Some 86,000 men and women arrived in Britain under this scheme, which
was one of several recruiting Europeans, including bulk recruitment from
Italy and a 1946 Ministry of Labour scheme to recruit Irish workers for coal
mines. European Volunteer Workers were refugees who had ended the war
in what were called 'displaced persons' camps' in Germany and Austria, but
the government argued that 'displaced person' was a pejorative term, and
renamed them 'volunteer workers'.

Initially, those arriving under this scheme were mainly Poles, Ukrainians,
Yugoslavians, Estonians, Latvians, and Lithuanians. Recruitment was later
extended to Sudeten Germans and Austrians. Intermarriage, which had led
the Royal Commission on Population to rule out the recruitment of non-
white people from the empire, was canvassed in a Parliamentary debate in
1947 as a positive benefit of the recruitment of men from displaced persons'

camps, 'We are suffering from the falling birth-rate of the late 20s and 30s and have no fewer than 200,000 numerically surplus women. I believe that is an unfortunate sociological factor... On the assumption that we should take mainly single men, there are the strongest possible reasons for having an infusion of vigorous young blood from overseas at the present time'.[14]

European Volunteer Workers were widely labelled 'suitable' or ideal' immigrants—in Parliament, in the press, and by the Royal Commission on Population.[15] A leading article about the scheme, in *The Times* in 1947, argued that 'without the aid of suitable immigrants a serious deficiency of mobile and adaptable workers cannot be avoided in years to come'. For the government, as well as *The Times*, the flexibility of the workforce it recruited was a main advantage of the scheme. As aliens employed on a contract basis, European Volunteer Workers could be directed into 'essential industries' where there were shortages of labour. The leaflet issued in displaced persons' camps told them:

> Workers will enter Great Britain for an initial period of twelve months subject to good behaviour and to the specific condition that they undertake only employment selected by the Ministry of Labour and National Service, and on the clear understanding that they will only be allowed to change their employment with the consent of that department.[16]

The employment selected by the Ministry of Labour was in limited areas—70 per cent of European Volunteer men were directed into agriculture and mining, and 90 per cent of women into textiles and institutional domestic service.[17] As aliens, European Volunteer Workers had to report to the police when they wanted to change their address or job. If unsatisfactory, they could be deported. Historian Kathleen Paul argues that 'Britain maintained its image as a liberal democratic country even as aliens were compelled to accept specific jobs in designated areas'.[18] But this was not the idea of Britain that a Serbian man who was recruited to work in the Scottish coalfields remembers:

> After the [first] year, I was expecting I'll be free and I can change the job. On the contrary, I was called in by the police and told I cannot leave the present job. I have to stay another two years. I was astounded, I couldn't believe... The policeman told me that if you leave without our knowledge be assured that wherever you go the police will get you and you'll be brought back to this place... And it came to my mind, what country am I in? Am I in a free democratic Britain or somewhere else?[19]

Few Jews who had ended the war in displaced persons' camps were recruited as European Volunteer Workers. The Foreign Office instructed that: 'the situation in Palestine, and anti semitics (*sic*), clearly prevent the recruitment of Jews'.[20] Most of the very limited numbers of Jewish survivors of the Holocaust who were admitted to Britain came under a scheme allowing 'distressed foreigners' to join relatives in Britain, which was designed so that the numbers who would qualify 'would be in 100s rather than 1000s'. The Foreign Secretary, voicing anxieties about 'the concentration of large numbers of refugees, especially Jewish refugees, in the towns', suggested that to avoid such concentration, young Jewish men should be encouraged to work in agriculture, and Jewish women steered into hospital work.[21] The persistence of anti-Semitism in Britain in the aftermath of war is demonstrated by the anti-Jewish riots in Manchester, Liverpool, Eccles, and Salford in 1947, following the hanging of two British sergeants in Palestine by the Jewish paramilitary Irgun group.[22]

In 1949, the Royal Commission on Population welcomed the possibility of continued immigration from Ireland. Between 1945 and 1951, 70,000–100,000 Irish arrived in Britain, most of them seeking work.[23] During the war, the government of Éire had been anxious that Irish war workers and Irish volunteers for the British forces would return to Ireland in large numbers when the war ended, saturating the job market in Éire. In 1942, Éamon De Valera, the Irish Taoiseach, writing to the Finance Minister, anticipated that this might involve the return of as many as 250,000 men and women. These anxieties proved unfounded. Historian Bernard Kelly comments, 'Despite the apocalyptic fears of the De Valera government, the mail boats from Holyhead to Dun Laoghaire were not crammed with Irish returnees in 1945. Britain was rebuilding in 1945 and needed workers from all over Europe. The Irish answered in their droves'.[24] Those who had returned to Éire when the war was over were often attracted back to Britain by the prospect of jobs. It was not easy to get jobs in Ireland, as the *Irish Times* reported in January 1947:

> Southern Ireland is a depressed area for ex-Servicemen. Their chances of obtaining employment are understandably small, with the competition of men released from the [Irish] Defence Forces here, and it is no secret that great numbers of them have been compelled to return to England, after the expiration of the demob leave, to seek employment there.[25]

Irish women also migrated to Britain—the majority of Irish migrants to Britain in the twentieth century were female, most of them young single migrant workers. Some arrived—as Mary Mulry had arrived earlier—to train as nurses. By 1951, 11 per cent of nurses and midwives in Britain were Irish.[26]

Schemes to recruit labour from the colonies were very limited. In discussions about the possibility of such recruitment in 1948, a government working party set out the range of Europeans recruited to the British labour market since the war, but recommended only a very limited and experimental scheme to bring in women from British colonies to work as hospital domestics, noting that 'a large majority of any workers brought here would be coloured, and this fact has been borne in mind throughout our discussions'. The report ruled out the possibility of recruiting women from the Caribbean to work in textiles: 'It is unlikely that West Indian women could stand up to the Lancashire climate for any length of time ... [and] ... it was understood that most of the women available were illiterate and thus unlikely to make suitable textile operatives'.[27]

When the *Empire Windrush* arrived in 1948—with 492 West Indian men on board and a woman stowaway—eleven Labour Members of Parliament wrote to Clement Attlee, the Labour Prime Minister, that 'an influx of coloured people domiciled here is likely to impair the harmony, strength and cohesion of our public and social life'. Their letter suggested control of immigration 'by legislation if necessary'.[28] The post-war Labour government ruled out legislation—they wanted to avoid strengthening colonial nationalist movements or damaging Commonwealth unity. But they set up a committee in 1950 to review 'further means which might be adopted to check the immigration into this country of coloured people from British Colonial Territories'.[29] A similar committee, set up by the Conservative government in 1955, to look at the possibility of immigration controls noted that 'coloured immigration has become an ominous problem which cannot now be ignored', but decided against legislation.[30] These committees were secret.[31] In 1954, the Home Secretary advised against the announcement of a committee, because 'even to contemplate restricting immigration from the Colonies would be a step toward breaking up the Empire, and in other quarters it would be regarded as evidence that the Government are in favour of a colour bar'.[32]

Both the Labour government, from 1950, and subsequent Conservative administrations used informal methods to discourage black and Asian migration to Britain, particularly through requests to colonial governments to restrict the issue of passports and other travel documents.[33] Even so, the war generated some limited migration to Britain. In the 1950s the commander of a unit of Punjabi Sikhs, who needed labour to make car accessories in his family firm in Southall, drew on his old servicemen's networks to recruit Sikhs from Jullundur.[34] A number of West Indians who had served in the forces in wartime Britain and who were demobbed back home when the war was over subsequently returned to Britain—some of them on board the *Empire Windrush*.

The return of West Indians had not been anticipated in government plans to discourage them from staying on in Britain when the war was over. The War Cabinet's recommendation in 1942—that service departments should reduce opportunities for West Indian servicemen to be demobilized in Britain to a minimum—was followed in 1945 by similar recommendations at the Ministry of Labour on the future of West Indian technicians doing war work in Britain, 'As they are British subjects we cannot force them to return, but it would be undesirable to encourage them to remain in this country. We should, therefore, take immediate advantage of every expression in favour of repatriation as the longer the men stay here, the less ready they will be to go'.[35]

There were no reservations about forcing Chinese seamen who had served in the wartime merchant navy to return (see Figure 7.1.). Their repatriation and deportation is a comparatively little-known and shameful episode in post-war British history. Government plans were made soon after the war ended in October 1945:

[I]t has not hitherto been possible to get rid of them. Now, however, the China coast is open again and it is proposed to set in motion the usual steps for getting rid of foreign seamen whose presence here is unwelcome. All these men are on temporary landing conditions and the shipping companies whom they have served and who are supporting most of them can now provide ships to take them back to China. It is proposed, therefore, that those who are here temporarily should have their landing conditions varied so as to require them to depart by the ships in question. If they refuse to do so, it will be necessary to make Deportation Orders against them.[36]

A report by an Immigration Officer shows a thoroughgoing operation in 1946:

In order to spread the net as widely as possible I have, within the last few days circulated all Chief Constables throughout Great Britain. Pool deserters and other Chinese seamen engaged in unauthorised shore employment have been located as far afield as Hereford and Greenock and when the operation is completed within the next few days I shall be satisfied that every possible step has been taken to secure a maximum repatriation of Chinese.[37]

By July 1946, this operation had secured the repatriation of 1,362 Chinese seamen.[38] Some had British-born wives and partners, who organized a defence association in Liverpool to campaign for the rights of seamen's families. Marion Lee, organizer of the association, stated: 'We are left to live on public aid, charity, and the help of our families'.[39] British-born wives and partners had no information about what had happened—many thought their men had abandoned them. Most British-born wives, partners, and children of Chinese seamen who were repatriated and deported never saw them again.

Staying On

In the immediate aftermath of war there was little support—in either official or popular opinion—for the idea that people who had arrived in Britain in wartime should be able to stay on. The deportation of Chinese seamen by the government was kept secret, but there was considerable support for the idea of repatriation of other groups. In September 1945, *The Times* carried a message for refugees from the continent who had spent the war in Britain. They should now go back:

> Many people are concerned at the continued presence in this country of so many foreign refugees. While they were welcomed when their countries were overrun by the Germans, it is felt that the time has arrived when special efforts should be made to repatriate them now that their homelands have been liberated. The countries of which they are nationals need their services for the tasks of reconstruction, and yet they are allowed to remain undisturbed.[40]

The article made clear that those who should go back included people who had served in the armed forces, and named Poles, Czechs, and German Jews as groups that were occupying houses 'badly wanted by homeless Britons'.

This message in *The Times* corresponded closely to wartime government thinking. The Home Secretary, Herbert Morrison, had reservations about Polish settlement in Britain, expressing concerns about the effect this would have on 'all those many aliens who desire to stay here and claim they have rendered assistance to the war effort'.[41] During the war, Morrison had also forbidden naturalization to Austrians and Germans who had come to Britain as refugees and refused to offer any guarantee of settlement, even for those serving in the British forces.

Germans and Austrians who fought their way back to Germany and served in the British army of occupation rarely wanted to stay on in Germany after they were demobbed. German refugees in Britain rarely wanted to return to Germany. A press statement issued by the Association of Jewish Refugees in June 1945 stated, 'To the Jews from Germany their former country is the graveyard of their families. There are no bonds left between them and Germany. In their overwhelming majority they have no desire to return to the country where these atrocities were committed and be compelled to live amongst people who perpetrated the murder of the Jews or connived in these crimes. They prefer to live anywhere else in the world rather than in Germany'.[42]

The continued status of Germans who served in the British army of occupation in Germany as aliens meant that return to Britain after demob brought problems of adjustment. A demobbed officer wrote:

> Those of us who have served abroad cannot quite free ourselves from a feeling of disillusion. Yesterday, we were still members of that conquering British Army, true 'masters' in Germany; now, at the Dispersal Centre, it was driven home to us with a bang: Special questionnaires for Aliens! A few days later, we had to queue for our little grey identity book.[43]

Peter Sinclair, who had come to Britain on the *Kindertransport* and volunteered for the Royal Fusiliers in 1943, remembers:

> When I was demobbed at the end of 1947, I had to report to Hampstead police station as an alien. And the police sergeant looked at me and said 'How bloody stupid'. Anyway, I became an alien. Twenty-four hours later, I had to report to a Justice of the Peace, behind the police station, to swear allegiance to King George VI and his successors. But it just goes to show, I was an alien again for twenty-four hours after having served in the army.[44]

Mark Lynton, who had been interned in 1940 under the government's mass interment policy, was also naturalized in 1947. He writes, 'On March 17, 1947, having been in British uniform for just over six years, an officer of His Majesty's Forces for over three, and dealing with rather complex Intelligence matters for eighteen months, I swore the Oath of Allegiance and became a British subject in due form. It was frankly no longer as much of a thrill as it should have been'.[45]

Austrians and Germans in Britain had begun campaigning against repatriation in 1944. Herbert Morrison's opposition to their naturalization was not shared by other officials at the Home Office and his wartime policy was effectively overruled by Churchill's two-word reply to a question in the

House of Commons, asking whether arrangements could be made for the immediate repatriation of Jewish refugees, 'No sir'. Applications for British naturalization burgeoned after the war ended. The majority of Austrians and Germans decided to remain in Britain, not only in preference to returning to Germany, but also in preference to emigrating elsewhere. By 1950, many had applied for and been granted British naturalization.[46]

Morrison's reservations about Poles staying on in Britain were also subject to Churchill's intervention. On his return from the Yalta Conference, which had agreed that almost half of Polish territory would be consigned to the Soviet Union's sphere of influence, Churchill made a speech in the House of Commons, subsequently known as 'Churchill's pledge'. The speech expressed his earnest hope that Polish forces that had fought under the British flag might, if they desired, be offered citizenship of the British Empire. 'We should think it an honour' he stated 'to have such . . . faithful and valiant warriors dwelling among us as if they were men of our own blood'.[47]

The Yalta agreement was condemned by the Polish government-in-exile in London and regarded by most Poles in Britain as a shameful betrayal. On the day that the agreement was announced, a Polish pilot wrote to a friend, 'If the Germans get me now, I won't even know what I'm dying for. For Poland, for Britain, or for Russia?' The pilot was from the city of Lwow, which had been consigned to the Soviet Union under the Yalta agreement. He was killed over Germany ten days later.[48] Postal Censorship reported that the decisions made at the Conference 'have evoked a terrible shock amongst the Polish troops . . . they find that they are lost and betrayed'.[49] A censored letter by a Polish officer read:

> Now I want to tell you a few words as a Pole have to tell to his Britisher friend. When this morning we heard the news about the statements from the Big Three meeting [the Yalta Conference] we got deadly silent. Up to now I was one of the most trusting Pole (sic) in your policy which now I can call only as the policy of an ostrich hiding its head into the sand. You can think about our 'small' and 'too proud' nation as you like . . . but you just can't treat us worse than you treat countries which didn't put up any effort at all to help you against Germany. We sacrificed most of all countries—more than you even. We trusted you so much, and what have we got. Our biger (sic) friend let us go down.[50]

Another Polish soldier wrote, 'For the last few days I have been in a state of dumb bewilderment . . . It is the Fifth Partition of Poland, and what we are living through, mentally, I cannot tell you'.[51]

The Yalta agreement meant that Polish responses to the end of the war in Europe were very far from celebratory. On the day that Germany surrendered, an entry in the Diary of 305 Polish Bomber Squadron recorded, ' "Victory!" every Anglo-Saxon says in greeting instead of the traditional "Hello!". The word "Victory!" is devoid of meaning, power and any sense today only for the Poles'.[52] A Polish officer wrote in a censored letter:

> When the loudspeakers announced the end of the war—I was not happy. I abstained with difficulty from the weeping. The weeping of an immeasurable pain. I am an old soldier. I took part in a number of battles. And I was happy that I was left alive. I did it because I was sure that it happened for my destination for a beautiful future and now? The end of the war indicates for me:—the certainty that I'll never more see my beautiful fatherland—the certainty that I'll never see my family and friends—the certainty that the ideas for which I fought about 6 years never have existed—the beginning of leading a homeless life. Bitter words. Bitter minds. But can they be other?[53]

Despite Churchill's post-Yalta pledge in February 1945, the Labour government elected in July encouraged Poles to go back to Poland. A letter sent by Foreign Secretary Ernest Bevin to all Polish forces under British command told them that no guarantees could be offered on settlement in British territory at home or overseas. The main burden of Bevin's message was clear: 'They [His Majesty's Government] consider it to be the duty of all members of these [Polish] forces who possibly can do so to return to their home country without further delay under the conditions now offered them in order that they may make their contribution to the restoration of the prosperity of liberated Poland. Only thus can they serve their country in a manner worthy of her great traditions'.[54]

The decision about returning or staying was not an easy one for Poles who had already been living in exile for several years. Many were from Eastern Poland and, like Zbigniew Siemaszko, had been deported to the Soviet Union after the Soviet invasion of Eastern Poland in 1939. They had little reason to believe Stalin's promise of 'free elections' in Poland at the Yalta Conference, or his statement that 'it is not only a question of honour for Russia, but one of absolute necessity, to have Poland independent, strong and democratic'. Postal Censorship reported, 'thousands of letters written by Polish soldiers in the last days repeats as a cardinal topic that to Poland governed by communist they won't return'. One soldier wrote, 'I will never go back to Poland if she is under Russian control because I don't want to be in the Red Russian Paradise. It is better to die than to go there'. Another stated, 'Believe me it's no good at all to go to sovietised Poland where anyone even with British passport can be very easy (*sic*) sent to Siberia for many years'. A third wrote, 'I wonder what we shall do, now that all our hopes have proved in vain. Under these conditions I do not want to go back to Poland. Being still a Pole, my place could only be Siberia, and I would sooner commit suicide than go there again'.[55]

Stanisław, who had been deported to Siberia by the Soviet Union and came out under the 'amnesty' of 1941 to join the Polish army in Palestine, remembers:

> When I was in Siberia I was planning in my head to run to Poland, because...Siberia was terrible. We had no food. I was dreaming to go back to Poland. I would have gone on foot. At the end of the war I was hoping we would go back to Poland, because the war finished. But at that time my territory was occupied by the Russians. Well who wants to go back to the Russians when they gave me so much suffering in my lifetime, who wants to go to Poland when the Russians were occupying. If Poland was free I would have gone back when the war finished.[56]

The Labour government finally honoured 'Churchill's pledge' in autumn 1946 through the establishment of the Polish Resettlement Corps as a non-combatant unit of the British army under War Office command. In 1947, the Polish Resettlement Act allowed Poles who stayed on to take up permanent residence in Britain. According to historian Jerzy Zubrzycki's figures, 86,000 Poles had returned to Poland from the United Kingdom by 1948 and 114,000 Polish soldiers had enlisted in the Polish Resettlement Corps—17,000 officers, 92,000 men, and 5,000 women. By 1949, they had been joined by 31,800 dependants.[57] These included many children, deported to Siberia by the Soviet Union with their parents, who had come out of the Soviet Union under the so-called 'amnesty' and spent the war in refugee camps in Iran, Palestine, Pakistan, India, and East Africa.

The government's initial willingness to repatriate Polish soldiers when the war was over contrasted with its unwillingness to repatriate German prisoners of war. The numbers of prisoners held in Britain actually increased once the war was over and the numbers of German prisoners in employment peaked at 362,000 in the summer of 1946. To meet shortages of labour, particularly in agriculture, the government brought in 118,000 prisoners of war from the United States and Canada.[58] Fritz Zimmerman was one of these. Held in Africa and then in Canada, he was told in July 1946 that he would be going home soon. Instead, he was shipped to Britain and put to work potato-picking.

He was not released until August 1947.[59] There were also government schemes for Italian and German prisoners of war to stay on in Britain, designed mainly to address the shortage of labour on farms. In 1946, Italian ex-prisoners could stay on under a scheme that bound them to work in agriculture for four years.[60] A similar scheme for German prisoners of war, introduced in 1947, also required them to commit themselves to agriculture.

The very slow rate of repatriation of prisoners and the increase in the numbers held in Britain caused considerable controversy. There were campaigns and petitions to release the prisoners. Accusations that they were being used as slave labour were made in the press and in Parliament. An article in the *Daily Mirror* arguing that prisoners should be given a release date was entitled 'Slaves'. Richard Stokes, a Labour Member of Parliament, said in the House of Commons in March 1946 that, 'They [Allied governments] are doing some of those very things for which we are trying the war criminals at Nuremberg, such as forcible detention and slave labour—because it is nothing else when German nationals are detained as they are here'. The *Manchester Guardian* called the work done by prisoners of war 'a form of forced or conscript labour that is absolutely repugnant to British traditions and especially to the traditions of the British Labour movement'.[61]

When Bob Moore comments that the British government turned prisoners of war from 'liabilities into assets', he is writing about wartime policies and the wartime need for labour.[62] The government had also turned Austrian and German refugees into assets in wartime, recruiting them to the British forces and to war work. In the aftermath of war, the government once more used prisoners of war and refugees to meet demands for labour in 'essential industries'. Schemes to recruit people from displaced persons' camps as European Volunteer Workers, to bring in prisoners of war when the war was over, and to recruit prisoners to stay on and work on farms, demonstrate a continuation of wartime policies. The government was able not only to recruit but also to control this labour, turning prisoners and refugees from liabilities into assets, both during the war and in its aftermath.

Change of Climate

Many people who spent time in wartime Britain remember facing greater discrimination and hostility when the war was over. Sam King, who served in the RAF, returned to Jamaica at the end of the war, but then sailed back to Britain on the *Empire Windrush*. He noticed a change from wartime attitudes when he returned, with people 'more aggressive' and 'trying to say that you shouldn't be here'.[63] The question, 'Why don't you go back to Poland?' and the phrases 'bloody Pole' and 'bloody foreigners' recur in accounts by Polish people of their reception in Britain in the late 1940s.[64] A Polish soldier who had been stationed in Scotland remembers, 'After the war, the Scottish people who, during the war, were very, very friendly, said 'why don't you go back to Poland?'[65] Miners in Fife organized a 'Poles Go Home' campaign.[66]

It was not only people who stayed on or returned who faced hostility. A Polish woman who was recruited as a European Volunteer Worker remembers, 'they treat us like a second class citizen. Sometimes they ask us why we not back to Poland'.[67] Another Polish woman records that a woman at her workplace said, 'I told you, you bloody foreigner, go away from here'.[68] In 1948, a *Daily Mirror* editorial, under the headline 'Let Them Be Displaced', described European Volunteer Workers as black marketeers and criminals. 'In taking in Displaced Persons wholesale', the editorial writer declared, 'we have had a bad deal. Too many are living or working in some dubious way. Some no doubt are in the Black Market. They live on our rations—and live very well. They add to our discomfort and swell the crime wave. This cannot be tolerated. They must now be rounded up and sent back'.[69]

In an unprecedented move, and one that was never subsequently extended to any other group of migrants, the Ministry of Labour set up a Committee on Publicity for the Education of Popular Opinion on Foreign Workers in 1947, with the intention of encouraging more favourable attitudes—not only to European Volunteer Workers, but also to other groups from the continent. They encouraged positive media coverage and appointed a Public Relations Officer to orchestrate such publicity. The Committee found that popular opinion about European Volunteer Workers included the view that they were Fascists who had fought for the Germans, 'some of the scum of Europe' and 'the Jews of Europe'.[70]

One product of the Ministry of Labour's efforts was a documentary made by the Central Office of Information and also shown on television—*Code Name: Westward Ho!* (1949).[71] The film drew on the Committee's findings to rehearse a number of objections to European Volunteer Workers through a range of British voices commenting on their arrival and employment. These hostile voices accuse them of black marketeering and fighting on the side of the Germans in the Second World War and call them 'the scum of Europe', but are countered by other British voices stating that 'really, they're like us'—a main message of the film. A BBC programme entitled 'Focus on European Workers' also attempted to incorporate a range of views and to answer criticisms and allegations. But a substantial proportion of letters received by the BBC about this programme expressed the view that charity begins at home and that the writers were 'tired of foreigners in Britain and what about putting Britain first'.[72]

The view that some of those who arrived as European Volunteer Workers had fought for the Germans was not without foundation. War criminals of a range of nationalities entered Britain under this scheme.[73] In 1948, the *Daily Mirror* carried a front-page story on the 8,000 Ukrainians in Britain, who had arrived in Britain in the spring of 1947 as prisoners of war, but had their status changed to that of European Volunteer Workers. The reporter quoted what a police inspector had told him about his encounter with Ukrainians, 'Some of them, who speak a little English, after getting drunk, tell us they fought against us in the Ukrainian Division of the *Wehrmacht*. Some of our local boys did some fighting too, and naturally they don't like that sort of talk'.[74]

Accusations that they were Fascists who had fought with the Germans were also made against Poles in Britain. This accusation came in the context of widespread British admiration for the Soviet war effort, and the reluctance of many Poles to return to their country after the Yalta agreement. As early as 1944, four Polish mechanics serving in 307 Squadron RAF, who visited the De Havilland works, were booed by workers there—many of these workers wore red stars.[75] One Trade Union official reported that 'when urging the employment of Poles he was frequently met at meetings with the statement that Poles were ex-Fascists'.[76] The Communist Party of Great Britain claimed that at least one third of Poles in Britain had fought with the Germans, and published a leaflet entitled *No British Jobs for Fascist Poles*. Anti-Catholicism also occasionally surfaced in reaction to Poles settling in Britain. Rumours circulated about the conspiracies of Polish Catholics to widen the influence of the papacy in Britain.[77]

In 1944, Postal Censorship reported the development of increasing animosity against Polish soldiers expressed in letters by British soldiers, in contrast to their previous admiration for Polish martial qualities. The report explained that this development 'in some cases…appears to be due to the Polish attitude vis-á-vis Russia'. One British soldier wrote, 'The Polish

soldiers I have met have on the whole disgusted me by their attitude to the
Soviet Union...It is quite evident that they one and all have a deep rooted
hatred against the USSR, and try to quote their own personal experiences
to justify it'.[78] There was nevertheless some support for Churchill's description of 'faithful and valiant warriors'. A letter to the *Lancashire Evening Post*
commented, 'No British soldier who has fought alongside the Polish troops
in the Eighth Army in Africa, at Arnhem, Monte Cassino etc. would deny
that they are entitled to the same consideration as any of our own lads...The
services rendered by the 400 Polish pilots who fought in the Battle of
Britain will never be forgotten by decent minded people'.[79]

Many people did forget these services, airbrushing Poles from the history
of the Battles of Britain, Tobruk, Arnhem, Falaise, and Monte Cassino. They
included a delegate at the Brighton Trades Union Congress Conference
who asked, 'How do the people of Liverpool feel when they see these
Poles...strutting about our streets, when our...heroes from Arnhem,
pilots from the Battle of Britain, have to take their wives and families and
go squatting? How do they feel when accommodation is supplied for these
people?'[80] Representatives at this Conference were opposed to members of
the Polish army staying on in Britain. The Gallup Poll in the same year
which found that 56 per cent of respondents did not agree that Poles who
wanted to stay in Britain should have the right to do so showed considerable
support for this view.[81]

The accommodation that was supplied for Poles who joined the Polish
Resettlement Corps and was condemned by the Conference delegate was
in vacated British, American, or Canadian barracks, which were renamed
'workers' hostels'.[82] It was generally under this name that ex-barrack and
prisoner-of-war camps were also used to accommodate European Volunteer
Workers, Italians who came to Britain under bulk recruitment schemes,
and some Irish migrants. In the late 1940s, many migrant workers therefore
lived in Nissen huts, ate communally, and slept in dormitories. There was
little comparable provision for non-white migrants, who usually had to make
their own arrangements. In their search for rooms to let, many of them
encountered the view that there was no longer a place for them in Britain.
Advertisements for private rentals regularly announced 'no coloureds'. As
late as 1965, the Milner Holland report on housing in London found that
only 11 per cent of accommodation advertised for private rental did not
include these words.[83]

Discrimination in the housing market was not confined to non-white people. 'No coloureds, no Irish' was a common sign on rooms to let. Others read 'no Irish, no Poles' and in some areas 'no Poles or East Europeans'.[84] A Pole who had served in the RAF remembers:

> Victoria Station holds different memories for different people. To me it is the place where I realised that after twelve years in the air force (Polish, French and Royal Air Force) I was now a civilian in a brand new demob suit...First was a visit to my future employer in Earls Court who had to sign one of my documents...A police station had to be notified of my presence in London...I looked for a bedsit...some adverts in shop windows clearly stated 'Room to let but Irish and Polish need not apply'.[85]

Discrimination was also encountered in the search for employment. Eddie Noble—a Jamaican airman who arrived in Britain in 1943 to join the RAF—made many applications for civilian jobs after discharge from the RAF, but was always rejected. In one interview he was told that the post had been wrongly advertised as 'senior clerk', when it was in fact for 'junior clerk' and would not pay enough for him to live on. Noble, calling his interviewer's bluff, invented 'private means', which he said, meant that he was prepared to accept a modest salary. Even so, he was rejected for the post, on the grounds that colleagues would refuse to work with him:

> When it was a question of risking my life fighting for this country, the colour of my skin was irrelevant, now that the war was over it was a different ball game altogether. I was so livid, I told him exactly what I thought of his lame excuses and what he could do with his offer to reimburse my fares and, believe me when I tell you, it was unprintable.[86]

Eventually Noble rejoined the RAF. There were riots against black communities in London in 1947 and in Liverpool in 1948.[87]

Gerald Beard, who had joined the RAF in 1943, went back to Jamaica when the war was over, but subsequently returned to Britain. He remembers the contrast between wartime and post-war attitudes, 'Well, they actually turned on us after the War, saying "the War is over now, we don't want you"...In the Air Force we did not come up against a lot of prejudice because we were secluded. We didn't have to go looking for a job, we didn't have to go and look for accommodation...but once you came out in civilian life you had to come up against them. You had to find a job and find a place to live and that sort of thing...we found a lot of prejudice'.[88]

Renee Webb served as an airman, first in Jamaica and then in Britain from 1944 to 1945, and has similar memories:

> I was terribly concerned at that time that people should have forgotten so easily...I was terribly upset and concerned about it, when they began to call you names. I mean some of the many questions that were asked of me, one of the main ones was, 'When are you going back'?[89]

Not all memories are of prejudice and discrimination. Eddie Noble records a conspicuous act of kindness after he rejoined the RAF, when he lost his wallet late at night, could not get back to his camp without a ticket, and went to the Women's Voluntary Service all-night canteen to ask for help. One of the volunteers there told him:

> She...had a car of rather ancient vintage (her words), and was allowed sufficient petrol to go about her WVS work. As soon as her relief arrived at 5 am she would drive me to camp herself; which indeed she did. About a week later I paid another visit to the canteen in order to thank her...my benefactress was not on duty, but I learnt that that kind lady by driving me to camp had used up all her petrol allowance for the rest of the month and had to use public transport or walk to go about her charitable work.[90]

In telling the story of his life in the war years and the aftermath of war, Noble says that what he tries to do is to relate an incident of friendship and kindness for every incident of discrimination that he experienced or heard about.[91] Even so, he begins his account, 'this is the story of my life as an airman and the rejection I met as a civilian once the war was over'.[92] The rejection he experienced was part of a wider pattern of discrimination and hostility experienced by people who had served in the Allied war effort and a wider forgetting of their contributions that was very evident in the British media and in public memories of the war.

'Allies' War' Ends

The True Glory (1945)—the Anglo-American documentary that tells the story of the Allied victory in Europe from D-Day to German surrender—registers the end of the war in Europe by the sound of loud firing gradually fading out. A British voice comments, 'At one minute after midnight, May 9th 1945, the guns stopped'. Then, against shots of uniformed men at a conference table, an American voice comments, 'Now it starts. All the arguments about who won the war. Well here's what I say, that no country on earth could have won it alone. So what does that mean? That anybody who wants to take a bow by himself is not only boasting, but nuts'. By these standards, many Allied nations proved to be 'nuts'. The vision of an 'allies' war' and the wartime 'culture of tribute' both faded rapidly in the aftermath of war as the British, like the Americans and the Soviets, increasingly took a bow by themselves.

British cinema produced a prolific cycle of films on the Second World War in the 1950s, but their tributes were mainly confined to the British war effort and to the military, largely dispensing with attention to wartime allies, to women and to civilians. They installed British military heroes—often officers—at the centre of exciting action. Post-war government publications downplayed the Allied contribution to the war effort in favour of the British.[93] On VE (Victory in Europe) day, the walls of Broadcasting House were festooned with the flags of the Allied nations. Inside the building, the BBC was less celebratory of the Allied effort. In an early memorandum on plans for Victory Day, Basil Nicolls, the BBC's Programme Controller, urged his production heads to focus on the British war effort, 'In the course of the celebrations there will no doubt be the usual tendency in this country to praise everyone but ourselves. In spite of this we should keep in our minds as a background to our programmes the fact that we stood alone in 1940 and there would have been no victory if it had not been for our resistance then and since.[94] In 1940, Nicolls had instructed departments to emphasize the war effort as Allied, not British. Now that was reversed. Nicolls's view in 1945 that 'we stood alone in 1940' was in strong contrast to the view he took in 1940, but was widely circulated in the aftermath of war. When the fighting was over, the focus was on national victory and national heroes and the wartime vision of a multinational community of allies receded.

Other nations also focused on national victory and heroes, and in Britain there was increasing concern about Americans taking 'a bow by themselves', ignoring the British–American alliance and the British war effort. The Hollywood production *Objective Burma!* (1945), which presented the Burma campaign as one fought by American troops, produced a storm of protest from reviewers.[95] Three popular newspapers advocated withdrawal of the film when it was first screened in Britain in September 1945. A cartoon in the *Daily Mirror* by Philip Zec showed a Hollywood mogul seated in a studio chair, surrounded by scripts proclaiming the all-American defence of London, the all-American defence of Stalingrad, and the all-American Burma front. Tiny crosses stick up under his chair, labelled 'Britain's sacrifice for world freedom' and a man pointing to them tells him, 'Excuse me but you're sitting on some graves'.[96]

E. Arnot Robertson, reviewing Objective Burma! in the Daily Mail, wrote:

> After seeing Errol Flynn at the head of his band of American Commandos, liberating the jungle practically single-handed—that is until just before the end, when he is supported by masses of American infantry, American tanks and the might of the US Air Force—after this I shall no longer be surprised if a film is produced in which the Eagle Squadron wins the Battle of Britain for us by itself.[97]

Alvah Bessie, one of the team of scriptwriters, later explained why Objective Burma! showed Americans liberating Burma 'practically single-handed':

> My job was to go back to my office and work up an original story for Errol Flynn. So you call up the research department and ask them to send over everything they have on the war in Burma. And it does not take more than an hour's reading to discover that the war in Burma is strictly a British operation, so you call up your producer and say, 'Look, Jerry, there are no American troops in Burma', and he says, 'so what? It's only a moving picture'. It was a good story, if you don't mind the fact that Burma was a British show and was not commanded by Errol Flynn.[98]

Americans taking a bow by themselves became a government concern in 1952, when the first documentary series about the war shown on BBC television was an American import—the twenty-six-part Victory at Sea, made by the American National Broadcasting Company. When executives from the Company arranged for three episodes of Victory at Sea to be screened for Winston Churchill at Chartwell, where he often watched films, his principal private secretary reported that he 'went up in smoke'. Victory at Sea commentaries on the British war at sea in 1940–41—years when Churchill had been First Lord of the Admiralty and then Prime Minister—were hardly designed to please him, with their judgement that this was 'a pitiful, feeble way of making war; hoping, praying, to dodge the enemy'. The Victory at Sea episode on D-Day was equally unlikely to go down well with Churchill. It made only one reference to the British forces.[99]

The BBC hired a naval historian to provide an introduction to the series, in an attempt to correct its pro-American perspective.[100] Screening of the series led to demands for a British series and there were questions in the House of Commons urging Service Ministries to release their wartime news films to the BBC, or other documentary producers, so that British films could be produced to balance the American production. 'Victory in the Air' and 'Victory on Land' were suggested titles.[101] When a British television series was eventually produced on the history of air warfare in the Second World War, the Director General of the BBC intervened to ensure that 'Victory in the Air' was not chosen as the title. He told the Director of Television Broadcasts, 'I have a feeling that it would be a good thing if we could find a title which was not so clearly a copy of Victory at Sea. Would something like Air Power do?'[102]

This fifteen-part BBC television documentary series—the first British television production on the history of the Second World War—was eventually named *War in The Air* and was shown on BBC television in 1954.[103] The series was highly praised by most reviewers and widely welcomed as a challenge to the earlier US production. The *Daily Sketch* called it 'the BBC's answer—and a complete answer too—to that fascinating American epic *Victory at Sea*'.[104] *The Times* commented: 'Already it is plain that the venture will rival in its absorbing interest its American counterpart, Victory at Sea'.[105] The *Daily Mail* expressed the 'earnest hope' that 'Americans who learned the story of Britain's war from the American series "Victory at Sea" will be shown this account too'.[106] The *Evening Standard* reviewer said: 'These are wonderful films which offer a challenge to the *Victory at Sea* series the Americans sent to us'.[107] *Reynolds News* hailed the programmes as 'Britain's answer to . . . *Victory at Sea* with its "alone-we-did-it" message to the world. *War in the Air* will tell British televiewers a different story to the narrative whose one-sidedness stirred up some resentment this side of the Atlantic'.[108]

Official concerns about *War in the Air* were rather different, shaped by the Cold War rather than Anglo-American rivalries. In the context of debates about the rearmament of West Germany, the British government was anxious not to cause offence to the West German government and considered censoring one episode of *War in the Air* because it showed Germany as a militaristic power. In correspondence about this proposal, Lord Salisbury made a succinct and revealing comment, 'It is of course true that the Germans are a warlike nation. That is why we want them on the side of the West'.[109]

Two years earlier, there had been similar concerns about the Soviet film, *The Fall of Berlin*, which portrayed the German invasion of the Ukraine, with shots of German brutality. At the Foreign Office, Frank Roberts thought that 'it was perhaps unfortunate that this 1949 film should appear at this time [1952] to revive memories of hostility towards Germany. On the other hand the film is hostile only to Hitler's Nazism and not to the German people'.[110] Censorship was considered and rejected, but there were concerns about the Soviet Union taking a bow by itself. The film told the story of the Great Patriotic War in which the Eastern front was the only significant battle, and opened at a major West End cinema—the first screening outside small cinemas and private showings of a Soviet propaganda film. Churchill asked for an introduction to be added to the film, 'to the effect that it gave only one aspect of the allied war effort'. The introduction pointed out that America and Britain had materially helped Russia, that this essential aid would never have reached the Red Army but for the courage and skill of the Royal Navy and the Merchant Navy, and that vital and courageous assistance had included the RAF's strategic bombing of Germany and Montgomery's victories in North Africa.[111]

In 1954, when the government was considering censoring the first episode of *War in the Air* because it showed Germany as a militaristic power, Churchill was once more involved. He minuted that he had watched the 'offending film' and continued, 'compared to the harm done by Lord Russell of Liverpool's book it is trivial'.[112] On the same day, apparently having difficulty in bringing himself to name the title of this book, he informed the Foreign Office, 'Lord Russell of Liverpool's book has already sold 60,000 copies and is being reprinted as fast as possible as the demand is very great'.[113] It is possible that Churchill, himself a substantial author, was offended by these sales figures, as well as by the book.

The title of Lord Russell's book published in 1954 was *The Scourge of the Swastika: A Short History of Nazi War Crimes.* Earlier that year, the government had attempted to prevent its publication. This attempted censorship was in the context of the Cold War and, as one official noted, a commitment to 'controlled German rearmament, and to a policy which contains, as an important element, belief in the possibility of a free Germany reborn on democratic lines'.[114] The book was therefore deemed 'offensive' because 'there is no doubt that many Germans would now be frightfully hurt by this book' and because 'it does little good to rake over the ashes of the past'.[115] *The Scourge of the Swastika* went through seven editions by 1955 and came out in paperback from Corgi in 1956. The initial demand for it, noted by Churchill, was probably fuelled by the considerable press coverage it received as a result of the government's attempt to ban it. The *Daily Express*, reporting this attempt under the headline 'Monstrous Act of Censorship' proceeded to serialize the book.[116]

Soviet successes on the Eastern Front had been widely celebrated in wartime Britain. Forgettings of these successes in the aftermath of war are striking. A report on public opinion polls in 1947 suggested that popular attitudes were slow to shift away from wartime admiration. Anti-Russian feeling was hardening 'slowly, painfully, but steadily', the report commented, while the large number of 'don't know' responses to questions could be attributed not only to lack of interest but also to hesitancy, in a context where news sources were distrusted as propagandist.[117] Some British reviewers of *The Fall of Berlin* criticized British neglect of the Soviet successes that the film celebrated. The *Sunday Times* and the *Evening Standard* not only commented on the film's silence about American and British aid to Russia in the early days of 1941–2, but also argued that this was no more reprehensible than the equal silence of most British and American war films on Russia's contribution to victory in 1943–4.[118] A review in *The Times* criticized the film's 'almost complete silence as to any part the British and Americans may have had in the successful outcome of the European war', but also noted that 'Russia is not the only nation to indulge in some exaggeration when recalling to its people the success of the national arms'.[119]

In the aftermath of war, the 'success of the national arms' became a dominant theme of public memories in Britain. This theme left little space for memories of the diversity of the population in wartime Britain and the diversity of forces that had fought with or alongside the British. Many of those who contributed to the Allied war effort in Britain were doubly forgotten—by the British and by their compatriots.

Remembering and Forgetting

A photograph of Miroslav Liskutin featured in *There's Freedom in the Air*, a pamphlet published by the British government in 1944. The pamphlet told 'a stirring and ennobling story' of Allied airmen from continental Europe who were fighting with the British. It offered fulsome praise of their heroism, their determination to continue the fight, their daring escapes from occupied Europe, and their role in the Battle of Britain. They had 'given their all in the cause of liberty and freedom'. The pamphlet urged: 'we on our side must never forget this'.[120]

In 1940, Churchill had viewed Allied contingents who arrived in Britain from occupied Europe as a significant asset, giving the war a 'broad, international character', which would 'add greatly to our strength and prestige'.[121] During the war, the British media regularly told stories like the ones that featured in *There's Freedom in the Air*, but these stories were rarely told after 1945. When the war was over, there was no further need to give the war a 'broad international character' and the message of *There's Freedom in the Air*— 'we on our side must never forget this'—was itself forgotten. Stirring and ennobling stories about the war continued to be told, but were now rarely about a multinational community of allies. The focus shifted to the war fought by the British—their courage and resolve, their finest hour, their victory.

Poles were excluded from the Victory Parade in London, held in June 1946. A woman interviewed by Michelle Winslow for an oral history of Polish émigrés remembers:

> Most of my compatriots are still very, very bitter about how the Polish forces were treated...my husband, who was in the Polish army under the British command, was not at the victory parade and we felt, well, betrayed if you want...Of course, one can understand that the political situation was such that Churchill probably didn't have any other choice, but it was very painful and it still is for very elderly people, still is a wound which is not cleaned at all.[122]

In contrast, Zbigniew Siemaszko had no wish to march in a parade which was about victory. He writes:

> June 8th [1946] was Victory Day...There were no public events to mark this in our camp. I went to Kinross and there too, everything was quiet. Polish army units in Scotland did not celebrate this anniversary because the Second World War had not provided the outcome we had hoped for and its ending was a complete defeat of the ideal of [Polish] independence. The overwhelming majority of Polish soldiers in the West were not fighting simply for the destruction of Nazi Germany, but rather, and above all, for the restoration of their country's independence. We felt it very strongly. For us, the war had ended in catastrophe. Personally, if I had been ordered to take part in the Parade, I would have done everything in my power to avoid it. Because for me, it would have been the 'Parade of Defeat'.[123]

Different explanations of the British government's failure to invite Polish contingents to march in the Victory Parade have been offered, including compliance with a request from the Soviet Union and a desire to avoid offending the Soviet Union.[124] General Władysław Anders, commander of the Polish Second Corps, which had fought in North Africa and Italy, records that twenty-five Polish airmen who had fought in the Battle of Britain were invited, but refused to attend a ceremony from which the Polish Army was excluded.[125] Norman Davies offers a different version of events. In July 1945, the British and American governments had withdrawn recognition from the Polish government-in-exile in London in favour of the Warsaw regime. This meant that, although Polish forces were invited to march, the invitation went to the Warsaw regime. According to Davies, it was only when the British government realised that Warsaw would not be sending representatives that it issued last-minute invitations to Polish Chiefs of Staff. These were courteously declined.[126]

Poles and Czechs who fought in the West were also increasingly forgotten in their own countries, which became satellites of the Soviet Union in the aftermath of war. After 1948, Miroslav Liskutin's fight and those of his compatriots in Britain not only went without honour in Czechoslovakia, but also made them liable to arrest. In Poland, the Battle of Lenino on the Eastern Front, where Poles and Soviets fought side by side, was officially remembered, while Poles who had fought in the Battles of Britain, Tobruk, Arnhem, Falaise, and Monte Cassino were forgotten.

Like Poles and Czechs who fought on the Western Front, Irish volunteers who served in the British forces were doubly neglected in the aftermath of war. Churchill had expressed his admiration for the Irish pilot, Brendan Finucane, in wartime and reiterated this expression of admiration in 1948 in the House of Commons, 'If ever I feel a bitter feeling rising in me in my heart about the Irish the hands of heroes like Finucane seem to stretch out to soothe it away'.[127] But this post-war tribute to Irish heroism was exceptional. When the war was over, Irish volunteers who had fought with the British were mostly forgotten heroes. At times, the idea that the Irish spied for the enemy, noted by Home Intelligence in wartime reports, resurfaced. Two British films released in the aftermath of war—*I See A Dark Stranger* (1946) and *Against the Wind* (1947)—show Irish women working as spies for Germany.[128]

In Ireland, the end of the war brought a relaxation of censorship and celebration of Irish volunteers in the British forces, including the publication of Rolls of Honour in some Irish newspapers. But Deputy Colley of Fianna Fáil, speaking in the Irish Dáil, described volunteers in the British army as 'people who think that the policy of neutrality adopted by the huge majority of our people was not sufficient for them'. He said, 'it is necessary to show them that their duty was first to their own country'.[129] Colley was speaking in support of an Order under the Emergency Powers Act, which sentenced deserters from the Irish army to seven years 'civil disability' if they returned to Ireland. Under this Order, the Irish government denied all soldiers who had deserted the Irish army, including those who had subsequently joined the British army, any rights to pay and pensions, and banned them from government employment for seven years.

Colley's views were echoed in the Irish newspaper, *The Leader*. 'Every citizen of this neutral state who joined a foreign army did an actual or potential wrong to his own country. The only place of honour and duty for an Irish soldier during the war was in the Irish army'.[130] Irish volunteers who served in the British forces and returned to Ireland when the war ended were occasionally treated with hostility, but historian Bernard Kelly argues that the main response to them was indifference.[131] In the dominant post-war Irish narrative of Ireland's war, neutrality had successfully asserted independence from Britain, maintained national unity, and enjoyed widespread popular support.[132] Within this narrative, there was no place for Irish volunteers who had worn British uniform.

Other groups who wore British uniform have also been doubly forgotten. The story of Jewish Germans who escaped to Britain and served in the British army is little known outside the community of German refugees and their descendants in Britain.[133] The dramatic story of Germans serving in the British army, who re-entered Germany as victors, with considerable authority over their former persecutors, has never been told on stage or screen. German Jews serving with the British were portrayed in an American film— *Tobruk* (1967)—but this portrayal has no counterpart in British cinema.[134] Most Italians who served in the British forces were also forgotten. Dennis Donnini continued to be honoured in Easington, and was listed in '100 North East heroes' in 2006, but this was exceptional. The focus of memorialization by the Italian community in Britain was on Italians who died when the *Arandora Star* went down and on Italian prisoners of war who died while they were held in Britain. Historian Wendy Ugolini argues that these dominant memories consign second- and third-generation Italians who served in the British armed forces to a 'commemorative no man's land'.[135]

Public memories have a history. Changes in the ways in which the Second World War was remembered are particularly apparent in the context of the Cold War thaw in the late twentieth century. Poles had been excluded from the Victory Parade in 1946 and were also excluded from ceremonies in

Britain marking the fortieth anniversary of the D-Day landings, in 1984. Ten years later, after the collapse of the Soviet Union, fiftieth-anniversary ceremonies were very different. One in Portsmouth, attended by the Queen, was also attended by Presidents Lech Wałęsa of Poland, Michal Kováč of Slovakia, and Václav Havel of the Czech Republic. They honoured the invited contingents of Czech, Polish, and Slovakian soldiers and airmen.

The Cold War thaw also meant that Poles and Czechs who fought on the Western Front were increasingly honoured in Poland and Czechoslovakia. In 1992 on 'soldier's day' in Poland, a victory parade in Warsaw united those who had fought on both the Eastern and the Western Fronts. They marched together.[136] *Dark Blue World*—a film about Czech airmen in the RAF and their subsequent imprisonment in Czechoslovakia—came out in 2001.[137] The film broke box-office records, after a state opening by President Havel, attended by dozens of veterans. Jan Sverak, director of the film, said 'It gives Czech airmen something they were not given by our society. It's a "thank-you". And a "sorry". The film immortalises them'.[138] In 2014, memorials to Czechs and Slovaks who fought in the RAF were unveiled in Prague and Bratislava.

A remaking of national memories was also apparent in Ireland, following the peace process of the 1990s. In April 1995 the Irish Taoiseach, John Burton, speaking at the Islandbridge National War Memorial, paid tribute to those Irish people, from North and South, who 'volunteered to fight against Nazi tyranny in Europe, at least 10,000 of whom were killed while serving in British uniforms'. He said that 'in recalling their bravery we are recalling a shared experience of Irish and British people... we remember a British part of the inheritance of all who live in Ireland'. In 2012, the Irish government apologized for the way those who deserted the Irish army to join the British army had been treated. In 2013, the Irish Dáil passed a bill granting them a pardon. Alan Shatter, Minister for Defence, said that this 'would help to make amends for the shameful way they were treated after World War II'.[139] Speaking of Irish volunteers in the British armed forces in the Second World War, he told the Dáil:

> For too long in this State we failed to acknowledge their courage and their sacrifice and for too long their contribution was airbrushed out of history as taught in our schools... In recent years this has changed and the role played by them has been documented and written about. That is as it should be. I hope this Bill provides a statutory foundation to ensure they are never again ignored or forgotten in narratives covering the Ireland of 1939 to 1945.[140]

In 2014, the Irish government was asked to lay a wreath at London's Cenotaph on Remembrance Sunday. Dan Mulhall, Ireland's ambassador to Britain, laid the wreath. The Irish Taoiseach commented that this was a mark of a more united people, signifying a stronger relationship between Ireland and Britain.

In the twenty-first century, there was increasing recognition of the contributions made by people of colour to the British forces. 'We Were There'—an exhibition sponsored by the Ministry of Defence—celebrated diverse contributions to the British military. A publication for schools, associated with the exhibition, bore the subtitle 'for 200 Years Ethnic Minorities Have Fought for Britain All Over the World '.[141] An exhibition at the RAF Museum in Cosford, entitled 'Diversity in the Royal Air Force', opened in 2009. Mohinder Singh Pujii—one of eighteen Indian pilots who joined the RAF in 1940—was the guest of honour at the opening of the exhibition and commented that he was 'still disgusted at the lack of recognition given to the role of black and Asian airmen and women during the war'.[142] Both exhibitions were subsequently criticized for skating over the history of racism in the British forces.[143]

The Memorial Gates on the top of Constitution Hill in London were unveiled by the Queen in 2002. The main inscription reads, 'In memory of the five million volunteers from the Indian sub-continent, Africa and the Caribbean who fought with Britain in the two World Wars'. A statue of Noor Inayat Khan—the Muslim woman of mixed Indian and American parentage who was murdered at Dachau concentration camp while serving in the Special Operations Executive—was unveiled in 2011 in Gordon Square, London, by Princess Anne. An exhibition on West Indians in the Royal Air Force, entitled 'Pilots of the Caribbean', opened at the RAF Museum in Hendon in October 2013. A memorial to African and Caribbean servicemen and servicewomen who fought in the First and Second World Wars was unveiled in Windrush Square, London, in June 2017.

T-shirts, as well as monuments, are sites of twenty-first-century memorialization. The diversity of the wartime RAF featured in an advertisement for a T-shirt sold by *The Guardian* newspaper, during the seventy-fifth anniversary of the Battle, in 2015, which told readers:

> Aircrews from across Europe, the USA, Australia, New Zealand, Canada, South Africa and all parts of what was then the British Empire joined the RAF in its 1940 battle for freedom. Polish aircrews made up the second largest nationality

among the 'The Few'. Proportional to their numbers, Polish battle successes and losses were higher than for any other nationality.

The T-shirt bore the names of all the Polish aircrew killed in action during the Battle of Britain under their air-force symbol and the slogan 'Za wolność' ('For Freedom').[144]

The twenty-first century also brought memorialization of the Polish Navy and Army. In 2013, a plaque commemorating the contribution of the Polish Navy to the Battle of the Atlantic was unveiled in Liverpool. In 2014, Polish soldiers were among those making a commemorative parachute jump, to mark the seventieth anniversary of the Battle of Arnhem.

Nine of the Polish names that featured on the Guardian T-shirt also appeared on an image widely circulated on Facebook and Twitter in 2014. The image showed a group of Polish pilots, in No. 303 Squadron, walking towards the camera from a Hawker Hurricane, at RAF Leconfield in October 1940. The photograph is part of the Air Ministry's Second World War collection, but the image on Facebook carried a caption which gave it a twenty-first century meaning—'Bloody Poles, coming over here, protecting our women and children'.

Jacek Saryusz-Wolski, the Polish politician whose father served in the Polish army-in-exile in Britain during the war, wrote another caption to the same photograph, with a distinctive twenty-first-century meaning. Using the hashtag, 'Brexit', he tweeted 'Bloody Poles, coming over here, taking away our jobs and social benefits!' A post on the website advertising the Guardian T-shirts made a similar connection between Poles who served in the wartime RAF and attitudes to Polish migrants who arrived in Britain after Poland joined the European Union in 2004, 'Bought this [T-shirt] for my son whose Polish grandfather served in the RAF during WWII. My father who later became naturalised and then a UK citizen would be saddened to hear the derogatory way that Poles are often talked about now'.[145]

Most twenty-first-century memorialization—whether in official ceremonies, in museum exhibitions, or on T-shirts—was of people who came to wartime Britain in uniform. Like wartime imagery of an 'allies' war', the main focus of such memorialization is on martial masculinity, sidelining women and those who arrived as civilians, émigrés, exiles, and refugees. However prominent as themes in the history of Britain in wartime and its aftermath, the movements of these groups to Britain are neglected in histories and memories dominated by a national frame of reference. Jewish refugees who escaped to Britain, especially the children who came on the *Kindertransport*, are more widely remembered. But these memories are select-ive, focusing on the sanctuary given by Britain and not the subsequent introduction of mass internment of enemy aliens, nor the deportations to Australia and Canada, nor the persistence of anti-Semitism in wartime, nor the anti-Jewish riots of 1947.

Civilians who served in the merchant navy have also been memorial-ized—the merchant navy had a higher death rate than any of the fighting services. As the generation that witnessed the war diminishes in number, the generations born during the war and in its aftermath have been increasingly involved in memorialization of their parents' generations. Two campaigns in Liverpool call for more recognition to be given to Norwegians and Chinese who served in the merchant navy. Maria Cunningham is the daughter of a Norwegian seaman and never knew her father, who died when his ship—the *Brant County*—was torpedoed and sunk in the Atlantic, in March 1943. Yvonne Foley is the daughter of a Chinese seaman and, like Maria Cunningham, never knew her father. She believes that he was one of the Chinese seamen deported by the British government at the end of the war.

Maria Cunningham pays tribute to Norwegian seamen:

> Thousands of them lost their lives and they helped you so much during the war...I think their families have got a right to grow up with the pride of what they did. That old saying 'All that it takes for evil to survive in the world is for good men to do nothing'. And I think these were good men, and I think they've done plenty.[146]

Yvonne Foley pays tribute to Chinese seamen:

> They brought the food in and out of the country, some of them died on board ship, quite a substantial number died, some of them were burnt, injured, and some of them were torpedoed and spent time at sea. They were kind of ignored. And what we set out to do was to acknowledge that they did exist. Aboard those ships, there were laundry men and nine times out of ten they were Chinese. The kitchen staff—nine times out of ten were Chinese. There were so many there, but do you ever see them? No you don't...Recognition should be given. Our way was putting up a memorial plaque.[147]

The plaque, shown in Figure 7.2, was installed at Liverpool Pier Head in 2006. Its inscription is in Chinese and English:

> To the Chinese Merchant Seamen who served this country well during both world wars.

Figure 7.2 The memorial plaque to Chinese merchant seamen, Liverpool Pier Head (by kind permission of Mark McNulty).

For those who gave their lives for this country—Thank You.

To the many Chinese Merchant Seamen who after both world wars were required to leave.

For their wives and partners who were left in ignorance of what happened to their men.

For the children who never knew their fathers. This is a small reminder of what took place. We hope nothing like it will ever happen again.

FOR YOUR MEMORY

Notes

INTRODUCTION

1. Mixing It: The Changing Faces of Wartime Britain, Imperial War Museum North.
2. Inge Weber-Newth and Johannes Dieter Steinert, *German Migrants in Post-war Britain: An Enemy Embrace* (London: Routledge, 2006), 24.
3. http://www.theguardian.com/politics/2016/jun/29/polish-war-veteran-saw-countrymen-give-lives-change-europe-for-better. Accessed 20 September 2016.
4. https://www.bnp.org.uk/news/national/bnp-policies-%E2%80%93-immigration-1. Accessed 17 October 2016. https://bnp.org.uk/policies/immigration/ Accessed 22 September 2017.
5. *Daily Express*, 20 May 1948.
6. File note, 18 May 1939, AIR 2/3654, The National Archives (TNA).
7. I am very grateful to Kawana (Kae) Pohe for permission to use this material about his brother.
8. http://www.nzonscreen.com/title/turangaarere-the-john-pohe-story-2008. Accessed 22 April 2015.
9. Ibid.
10. Bernard Kelly, *Returning Home: Irish Ex-Servicemen after the Second World War* (Dublin: Merrion, 2012), 100.
11. David Reynolds, *Rich Relations: The American Occupation of Britain, 1942–1945* (London: HarperCollins, 1995), 432–3.
12. *The True Glory* (Carol Reed and Garson Kanin, 1945).
13. Mollie Panter-Downes, ed. William Shawn, *London War Notes 1939–1945* (London: Longman, 1972), 318, 322.
14. Neil Wynn, ' "Race War": Black American GIs and West Indians in Britain during the Second World War', *Immigrants and Minorities*, 24/3 (2006), 324.
15. Colin Holmes, 'British Government Policy towards Wartime Refugees', in Martin Conway and José Gotovitch, eds., *Europe in Exile: European Exile Communities in Britain 1940–1945* (Oxford: Berghahn Books, 2001), 14.
16. Louise London, *Whitehall and the Jews, 1933–1948: British Policy and the Holocaust* (Cambridge: Cambridge University Press, 2000), 12.
17. Brian Read, *No Cause for Panic: Channel Islands Refugees 1940–1945* (Bradford on Avon: Seaflower Books, 1995), 2.

18. Johannes Kramer, *English and Spanish in Gibraltar* (Hamburg: Helmut Buske, 1986), 39.

19. Robert Allen, *Churchill's Guests: Britain and the Belgian Exiles During World War II* (Westport, CT: Praeger, 2003), 45.

20. I am grateful to Frank Grombir for this information.

21. John Seed, 'Limehouse Blues: Looking for Chinatown in the London Docks, 1900–40', *History Workshop Journal*, 62/1 (2006), 66, 68.

22. *Manchester Guardian*, 9 October 1941.

23. Madeleine Bunting, *The Model Occupation: The Channel Islands under German Rule 1940–1945* (London: HarperCollins, 1995), 148–54; 179–90.

24. David Howard, *The Shetland Bus* (Morley: Elmfield Press, 1976, first published 1951). I am grateful to Mike Paris for telling me about the Shetland Bus.

25. Philip Paris, *Orkney's Italian Chapel: The True Story of an Icon* (Edinburgh: Black and White Publishing, 2010).

26. Lucio Sponza, *Divided Loyalties: Italians in Britain during the Second World War* (Bern: Peter Lang, 2000), 231.

27. Tony Kushner and Kenneth Lunn, *The Politics of Marginality: Race, the Radical Right and Minorities in Twentieth Century Britain* (London: Frank Cass, 1990), vii; Panikos Panayi, 'The Historiography of Immigrants and Ethnic Minorities: Britain compared with the USA', *Ethnic and Racial Studies*, 19/4 (1996), 834–5; Kathy Burrell and Panikos Panayi, 'Immigration, History and Memory in Britain', in Kathy Burrell and Panikos Panayi, eds., *Histories and Memories: Migrants and their History in Britain* (London: I. B. Tauris, 2006), 16; Tony Kushner, *Remembering Refugees: Then and Now* (Manchester: Manchester University Press, 2006).

28. Michelle Hilmes, *Network Nations: A Transnational History of British and American Broadcasting* (New York and London: Routledge, 2012), 5.

29. Isabel Hofmeyr, 'AHR Conversation: On Transnational History', *American Historical Review*, 111/5 (2006), 1444; Marilyn Lake and Ann Curthoys, eds., *Connected Worlds: History in Transnational Perspective* (Canberra: ANU E Press, 2005), 5.

30. 'Allies in the Air War: Building an International Force', *The Times*, 14 March 1941.

31. http://genome.ch.bbc.co.uk/8a7eb7435e2643fb8e5deb5c2af39ec3.   Accessed 14 October 2015.

32. Jean Offenberg, *Lonely Warrior: The Action-journal of a Battle of Britain Fighter Pilot* (St. Albans: Mayflower Books, 1969, first published 1956), 54.

33. Pierre Lefranc, 'A Member of the Free French bears Witness', in Anne Corbett and Douglas Johnson, eds., *A Day in June: Britain and De Gaulle 1940* (London: Franco-British Council, 2000), 13.

34. Tadeusz Szumowski, *Through Many Skies: The Flying Days of One Polish Pilot* (Beverley: Highgate Publications, 1993), 70.

35. Robert Murray, *Lest We Forget: The Experiences of World War II Westindian Ex-Service Personnel* (Nottingham: Westindian Combined Ex-Services Association, 1996), 58.

36. Offenberg, *Lonely Warrior* (see n. 32), 96.
37. *Tree Fellers* (Sana Bilgrami, 2006). I am grateful to Marika Sherwood for lending a copy of this film.
38. 'Feelings about America and the Americans', 22 January 1943, Report no. 1569, Mass Observation Archive (MOA).
39. File Report 1885, August 1943, MOA.
40. Quoted in Steven O'Connor, 'Irish Identity and Integration within the British armed forces, 1939-1945', *Irish Historical Studies*, 39/155 (2015), 417–38.
41. Marika Sherwood, *Many Struggles: West Indian Workers and Service Personnel in Britain (1939–45)* (London: Karia Press, 1985); Tony Kushner, *The Persistence of Prejudice* (Manchester: Manchester University Press, 1989); Tony Kushner and David Cesarani, eds., *The Internment of Aliens in Twentieth-century Britain* (London: Frank Cass, 1993); Tony Kushner, *The Holocaust and the Liberal Imagination: A Social and Cultural History* (Oxford: Blackwell, 1994); Reynolds, *Rich Relations* (see n. 11); Louise London, *Whitehall and the Jews*; Gavin Schaffer, 'Re-thinking the History of Blame: Britain and Minorities during the Second World War', *National Identities* 8/4 (2006), 401–19; Tony Kushner, ' "Without Intending any of the Most Undesirable Features of a Colour Bar": Race Science, Europeanness and the British armed forces during the Twentieth Century', *Patterns of Prejudice*, 46/3–4 (2012), 339–74; John Belchem, *Before the Windrush: Race Relations in 20th-Century Liverpool* (Liverpool: Liverpool University Press, 2014).
42. Paul Addison and Jeremy Crang, eds., *Listening to Britain: Home Intelligence Reports on Britain's Finest Hour* (London: Bodley Head, 2010), 94.
43. Tony Kushner, *We Europeans? Mass Observation, 'Race' and British Identity in the Twentieth Century* (Aldershot: Ashgate, 2004), 219.
44. M50C, interviewed 29 June 1943, TC25 3/G, MOA.
45. Cy Grant, *A Member of the RAF of Indeterminate Race: World War Two Experiences of a West Indian Officer in the RAF* (Bognor Regis: Woodfield Publishing, 2006), 27.
46. Szumowski, *Through Many Skies* (see n. 34), 49–68.
47. Alan Wilmot, Imperial War Museum Sound Archive, Interview no. 31047, Reel 3.
48. Adam Zamoyski, *The Forgotten Few: The Polish Air Force in the Second World War* (London: John Murray, 1995), 206.
49. Tony Sosna interview, Kirklees Sound Archive, 036 PL, 12 February 1986.
50. Weber-Newth and Steinert, *German Migrants* (see n. 2), 24.
51. Richard Dove, *Journey of No Return: Five German-speaking Literary Exiles in Britain, 1933–1945* (London: Libris, 2000), 74–6.
52. Colin Holmes, *John Bull's Island: Immigration and British Society 1871–1971* (Basingstoke: Macmillan, 1988), 168.
53. Offenberg, *Lonely Warrior* (see n. 32), 94–5.
54. Ibid., 129.
55. Ibid., 98, 137, 203.
56. http://www.vieillestiges.be/files/memorials/MAB_Offenberg_FR.pdf. Accessed 23 September 2017. When the war was over Offenberg's body was reinterred in the Belgian airmen's field of honour at Brussels cemetery.

57. Sherwood, *Many Struggles* (see n. 41); Charles Stacey and Barbara Wilson, *The Half Million:The Canadians in Britain, 1939–1946* (Toronto: University of Toronto Press, 1987); Reynolds, *Rich Relations* (see n. 11); Zamoyski, *The Forgotten Few* (see n. 48); Sponza, *Divided Loyalties* (see n. 26); Conway and Gotovitch, *Europe in Exile* (see n. 15); Allen, *Churchill's Guests* (see n. 9); Nicholas Atkin, *The Forgotten French: Exiles in the British Isles, 1940–44* (Manchester: Manchester University Press, 2003); Richard Doherty, *Irish Volunteers in the Second World War* (Dublin: Four Courts Press, 2003); Anthony Grenville, *Jewish Refugees from Germany and Austria in Britain 1933–1970* (London: Vallentine Mitchell, 2010); Kelly, *Returning Home* (see n. 10); Wendy Ugolini, *Experiencing War as the 'Enemy Other': Italian Scottish Experience in World War II* (Manchester: Manchester University Press, 2011).

58. 'Public feeling on aliens', Report no. 79, 25 May 1940; 'Feelings about America and the Americans', Report no. 1569, 22 January 1943; 'Feelings about Australians', Report no. 1094, 13 February 1942; 'Feelings about the Czechs', Report no, 1664, 23 April 1943; 'Feelings about foreigners', TC25 2/O, 1943, MOA.

59. 'Feelings about the Czechs', MOA.

60. 'Feelings about foreigners', MOA.

61. M40B interview in ibid.

62. File Report 1885, August 1943, MOA.

63. F40C, interviewed in Hampstead, 15 January 1943, TC25 2/O, MOA.

64. *Daily Mirror*, 31 July 1940.

65. These reports have been made accessible through Paul Addison and Jeremy Crang's edited volume, Addison and Crang, *Listening to Britain* (see n. 42).

66. See Chapter 4.

67. For BBC Listener Research, see Sian Nicholas, 'The Good Servant: the Origins and Development of BBC Listener Research 1936-1950', available at http://www.microform.co.uk/guides/R50035.pdf. Accessed 24 April 2015.

68. Supplement B to Special Security Report, no, 27 of 25 February 1941, 4 March 1941, DEFE 1/335, TNA.

69. Postal Censorship Report, no. 11, 3 October 1940, DEFE 1/335, TNA.

70. Quoted in Mark Ostrowski, '"To Return to Poland or Not to Return": the Dilemma facing the Polish Armed Forces at the End of the Second World War', Ph.D dissertation, University of London, nd, 74–5.

CHAPTER I: 1940

1. Mary Morris, *A Very Private Diary: A Nurse in Wartime* (London: Weidenfeld and Nicholson, 2014), 30.

2. Ibid., 3–4.

3. Ibid., 5.

4. Ibid., 6–7.

5. Ibid., 24.

6. Ibid., 1–36.

7. Ibid., 11, 18.

8. WO 106/1615, TNA.

9. This phrase was used by Churchill in a speech in the House of Commons on 4 June 1940 and taken up on 5 June by several newspapers, including *The Times*, which used it as the headline for an editorial on Churchill's speech.

10. *Daily Express*, 26 June 1940.

11. J. B. Priestley, *Postscripts* (London: William Heinemann, 1940), 2–3. For Ministry of Information instructions on avoiding a focus on England, see Sian Nicholas, *The Echo of War: Home Front Propaganda and the Wartime BBC, 1939–45* (Manchester: Manchester University Press, 1996), 231.

12. Hansard, House of Commons Debate, 4 June 1940, vol, 361, cc 787–98.

13. P. M. H. Bell, *A Certain Eventuality: Britain and the Fall of France* (Farnborough: Saxon House, 1974), 18.

14. Martin Gilbert, *The Second World War: A Complete History* (London: Phoenix, 2009), 80–1.

15. Norman Bentwich, 'Belgian Refugees in Britain', *Message*, February 1942, 50.

16. Zamoyski, *The Forgotten Few* (see Introduction, n. 48), 66.

17. C. B. Glenister to R. M.Y. Gleadowe, 13 December 1940, MT 9/3431, TNA.

18. Marcus Cowper, *The Words of War: British Forces Personal Letters and Diaries During the Second World War* (Edinburgh: Mainstream Publishing, 2009).

19. Zamoyski, *The Forgotten Few* (see Introduction, n. 48), 53.

20. 'Extract from War Cabinet Conclusions', 17 June 1940, FO 371/24285/7334, TNA.

21. Offenberg, *Lonely Warrior* (see Introduction, n. 32), 26.

22. Luc de Vos, 'The Reconstruction of Belgian Military Forces in Britain', in Conway and Gotovitch, *Europe in Exile* (see Introduction, n. 15), 86.

23. 'Airmen From Czecho-slovakia: How They Fought Their Way to Britain', *Manchester Guardian*, 10 September 1940.

24. Antoni Slonimski, 'The Bread and the Smile of England', in F. B. Czarnomski, ed., *They Fight for Poland: The War in the First Person*, 281 (London: George Allen and Unwin, 1941).

25. Janina Struk, 'My Father's Miraculous Wartime Escape', *The Guardian*, 21 December 2013.

26. Alan Brown, 'The Czechoslovak Armed Forces in Britain', in Conway and Gotovitch, *Europe in Exile* (see Introduction, n. 15), 168.

27. Allen, *Churchill's Guests* (see Introduction, n. 9), 46.

28. Atkin, *The Forgotten French* (see Introduction, n. 57), 117,

29. M. A. Liskutin, *Challenge in the Air: A Spitfire Pilot Remembers* (London: William Kimber, 1998), 60–2.

30. Ibid., 62–4.

31. 'Airmen From Czecho-slovakia' (see n. 23).

32. Szumowski, *Through Many Skies* (see Introduction, n. 34), 68.
33. Brown, 'The Czechoslovak Armed Forces' (see n. 26), 181. The Grand Duchess of Luxembourg and her government did not arrive until 1941, having initially set up a government-in-exile in Canada. King Peter II of Yugoslavia and his government and King George II of Greece and his government also arrived in 1941.
34. Allen, *Churchill's Guests* (see Introduction, n. 9), 13.
35. Ibid., 17–23.
36. Quoted in Atkin, *The Forgotten French* (see Introduction, n. 57), 39.
37. Ibid.
38. Squadron Leader A.D.C. 'I Climbed to Attack' in Allan Michie and Walter Graebner, eds., *Lights of Freedom* (London: George Allen and Unwin, 1941), 155.
39. ' "From Berlin to the Maginot Line", as told by Joseph Lipski to F. B. Czarnomski' in F. B. Czarnomski, ed., *They Fight for Poland: The War in the First Person*, 166–9 (London: George Allen and Unwin, 1941).
40. Bohuš Beneš, ed., *Wings in Exile: Life and Work of the Czechoslovak Airmen in France and Great Britain* ('The Czechoslovak' Independent Weekly: London, 1942), 73–4.
41. 'List of Vessels Lost during 'Dynamo', 'Cycle' and 'Aerial' Operations', WO 361/21, TNA.
42. N. David J. Barnouw, 'Dutch Exiles in London', in Conway and Gotovitch, *Europe in Exile* (see Introduction, n. 15), 234.
43. Allen, *Churchill's Guests* (see Introduction, n. 9), 33–4.
44. Arthur Lamsley, 'Belgian School for Fishermen: Unique Adventure in Britain', *Message*, June 1944.
45. 'Summary of situation in regard to foreign small craft, not cargo carrying, in the UK', 26 June 1940, ADM 1/11230, TNA; Luis Angel Bernardo y Garcia and Matthew Buck, 'Belgian Society in Exile: An Attempt at a Synthesis', in Conway and Gotovitch, *Europe in Exile* (see Introduction, n. 15), 55.
46. Atkin, *The Forgotten French* (see Introduction, n. 57), 54.
47. David Howarth, *The Shetland Bus* (Morley: Elmfield Press, 1976, first published 1951), 1–5.
48. Jonathan Fenby, *The Sinking of the Lancastria: Britain's Greatest Maritime Disaster and Churchill's Cover-Up* (London: Simon and Schuster, 2005).
49. Quoted in Gilbert, *The Second World War* (see n.14), 98.
50. 'List of Vessels Lost during 'Dynamo', 'Cycle' and 'Aerial' Operations', WO 361/21, TNA.
51. Charles Williams, *The Last Great Frenchman: A Life of General de Gaulle* (New York: John Wiley, 1993), 123.
52. Ralph Barker, *Children of the Benares: A War Crime and its Victims* (London: Methuen, 1987), 160.
53. Norman Angell, 'Refugees: Enemies or Allies', *Picture Post*, 6 April 1940.
54. *Picture Post*, 27 April 1940.
55. 'Hitler's Prisoner on the Air', *Picture Post*, 1 June 1940.

56. Michael Hallett, *Stefan Lorant, Godfather of Photojournalism* (Lanham, MD: Scarecrow Press, 2006), 81.

57. 'Alien Restrictions on Refugees', *The Times*, 23 May 1940.

58. Hallett, *Stefan Lorant* (see n.56), 85–6.

59. Ibid., 124.

60. 'The Twentieth Week: Diary of the War', *Picture Post*, 10 February 1940.

61. Miriam Kocham, *Britain's Internees in the Second World War* (London: Macmillan, 1983), 19.

62. Hansard, House of Commons Debate, 1 March 1940, vol. 357, cc 2410–1 W.

63. Susan Pedersen, *Eleanor Rathbone and the Politics of Conscience* (New Haven, CT: Yale University Press, 2004), 313.

64. See, for example, letter from Fritz Frank to *The Times*, 16 July 1940.

65. Quoted in Francois Lafitte, *The Internment of Aliens* (Harmondsworth: Penguin, 1940), 165–6.

66. David French, 'Spy Fever in Britain, 1900–1915', *Historical Journal* 21/2 (1978), 355–70.

67. Addison and Crang, *Listening to Britain* (see Introduction, n. 42), 74.

68. Report 276, 16 July 1940, MOA.

69. Hansard, House of Commons Debate, 22 August 1940, vol. 364, cc 1542–4.

70. Hansard, House of Commons Debate, 22 August 1940, vol. 364, cc 1543–4.

71. David Cesarani, 'An Alien Concept? The Continuity of Anti-Alienism in British Society Before 1940', in David Cesarani and Tony Kushner, eds., *The Internment of Aliens in Twentieth Century Britain*, 45 (London: Frank Cass, 1993).

72. *News Chronicle*, 13 May 1940.

73. *Manchester Guardian*, 13 May 1940.

74. 'Feelings about Aliens', Report 107, 14 May 1940, MOA.

75. Ibid.

76. 'Internment', Report 118, 18 May 1940, MOA.

77. Tom Harrisson, *New Statesman*, 13 July 1940, quoted in Lafitte, *The Internment* (see n. 65), 167.

78. Addison and Crang, *Listening to Britain* (see Introduction, n. 42), 9, 16, 19–20, 34, 43, 47, 50–1, 72, 74, 81, 85, 87, 89, 94, 102, 129, 133, 141.

79. Ibid., 16, 19, 34, 43.

80. Ibid., 80.

81. Maxine Seller, *We Built Up Our Lives: Education and Community among Jewish Refugees Interned by Britain in World War II* (Westport, CT: Greenwood Press, 2001), 59.

82. Connery Chappell, *Island of Barbed Wire: The Remarkable Story of World War Two Internment on the Isle of Man* (London: Robert Hale, 2005), 33.

83. Home Intelligence Reports, 30 May & 3, 7, 8 June 1940 in Addison and Crang, *Listening to Britain* (see Introduction, n. 42), 54, 71, 89, 93.

84. Ibid., 102.

85. Ugolini, *Experiencing War* (see Introduction, n. 57), 2.

86. Observer's report, 10 June 1940, TC25 1/G, MOA.

87. Addison and Crang, *Listening to Britain* (see Introduction, n. 42), 101, 107, 108.

88. Mass Observation report on Italy, 12 June 1940, MOA.

89. Ibid.

90. October directive 1940, TC25 1/G, MOA.

91. TC25 1/G, MOA; Sponza, *Divided Loyalties* (see Introduction, n. 26), 80–1.

92. Home Intelligence Report, 24 June 1940, in Addison and Crang, *Listening to Britain* (see Introduction, n. 42), 149–50.

93. 'Attitudes to Aliens', TC25 1/C, MOA.

94. *The First Days* (Humphrey Jennings & Harry Watt, 1939).

95. 'War Refugees', 17 January 1940, AST 11/70, TNA.

96. Peter Davison, ed., *George Orwell Diaries* (London & New York: W. W. Norton, 2009), 278.

97. Addison and Crang, *Listening to Britain* (see Introduction, n. 42), 78, 86.

98. Ibid., 86, 78.

99. Ibid., 85, 151.

100. 'Note on Spy Mania', 14 September 1940, TC25 1/G, MOA.

101. Addison and Crang, *Listening to Britain* (see Introduction, n. 42), 19, 26, 111, 199, 359.

102. Ibid., 19, 26.

103. Report by Observer, 31 May 1940, TC25 1/G, MOA.

104. H. A. Crowe, Mayor of Wimbledon, 'To the Burgesses of Wimbledon', 10 May 1940, TC25 2/E, MOA.

105. Quoted in Read, *No Cause for Panic* (see Introduction, n. 17), 36.

106. Bill Williams, *'Jews and Other Foreigners': Manchester and the Rescue of the Victims of European Fascism, 1933–1940* (Manchester: Manchester University Press, 2011), 364–5.

107. Craig Armstrong, 'Aliens in Wartime: A Case Study of Tyneside 1939–45', *Immigrants & Minorities*, 25/2 (2007), 121–3.

108. Helen Jones, 'National, Community and Personal Priorities: British women's responses to refugees from the Nazis, from the mid-1930s to early 1940s', *Women's History Review*, 21/1 (2012), 127.

109. Ibid., 136.

110. Ibid.

111. 'Second Report from Mass-Observation on Refugees', 29 May 1940, TC25 1/D, MOA.

112. Pedersen, *Eleanor Rathbone* (see n. 63), 296–7, 319.

113. Williams, *Jews and other Foreigners* (see n. 106), xi, 6.

114. Slonimski, 'The Bread and the Smile' (see n. 24), 281.

115. Zamoyski, *The Forgotten Few* (see Introduction, n. 48), 67, 60.

116. Addison and Crang, *Listening to Britain* (see Introduction, n. 42), 189–90.

117. Ibid., 142, 144, 158, 216.

118. Atkin, *The Forgotten French* (see Introduction, n. 57), 67.

119. Addison and Crang, *Listening to Britain* (see Introduction, n. 42), 107–8, 139, 141, 151, 154.

120. European Service broadcast, 18 June 1940 in Henning Krabbe, ed., *Voices from Britain: Broadcast History 1939–45* (London: George Allen and Unwin, 1947), 55–6.

121. Martyn Cornick 'Free France and the BBC', in Anne Corbett and Douglas Johnson eds., *A Day in June: Britain and De Gaulle 1940*, 43 (London: Franco-British Council, 2000).

122. Pierre Lefranc 'A Member of the Free French Bears Witness', in ibid., 13.

123. Atkin, *The Forgotten French* (see Introduction, n. 57), 93.

124. Churchill to General Ismay, 12 July 1940, PREM 3/43, TNA.

125. Atkin, *The Forgotten French* (see Introduction, n. 57), 112, 118.

126. Churchill to General Ismay (see n. 124).

127. Panter-Downes, *London War Notes* (see Introduction, n. 13), 75.

128. Atkin, *The Forgotten French* (see Introduction, n. 57), 127–8.

129. Report on the October directive, Question 4… Allies', 10 December 1940, MOA.

130. Ibid.

131. File Report 1885, August 1943, MOA.

132. Lieutenant-Colonel Jan Ambruz, 'The RAF Have the Finest Training', in Beneš, *Wings in Exile*, 97–8 (see n. 40).

133. Zamoyski, *The Forgotten Few* (see Introduction, n. 48), 87.

134. Brown, 'The Czechoslovak Armed Forces' (see n. 26), 169; Alan Brown, *Flying for Freedom: The Allied Air Forces in the RAF 1939–45* (Stroud: The History Press, 2000), 50.

135. ADM 199/615, TNA. I am grateful to Steven O'Connor for this information.

136. 'Allied Aliens in Britain', ADM 1/11230, TNA.

137. Churchill to General Ismay (see n. 124). See also Churchill to General Ismay, AIR 8/370, TNA.

138. 'Record of a Conference held at the Air Ministry on 14th July 1940 to discuss the disposal of Allied Air Force Personnel now in the UK', AIR 8/370, TNA.

139. *The Times*, 15 July 1940.

140. Halik Kochanski, *The Eagle Unbowed: Poland and the Poles in the Second World War* (Cambridge, MA: Harvard University Press, 2012), 225.

141. Churchill to General Ismay (see n. 124).

142. *Evening Standard*, 18 June 1940.

143. Angus Calder, *The Myth of the Blitz* (London: Pimlico, 1992), 30.

144. http://genome.ch.bbc.co.uk/8beff3c76e404ca296a907fcd1234d9e. Accessed 2 February 2016.

145. *Punch*, 17 July 1940.

146. 'Australian Airmen Arrive', *British Paramount News*, 1 January 1940; 'Aussies Arrive in Britain', *British Pathé*, 1 January 1940; 'Making Themselves at Home', *Universal News*, 4 January 1940; 'Australia Sends First Instalment', *British Paramount News*, 1 January 1940; 'New Zealanders Arrive', *Universal News*, 4 January 1940; 'Lumberjacks Cross Atlantic to Help', *British Paramount News*, 29 January 1940; 'Newfoundland Lumberjacks Over Here', *Universal News*, 29 January 1940; 'Brisk Job by Loggers from Newfoundland', *British Movietone*

News, 29 January 1940; 'Mr. Anthony Eden Welcomes Australians', *British Pathé*, 18 January 1940; 'New Year Sees Empire Gathering of the Clans', *British Paramount News*, 4 January 1940.

147. 'Defenders of the Empire', *Pathé Gazette*, 4 January 1940.

148. Mass Observation interview, 28 May 1940, TC 25 2/E, MOA.

149. 'Note for Lord Strabolgi's Motion', 8 July 1940, FO 371/29602, TNA.

150. Listener Research, Weekly Report, no 17, 4 Jan 1941, R9/1/1, BBC, WAC.

151. '14th July, 1940 - France's National Day', *British Pathé*, 18 July 1940; 'Free French Swear to Free France', *British Paramount News*, 18 July 1940.

152. Basil Nicolls, 'Programme Directive No. 36: France', 2 September 1940, R 34/953, WAC. I am grateful to Thomas Hajkowski for this reference.

153. 'Czechs are Fighting Beside Britain', *Gaumont British News*, 12 August 1940. See also, 'Polish Airmen Somewhere in England', *Pathé Gazette*, 1 February 1940; 'Poland's Air Force in Britain', *Gaumont British News*, 1 May 1940; 'More Polish and Czech Troops Arrive', *Pathé Gazette*, 11 July 1940; 'President Benes with Czech Air Force', *Pathé Gazette*, 12 August 1940.

154. 'The King visits Canadian and Polish airmen in Britain', *Gaumont British News*, 30 September 1940.

155. *The Manchester Guardian*, 10 September 1940.

156. *The Times*, 6 September 1940.

157. Alexander Hardinge to Lord Hamilton of Dalzell, in Edward Raczynski, *In Allied London* (London: Charles Birchall & Sons, 1962), 70.

158. Quoted in Lynne Olson and Stanley Cloud, *For Your Freedom and Ours: The Kościuszko Squadron: Forgotten Heroes of World War II* (London: Arrow Books, 2003), 142.

159. http://genome.ch.bbc.co.uk/search/0/20?adv=0&q=%22fights+on%22& media=all&yf=1923&yt=2009&mf=1&mt=12&tf=00%3A00&tt=00%3A00. Accessed 30 November 2016.

160. http://genome.ch.bbc.co.uk/search/0/20?adv=0&q=comrades+for+freedom &media=all&yf=1923&yt=2009&mf=1&mt=12&tf=00%3A00&tt=00 %3A00. Accessed 30 November 2016.

161. 'Queen Wilhelmina to Holland', BBC European Service, 28 July 1940, in Krabbe, *Voices from Britain*, 71–3 (see n. 120).

162. 'King Haakon to Norway', BBC European Service, 26 September 1940, in ibid., 73.

163. Asa Briggs, *The History of Broadcasting in the United Kingdom, Vol. III: The War of Words, 1939–1945* (Oxford: Oxford University Press, 1995), 74.

164. John Salt, 'The European Service', *BBC Handbook*, 1941, 39–40.

165. Cornick 'Free France and the BBC' (see n. 121), 38.

166. Jennifer Taylor, 'The Propagandists' Propagandist: Bruno Adler's 'Kurt und Willi' Dialogues as Expression of British Propaganda Objectives' in Charmian Brinson, Richard Dove, Jennifer Taylor, eds., *'Immortal Austria'?: Austrians in Exile in Britain*, 20 (Amsterdam: Rodopi, 2006).

167. *The Air is Our Sea*, transcript. The programme was broadcast in the Home Service on 1 August 1940. See R19/239, BBC, WAC.

168. Basil Nicolls, 'Programme Directive No. 3: Propaganda', 7 June 1940, R34/953, BBC, WAC. I am grateful to Thomas Hajkowski for this reference.

169. 'Public Feeling on Aliens', Report 79, 25 May 1940, MOA.

170. Home Intelligence Report, 6 July 1940 in Addison and Crang, *Listening to Britain* (see Introduction, n. 42), 198.

171. *Evening Standard*, 17 July 1940.

172. *Evening Standard*, 19 July 1940.

173. *Evening Standard*, 23 July 1940.

174. Hansard, House of Commons Debate, 10 July 1940, vol. 362, cc 1225–6.

175. Hansard, House of Lords Debate, 6 August 1940, vol. 117, cc 132–3.

176. Hansard, House of Commons Debate, 22 August 1940, vol. 364, cc 1538–9.

177. Hansard, House of Commons Debate, 10 July 1940, vol. 362, cc 1209–10.

178. Joshua Levine, *The Secret History of the Blitz* (London: Simon and Schuster, 2015).

179. *The Times*, 24 August 1940.

180. Addison and Crang, *Listening to Britain* (see Introduction, n. 42), 294, 361.

181. 'Impressions', 2 August 1940, TC25 1/G, MOA.

182. Report 324, 5 August 1940, MOA.

183. See, for example, *The Black Sheep of Whitehall* (Will Hay/Basil Dearden, 1941); *The Ghost of St Michael's* (Marcel Varnel, 1941); *Back Room Boy* (Herbert Mason, 1942).

184. Panter-Downes, *London War Notes* (see Introduction, n. 13), 59, 63, 88.

CHAPTER 2: ENEMIES AND NEUTRALS

1. Susanne Medas, interview with Janette Martin for the 'Mixing It' project, 2015. The full interview is available at http://www.iwm.org.uk/collections/item/object/80033222.

2. Ibid.

3. Ibid.

4. Ibid.

5. Chappell, *Barbed Wire* (see Introduction, n. 82), 143; Keiko Itoh, *The Japanese Community in Britain: From Integration to Disintegration* (London: Routledge, 2001), 185.

6. Sponza, *Divided Loyalties* (see Introduction, n. 26), 51.

7. Wendy Ugolini, '"The Sins of the Fathers": The Contested Recruitment of Second-Generation Italians in the British Forces', *Twentieth-Century British History* 24/3 (2013), 377. This figure includes between 10,000 and 15,000 children born in Britain, many of whom were of dual British-Italian nationality.

8. Bob Moore, 'Axis Prisoners in Britain during the Second World War: A Comparative Survey', in Bob Moore and Kent Fedorowich, eds., *Prisoners of War and their Captors in World War II*, 19 (Oxford: Berg, 1996).

9. Enda Delaney, *Demography, State and Society: Irish Migration to Britain, 1921–1971* (Montreal: McGill-Queen's University Press, 2000), 130, 149.

10. Cormac Kavanagh,'Irish and British Government Policy towards theVolunteers', in Brian Girvin and Geoffrey Roberts, eds., *Ireland and the Second World War: Politics, Society, Remembrance* (Dublin: Four Courts Press, 2000), 86; Robert Cole, *Propaganda, Censorship and Irish Neutrality in the Second World War* (Edinburgh: Edinburgh University Press, 2006), 181.

11. 'Eire menaced by Germany', *Pathé Gazette*, 8 July 1940; 'Eire stands guard on her coasts', *Gaumont British News*, 6 July 1940.

12. Cole, *Propaganda* (see n. 10), 50.

13. 'Plan of Propaganda to Eire', Overseas Planning Committee Paper, no. 329, 10 February 1943, INF 1/562, TNA.

14. 'Behind the Crisis with Eire: The Northern Ireland Base We Must Protect', *Picture Post*, 25 March 1944.

15. Brian Inglis, *West Briton* (London: Faber and Faber, 1962), 191.

16. These histories have recently begun to be the subject of a considerable academic literature. Key works on Austrian and German refugees after 1940 include Marion Berghahn, *Continental Britons: German-Jewish Refugees from Nazi Germany* (New York: Berghahn Books, 1984); Ian Wallace, ed., *German-speaking Exiles in Great Britain* (Yearbook of the Research Centre for German and Austrian Exile Studies, Vol. 1, Amsterdam: Rodopi 1999); Grenville, *Jewish Refugees* (see Introduction, n. 57). For their service in the British forces see Peter Leighton-Langer, *The King's Own Loyal Enemy Aliens: German and Austrian Refugees in Britain's Armed Forces, 1939–1945* (London: Vallentine Mitchell, 2006); Helen Fry, *The King's Most Loyal Enemy Aliens: Germans who fought for Britain in the Second World War* (Stroud: Sutton Publishing, 2007). For Italians see Sponza, *Divided Loyalties* (see Introduction, n. 26); Ugolini, *Experiencing War* (see Introduction, n. 57). For Irish volunteers and war workers see Richard Doherty, *Irish Men and Women in the Second World War* (Dublin: Four Courts Press, 1999); Doherty, *Irish Volunteers* (see Introduction, n. 57); Girvin and Roberts, eds., *Ireland* (see Chapter 2, n. 10): Robert Cole, *Propaganda* (see n. 10), Clair Wills, *That Neutral Island: A Cultural History of Ireland during the Second World War* (London: Faber and Faber, 2007); Kelly, *Returning Home* (see Introduction, n. 10).

17. Ugolini, *Experiencing War* (see Introduction, n. 57), 240.

18. Maxine Seller, *We Built Up Our Lives* (see Chapter 1, n. 81), 218.

19. Winston Churchill to General Ismay, 21 June 1940, CAB 120/243, TNA.

20. Ismay to Churchill, 22 July 1940, CAB 120/243, TNA.

21. Reports of intake of men of enemy nationality, 30 August 1940, CAB 120/243, TNA.

22. Lucio Sponza, 'The Internment of Italians in Britain', in Franca Iacovetta, Roberto Perin and Angelo Principe, eds., *Enemies Within: Italian and other Internees in Canada and Abroad*, 262 (Toronto: University of Toronto Press, 2000).

23. Lafitte, *The Internment of Aliens* (see Chapter 1, n. 65), 202.

24. Hansard, 22 August 1940.

25. *The Times*, 16 July 1940.

26. This comment came from Yvonne Kapp and Margaret Mynatt in their 1940 study, which remained unpublished until 1997. Yvonne Kapp and Margaret Mynatt, *British Policy and the Refugees 1933-1941* (London: Frank Cass, 1997), 78.

27. Mark Lynton, *An Accidental Journey: A Cambridge Internee's Memoir of World War II* (Woodstock, NY: Overlook Press, 1996), 64, 78.

28. Peter Masters, *Striking Back: A Jewish Commando's War Against the Nazis* (Novato, CA: Presidio Press, 1997), 41.

29. Fry, *The King's Most Loyal* (see n. 16), 95.

30. George Clare, *Berlin Days 1946-7* (London: Pan Books, 1990), 45, 68.

31. Postal Censorship Report, no. 11, 3 October 1940, HO 215/291, TNA

32. Ibid.

33. Ibid.

34. Lynton, *An Accidental Journey* (see n. 27), 82.

35. Norman Bentwich, *I Understand the Risks: The Story of the Refugees from Nazi Oppression who Fought in the British Forces in the World War* (London: Victor Gollancz, 1950), 54.

36. 'Supplement B to the Special Security Report, no. 36 of June 21 1941', Postal Censorship Report, no. 29, July 1 1941, DEFE 1/335, TNA.

37. Chappell, *Barbed Wire* (see Introduction, n. 82), 111.

38. Martin Sugarman, 'Jewish RAF Special Operators in Radio Counter Measures with 101 Squadron', at http://www.jewishvirtuallibrary.org/jsource/ww2/sugar1.html. Accessed 7 March 2013. I am grateful to Richard Morris for this reference.

39. Bentwich, *I Understand the Risks* (see n. 35), 118, 158.

40. Simona Tobia, 'Questioning the Nazis: languages and effectiveness in British war crime investigations and trials in Germany, 1945-48', *Journal of War and Culture Studies*, 3/1 (2010), 123-36.

41. Ugolini, *Experiencing War* (see Introduction, n. 57), 193.

42. Home Intelligence Weekly Report, no. 216, 23 November 1944, INF 1/292, TNA.

43. Editorial, *Daily Mail*, 21 April 1945.

44. *Daily Telegraph*, 18 April 1945. See also *Daily Mail*, 25 April 1945.

45. *Sunday Express*, 22 April 1945.

46. *Daily Mail*, 25 April 1945.

47. Home Intelligence Weekly Reports, no. 213, 2 November 1944; no. 190, 25 May 1944, and no. 215, 16 November 1944, INF 1/292, TNA.

48. Sponza, *Divided Loyalties* (see Introduction, n. 26), 211-12; Home Intelligence Weekly Reports, no. 207, 21 September 1944; no. 208, 28 September 1944, INF 1/292, TNA.

49. Home Intelligence Weekly Report, no. 190, 25 May 1944, INF 1/292, TNA.

50. Home Intelligence Monthly Review, 14 September 1944; Weekly Report, no. 202, 17 August 1944, INF 1/292, TNA.

51. Bob Moore, '"Turning Liabilities into Assets": British Government Policy towards German and Italian Prisoners of War during the Second World War', *Journal of Contemporary History*, 32/1 (1997), 131.

52. Ibid., 117–36.

53. *The Times*, 26 September 1941.

54. Churchill to Secretary of State for War and Secretary of State for Air, 8 October 1941, PREM 3/129/5, TNA.

55. Morris, *A Very Private Diary* (see Chapter 1, n. 1), 26.

56. Moore, 'Axis Prisoners' (see n. 8), 29.

57. Home Intelligence Reports, 10 and 12 June 1940 in Addison and Crang, *Listening to Britain* (see Introduction, n. 42), 98, 106.

58. Lafitte, *The Internment of Aliens* (see Chapter 1, n. 65), 144.

59. Home Intelligence Weekly Report, no. 104, 1 Oct 1942, INF 1/292, TNA.

60. Home Intelligence Weekly Report, no. 181, 23 March 1944, INF 1/292, TNA.

61. Delaney, *Demography* (see n. 9), 145, 144, 139.

62. Home Intelligence Weekly Report, no. 19, 5 February 1941, INF 1/292, TNA.

63. Letter from County Wicklow to Surrey, 25 December 1941, Postal Censorship Reports, Secret Series B, no. 24, 1 February 1942, CJ 4/30, TNA.

64. Letter from County Mayo to Windsor, 4 January 1942, Postal Censorship Reports, Secret Series B, no. 24, 1 February 1942, CJ 4/30, TNA.

65. 'Dr Evatt Meets Famous Squadron and Leader', *Movietone War Time News*, Issue 677A, 28 May 1942.

66. Cole, *Propaganda* (see n. 10), 131.

67. *The 'Man in the Street' (of the B.B.C.) Talks to Europe* (London: P.S. King and Staples, 1945), 184–5.

68. 'RAF Heroes Named', *Movietone War Time News*, Issue 721A, 1 April 1943.

69. 'Plan of Propaganda to Eire', Overseas Planning Committee Paper, no. 329, 10 February 1943, INF 1/562, TNA; 'Volunteers from Eire who have won distinctions serving with the British Forces', INF 2/8, TNA.

70. For the press, see Cole, *Propaganda* (see n. 10), 131.

71. 'Plan of Propaganda to Eire', Overseas Planning Committee Paper, no. 329, 10 February 1943, INF 1/562, TNA.

72. Personal Telegram from Prime Minister to Foreign Secretary, 5 September 1943, Churchill Archives CHAR 20/129.

73. Quoted in Wills, *That Neutral Island* (see n. 16), 384.

74. 'Winston Churchill's Survey of the War', BBC Home Service, 13 May 1945 in Krabbe, *Voices from Britain* (see Chapter 1, n. 120), 287–8.

75. Ibid.

76. Inglis, *West Briton* (see n. 15), 67.

77. *Halfway House* (Basil Dearden, 1944).

78. For their work in the BBC Monitoring Service, see Hamid Ismailov, Marie Gillespie, and Anna Aslanyan, *Tales from Bush House* (London: Hertfordshire Press, 2012).

79. Kristina Meier, 'The German Service of the BBC during the Second World War: Attitudes towards Satire as a Weapon of War', paper to World War II and the Media Symposium, University of Chester, June 2011.

80. Jennifer Taylor, 'The 'Endsieg' as Ever-receding Goal: Literary Propaganda by Bruno Adler and Robert Lucas for BBC Radio', in Ian Wallace, ed., *German-speaking Exiles in Great Britain*, 43–58 (Amsterdam: Rodopi, 1999).
81. Meier, 'The German Service' (see n. 79).
82. Hugh Rorrison, 'German Theatre and Cabaret in London, 1939–45', in Günter Berghaus, ed., *Theatre and Film in Exile: German Artists in Britain, 1933–1945*, 54–5 (Oxford: Berg, 1989).
83. http://genome.ch.bbc.co.uk/5f20f7ee9cb14311943aec8e8bdeeac3. Accessed 12 January 2016. http://genome.ch.bbc.co.uk/5e67d06c0beb4c109f4b2d82e0 36830d. Accessed 12 January 2016.
84. Charmian Brinson and Richard Dove, eds., *'Stimme der Wahrheit': German-language Broadcasting by the BBC* (Amsterdam: Rodopi, 2003).
85. Dove, *Journey* (see Introduction, n. 15), 197–202; Tom Harrisson, 'Radio', *The Observer*, 10 May 1942.
86. Sponza, *Divided Loyalties* (see Introduction, n. 26), 167–8.
87. Fry, *The King's Most Loyal* (see n. 16), 192; Sponza, *Divided Loyalties* (see Introduction, n. 26), 171.
88. Fry, *The King's Most Loyal* (see n. 16), 188–93. See also Robert Clark, *Intelligence Collection* (London: Sage, 2014), 27; Sefton Delmer, *Black Boomerang: An Autobiography*, vol. 2 (London: Secker and Warburg, 1962).
89. Brinson, *Stimme der Wahrheit* (see n. 84), 13.
90. Ministry of Information Policy Committee, 22 January 1941, INF 1/849.
91. *Lift Your Head, Comrade* (Michael Hankinson, 1943); Bentwich, *I Understand the Risks* (see n. 35), 56.
92. *Documentary Newsletter*, January 1943, 165.
93. Transcript of *The Fingers of Private Spiegel*, BBC radio broadcast, Home Service, 9 December 1942, BBC, WAC.
94. Ian McLaine, *Ministry of Morale: Home Front Morale and the Ministry of Information in World War II* (London: George Allen and Unwin, 1979), 166–70.
95. Ilaria Favretto and Oliviero Bergamini, ' "Temperamentally Unwarlike": The Image of Italy in the Allies' War Propaganda, 1943–45', in Mark Connelly and David Welch, eds., *War and the Media: Reportage and Propaganda 1900–2003* (London: I. B. Tauris, 2005), 114.
96. Report on October directive, 10 December 1940, MOA; Report 1669Q, April 1943, MOA.
97. *The Times*, 21 March 1945.
98. Ugolini, *Experiencing War* (see Introduction, n. 57), 241.
99. *Daily Express*, 21 March 1945.
100. *Daily Mail*, 16 April 1941; *Daily Mirror*, 16 April 1941; *Daily Express*, 16 April 1941.
101. *The Times*, 16 April 1941.
102. Leighton-Langer, *The King's Own* (see n. 16), 51.
103. Sugarman, 'Jewish RAF Special Operators' (see n. 38).

104. Kavanagh, 'Irish and British Government Policy' (see n. 10), 82.

105. Ian Wood, *Britain, Ireland and the Second World War* (Edinburgh: Edinburgh University Press, 2010), 90.

106. Inglis, *West Briton* (see n. 15), 57–8.

107. Wills, *That Neutral Island* (see n. 16), 226.

108. Wood, *Britain, Ireland* (see n. 105), 164–5.

109. Doherty, *Irish Men and Women* (see n. 16), 50–1.

110. Kelly, *Returning Home* (see Introduction, n. 10), 44.

111. Ibid. 46.

112. Inglis, *West Briton* (see n. 15), 67.

113. Wood, *Britain, Ireland* (see n. 105), 152.

114. Kavanagh, 'Irish and British Government Policy' (see n. 10), 77; Tim Pat Coogan, *De Valera: Long Fellow, Long Shadow* (London: Arrow Books, 1995), 521.

115. Kelly, *Returning Home* (see Introduction, n. 10), 189.

116. Home Intelligence Weekly Report, no. 73, 25 Feb 1942, INF 1/292, TNA. The newsreel was 'Ireland—the Plain Issue', *British Paramount News*, 2 February 1942.

117. Home Intelligence Weekly Report, no. 180, 16 March 1944, INF 1/292, TNA.

118. Home Intelligence Weekly Report, no. 182, 30 March 1944, INF 1/292, TNA.

119. Romie Lambkin, *My Time in the War: An Irishwoman's Diary* (Dublin: Wolfhound Press, 1992), 45; 36–7; 62.

120. Ibid., 62–3.

121. Ibid., 39.

122. For discussion of this community in the diary of Mary Morris (see Chapter 1, n. 1) as well as Romie Lambkin, see Carol Acton, ' "Stepping into history": Reading the Second World War through Irish Women's Diaries', *Irish Studies Review*, 18/1 (2010), 39–56.

123. Ugolini, *Experiencing War* (see Introduction, n. 57), 163–5; 192–4.

124. Sponza, *Divided Loyalties* (see Introduction, n. 26), 264, 320–1.

125. Wendy Ugolini, 'The Embodiment of British Italian War Memory? The Curious Marginalisation of Dennis Donnini, VC', *Patterns of Prejudice*, 46/3–4 (2012), 401; 414–15; Ugolini, *Experiencing War* (see Introduction, n. 57), Chapters 5 and 6.

126. Sponza, *Divided Loyalties* (see Introduction, n. 26), 320–1.

127. Ugolini, *Experiencing War* (see Introduction, n. 57), 190.

128. Masters, *Striking Back* (see n. 28), 41.

129. Quoted in Fry, *The King's Most Loyal* (see n. 16), 210.

130. Seller, *We Built Up Our Lives* (see Chapter 1, n. 81), 217–18.

131. Masters, *Striking Back* (see n. 28), 27; 42; x–xii.

132. Seller, *We Built Up Our Lives* (see Chapter 1, n. 81), 51–2.

133. Letter to the *Melbourne Herald*, quoted in Cyril Pearl, *The Dunera Scandal: Deported by Mistake* (London: Angus and Robertson Publishers, 1983), 212.

134. Leighton-Langer, *The King's Own* (see n. 16), 46–8.

135. Lynton, *Accidental Journey* (see n. 27), 232.

136. Ibid., 168, 118.

137. Quoted in Tobias, 'Questioning' (see n. 40), 129–30.

138. Ibid., 218.

139. Gerhart Friedlander and Keith Turner, *Rudi's Story: The Diary and Wartime Experiences of Rudolf Friedlaender* (London: Jedburgh Publishing, 2006), 129.

140. L. G. Scala to Emilio Scala, 9 May 1941, Supplement B to the Special Security Report, no. 34 of 24 May 1941, 3 June 1941, DEFE 1/335, TNA.

141. Hansard, House of Commons Debate, 10 July 1940, vol. 362, cc 1229–1231.

142. https://mentionthewar.wordpress.com/world-war-ii-1939-1945/italian-internment/silvestro-dambrosio/. Accessed 24 January 2015.

143. Joe Pieri, *Isle of the Displaced: An Italian-Scot's Memoirs of Internment in the Second World War* (Glasgow: Neil Wilson Publishing, 1997), 8.

144. Ibid., 9–10.

145. Ugolini, *Experiencing War* (see Introduction, n. 57), 163.

146. Letter of 10 November 1941, Supplement B to the Special Security Report, no. 55 of December 13 1941, 15 December 1941, DEFE 1/335. TNA.

147. Steven O'Connor, *Irish Officers in the British Forces, 1922–45* (Basingstoke: Palgrave, 2014), 50.

148. Wills, *That Neutral Island* (see n. 16), 64–5.

149. Stephen Kennedy, Imperial War Museum Sound Archive, interview, 19089.

150. Morris, *A Very Private Diary* (see Chapter 1, n. 1), 231.

151. Benzion Patkin, *The Dunera Internees* (Melbourne: Cassell, 1979), 16.

152. Lafitte, *The Internment of Aliens* (see Chapter 1, n. 65), 77; Pearl, *The Dunera Scandal* (see n. 133), 15.

153. Masters, *Striking Back* (see n. 28), 35.

154. Hansard, House of Commons Debate, 10 July 1940, vol. 362, cc 1261–1262.

155. Lucy Lethbridge, *Servants: A Downstairs View of Twentieth-Century Britain* (London: Bloomsbury, 2013), 241.

156. Bronka Schneider, *Exile: A Memoir of 1939*, ed. Erika Bourguignon and Barbara Hill Rigney (Columbus, OH: Ohio State University Press, 1998).

157. Ugolini, *Experiencing War* (see Introduction, n. 57), 200–4.

158. Chappell, *Barbed Wire* (see Introduction, n. 82), 67.

159. Postal Censorship, Supplement B to the Special Security Report, no. 36 of 21 June 1941, 1 July 1941, DEFE 1/335, TNA.

160. K. K. Berliner, Blackwell Heath Bucks to Miss M. Allison, New York, 6 March 1941, Postal Censorship, Supplement B to the Special Security Report of April 29th 1941, 3 May 1941, DEFE 1/335, TNA.

161. Oskar Marmorek to Miss Joyce Enfield, 23 October 1940, Postal Censorship Report, no. 14, 9 November 1940, HO 215/291, TNA.

162. Seller, *We Built Up Our Lives* (see Chapter 1, n. 81), 27, 230.

163. Ibid., 230.

164. Lore Groszmann's testimony in *The Children who Cheated Hitler* (Sue Read and Jim Goulding), Channel 4, 2000.

165. Lethbridge, *Servants* (see n. 155), 240–1.
166. Bill Williams, *Jews and Other Foreigners* (see Chapter 1, n. 106), 344–55.
167. Vera Gissing's testimony in *The Children who Cheated Hitler* (see n. 164).
168. Emmy Mogilensky's testimony in ibid.
169. Tony Kushner and Katharine Knox, *Refugees in an Age of Genocide: Global, National and Local Perspectives During the Twentieth Century* (London: Frank Cass, 1999), 156.
170. Max Dickson, *The Memories of Max Dickson formerly Max Dobriner* (Privately printed, 1992), 4.
171. Ibid., 7.
172. Ibid., 16–17.
173. Ibid., 16.
174. Susanne Medas interview.

CHAPTER 3: THE EMPIRE COMES TO BRITAIN

1. http://www.overgrownpath.com/2007/04/berlin-philharmonics-first-black.html. Accessed 10 August 2016; Rudolph Dunbar obituary, *The Musical Times*, 129/1749 (November 1988), 619.
2. *The Times*, 22 August 1934, 13 October 1934; 'First broadcast of all-British coloured band', *Topical Times*, 11 August 1934.
3. Directive reply by Respondent no. 3483, 'Directive on Attitudes towards People of Colour, June 1943, MOA.
4. *The Times*, 10 April 1942, 18 April 1942, 28 November 1942; Judith Still, Michael Dabrishus, and Carolyn Quin, *William Grant Still: A Bio-bibliography* (Westport, CT: Greenwood Press, 1996), 51–2; *The Times*, 14 September 1942.
5. *The Times*, 28 April 1942.
6. Bernard Bracken, 'Colour Bar Must Go', *Sunday Express*, 20 September 1942.
7. Still, *A Bio-Bibliography* (see n. 4), 52.
8. Noel Sabine to BBC, 15 July 1942, Rudolph Dunbar contributor file, BBC, WAC.
9. Noel Sabine, Colonial Office Minute, 10 January 1942, CO 875/11/14, TNA.
10. Rudolph Dunbar 'Men and Women of Color Continue Rapid Rise to Prominence in England', London Bureau, Associated Negro Press, 27 June 1941, CO 875/11/14, TNA.
11. Colonial Office to George Barnes, BBC, 31 January 1942, CO 875/11/14, TNA.
12. Ibid.
13. Noel Sabine, Colonial Office Minute, 10 January 1942, CO 875/11/14, TNA.
14. Rudolph Dunbar contributor file, BBC, WAC.
15. *Picture Post*, 6 October 1945.
16. 'W. Rudolph Dunbar: Pioneering Orchestra Conductor', *The Black Perspective in Music*, 9/2 (Autumn, 1981), 193–225.
17. http://www.overgrownpath.com/2007/04/berlin-philharmonics-first-black.html. Accessed 10 August 2016.

18. Director of Music to Music Booking Manager, 9 August 1945, Rudolph Dunbar contributor file, BBC, WAC.

19. Kenneth Wright to Monsieur Henry Barraud of Radiodiffusion Française, 15 April 1946, Rudolph Dunbar contributor file, BBC, WAC.

20. 'At the BBC Canteen', *Picture Post*, 27 November 1943, 19–21.

21. Simon Potter, 'The Colonisation of the BBC: Diasporic Britons at the BBC External Services, c. 1932–1936', in Marie Gillespie and Alban Webb, eds., *Diasporas and Diplomacy: Cosmopolitan Contact Zones at the BBC World Service (1932–2012)*, 46–7 (London: Routledge, 2013).

22. Ibid., 47.

23. Venu Chitale to Eileen Blair, 23 October 1942, in Peter Davison, ed., *Keeping Our Little Corner Clean 1942–1943*, 125 (London: Secker & Warburg, 2001).

24. http://www.open.ac.uk/researchprojects/makingbritain/content/indira-devi. Accessed 15 January 2017.

25. Peter Davison, ed., *All Propaganda is Lies 1941–1942*, The Complete Works of George Orwell, vol. 13 (London: Secker and Warburg, 1998), 271.

26. 'Indians Train Here to Make Munitions', *British Paramount News*, 29 May 1941; 'Indians to Learn Munitions Making', *British Movietone News*, 29 May 1941; 'Royal Visit to Indian Trainees', *British Movietone News*, 2 October 1941.

27. Shompa Lahiri, 'Divided Loyalties', *History Today*, 57/5 (2007), 57.

28. http://genome.ch.bbc.co.uk/8beff3c76e404ca296a907fcd1234d9e. Accessed 22 November 2016.

29. Thomas Hajkowski, 'The BBC, the Empire, and the Second World War, 1939–1945', *Historical Journal of Film, Radio and Television* 22/2 (2002), 147–51; Sian Nicholas, ' "Brushing Up Your Empire": Dominion and Colonial Propaganda on the BBC's Home Services, 1939–45', *Journal of Imperial and Commonwealth History* 31 (May 2003), 207–30.

30. Nicholas, 'Brushing Up Your Empire' (see n. 29).

31. *Daily Express*, 19 February 1944.

32. G. R. Barnes to A. P. Ryan, 14 October 1941, R51/423/1, BBC, WAC.

33. Director of Talks to R. B. Pugh, Dominions Office, 15 November 1941, R51/423/1, BBC, WAC.

34. Listener Research Report, 17 November 1941, R9/65/1, BBC, WAC.

35. Listener Research Report, 24 September 1941, R9/65/1, BBC, WAC.

36. Listener Research Report, 5 November 1941, R9/65/1, BBC, WAC.

37. Listener Research Report, 14 January 1942, R9/65/1, BBC, WAC.

38. Noel Sabine, Colonial Office Minute, 10 January 1942, CO 875/11/14, TNA.

39. Memorandum from the Director of Talks, G. R. Barnes, 8 July 1943, Learie Constantine, Talks, File 1, 1939–62, BBC, WAC.

40. For the 'people's empire', see Wendy Webster, *Englishness and Empire, 1939–1965* (Oxford: Oxford University Press, 2005), chapters 2 and 3.

41. Scott Worthy, 'A Martial Race? Maori and Pakeha New Zealand Soldiers of the Great War in Imperial Context', paper delivered to British World Conference II, University of Calgary, July 2003; Timothy Parsons, *The African Rank-and-File: Social Implications of Colonial Military Service in the King's African Rifles 1902–1964*

(Portsmouth: Heinemann, 1999), 53–103; Heather Streets, *Martial Races: The Military, Race and Masculinity in British Imperial Culture, 1857–1914* (Manchester: Manchester University Press, 2004).

42. 'King and Queen with Indian Troops', *British Pathé Gazette*, 12 August 1940; 'A Day with the Australians', *British Pathé Gazette*, 8 July 1940; 'Former Indian POWs Cheer King', *British Paramount News*, 28 June 1945.

43. *Africa's Fighting Men* (Colonial Film Unit, 1943).

44. INF 6/1328, TNA; *West Indies Calling* (John Page, 1943).

45. For the radio programme see SC 19/28; R 46/92, BBC, WAC.

46. Holmes, *John Bull's Island* (see Introduction, n. 52), 168.

47. 'Demobilisation and Resettlement, Extract from War Cabinet paper', 16 Nov, 1942, AIR 20/9051, TNA.

48. Anand to Sir Malcolm Darling, 22 March 1941, in W. J. West, ed., *Orwell: The War Broadcasts* (London: Duckworth, 1985), 15.

49. Ibid.

50. Quoted in Susheila Nasta, 'Sealing a Friendship: George Orwell and Mulk Raj Anand at the BBC', *Wasafiri*, 26/4 (2011), 15–16.

51. *The Times*, 26 September 1942; *The Times*, 17 September 1942.

52. Ruvani Ranasinha, 'South Asian Broadcasters in Britain and the BBC: talking to India' (1941–1943)', *South Asian Diaspora*, 2/1 (2010), 58.

53. Shompa Lahiri, 'Clandestine Mobilities and Shifting Embodiments: Noor-un-nisa Inayat Khan and the Special Operations Executive, 1940–44', *Gender & History*, 19/2 (2007), 308.

54. 'West Indian Trainees and Technicians, Discrimination', 24 July 1944, LAB 26/55, TNA.

55. Ibid.

56. *Daily Mail*, 2 August 1944. See also *The Manchester Guardian*, 2 August 1944.

57. *Daily Mail*, 2 August 1944.

58. *The Times*, 10 August 1944.

59. 'Colour Discrimination in the UK', CO 537/1224, TNA.

60. *The Manchester Guardian*, 13 September 1943.

61. *The Manchester Guardian*, 19 June and 4 July 1941.

62. Home Intelligence Weekly Report, no. 153, 9 September 1943, INF 1/292, TNA.

63. Home Intelligence Weekly Report, no. 153, 9 September 1943; no. 154, 16 September 1943, INF 1/292, TNA.

64. *Daily Mirror*, 24 September 1943.

65. Peter Fryer, *Staying Power: The History of Black People in Britain* (London: Pluto Press, 1984), 364.

66. Mass Observation, *Fortnightly Bulletin*, 11 October 1943, MOA.

67. Ibid.

68. *The Times*, 20 June 1944; *Daily Mail*, 20 June 1944.

69. 'West Indian Trainees and Technicians, Discrimination', 24 July 1944, LAB 26/55, TNA.

70. *The Times*, 29 June 1944.
71. Bracken, 'Colour Bar Must Go' (see n. 6).
72. Reynolds, *Rich Relations* (see Introduction, n. 11), 217.
73. Minute Sheet, 27 August 1945, AIR 2/13437, TNA.
74. Murray, *Lest We Forget*, 127–8 (see Introduction, n. 35).
75. Walter White, *A Rising Wind* (New York: Doubleday, Doran and Co, 1945), 28.
76. Sonya Rose, *Which People's War?: National Identity and Citizenship in Wartime Britain 1939–1945* (Oxford: Oxford University Press, 2003), 245.
77. J. L. Keith, 20 September 1943, CO 876/15, TNA.
78. See *The Manchester Guardian*, 19 September 1943.
79. Rose, *Which People's War?* (see n. 76), 265.
80. Susan Pennybacker, *From Scottsboro to Munich: Race and Political Culture in 1930s Britain* (Princeton, NJ and Oxford: Princeton University Press, 2009), 254.
81. Respondent no. 3478, File Report 1885, August 1943, MOA.
82. 'Feelings About Australians', Report 1094, 13 February 1942, MOA.
83. Ibid.
84. Hank Nelson, *Chased by the Sun: The Australians in Bomber Command in World War II* (Crows Nest: Allen and Unwin, 2006), 137, 57.
85. Stacey and Wilson, *The Half Million* (see Introduction, n. 57), 58.
86. Mary Muldowney, *The Second World War and Irish Women: An Oral History* (Dublin: Irish Academic Press, 2007), 94.
87. *Manchester Guardian*, 5 September 1943.
88. Murray, *Lest We Forget* (see Introduction, n. 35), 106.
89. Reynolds, *Rich Relations* (see Introduction, n. 11), 137.
90. Home Intelligence Weekly Report, no. 48, 27 August 1941, INF 1/292, TNA.
91. Appreciation and Censorship Report, no. 51, for period 16–31 August 1944, WO 204/10381, TNA.
92. Nelson, *Chased by the Sun* (see n. 84), 85.
93. Iain Johnston, 'The British Commonwealth Air Training Plan and the Shaping of National Identities in the Second World War', *Journal of Imperial and Commonwealth History* 43/5 (2015), 910–14.
94. Grant, *A Member of the RAF* (see Introduction, n. 45), 28–35, 59.
95. Nelson, *Chased by the Sun* (see n. 84), 137.
96. Ibid., 64–5.
97. Doris Carter, *Never Leave Your Head Uncovered: A Canadian Nursing Sister in World War Two* (Stoney Creek, Ontario: Potlatch Publications, 1999), 25.
98. Wartime diary of Leonard George Peake, entries for 6, 7, and 16 October and 29 November 1942, 17 January, 4 and 20 February, 6 March, 27–29 April, 20–21 June, 16, 18 August, 12 December 1943, 1 January, and 12–14 February 1944, Imperial War Museum manuscript collection, 416453.
99. Nelson, *Chased by the Sun* (see n. 84), 65.
100. Murray, *Lest We Forget* (see Introduction, n. 35), 97.
101. Ibid. 72.
102. Reynolds, *Rich Relations* (see Introduction, n. 11), 133.

103. Ibid.
104. Michael Ockenden, *Canucks by the Sea: The Canadian Army in Eastbourne during the Second World War* (Eastbourne Local History Society, 2009), 29.
105. Reynolds, *Rich Relations* (see Introduction, n. 11), 150–1.
106. Ibid., 134–5.
107. Home Intelligence Weekly Report, no. 59, 19 November 1941, INF 1/292, TNA.
108. Reynolds, *Rich Relations* (see Introduction, n. 11), 339.
109. Christopher Somerville, *Our War: How the British Commonwealth Fought the Second World War* (London: Weidenfeld and Nicolson, 1998), 237.

CHAPTER 4: ALLIES

1. Halik Kochanski, *The Eagle* (see Chapter 1, n. 140), 169; Thomas Lane, *Victims of Stalin and Hitler: The Exodus of Poles and Balts to Britain* (Basingstoke: Palgrave, 2004), 6–7.
2. Zbigniew Siemaszko, interview by Rob Light for the 'Mixing It' project, 2015. The full interview is available at http://www.iwm.org.uk/collections/item/object/80033328.
3. Katherine Jolluck, *Exile and Identity: Polish Women in the Soviet Union during World War II* (Pittsburgh, PA: University of Pittsburgh Press, 2002), 9.
4. Zbgniew Siemaszko, interview (see n. 2).
5. Zbigniew Siemaszko, interview (see n. 2).
6. Zbigniew S. Siemaszko, *Pod Sowiecką Władzą, 1939–1942* (London: Polish Cultural Foundation, 2001). I am very grateful to Anna Siemaszko for translation of passages from her father's memoirs.
7. Ibid., 126–7.
8. Ibid., 128.
9. Kochanski, *The Eagle* (see Chapter 1, n. 140), 190.
10. http://www.polishresettlementcampsintheuk.co.uk/stories/turowicz.htm. Accessed 7 December 2015.
11. http://www.polishresettlementcampsintheuk.co.uk/stories/danutaprzeleska.htm. Accessed 7 December 2015.
12. Kochanski, *The Eagle* (see Chapter 1, n. 140), 182.
13. Raczynski, *In Allied London* (see Chapter 1, n. 157), 130.
14. Rose Macaulay, 'Consolations of the War', the *Listener*, 16 January 1941, in Jenny Hartley, ed., *Hearts Undefeated: Women's Writing of the Second World War*, 225 (London: Virago, 1994).
15. Panter-Downes, *London War Notes* (see Introduction, n. 13), 233.
16. William Sansom, *Westminster in War* (London: Faber and Faber, 1947), 167.
17. Home Intelligence Special Report, no. 32, 16 October 1942, INF 1/293, TNA.
18. Ibid.
19. 'Polish Airmen in Training in Britain', *Gaumont British News*, 1 May 1940.
20. Rose, *Which People's War* (see Chapter 3, n. 76), Chapter 5.

21. 'Attitudes to Foreigners', Report 1669Q, April 1943, MOA; 'Feelings About Australians', Report 1094, 13 February 1942, MOA.
22. *The Way to the Stars* (Anthony Asquith, 1945).
23. 'A Report on Home Opinion', no. 28 (Part 1) Secret Series A, Postal Censorship Report, 4 April 1942, PREM 4/100/1, TNA.
24. Ibid.
25. Home Intelligence Weekly Report, no. 125, 25 February 1943, INF 1/292, TNA.
26. Churchill to Layton, 17 July 1943, PREM 4/66/2, TNA.
27. Report of Gallup Poll on 'Who Won the War', published in the News Chronicle, 17 July 1943, PREM 4/66/2, TNA.
28. A Report on Home Opinion, no. 28, part 1, 4 April 1942, PREM 4/100/1, TNA; Home Intelligence Weekly Report, no. 151, 26 August 1943; no. 176, 17 Feb 1944, INF 1/292, TNA.
29. Home Intelligence Weekly Report, no. 151, 26 August 1943, INF 1/292, TNA.
30. A Report on Home Opinion, no. 24, 1 December 1941, PREM 4/100/1, TNA.
31. Home Intelligence Weekly Report, no. 162, 11 Nov 1943, INF 1/292, TNA.
32. 'The Soviet Youth Delegation', Home Intelligence Special Report, no. 36, 9 December 1942, INF 1/293, TNA.
33. Home Intelligence Weekly Report, no. 78, 1 April 1942, INF 1/282, TNA.
34. '25th Birthday of USSR', *The Times*, 9 November 1942; 'London's Tribute', *The Manchester Guardian*, 8 November 1942.
35. Home Intelligence Periodic Review, 25 November 1943; Weekly Report, no. 144, 8 July 1943, INF 1/292; Special Report, no. 32, 16 October 1942 INF 1/293, TNA.
36. Home Intelligence Weekly Report, no. 144, 8 July 1943, INF 1/292, TNA.
37. Letter from Northern Ireland to Liverpool, 28 December 1942, Postal Censorship Report, no. 36, 8 February 1943, CJ 4/30, TNA.
38. Home Intelligence Weekly Report, no, 104, 1 Oct 1942; Home Intelligence Monthly Review, 8 June 1944, INF 1/292, TNA.
39. Home Intelligence Weekly Report, no. 220, 21 December 1944, INF 1/292, TNA.
40. Home Intelligence Weekly Report, no. 205, 7 September 1944, INF 1/292, TNA.
41. Appreciation and Censorship Report, no. 51, for period 16–31 August 1944, WO 204/10381, TNA.
42. Home Intelligence Weekly Report, no. 204, 31 August 1944, INF 1/292 TNA.
43. Home Intelligence Weekly Report, no. 194, 22 June 1944, INF 1/292, TNA.
44. Home Intelligence Weekly Report, no. 206, 14 September 1944, INF 1/292, TNA.
45. Home Intelligence Weekly Report, no. 205, 7 September 1944, INF 1/292, TNA.
46. File Report 1656–7, April 2 1943, MOA.
47. Paul Ward, *Britishness Since 1870* (London: Routledge, 2004), 90.
48. Rose, *Which People's War* (see Chapter 3, n. 76), 97–101.

49. M35C to F30C, TC62 1/H, MOA.

50. Home Intelligence Weekly Report, no. 1, 30 September 1940, INF 1/292, TNA.

51. Home Intelligence Special Report on conditions in Merseyside, 9 July 1941, INF 1/292, TNA.

52. Home Intelligence Periodical Review, 27 July 1944, INF 1/292, TNA.

53. 'Recent trends in anti-Semitism', Report 1648, March 1943, MOA. Emphasis in original.

54. Home Intelligence Special Report, no. 1, 15 January 1942, INF 1/293, TNA.

55. F50D, 'Recent trends in anti-Semitism', Report no. 1648, 10 March 1943, MOA.

56. Home Intelligence Weekly Report, no. 120, 21 January 1943, INF 1/292, TNA.

57. Rose, *Which People's War* (see Chapter 3, n. 76), 106.

58. Home Intelligence Monthly Review, 8 June 1944, INF 1/292, TNA.

59. Home Intelligence Weekly Report, no. 199, 27 July 1944, INF 1/292, TNA.

60. Letter from Northern Ireland to Melton Mowbray, 25 December 1942, Postal Censorship Report, no. 36, 8 February 1943, CJ 4/30, TNA.

61. Beneš, *Wings in Exile* (see Chapter 1, n. 40), 93.

62. Ibid., 80–1.

63. 'Allies in the Air War: Building an International Force', *The Times*, 14 March 1941.

64. 'Bombing Boulogne: The Diary of Z. P. transcribed by F. B. Czarnomski' in F. B. Czarnomski, ed., *They Fight for Poland: The War in the First Person*, 271 (London: George Allen and Unwin, 1941).

65. Liskutin, *Challenge in the Air* (see Chapter 1, n. 29), 78.

66. Fry, *The King's Most Loyal* (see Chapter 2, n. 16), 45–52; *Churchill's German Army* at http://www.youtube.com/watch?v=SDkxq5gbRoE. Accessed 6 March 2014.

67. Appreciation and Censorship Report of the Polish Base Censor for period 27 June to 12 July 1944, WO 204/711, TNA.

68. Kelly, *Returning Home* (see Introduction, n. 10), 36.

69. Allen, *Churchill's Guests* (see Introduction, n. 9), 53.

70. Atkin, *The Forgotten French* (see Introduction, n. 57), 128.

71. Lefranc, 'A Member of the Free French' (see Introduction, n. 33), 14.

72. Reynolds, *Rich Relations* (see Introduction, n. 11), 197. See also 149–51, 183–4.

73. Home Intelligence Weekly Report, no. 148, 5 August 1943, INF 1/292, TNA.

74. Ibid.

75. Reynolds, *Rich Relations* (see Introduction, n. 11), 324.

76. Graham Smith, *When Jim Crow met John Bull: Black American Soldiers in World War II Britain* (London: I. B. Tauris, 1987), 134.

77. See for example Home Intelligence Weekly Report, no. 206, 23 November 1944, INF 1/292, TNA.

78. George Orwell, 'As I please', *Tribune*, 3 December 1943.

79. White, *Rising Wind* (see Chapter 3, n. 75), 33–4.

80. Ibid., 34, 21.

81. 'An American looks at American Troops in Britain', Home Intelligence Special Report no. 40, 11 March 1943, INF 1/293, TNA.

82. Home Intelligence Weekly Report, no. 144, 8 July 1943, INF 1/292, TNA; Zamoyski, *The Forgotten Few* (see Introduction, n. 48), 160, 63.

83. Smith, *When Jim Crow* (see n. 76), 140–1.

84. 'Relationships between American white soldiers and British coloured civilians in Liverpool', no date, CO 876/15, TNA.

85. Learie Constantine to Arnold Watson, 12 January 1943, CO 876/15, TNA.

86. BBC Listener Research Report on the changes in the state of British Public Opinion on the USA during 1942 and 1943, 7 February 1944, R9/9/7 BBC, WAC.

87. Home Intelligence Weekly Report, no. 92, 9 July 1942, INF 1/292, TNA.

88. Home Intelligence Weekly Report, no. 94, 23 July 1942, INF 1/292, TNA.

89. Secretary of State for War to Prime Minister, 21 October 1943, PREM 4/26/9, TNA.

90. Ibid.

91. Smith, *When Jim Crow* (see n. 76), Chapter 3.

92. Memorandum from Assistant Director, Features, 21 July 1942, R/19/1076/1, BBC, WAC. 'Salute to Mexico' was broadcast on 26 July 1942.

93. Panter-Downes, *London War Notes* (see Introduction, n. 13), 156.

94. For propaganda about the Soviet Union see McLaine, *Ministry of Morale* (see Chapter 4, n. 92), 197–208.

95. John Martin to Oliver Harvey, 21 January 1942, FO 371/32960, TNA. For the ban on enemy anthems see Robert Mackay, 'Being Beastly to the Germans: Music, Censorship and the BBC in World War II', *Historical Journal of Film, Radio and Television*, 20/4 (2000), 513–25.

96. *Daily Mail*, 22 February 1943.

97. Victor de Laveleye, 'The V sign', *Message*, January 1944, 20–24. For De Laveleye's choice of the letter 'V', see European Intelligence Papers, Series 2, no. 2, 8 October 1941, E2/188/1, BBC, WAC.

98. De Laveleye, 'The V sign' (see n. 97).

99. Martin Gilbert, *The Churchill War Papers: Vol. 3, The Ever Widening War, 1941* (London: William Heinemann, 2000), 1265.

100. Briggs, *The War of Words* (see Chapter 1, n. 163), 239–57; Gerard Mansell, *Let Truth Be Told: 50 Years of BBC External Broadcasting* (London: Weidenfeld and Nicolson 1982), Chapter 7; Cornick, 'Free France and the BBC' (see Chapter 1, n. 121); Peter Mangold, *Britain and the Defeated French: From Occupation to Liberation, 1940–1944* (London: I. B. Tauris, 2012), Chapter 8; Kay Chadwick, 'Our enemy's enemy: Selling Britain to Occupied France on the BBC French Service', *Media History*, 21/4 (2015), 426–42.

101. http://genome.ch.bbc.co.uk/326b4e1085014e759e121ccfe3dbdc42. Accessed 11 September 2016.

102. 'BBC Pep Up Features', *Daily Mail*, 20 March 1942.

103. Albert Rasmussen, 'The Listening Post' and 'The Norwegian Tankers and their Crews', in Krabbe, *Voices from Britain* (see Chapter 1, n. 120), 128–30; 137–41; Briggs, *The War of Words*, 439 (see Chapter 1, n. 163).

104. Tahu Hole to Françoise Rosay, 18 July 1944; Booking Form for talk on 'What Happened to French Films'? 16 March 1944, Françoise Rosay contributor file, BBC, WAC.
105. Listener Research Bulletin, no. 165, 16 Nov 1943, R9/1/3, BBC, WAC; Home Intelligence Weekly Report, no. 162, 11 Nov 1943, INF 1/292, TNA.
106. Michael Balcon, *Michael Balcon Presents a Lifetime in Film* (London: Hutchinson, 1969), 150.
107. Home Intelligence Weekly Report, no. 168, 23 Dec 1943, NA, INF 1/292; Listener Research Bulletin, no. 170, 20 Dec 1943, R9/1/3, BBC, WAC.
108. 'Holland under German Occupation', Home Service, 13 February 1944, in Krabbe, *Voices from Britain* (see Chapter 1, n. 120), 188–91; Listener Research Bulletin, no. 180, 29 Feb 1944, R9/1/4, BBC, WAC.
109. What 'Friendship' Means in Poland, Home Service, February 1944 in Krabbe, *Voices from Britain* (see Chapter 1, n. 120), 184–8; Listener Research Bulletin, no. 184, 27 March 1944, R9/1/4, BBC, WAC.
110. Listener Research Report, 14 July 1941, R9/65/1, BBC, WAC.
111. *Daily Mail*, 30 June 1941.
112. Listener Research Report, 30 August 1941, R9/1/1, BBC, WAC.
113. Home Intelligence Weekly Report, no. 89, 18 June, 1942, INF 1/292, TNA.
114. INF 6/607, TNA.
115. *Polish Bomber's Holiday* (Polish Film Unit 1942); *The Shortest Route* (Polish Film Unit 1942); *Strangers* (Polish Film Unit, 1944).
116. *Diary of a Polish Airman* (Concanen, 1942).
117. Home Intelligence Special Report, no. 28, 22 August 1942, INF 1/293, TNA.
118. See, for example, responses to 1943 survey on feelings about foreigners, TC25 2/O, MOA.
119. Martin Francis, *The Flyer: British Culture and the Royal Air Force 1939–1945* (Oxford: Oxford University Press), 30–1.
120. *The Gentle Sex* (Leslie Howard and Maurice Elvey, 1943).
121. *Fighting Allies* (Louise Birt, 1941).
122. A. E. Barker, 'Visit of Jewish delegation', 1 May 1942, R28/20, BBC, WAC.
123. *The 'Man in the Street' (of the B.B.C.) Talks to Europe* (London: P.S. King and Staples, 1945), 63. This series of talks ran on the European Services from 1941 to 1944.
124. Anthony Eden's speech was widely reported in the media on 17 and 18 December 1942.
125. Jeremy Harris, 'Broadcasting the Massacres: An Analysis of the BBC's Contemporary Coverage of the Holocaust', in David Cesarani, ed., *Holocaust: Critical Concepts in Historical Studies*, 308 (London: Routledge 2004).
126. Home Intelligence Weekly Report, 7 January 1943, R34/277, BBC, WAC.
127. See for example 'Record of interview with Commander O. Locker Lampson signed by R. Maconachie, 7 June 1943'; 'Sir Richard Maconachie to Lady Violet Bonham Carter, 27 October 1943', R34/277, BBC, WAC.
128. Memorandum from Sir Richard Maconachie, 27 April 1943, R34/277, BBC, WAC.

129. Programme Policy Minutes, P 54/43, R 34/614/2, BBC, WAC.
130. R34/277, BBC, WAC.
131. R. A. Rendall to Edward Wilkinson, 28 August 1947, R34/277, BBC, WAC.
132. Paul Davenport, 'Dangerous, Courageous, Invisible: Non-white Seafarers in the Merchant Navy of the 1940s and 1950s', *Journal of War and Culture Studies* 4/1 (2011), 51–64.
133. 'Lived 133 days on a raft in Atlantic', *Daily Mail*, 14 July 1943.
134. *The Chinese in Wartime Britain* (Carl Heck), INF 6/615, TNA.
135. Immigration Officer's Report, 15 July 1946, HO 213/926, TNA.
136. Minute in file, 22 October 1945, HO 213/926, TNA.

CHAPTER 5: LANGUAGE, SPEECH, AND SOUND

1. Dove, *Journey* (see Introduction, n. 15), 19.
2. Michael Kerr, *As Far as I Remember* (Oxford and Portland, OR: Hart Publishing, 2002), 51, 121.
3. Ibid., 55.
4. Judith Kerr, *The Other Way Round* (London: Fontana, 1977), 191–2.
5. Kerr, *As Far as I Remember* (see n. 2), 174.
6. Kerr, *The Other Way Round* (see n. 4), 153–4. This was later retitled *Bombs on Aunt Dainty*.
7. Dove, *Journey* (see Introduction, n. 15), 38–9.
8. Tobias Hochscherf, *The Continental Connection: German-speaking émigrés and British Cinema, 1927–45* (Manchester: Manchester University Press, 2011), 106–7.
9. Kerr, *The Other Way Round* (see n. 4), 178.
10. Dove, *Journey* (see Introduction, n. 15), 19; Kerr, *As Far as I Remember* (see n. 2), 39.
11. Kerr, *As Far as I Remember* (see n. 2), 163.
12. Ilse Newbery, 'Alfred Kerr und die BBC', *German Life and Letters*, 38/3 (1985), 260–3.
13. Deborah Vietor-Englander, 'Alfred Kerr and Marcel Reich-Ranicki: Critics and Power in Germany in the Weimar Republic and the Federal Republic', in Dagmar Lorenz and Renate Posthofen, eds., *Transforming the Center, Eroding the Margins: Essays on Ethnic and Cultural Boundaries in German-speaking Countries*, 159 (Columbia, SC: Camden House, 1998).
14. Kerr, *As Far As I Remember* (see n. 2), 52.
15. Churchill to Bracken, 16 September 1944; Bracken to Churchill, 18 September 1944, PREM 4/68/8, TNA.
16. Robert Wybrow, *Britain Speaks Out, 1937–87: A Social History as Seen Through the Gallup Data* (Basingstoke: Macmillan, 1989), 132.
17. Zamoyski, *The Forgotten Few* (see Introduction, n. 48), 117–18.
18. *While You Are in England: Helpful Information and Guidance for Every Refugee* (London: The German Jewish Aid Committee, no date), 12.
19. TC25 1/D, MOA. Emphasis in original.

20. Seller, *We Built Up Our Lives* (see Chapter 1, n. 81), 222.
21. F50D, interviewed in Hampstead, 15 January 1943, TC25 2/O, MOA.
22. F35D, interviewed in Hampstead, 16 January 1943; F35D, interviewed in Bayswater, 15 January 1943, TC25 2/O, MOA.
23. Report 118, 18 May 1940, MOA.
24. Attitudes to Aliens survey, TC25 I/J, MOA; Response to 1943 survey on feelings about foreigners, TC25 2/O, MOA.
25. Stephen Youngkin, *The Lost One: A Life of Peter Lorre* (Lexington, KY: University Press of Kentucky, 2005), 91.
26. Letter to Sydney Attwood, no date, Lucie Mannnheim contributor file, BBC, WAC.
27. Alan Brown, *Flying for Freedom* (see Chapter 1, n. 134), 23.
28. Brown, *Flying for Freedom* (see Chapter 1, n. 134), 23; Brown, 'The Czechoslovak Armed Forces' (see Chapter 1, n. 26), 175, 181.
29. Sponza, *Divided Loyalties* (see Introduction, n. 26), 211.
30. Ibid.
31. Ibid., 204.
32. Annette Kobak, *Joe's War: My Father Decoded* (London: Virago, 2004), 256–7.
33. Paris, *Orkney's Italian Chapel* (see Introduction, n. 2), 144–5.
34. Brown, *Flying for Freedom* (see Chapter 1, n. 134), 11.
35. Offenberg, *Lonely Warrior* (see Introduction, n. 32), 38.
36. Diane Collins, 'Acoustic Journeys: Exploration and the Search for an Aural History of Australia', *Australian Historical Studies*, 37/128 (2006), 11.
37. Wartime diary of Leonard George Peake, entries for 25 and 26 May 1944, 27 July 1943, Imperial War Museum manuscript collection, 416453.
38. *Night Train to Munich* (Carol Reed, 1940).
39. British Board of Film Censors, Report on scenario for *The Exiles*, 28 May 1938, British Film Institute Library.
40. British Board of Film Censors, Report on scenario for *Pastor Hall*, 14 July 1939, British Film Institute Library.
41. British Board of Film Censors, Report on scenario for *Report on a Fugitive*, 15 November 1939, British Film Institute Library.
42. Hochscherf, *The Continental Connection* (see n. 8), 87–8.
43. *The Scarlet Pimpernel* (Harold Young, 1934); *Contraband* (Michael Powell and Emeric Pressburger, 1940); *The Gentle Sex* (Leslie Howard, 1943); *The New Lot* (Carol Reed, 1943).
44. Andrew Moor, 'Dangerous Limelight: Anton Walbrook and the Seduction of the English', in Bruce Babington, ed., *British Stars and Stardom*, 85 (Manchester: Manchester University Press, 2001); *Dangerous Moonlight* (Brian Desmond Hurst, 1941).
45. C. A. Lejeune, 'Misunderstanding', *Observer*, 28 August 1949.
46. http://users.telenet.be/kurt.weygantt/worldwariiaces.index.html_daniel-leroyduvivier.htm. Accessed 13 May 2015.

47. *Crook's Tour* (John Baxter, 1941). *Crook's Tour* was broadcast on BBC radio between 16 August and 20 September 1941.

48. *The Secret Mission* (Harold French, 1942).

49. *One of Our Aircraft is Missing* (Michael Powell and Emeric Pressburger, 1942).

50. Emeric Pressburger, *One Of Our Aircraft is Missing* (Anglo-American Film Corporation, 1942). This is a pamphlet about the film.

51. Kevin Gough-Yates, 'The British Feature Film as a European Concern: Britain and the Émigré Film Maker, 1933-45', in Günter Berghaus, ed., *Theatre and Film in Exile: German Artists in Great Britain, 1933–45*, 156 (Oxford, Berg, 1989).

52. *I Know Where I'm Going* (Michael Powell and Emeric Pressburger, 1945).

53. George Mikes, *How to be an Alien* (London: Allan Wingate, 1949, first published 1946), 83, 85.

54. *The 49th Parallel* (Michael Powell and Emeric Pressburger, 1941); *The Life and Death of Colonel Blimp* (Michael Powell and Emeric Pressburger, 1943).

55. Gough-Yates, 'The British Feature Film' (see n. 51), 156.

56. Quoted in Robert Murphy, *British Cinema and the Second World War* (London: Continuum, 2000), 143.

57. Humphrey Jennings, 'The Silent Village', BBC radio broadcast, Home Service, 26 May 1943, in Kevin Jackson, ed., *The Humphrey Jennings Film Reader*, 72–4 (Manchester: Carcanet Press, 1993).

58. Ibid., 67.

59. Press-cutting in INF 6/1916, TNA.

60. INF 5/90, TNA.

61. Australian National Library, Manuscript Collections, MS 5392.

62. Ruvani Ranasinha, 'South Asian Broadcasters in Britain and the BBC: talking to India' (1941–1943)', *South Asian Diaspora*, 2/1 (2010), 57–71.

63. Miles Hudson and John Stanier, *War and the Media: A Random Searchlight* (Stroud: Sutton Publishing, 1999), 68.

64. Airgram of 17 August 1944, Chester Wilmot papers, Ms 8436, Box 9, Australian National Library.

65. Airgram of 20 June 1944, Chester Wilmot papers, Ms 8436, Box 9, Australian National Library.

66. Lindsey Dodd, 'Some Elephants Collaborate: Babar the Free French Elephant and Children's Broadcasting from London (1941–1944)', Paper to Society for French Studies Conference, July 2011.

67. *London Can Take It!* (Harry Watt and Humphrey Jennings, 1940); *Christmas Under Fire* (Harry Watt, 1941).

68. For the British propaganda campaign addressed to America see Nicholas Cull, *Selling War: The British Propaganda Campaign against American 'Neutrality' in World War II* (Oxford: Oxford University Press, 1995).

69. Quoted in James Chapman, *The British At War: Cinema, State and Propaganda 1939–1945* (London: I. B. Tauris, 1998), 100.

70. Ministry of Information, 14 October 1940, INF 6/328, TNA.

71. Antonia Lant, *Blackout: Reinventing Women for Wartime British Cinema* (Princeton, NJ: Princeton University Press, 1991), 34.
72. http://www.screenonline.org.uk/film/id/500677/. Accessed 23 April 2016.
73. Una Marson, 'Talking it Through', Home Service 11 July 1940, transcript BBC, WAC.
74. BBC Listener Research, Weekly Report, no. 36, 28 May 1941; See also Weekly Report, no. 44, 28 July 1941, R9/1/1, BBC, WAC.
75. Stephen Bourne, *Elisabeth Welch: Soft Lights and Sweet Music* (Lanham, MD: Scarecrow Press, 2005), xvii, 35.
76. 'Colour Discrimination in UK', May 1946, CO 537/1224, TNA. Emphasis in original.
77. Amanda Bidnall, 'West Indian Interventions at the Heart of the Cultural Establishment: Edric Connor, Pearl Connor, and the BBC', *Twentieth Century British History*, 24/1 (2013), 65.
78. 'Art of an Ally', *Daily Express*, 29 September 1943.
79. 'Coloured Soldiers give a Concert at the Albert Hall', *Picture Post*, 16 October 1943.
80. Reynolds, *Rich Relations* (see Introduction, n. 11), 314.
81. David Reynolds, *From World War to Cold War: Churchill, Roosevelt, and the International History of the 1940s* (Oxford: Oxford University Press, 2006), 207.
82. 'How the BBC Covers the Invasion', *Picture Post*, 17 June 1944.
83. A. P. Ryan, 'Notes to Correspondents', 8 May 1944, Chester Wilmot papers, Ms 8436, Box 9, Australian National Library.
84. Chester Wilmot, Airgram of 3 October 1944, in Ibid.
85. *Listen to Britain* (Humphrey Jennings, 1942).
86. Report 118, 18 May 1940, MOA.
87. European Monthly Intelligence Report, 5 August 1940, E2/186/2, BBC, WAC.
88. 'Self-Portraits of European Listeners', European Intelligence Papers, Series 3, no. 1, 6 March 1942, E2/187, BBC, WAC.
89. Campbell Dixon, 'Voices that Lost us the US Market: Effeminate Accents Spoiling British Pictures', *Daily Telegraph and Morning Post*, 28 March 1938.
90. Joy Damousi, '"The Australian has a Lazy Way of Talking": Australian Character and Accent, 1920s–1940s', in Joy Damousi and Desley Deacon, eds., *Talking and Listening in the Age of Modernity: Essays on the History of Sound*, 86 (Canberra: ANU E Press, 2007).
91. 'An Examination of the Many Reasons for the Unfriendly Feelings of a Large Number of Americans Towards Great Britain', Postal and Telegraph Censorship Report on The United States of America, 11 September 1942, CO 875/18/11, TNA.
92. Simon Potter, *Broadcasting Empire: The BBC and the British World, 1922–1970* (Oxford: Oxford University Press, 2012), 96.
93. Ibid.
94. 'A report on Home Opinion', Postal Censorship Report, no. 24, 1 December 1941, PREM 4/100/1, TNA.

95. Respondent no. 3491 to June 1943 directive, File Report 1885, August 1943, MOA.

96. Home Intelligence Weekly Report, no. 92, 9 July 1942, INF 1/292, TNA.

97. Report on Quentin Reynolds's Postscript, Sunday 29 June 1941 'Are you Listening Dr. Goebbels'? 14 July 1942, R9/65/1, BBC, WAC.

98. Listener Research Report, 26 August 1941, R9/65/1, BBC, WAC.

99. Report 1569, January 1943, MOA.

100. Kathleen Hunt to Robert Menzies, 6 September 1939, SP 112/1, Australian National Archives, Canberra.

101. Kathleen Hunt to Sir Henry Gullett, 22 September 1939, SP 112/1, Australian National Archives, Canberra.

102. Letter to Wilmot from R. Anne Lister, Birmingham, 8 March 1945, in Chester Wilmot papers, Ms 8436, Box 9, Australian National Library.

103. Joy Damousi, '"The Filthy American Twang": Elocution, the Advent of American "Talkies", and Australian Cultural Identity', *American Historical Review*, 112 (2007), 395, 409.

104. Joy Damousi, 'The Australian' (see n. 90), 92, 94.

105. Harry Watt, 'Filming the Soldier: Australia's Turn Next', *Sydney Morning Herald*, 4 December 1943.

106. *The Overlanders* (Harry Watt, 1946).

107. *Sydney Morning Herald*, 8 December 1943.

108. Empire Talks Manager to Programme Directors, 13 January 1942, R34/282, BBC, WAC.

109. Memo from ADS to A/AC (A), 30 June 1941, R34/282, BBC, WAC.

110. Memo from Assistant Controller of Overseas Services to R.A. Rendall, 1 May 1943, R34/306, BBC, WAC.

111. Letter from Sidney Salomon, 3 February 1942, R28/20, BBC. WAC.

112. NRD Manchester to CHD Bristol, 11 February 1941, R28/20, BBC, WAC.

113. Letters to Sidney Salomon, 29 May 1943, R34/277; 17 June 1943, R28/20, BBC, WAC.

114. Memorandum from Head of Variety, 21 December 1950, R41/19/2, BBC, WAC.

115. Letters of 22 October 1941, 21 March 1944, 18 September 1944, INF 1/598, TNA.

116. Cull, *Selling War* (see Chapter 5, n. 68), 46.

117. Susan Brewer, *To Win the Peace: British Propaganda in the United States During World War II* (Ithaca, NY: Cornell University Press, 1997), 49.

118. Ibid.

119. Harry Watt, Imperial War Museum Sound Archive, Interview no. 5367, Reel 4.

120. Ibid.

121. Michel Chion, *The Voice in Cinema* (New York: Columbia University Press, 1999), 12; Webster, *Englishness and Empire* (see Chapter 3, n. 40), 45.

122. 'An Examination of the Many Reasons for the Unfriendly Feelings of a Large Number of Americans Towards Great Britain', Postal and Telegraph Censorship

Report on The United States of America, 11 September 1942, CO 875/18/11, TNA.

123. Quoted in Andrew Roberts, *A History of the English-speaking Peoples since 1900* (London: Weidenfeld and Nicolson, 2006), 1.

124. Wendy Webster, ' "The Whim of Foreigners": Language, Speech, and Sound in Second World War British Film and Radio', *Twentieth Century British History*, 23/3 (2012), 359–60.

125. Winston Churchill to Sir Alexander Cadogan, 16 February 1941; Foreign Office to J.M. Martin, 30 March 1944, PREM 4/68/8, TNA.

126. Empire Talks Manager to Programme Directors, 13 January 1942, R34/282, BBC, WAC.

127. Prime Minister's personal minute, 30 October 1942, PREM 4/68/8, TNA.

CHAPTER 6: SEXUAL PATRIOTISM

1. Arthur Walrond to Colonial Office, 29 June 1943, CO 876/15, TNA.
2. Ibid.
3. Miss P. G. Palmer to Colonial Office, 15 September 1943, CO 876/15, TNA.
4. J. L Keith to Air Ministry, 22 September 1943; Air Ministry to J. L. Keith, 5 October 1943, CO 876/15, TNA.
5. War Office to J. L. Keith, 1 November 1943, CO 876/15, TNA.
6. Reynolds, *Rich Relations* (see Introduction, n. 11), Chapter 18.
7. Belchem, *Before the Windrush* (see Introduction, n. 11), 93.
8. Home Intelligence Periodical Review, 27 July 1944, INF 1/292, TNA.
9. Appreciation and Censorship Report, no. 51, for period 16–31 August 1944, WO 204/10381, TNA.
10. Anthony Aldgate and Jeffrey Richards (1986) *Britain Can Take It: British Cinema in the Second World War* (Oxford: Blackwell), 66; Home Intelligence Weekly Report, no. 140, 10 June 1943, INF 1/292, TNA.
11. *The Gentle Sex* (Leslie Howard and Maurice Elvey, 1943).
12. *The Times*, 25 May 1940.
13. 'Women!' *Picture Post*, 30 August 1941.
14. *Daily Mirror*, 7 June 1940; 3 June 1940; *Manchester Guardian*, 15 November 1940; 6 June 1942, 15 April 1942.
15. Jeremy Crang, *The British Army and the People's War 1939–45* (Manchester: Manchester University Press, 2000).
16. Alan Allport, *Demobbed: Coming Home After the Second World War* (New Haven, CT: Yale University Press, 2009), 103–4. For the range of relationships between British military stationed in India and Indian women, see Yasmin Khan, 'Sex in an Imperial War Zone: Transnational Encounters in Second World War India', *History Workshop Journal*, 73 (2012), 240–58.
17. Home Intelligence Weekly Report, no. 176, 17 February 1944. See also Home Intelligence Report, no. 171, 13 January 1944, INF 1/292, TNA.

18. Lucio Sponza, 'Italian Prisoners of War in Great Britain, 1943–6', in Bob Moore & Kent Fedorowich, eds., *Prisoners of War and their Captors in World War II*, 212–13 (Oxford: Berg, 1996).

19. Home Intelligence Periodical Review, 14 December 1944, INF 1/292, TNA.

20. Home Intelligence Weekly Report, no. 191, 2 June 1944, INF 1/292, TNA.

21. Quoted in Allport, *Demobbed* (see n. 16), 6.

22. Wendy Webster, *Imagining Home: Gender, 'Race and National Identity, 1945–64* (London: UCL Press, 1998), 14.

23. Home Intelligence Periodical Review, 31 August 1944; Home Intelligence Weekly Report, no. 214, 9 November 1944, INF 1/292, TNA.

24. Home Intelligence Monthly Review, 8 June 1944, INF 1/292, TNA.

25. Home Intelligence Monthly Review, 8 June 1944; Home Intelligence Weekly Reports, no. 212, 26 October 1944; no. 202, 17 August 1944; no. 213, 2 November 1944; no. 207, 21 September 1944, INF 1/292, TNA.

26. Home Intelligence Monthly Review, 8 June 1944, INF 1/292, TNA.

27. Home Intelligence Report, no. 100, 3 September 1942, INF 1/292, TNA.

28. Home Intelligence Periodic Review, no. 164, 25 November 1943, INF 1/292, TNA.

29. Leanne McCormick, ' "One Yank and They're Off": Interaction Between U.S. Troops and Northern Irish Women, 1942-1945', *Journal of the History of Sexuality*, 15/2 (2006), 237.

30. Responses to 1943 surveys on attitudes to aliens and feelings about foreigners, TC25 1/J; TC25 2/O, MOA.

31. F35B, interviewed in Bolton, 25 March 1943, Attitudes to Aliens survey, TC25 I/J, MOA.

32. F35C, interviewed in Hampstead, 15 January 1943, Survey on feelings about foreigners, TC25 2/O, MOA.

33. Sheila Patterson, 'The Poles: An Exile Community in Britain', in J. Watson, ed., *Between Two Cultures: Migrants and Minorities in Britain*, 224 (Oxford: Blackwell, 1977); Stacey and Wilson, *The Half Million* (see Introduction, n. 57), 136–8; Reynolds, *Rich Relations* (see Introduction, n. 11), 420–2.

34. See for example, Home Intelligence Weekly Report, no. 144, 8 July 1943, INF 1/292, TNA.

35. *Millions Like Us* (Sidney Gilliat and Frank Launder, 1943).

36. Home Intelligence Monthly Review, 8 June 1944, INF 1/292, TNA.

37. Quoted in McCormick, 'One Yank' (see n. 29), 238–9.

38. *Welcome to Britain* (Anthony Asquith, 1943).

39. Smith, *When Jim Crow* (see Chapter 4, n. 76), 197.

40. Les Back, 'Syncopated Synergy: Dance, Embodiment, and the Call of the Jitterbug', in Vron Ware and Les Back, eds., *Out of Whiteness: Color, Politics, and Culture*, 187 (Chicago, IL: University of Chicago Press, 2002).

41. 'Inside London's Coloured Clubs', *Picture Post*, 17 July 1943.

42. 'What the Chapel Means', *Picture Post*, 1 January 1944.

43. Wendy Webster, 'Mumbo-jumbo, Magic and Modernity: Africa in British Cinema, 1946–65, in Lee Grieveson & Colin MacCabe, eds., *Film and the End of Empire*, 242–3 (Basingstoke: Palgrave Macmillan, 2011).

44. *The Proud Valley* (Pen Tennyson, 1939).

45. James Robertson, *The British Board of Film Censors: Film Censorship in Britain, 1896–1950* (London: Croom Helm, 1985), 60.

46. Sir Frederick Leggett to Sir George Gater, 6 March 1944, LAB 26/55, TNA.

47. Report on West Indian Technicians and Trainees N. W., 18 Dec 1943, LAB 26/55, TNA.

48. Janet Toole, 'GIs and the Race Bar in Wartime Warrington', *History Today*, 1 July 1993, 22.

49. 'West Indian Technicians and trainees N. W', 18 December 1943, LAB 26/55, TNA.

50. Ibid.

51. Ibid.

52. Allison Abra, 'On with the Dance: Nation, Culture, and Popular Dancing in Britain, 1918–1945', Ph.D dissertation, University of Michigan, 2009, 339.

53. Report on West Indian Trainees and Technicians, Discrimination, 24 July 1944, LAB 26/55, TNA.

54. Survey on feelings about foreigners, 1943, TC25 2/O, MOA.

55. 'United States Coloured Troops in the United Kingdom, Memorandum by the Secretary of State for War', September 1942, PREM 4/26/9, TNA.

56. Reynolds, *Rich Relations* (see Introduction, n. 11), 217.

57. Ibid.

58. Home Intelligence Weekly Report, no. 99, 27 August 1942; Home Intelligence Weekly Report, no. 102, 17 Sept 1942, INF 1/292 TNA.

59. John Keith to John Wyndham, 28 August 1942, CO 876/14, TNA.

60. 'United States Negro Troops in the United Kingdom', Memorandum by the Secretary of State for War, September 1942, PREM 4/26/9, TNA.

61. John Keith memo, 12 September 1942, CO 876/14, TNA.

62. Quoted in Smith, *When Jim Crow* (see Chapter 4, n. 76), 45.

63. 'United States Negro Troops in the United Kingdom', Memorandum by the Lord Privy Seal, 17 October 1942, Appendix A. PREM 4/26/9, TNA.

64. Report on West Indian Technicians and Trainees N. W., 18 Dec 1943, LAB 26/55, TNA.

65. *Timbermen from Honduras* (Colonial Film Unit, 1943).

66. Note on file, 17 August 1943, CO, 876/42, TNA.

67. The Secretary, Bristol, British Honduras Unit, Relations with white women, 6 July 1943, CO 876/42, TNA.

68. Petherick to Eden, 17 July 1943, quoted in Gavin Schaffer, 'Re-thinking the History of Blame: Britain and Minorities during the Second World War, *National Identities*, 8/4 (2006), 407–8.

69. Quoted in Paul Rich, *Race and Empire in British Politics* (Cambridge: Cambridge University Press, 1986), 152.

70. Winston Churchill to Secretary of State for War, 20 October 1943, PREM 4/26/9, TNA.
71. Duke of Marlborough to Winston Churchill, 21 October 1943, PREM 4/26/9, TNA.
72. Daniel Williams, *Black Skins, Blue Books: African Americans and Wales, 1845–1945* (Cardiff: University of Wales Press, 2012), 223.
73. https://robertwalshwriter.wordpress.com/2014/08/16/the-strange-case-of-leroy-henry/; *The Times*, 19 June and 7 July 1944. Accessed 14 November 2016.
74. *Daily Mirror*, 2 June 1944.
75. Home Intelligence Weekly Report, no. 196, 6 July 1944, INF 1/292, TNA.
76. http://www.theyworkforyou.com/debates/?id=1944-05-10a.1875.2. Accessed 26 April 2016.
77. Home Intelligence Monthly Review, 8 June 1944, INF 1/292, TNA.
78. *The Times*, 12 August 1944.
79. Susan Pennybacker, *From Scottsboro to Munich* (see chapter 3, n. 80), 239.
80. File Report 1885, August 1943, MOA.
81. Sonya Rose, 'Girls and GIs: Race, Sex, and Diplomacy in Second World War Britain', *International History Review*, 19/1 (1997), 154.
82. Home Intelligence Weekly Report, no. 101, 10 Sept 1942, INF 1/292, TNA.
83. *Sunday Express*, 8 April 1945.
84. Allport, *Demobbed* (see n. 16), 100–2.
85. *New York Times*, 22 June 1945, quoted in Inge Weber-Newth, 'Bilateral Relations: British Soldiers and German Women, in Louise Ryan and Wendy Webster, eds., *Gendering Migration: Masculinity', Femininity and Ethnicity in Post-War Britain* (Aldershot: Ashgate, 2008), 57.
86. Fabrice Virgili, *Shorn Women: Gender and Punishment in Liberation France* (Oxford: Berg, 2002), 57.
87. Home Intelligence Periodical Review, 21 September 1944, INF 1/292, TNA.
88. *Loughborough Echo*, 26 January 1945, quoted in Sponza, *Divided Loyalties* (see Introduction, n. 26), 282.
89. Madeleine Bunting, *The Model Occupation: The Channel Islands Under German Rule, 1940–1945* (London: HarperCollins, 1995), 252–60.
90. Doreen and Jack Stang, interviewed by Janette Martin for the 'Mixing It' project, 2015. The full interview is available at http://www.iwm.org.uk/collections/item/object/80033224.
91. Fritz Zimmermann, 'A Stranger in Three Continents: My Life from 1920 to 1951'. I am grateful to Peter Zimmermann for giving me this account of the life of his father.
92. http://www.telegraph.co.uk/news/uknews/1560340/Diamond-date-for-British-bride-of-German-PoW.html. Accessed 10 November 2016.
93. Peter Sinclair interviewed by Janette Martin for the 'Mixing It' project, 2015. The full interview is available at http://www.iwm.org.uk/collections/item/object/80033223.
94. Weber-Newth and Steinert, *German Migrants* (see Introduction, n. 2), 53.

95. Smith, *When Jim Crow* (see Chapter 4, n. 76), 206.
96. Reynolds, *Rich Relations* (see Introduction, n. 11), 231.
97. 'Britain's Brown Babies: Illegitimate Tots a Tough Problem for England', *Ebony Magazine*, 2/1 (November 1946), 15–19.
98. *Time*, 11 March 1946.
99. Quoted in Clive Harris, 'Images of Blacks in Britain 1930–1960', in Sheila Allen and Marie Macey, eds., *Race and Social Policy* (London ESRC: 1988), 37.
100. Webster, *Imagining Home*, 118–19 (see n. 22).
101. Tony Martin, interviewed for *Mixed Britannia*, Channel 4, 2011.
102. http://www.mix-d.org/museum/timeline/the-babies-they-left-behind-them. Accessed 13 October 2016.
103. Andrew Nocon, A Reluctant Welcome? Poles in Britain in the 1940s, *Oral History*, 24/1 (1996), 81.
104. *Lancashire Daily Post*, 10 December 1946.
105. Trevor Philpott, 'Would You Let Your Daughter Marry a Negro?' *Picture Post*, 30 October 1954; Colin MacInnes, 'A Short Guide for Jumbles to the Life of their Coloured Brethren in England', in Colin MacInnes, *England: Half English*, 25 (London: MacGibbon and Kee, 1961, first published 1956); *Daily Express*, 18 July 1956.
106. Clive Webb, 'Special Relationships: Mixed-race Couples in Post-war Britain and the United States', *Women's History Review*, 26/1 (2017), 113.
107. *Daily Telegraph*, 2 September 1958.
108. Susan Kingsley Kent, *Gender and Power in Britain, 1640–1990* (London: Routledge, 1999), 332.
109. Amanda Bidnall, 'West Indian Interventions at the Heart of the Cultural Establishment: Edric Connor, Pearl Connor and the BBC', *Twentieth Century British History*, 24/1 (2013), 73.
110. White, *Rising Wind* (see Chapter 3, n. 75), 11.
111. Clive Webb, 'Special Relationships' (see n. 106), 116.
112. Ibid.

CHAPTER 7: AFTERMATH

1. Liskutin, *Challenge* (see Chapter 1, n. 29), 183.
2. http://www.iwm.org.uk/collections/item/object/1060005806. Accessed 5 December 2015.
3. Liskutin, *Challenge* (see Chapter 1, n. 29), 186.
4. Ibid., 187.
5. Ibid., 204.
6. *Daily Express*, 20 May 1948.
7. *Daily Mirror*, 20 May 1948.
8. *The Times*, 20 May 1948.
9. *Manchester Guardian*, 21 May 1948.
10. BBC Yearbook 1945, 112.

11. Sponza, *Divided Loyalties* (see Introduction, n. 26), 316.

12. Royal Commission on Population, *Report* (London, HMSO, Cmd. 7695, 1949), Para. 329.

13. Ibid.

14. Hansard, 29 February 1947, Col. 758.

15. Wendy Webster, 'Defining Boundaries: European Volunteer Worker Women in Britain and Narratives of Community', *Women's History Review*, 9/2 (2000), 259–61.

16. J. A. Tannahill, *European Volunteer Workers in Britain* (Manchester: Manchester University Press, 1958), 51.

17. Kathleen Paul, *Whitewashing Britain: Race and Citizenship in the Postwar Era* (Ithaca, NY: Cornell University Press, 1997), 80.

18. Ibid.

19. B0129 cassette 3, side 2, Bradford Heritage Archive.

20. Quoted in Tony Kushner, *The Holocaust and the Liberal Imagination: A Social and Cultural History* (Oxford: Blackwell, 1994), 235.

21. LAB 8/99, TNA.

22. Tony Kushner, 'Anti-semitism and Austerity: the August 1947 Riots in Britain', in Panikos Panayi, ed., *Racial Violence in Britain in the Nineteenth and Twentieth Centuries* (London: Leicester University Press, 1996).

23. John Jackson, *The Irish in Britain* (London: Routledge and Kegan Paul, 1963), 14.

24. Kelly, *Returning Home* (see Introduction, n. 10), 103, 112.

25. Ibid., 89.

26. Sheila Patterson, *Immigrants in Industry* (Oxford: Oxford University Press, 1968), 20.

27. Report of Working Party on Employment in the UK of Surplus Colonial Labour, 1948, CO 1042/192, TNA.

28. Bob Carter, Clive Harris, and Shirley Joshi, 'The Racialization of Black Immigration', in Kwesi Owusu, *Black British Society and Culture: A Text Reader*, 22 (London: Routledge, 2000).

29. Kenan Malik, *The Meaning of Race: Race, History and Culture in Western Society* (Basingstoke: Macmillan, 1996), 20.

30. Cabinet Committee, Colonial Immigrants, 22 June 1956, CAB 129/81/45, TNA.

31. Malik, *The Meaning of Race* (see n. 29), 22.

32. Randall Hansen, *Citizenship and Immigration in Post-war Britain* (Oxford: Oxford University Press, 2000), 68.

33. Ian Spencer, 'The Open Door, Labour Needs and British Immigration Policy, 1945-55', *Immigrants and Minorities*, 15/1 (March 1996), 22–41; Hansen, *Citizenship* (see n. 32), 59; Shompa Lahiri, 'South Asians in Post-imperial Britain: Decolonisation and Imperial Legacy', in Stuart Ward, ed., *British Culture and the End of Empire*, 206 (Manchester: Manchester University Press, 2001); Stephen Brooke, 'The Conservative Party, Immigration and National Identity, 1948–1968', in Martin Francis and Ina Zweiniger-Bargielowska, eds.,

The Conservatives and British Society 1880–1990, 147–70 (Cardiff: University of Wales Press, 1996).

34. Judith Brown, *Global South Asians: Introducing the Modern Diaspora* (Cambridge: Cambridge University Press, 2006), 43–4.

35. Belchem, *Before the Windrush* (see Introduction, n. 11), 111.

36. 'Repatriation of Chinese Seamen', 22 October 1945, HO 213/926, TNA.

37. Immigration Officer's Report, 15 July 1946, HO 213/926, TNA.

38. http://www.halfandhalf.org.uk/dr.htm. Accessed 5 March 2014.

39. *News Chronicle*, 19 August 1946.

40. *The Times*, 4 September 1945.

41. Kushner and Knox, *Refugees in an Age of Genocide* (see Chapter 2, n. 169), 222.

42. Grenville, *Jewish Refugees* (see Introduction, n. 57), 57–8.

43. 'Problems of Adjustment', *AJR Information*, July 1946.

44. Peter Sinclair, interview with Janette Martin for the 'Mixing It' project, 2015. The full interview is available at http://www.iwm.org.uk/collections/item/object/80033223. Peter Sinclair left this information in a telephone message after the interview had been completed.

45. Lynton, *Accidental Journey* (see Chapter 2, n. 27), 265.

46. Grenville, *Jewish Refugees* (see Introduction, n. 57), Chapter 3.

47. Kushner and Knox, *Refugees in an Age of Genocide* (see Chapter 2, n. 169), 221–3; *The Times*, 28 February 1945.

48. Zamoyski, *The Forgotten Few* (see Introduction, n. 48), 198–9.

49. Appreciation and Censorship Report of the Polish Base Censor Unit for period 12 Feb 1945–27 Feb 1945, WO 204/711, TNA.

50. Ibid.

51. Appreciation and Censorship Report, no. 63, for period 15–28 February 1945, WO 204/10382, TNA.

52. Zamoyski, *The Forgotten Few* (see Introduction, n. 48), 198–200.

53. Mark Ostrowski, 'To Return to Poland' (see Introduction, n. 70), 79.

54. Ibid., Appendix B, 391–2.

55. Appreciation and Censorship Report of the Polish Base Censor for period 27 July–12 August 1944, WO 204/711; Appreciation and Censorship Report, no. 63, for period 15–28 February 1945, WO 204/10382, TNA.

56. Kathy Burrell, *Moving Lives: Narratives of Nation and Migration among Europeans in Post-war Britain* (Aldershot: Ashgate, 2006), 47.

57. Jerzy Zubrzycki, *Polish Immigrants in Britain: A Study of Adjustment* (The Hague: Martinus Nijhoff, 1956), 58, 90, 62.

58. Paul, *Whitewashing Britain* (see n. 17), 67.

59. Fritz Zimmermann, 'A Stranger in Three Continents: My Life from 1920 to 1951': I am grateful to Peter Zimmermann for sending me this account by his father.

60. Sponza, *Divided Loyalties* (see Introduction, n. 26), 319.

61. *Daily Mirror*, 9 August 1946; Hansard, House of Commons Debate, vol. 421, 27 March 1946; *The Guardian*, 13 September 1946.

62. Moore, 'Turning Liabilities into Assets' (see Chapter 2, n. 51).

63. Quoted in Mike Phillips and Trevor Phillips, *Windrush: The Irresistible Rise of Multi-Racial Britain* (London: HarperCollins, 1998), 82.

64. Nocon, 'A Reluctant Welcome?' (see Chapter 6, n. 103), 80–2.

65. Michelle Winslow, 'War, Resettlement, Rooting and Ageing: An Oral History Study of Polish Émigrés in Britain', Ph.D dissertation, University of Sheffield, 2001, 127.

66. Wendy Ugolini, ' "When are you going back"? Memory, Ethnicity and the British Home Front', in Lucy Noakes and Juliette Pattinson, eds., *British Cultural Memory and the Second World War*, 102 (London: Bloomsbury, 2014).

67. Kirklees Sound Archive, 330PL.

68. Winslow, 'War, Resettlement' (see n. 65), 128.

69. *Daily Mirror*, 20 July 1948.

70. Publicity for the Education of Popular Opinion on Foreign Workers, Minutes of Committee Meeting, 5 December 1947, LAB 12/513, TNA.

71. *Code Name: Westward Ho!* (Mary Beales, 1949), shown on BBC television 1 September 1949 and repeated 25 October 1949, INF 6/731, TNA.

72. 'Complaint about "Focus on European Workers" ', 8 July 1947, R 28/20, BBC, WAC.

73. David Cesarani, 'Lacking in Convictions: British War Crimes Policy and National Memory of the Second World War', in M. Evans and K. Lunn, eds., *War and Memory in the Twentieth Century* (Oxford: Berg, 1997).

74. *Daily Mirror*, 19 July 1948.

75. Zamoyski, *The Forgotten Few* (see Introduction, n. 48), 193.

76. Letter on Polish labour, 8 September 1947, LAB 12/513, TNA.

77. Janine Hanson, 'Sympathy, Antipathy, Hostility: British Attitudes to Non-Repatriable Poles and Ukrainians after the Second World War and to the Hungarian Refugees of 1956', Ph.D dissertation, University of Sheffield, June 1995, 2 vols; vol. 1, 144–206, vol. 2, 342; Thomas Lane, *Victims of Stalin and Hitler: The Exodus of Poles and Balts to Britain* (Basingstoke: Palgrave, 2004), 181.

78. Appreciation and Censorship Report, no. 51, for period 16–31 August 1944, WO 204/10381, TNA.

79. *Lancashire Evening Post*, 14 November 1946.

80. Quoted in Holmes, *John Bull's Island* (see Introduction, n. 52), 249.

81. Weber-Newth and Steinert, *German Migrants* (see Introduction, n. 2), 28, 190.

82. Keith Sword with Norman Davies and Jan Ciechanowski, *The Formation of the Polish community in Great Britain 1939–1950* (London: School of Slavonic and East European Studies, 1989) 271–2.

83. W. W. Daniels, *Racial Discrimination in England, based on the PEP Report* (Harmondsworth: Penguin, 1968), 154.

84. Nocon, 'A Reluctant Welcome?' (see Chapter 6, n. 103), 82.

85. Winslow, 'War, Resettlement' (see n. 65), 14.

86. E. Martin Noble, *Jamaica Airman: A Black Airman in Britain 1943 and after* (London: New Beacon Books, 1984), 65–6.

87. A. H. Richmond, *Colour Prejudice in Britain: A Study of West Indian Workers in Liverpool, 1941–1951* (London: Routledge, 1954), 102–8; Fryer, *Staying Power* (see Chapter 3, n. 65), 367–71.

88. Murray, *Lest We Forget* (see Introduction, n. 35), 132.

89. Ugolini, 'When are you going back' (see n. 66), 100.

90. Noble, *Jamaica Airman* (see n. 86), 62–3.

91. https://charmedlifecampaign.wordpress.com/2009/10/23/charmed-life-promo/. Accessed 13 November 2016.

92. Noble, *Jamaica Airman* (see n. 86), 7.

93. David Edgerton, *Britain's War Machine: Weapons, Resources and Experts in the Second World War* (London: Penguin Books, 2012), 272–3.

94. Nicolls, 'Programme Directive No. 113: Victory Programmes', 30 August 1944, R34/953, WAC. I am grateful to Thomas Hajkowski for this reference.

95. *Objective Burma!* (Raoul Walsh, USA, 1945).

96. *Daily Mirror*, 5 October 1945.

97. *Daily Mail*, 21 September 1945.

98. Ian Jarvie, 'Fanning the Flames: Anti-American reaction to Operation Burma (1945)', *Historical Journal of Film, Radio and Television*, 1/2 (1981), 79–80.

99. S. P. Mackenzie, 'War in the Air: Churchill, the Air Ministry and the BBC response to Victory at Sea', *Contemporary British History*, 20/4 (2006), 561.

100. John Colville to Basil Nicholls, 27 October 1952, PREM 11/408, TNA.

101. Hansard, House of Commons Debate, 25 February 1953, vol. 511, c2 056.

102. Director General to Director Television, 13 October 1953, T6/301/1, BBC, WAC.

103. The first episode of *Victory at Sea* was screened on BBC television, on 27 October 1952. The first episode of *War in the* Air was screened on 8 November 1954.

104. *Daily Sketch*, 31 October 1954.

105. *The Times*, 9 November 1954.

106. *Daily Mail*, 9 November 1954.

107. *Evening Standard*, 30 October 1954.

108. *Reynolds News*, 31 October 1954.

109. Letter, 30 October 1954, FO 371/109343, TNA.

110. Report by Frank Roberts to Sir W. Strang, 29 April 1952, FO 1110/528, TNA.

111. Foreign Office note, 30 April 1952, FO 1110/528, TNA.

112. Minute from the Prime Minister to the Foreign Secretary, 1 November 1954, FO 371/109343, TNA.

113. Minute from Prime Minister's Office, 1 November 1954, FO 371/109733, TNA.

114. Minute, 12 August 1954, FO 371/109733, TNA.

115. Minute, 12 August 1954, FO 371/109733, TNA; Memorandum, 30 July 1954, LCO 4/273, TNA.

116. *Daily Express*, 11 August 1954.

117. H. D. Willcock, 'Public Opinion: Attitudes towards America and Russia', *Political Quarterly*, 19 (1948), 70–2.

118. Tony Shaw, *British Cinema and the Cold War: The State, Propaganda and Consensus* (London: I. B. Tauris, 2006), 188.

119. *The Times*, 6 May 1952.

120. *There's Freedom in the Air* (London, HMSO, 1944).

121. Churchill to General Ismay, 12 July 1940, PREM 3/43, TNA. See also AIR 8/370, TNA.

122. Winslow, 'War, Resettlement' (see n. 65), 182.

123. Zbigniew S. Siemaszko, *I Co Dalej? 1945–1948* (Warsaw: LTW, 2016), 89–90. I am grateful to Anna Siemaszko for translation of this passage. Norman Davies, *Rising '44: The Battle for Warsaw* (London: Pan Books, 2004), 508.

124. Andrew Hempel, *Poland in World War II: An Illustrated Military History* (New York: Hippocrene Books), 106; Peter Stachura, '"God, Honour and the Fatherland": The Poles in Scotland 1940–50, and the legacy of the Second Republic', in T. M. Devine and David Hesse, eds., *Scotland and Poland: Historical Encounters, 1500–2010*, 105 (Edinburgh: Birlinn, 2011); Olson and Cloud, *A Question of Honour* (see Chapter 1, n. 158), 397.

125. Władysław Anders, *An Army in Exile: the Story of the Polish Second Corps* (London: Macmillan, 1949), 299.

126. Davies, *Rising '44* (see n. 123), 507.

127. Quoted in Doherty, *Irish Men and Women* (see Chapter 2, n. 16), 54.

128. *I See a Dark Stranger* (Frank Launder and Sidney Gilliat, 1946), *Against the Wind* (Charles Crichton, 1947).

129. Geoffrey Roberts, 'Three Narratives of Neutrality: Historians and Ireland's War', in Girvin and Roberts, *Ireland* (see Chapter 2, n. 10), 173.

130. Ibid., 174.

131. Kelly, *Returning Home* (see Introduction, n. 10), 4, 43–4.

132. Roberts, 'Three Narratives' (see n. 129), 165.

133. Research work on Austrian and German refugees in wartime Britain has been carried out particularly by the Association of Jewish Refugees and the Research Centre for German and Austrian Exile Studies.

134. *Tobruk* (Arthur Hiller, 1967).

135. Ugolini, *Experiencing War* (see Introduction, n. 57), 240–1.

136. Ostrowski, 'To Return to Poland' (see Introduction, n. 70), 37.

137. *Dark Blue World* (Jan Sverak, 2001).

138. http://www.telegraph.co.uk/culture/film/3576802/I-couldnt-let-the-veterans-down.html. Accessed 22 December 2015.

139. http://www.rte.ie/news/2013/0507/390710-soldier-amnesty/. Accessed 8 May 2016.

140. Quoted in O'Connor, *Irish Officers* (see Chapter 2, n. 147), 2.

141. Ministry of Defence, *We Were There: For 200 Years Ethnic Minorities Have Fought for Britain All Over the World* (London: Ministry of Defence Schools Presentation Team, 2004).

142. *The Guardian*, 15 January 2009.

143. Kushner, 'Without Intending' (see Introduction, n. 42), 344–5.

144. I am grateful to Anna Siemaszko for this information.
145. https://entertainment.guardianoffers.co.uk/i-cc-1220-xaa/battleofbritainpo-land-g/. Accessed 3 May 2016.
146. Maria Cunningham, interview by Janette Martin for the 'Mixing It' project, 2015.
147. Yvonne Foley, interview by Janette Martin for the 'Mixing It' project, 2015. The full interview is available at http://www.iwm.org.uk/collections/item/object/80033221.

Select Bibliography

UNPUBLISHED PRIMARY SOURCES

Archival collections

Australian National Library Archives, Canberra
    Chester Wilmot papers
BBC Written Archives Centre, Caversham Park, Reading
    BBC Contributor Files
    BBC European Intelligence Papers
    BBC Listener Research Files
    BBC Policy Files
    BBC Programme Files
    BBC Radio Scripts
    BBC Scriptwriter Files
    BBC Yearbooks
British Film Institute
    Reports on scenarios
Imperial War Museum, London
    Manuscript collections
    War time diary of Leonard George Peake
Kirklees Sound Archive
Mass Observation Archive, University of Sussex
    Directive replies
    File reports
    Topic collections
The National Archives, Kew
    Admiralty Files (ADM)
    Air Ministry Files (AIR)
    Cabinet Office Files (CAB)
    Colonial Office Files (CO)
    Ministry of Defence Files (DEFE)
    Foreign Office Files (FO)
    Home Office Files (HO)
    Ministry of Information Files (INF)
    Ministry of Labour and National Security Files (LAB)
    Ministry of Transport Files (MT)

Records of the Prime Minister's Office (PREM)
War Office Files (WO)

INTERVIEWS

Maria Cunningham interviewed by Janette Martin, 2015
Yvonne Foley interviewed by Janette Martin 2015
Stephen Kennedy, Imperial War Museum Sound Archive
Susanne Medas interviewed by Janette Martin 2015
Zbigniew Siemaszko interviewed by Robert Light 2015
Peter Sinclair interviewed by Janette Martin 2105
Tony Sosna, Kirklees Sound Archive interview, 1986
Jack and Betty Stang interviewed by Janette Martin 2015
Harry Watt, Imperial War Museum Sound Archive
Alan Wilmot, Imperial War Museum Sound Archive

PRINTED MEDIA: NEWSPAPERS AND MAGAZINES

Daily Express
Daily Mail
Daily Mirror
Daily Sketch
Daily Telegraph
Documentary Newsletter
Ebony Magazine
Evening Standard
Lancashire Daily Post
Lancashire Evening Post
Listener
Manchester Guardian
Message
News Chronicle
Observer
Picture Post
Punch
Radio Times
Reynolds News
Sunday Express
Sunday Telegraph
Sunday Times
Sydney Morning Herald
Time
The Times
Yorkshire Post

VISUAL MEDIA: NEWSREELS

British Movietone News
British Paramount News
British Pathé
Gaumont British News
Movietone War Time News
Pathé Gazette
Pathé News
Universal News
War Pictorial News

VISUAL MEDIA: FILMS AND TELEVISION PROGRAMMES

The Man who Knew Too Much (Alfred Hitchcock, 1934).
The Scarlet Pimpernel (Harold Young, 1934).
Secret Agent (Alfred Hitchcock, 1936).
Song of Freedom (James Elder Wills, 1936).
Big Fella (James Elder Wills, 1937).
The Lady Vanishes (Alfred Hitchcock, 1938).
The First Days (Humphrey Jennings & Harry Watt, 1939).
The Proud Valley (Pen Tennyson, 1939).
The Spy in Black (Michael Powell, 1939).
Britain Can Take It! (Harry Watt and Humphrey Jennings, 1940).
Contraband (Michael Powell, 1940).
Night Train to Munich (Carol Reed, 1940).
The 49th Parallel (Michael Powell and Emeric Pressburger, 1941).
The Black Sheep of Whitehall (Will Hay/Basil Dearden, 1941).
Christmas Under Fire (Harry Watt, 1941).
Crook's Tour (John Baxter, 1941).
Dangerous Moonlight (Brian Desmond Hurst, 1941).
Fighting Allies (Louise Birt, 1941).
The Ghost of St Michael's (Marcel Varnel, 1941).
Pimpernel Smith (Leslie Howard, 1941).
Target for Tonight (Harry Watt, 1941).
Back Room Boy (Herbert Mason, 1942).
Casablanca (Michael Curtiz, US 1942).
Diary of a Polish Airman (Concanen, 1942).
Joan of Paris (Robert Stevenson, US 1942).
Listen to Britain (Humphrey Jennings, 1942).
One of Our Aircraft is Missing (Michael Powell and Emeric Pressburger, 1942).
Polish Bomber's Holiday (Polish Film Unit, 1942).
The Secret Mission (Harold French, 1942).
The Shortest Route (Polish Film Unit, 1942).
Africa's Fighting Men (Colonial Film Unit, 1943).

Before the Raid (Jiri Weiss, 1943).
The Gentle Sex (Leslie Howard and Maurice Elvey, 1943).
The Life and Death of Colonel Blimp (Michael Powell and Emeric Pressburger, 1943).
Lift Your Head, Comrade (Michael Hankinson, 1943).
Millions Like Us (Sidney Gilliat and Frank Launder, 1943).
The New Lot (Carol Reed, 1943).
The Silent Village (Humphrey Jennings, 1943).
Timbermen from Honduras (Colonial Film Unit, 1943).
Welcome to Britain (Anthony Asquith, 1943).
West Indies Calling (John Page, 1943).
The Chinese in Wartime Britain (Carl Heck, 1944).
The Halfway House (Basil Dearden, 1944).
This Happy Breed (David Lean, 1944).
Strangers (Polish Film Unit, 1944).
Tawny Pipit (Charles Saunders and Bernard Miles, 1944).
I Know Where I'm Going (Michael Powell and Emeric Pressburger, 1945).
I See a Dark Stranger (Frank Launder, 1945).
Johnny Frenchman (Charles Frend, 1945).
Night and Day (Jiri Weiss, 1945).
Objective Burma! (Raoul Walsh, US, 1945).
The True Glory (Carol Reed and Garson Kanin, 1945).
The Way to the Stars (Anthony Asquith, 1945).
The Overlanders (Harry Watt, 1946).
Against the Wind (Charles Crichton, 1947).
The Lost People (Bernard Knowles and Muriel Box, 1949).
Victory at Sea (26-part US documentary series made by the American National Broadcasting Company, first episode screened on BBC television, 27 October 1952).
War in the Air (15-part BBC documentary series, first episode screened on BBC television, 8 November 1954).
Tobruk (Arthur Hiller, 1967).
Dark Blue World (Jan Sverak, 2001).
Tree Fellers (Sana Bilgrami, 2006).

AUTOBIOGRAPHY, BIOGRAPHY AND DIARIES

Doris Carter, *Never Leave Your Head Uncovered: A Canadian Nursing Sister in World War Two* (Stoney Creek, Ontario: Potlatch Publications, 1999).
George Clare, *Berlin Days 1946–7* (London: Pan Books, 1990).
Marcus Cowper, *The Words of War: British Forces Personal Letters and Diaries During the Second World War* (Edinburgh: Mainstream Publishing, 2009).
F. B. Czarnomski, ed., 'Bombing Boulogne: The Diary of Z. P. transcribed by F. B. Czarnomski' in F. B. Czarnomski, ed., *They Fight for Poland: The War in the First Person* (London: George Allen and Unwin, 1941), 268–76.

F. B. Czarnomski, ed., 'From Berlin to the Maginot Line', as told by Joseph Lipski to F. B. Czarnomski' in F. B. Czarnomski, ed., *They Fight for Poland: The War in the First Person* (London: George Allen and Unwin, 1941), 164–73.

Max Dickson, *The Memories of Max Dickson formerly Max Dobriner* (Privately printed, 1992).

Gerhart Friedlander and Keith Turner, *Rudi's Story: The Diary and Wartime Experiences of Rudolf Friedlaender* (London: Jedburgh Publishing, 2006).

Cy Grant, *A Member of the RAF of Indeterminate Race: World War Two Experiences of a West Indian Officer in the RAF* (Bognor Regis: Woodfield Publishing, 2006).

Brian Inglis, *West Briton* (London: Faber and Faber, 1962).

Judith Kerr, *The Other Way Round* (London: Fontana, 1977).

Michael Kerr, *As Far as I Remember* (Oxford and Portland, Oregon: Hart Publishing, 2002).

Annette Kobak, *Joe's War: My Father Decoded* (London: Virago, 2004).

Romie Lambkin, *My Time in the War: An Irishwoman's Diary* (Dublin: Wolfhound Press, 1992).

Pierre Lefranc, 'A Member of the Free French bears Witness', in Anne Corbett and Douglas Johnson, eds., *A Day in June: Britain and De Gaulle 1940* (London: Franco-British Council, 2000), 12–15.

Miroslav A. Liskutin, *Challenge in the Air: A Spitfire Pilot Remembers* (London: William Kimber, 1998).

Mark Lynton, *An Accidental Journey: A Cambridge Internee's Memoir of World War II* (Woodstock, NY: Overlook Press, 1996).

Peter Masters, *Striking Back: A Jewish Commando's War Against the Nazis* (Novato California: Presidio Press, 1997).

Mary Morris, *A Very Private Diary: A Nurse in Wartime* (London: Weidenfeld and Nicholson, 2014).

Robert Murray, *Lest We Forget: The Experiences of World War II Westindian Ex-Service Personnel* (Nottingham: Westindian Combined Ex-Services Association, 1996).

E. Martin Noble, *Jamaica Airman: A Black Airman in Britain 1943 and after* (London: New Beacon Books, 1984).

Andrew Nocon, 'A Reluctant Welcome? Poles in Britain in the 1940s', *Oral History*, 1/24 (Spring 1996), 79–87.

Jean Offenberg, *Lonely Warrior: The Action-journal of a Battle of Britain Fighter Pilot* (St. Albans: Mayflower Books, first published 1956).

Mollie Panter-Downes, ed. by William Shawn, *London War Notes 1939–1945* (London: Longman, 1972).

Joe Pieri, *Isle of the Displaced: An Italian-Scot's Memoirs of Internment in the Second World War* (Glasgow: Neil Wilson Publishing, 1997).

Bronka Schneider, *Exile: A Memoir of 1939*, ed., Erika Bourguignon and Barbara Hill Rigney (Columbus: Ohio State University Press, 1998).

Antoni Slonimski, 'The Bread and the Smile of England', in F. B. Czarnomski, ed., *They Fight for Poland: The War in the First Person* (London: George Allen and Unwin, 1941), 280–5.

Tadeusz Szumowski, *Through Many Skies: The Flying Days of One Polish Pilot* (Beverley: Highgate Publications, 1993).

Walter White, *A Rising Wind* (New York: Doubleday, Doran and Co, 1945).

Fritz Zimmermann, 'A Stranger in Three Continents: My Life from 1920 to 1951', unpublished manuscript.

Zbigniew S. Siemaszko, *Pod Sowiecką Władzą, 1939–1942* (London: Polish Cultural Foundation, 2001).

Zbigniew S. Siemaszko, *I Co Dalej? 1945–1948* (Warsaw: LTW, 2016).

BOOKS AND ARTICLES

Carol Acton, ' "Stepping into history": Reading the Second World War through Irish Women's Diaries', *Irish Studies Review*, 18/1 (2010), 39–56.

Paul Addison and Jeremy Crang, eds., *Listening to Britain: Home Intelligence Reports on Britain's Finest Hour* (London: Bodley Head, 2010).

Robert Allen, *Churchill's Guests: Britain and the Belgian Exiles During World War II* (Westport, Connecticut: Praeger, 2003).

Alan Allport *Demobbed: Coming Home After the Second World War* (New Haven: Yale University Press, 2009).

Nicholas Atkin, *The Forgotten French: Exiles in the British Isles, 1940–44* (Manchester: Manchester University Press, 2003).

John Belchem, *Before the Windrush: Race Relations in 20th-Century Liverpool* (Liverpool: Liverpool University Press, 2014).

Bohuš Beneš, ed., *Wings in Exile: Life and Work of the Czechoslovak Airmen in France and Great Britain* (London: "The Czechoslovak" Independent Weekly, 1942).

Norman Bentwich, *I Understand the Risks: The Story of the refugees from Nazi Oppression who fought in the British Forces in the World War* (London: Victor Gollancz, 1950).

Günter Berghaus, ed., *Theatre and Film in Exile: German Artists in Great Britain, 1933–45* (Oxford: Berg, 1989).

Amanda Bidnall, 'West Indian Interventions at the Heart of the Cultural Establishment: Edric Connor, Pearl Connor and the BBC', *Twentieth Century British History* 24/1 (2013), 58–83.

Asa Briggs, *The History of Broadcasting in the United Kingdom, Vol. III: The War of Words, 1939–1945* (Oxford: Oxford University Press, 1995).

Charmian Brinson and Richard Dove, eds., *'Stimme der Wahrheit': German-language Broadcasting by the BBC* (Amsterdam: Rodopi, 2003).

Alan Brown, *Flying for Freedom: The Allied Forces in the RAF 1939–45* (Stroud, Gloucestershire: The History Press, 2011).

Madeleine Bunting, *The Model Occupation: The Channel Islands Under German Rule, 1940–1945* (London: HarperCollins, 1995).

Connery Chappell, *Island of Barbed Wire: The Remarkable Story of World War Two Internment on the Isle of Man* (London: Robert Hale, 2005).

Robert Cole, *Propaganda, Censorship and Irish Neutrality in the Second World War* (Edinburgh: Edinburgh University Press, 2006).

Martin Conway and José Gotovitch, eds., *Europe in Exile: European Exile Communities in Britain 1940–1945* (Oxford: Berghahn Books, 2001).

Nicholas Cull, *Selling War: The British Propaganda Campaign Against American Neutrality in World War II* (Oxford: Oxford University Press, 1995).

Joy Damousi, ' "The Australian has a Lazy Way of Talking": Australian Character and Accent, 1920s-1940s', in Joy Damousi and Desley Deacon, eds., *Talking and Listening in the Age of Modernity: Essays on the History of Sound* (Canberra: ANU E Press, 2007), 83–96.

Norman Davies, *Rising '44: The Battle for Warsaw* (London: Pan Books, 2004).

Enda Delaney, *Demography, State and Society: Irish Migration to Britain, 1921–1971* (Montreal, QC, Canada: McGill-Queen's University Press, 2000).

Victor de Laveleye, 'The V sign', *Message*, January 1944, 20–4.

Richard Doherty, *Irish Volunteers in the Second World War* (Dublin: Four Courts Press 2003).

Richard Dove, *Journey of No Return: Five German-speaking Literary Exiles in Britain, 1933–1945* (London: Libris, 2000).

Martin Francis, *The Flyer: British Culture and the Royal Air Force 1939–1945* (Oxford: Oxford University Press, 2008).

Helen Fry, *The King's Most Loyal Enemy Aliens: Germans who fought for Britain in the Second World War* (Stroud, Gloucestershire: Sutton Publishing, 2007).

Brian Girvin and Geoffrey Roberts, eds., *Ireland and the Second World War: Politics, Society, Remembrance* (Dublin: Four Courts Press, 2000).

Anthony Grenville, *Jewish Refugees from Germany and Austria in Britain 1933–1970* (London: Vallentine Mitchell, 2010).

Michael Hallett, *Stefan Lorant, Godfather of Photojournalism* (Lanham, Maryland: Scarecrow Press, 2006).

Tobias Hochscherf, *The Continental Connection: German-speaking émigrés and British Cinema, 1927–45* (Manchester: Manchester University Press, 2011).

Colin Holmes, *John Bull's Island: Immigration and British Society, 1871–1971* (Basingstoke: Macmillan, 1988).

David Howarth, *The Shetland Bus* (Morley, Yorkshire: Elmfield Press, 1976, first published 1951).

Helen Jones, 'National, Community and Personal Priorities: British women's responses to refugees from the Nazis, from the mid-1930s to early 1940s', *Women's History Review*, 21/1 (2012), 121–51.

Bernard Kelly, *Returning Home: Irish Ex-Servicemen after the Second World War* (Dublin: Merrion 2012).

Halik Kochanski, *The Eagle Unbowed: Poland and the Poles in the Second World War* (Cambridge, MA: Harvard University Press, 2012).

Henning Krabbe, ed., *Voices from Britain: Broadcast History 1939–45* (London: George Allen & Unwin, 1947).

Tony Kushner, *The Holocaust and the Liberal Imagination: A Social and Cultural History* (Blackwell: Oxford, 1994).

Tony Kushner, ' "Without Intending any of the Most Undesirable Features of a Colour Bar": Race Science, Europeanness and the British armed forces during the Twentieth Century', *Patterns of Prejudice*, 46/3–4 (2012), 339–74.

Tony Kushner and Katharine Knox, *Refugees in an Age of Genocide: Global, National and Local Perspectives During the Twentieth Century* (London: Frank Cass, 1999).

Francois Lafitte, *The Internment of Aliens* (Harmondsworth: Penguin, 1940).

Shompa Lahiri, 'Clandestine Mobilities and Shifting Embodiments: Noor-un-nisa Inayat Khan and the Special Operations Executive, 1940–44', *Gender & History*, 19/2 (2007), 305–23.

Thomas Lane, *Victims of Stalin and Hitler: The Exodus of Poles and Balts to Britain* (Basingstoke: Palgrave, 2004).

Peter Leighton-Langer, *The King's Own Loyal Enemy Aliens: German and Austrian Refugees in Britain's Armed Forces, 1939–1945* (London: Vallentine Mitchell, 2006).

S. P. Mackenzie, 'War in the Air: Churchill, the Air Ministry and the BBC response to Victory at Sea', *Contemporary British History*, 20/4 (2006), 559–74.

Leanne McCormick, ' "One Yank and They're Off": Interaction Between U.S. Troops and Northern Irish Women, 1942–1945', *Journal of the History of Sexuality*, 15/2 (2006), 228–57.

Ian McLaine, *Ministry of Morale: Home Front Morale and the Ministry of Information in World War II* (London: George Allen and Unwin, 1979).

George Mikes, *How to be an Alien* (London: Allan Wingate, 1949, first published 1946).

Bob Moore, 'Axis Prisoners in Britain during the Second World War: A Comparative Survey', in Bob Moore and Kent Fedorowich, eds., *Prisoners of War and their Captors in World War II* (Oxford: Berg, 1996), 19–46.

Bob Moore, 'Turning Liabilities into Assets': British Government Policy towards German and Italian Prisoners of War during the Second World War', *Journal of Contemporary History*, 32/1 (1997), 117–36.

Hank Nelson, *Chased by the Sun: The Australians in Bomber Command in World War II* (Crows Nest NSW: Allen and Unwin, 2006).

Steven O'Connor, *Irish Officers in the British Forces, 1922–45* (Basingstoke: Palgrave, 2014).

Steven O'Connor, 'Irish Identity and Integration within the British armed forces, 1939–1945', *Irish Historical Studies*, 39/155 (2015), 417–38.

Mark Ostrowski, ' "To Return to Poland or Not to Return": the Dilemma facing the Polish Armed Forces at the End of the Second World War', Ph.D dissertation, University of London, no date.

Philip Paris, *Orkney's Italian Chapel: The True Story of an Icon* (Edinburgh: Black and White Publishing, 2010).

Kathleen Paul, *Whitewashing Britain: Race and Citizenship in the Postwar Era* (Ithaca: Cornell University Press, 1997).

Susan Pedersen, *Eleanor Rathbone and the Politics of Conscience* (New Haven: Yale University Press, 2004).

Susan Pennybacker, *From Scottsboro to Munich: Race and Political Culture in 1930s Britain* (Princeton, NJ: Princeton University Press, 2009).

Simon Potter, *Broadcasting Empire: The BBC and the British World, 1922–1970* (Oxford: Oxford University Press, 2012).

Edward Raczynski, *In Allied London* (London: Charles Birchall & Sons, 1962).

Ruvani Ranasinha, 'South Asian Broadcasters in Britain and the BBC: talking to India' (1941–1943)', *South Asian Diaspora*, 2/1 (2010), 57–71.

Brian Read, *No Cause for Panic: Channel Islands Refugees 1940–1945* (Bradford on Avon: Seaflower Books, 1995).

David Reynolds, *Rich Relations: The American Occupation of Britain, 1942–1945* (London: HarperCollins, 1995).

Sonya Rose, *Which People's War?: National Identity and Citizenship in Wartime Britain 1939–1945* (Oxford: Oxford University Press, 2003).

William Sansom, *Westminster in War* (London: Faber and Faber, 1947).

Maxine Seller, *We Built Up Our Lives: Education and Community among Jewish Refugees Interned by Britain in World War II* (Westport, CT: Greenwood Press, 2001).

Marika Sherwood, *Many Struggles: West Indian Workers and Service Personnel in Britain (1939–45)* (London: Karia Press, 1985).

Graham Smith, *When Jim Crow met John Bull: Black American Soldiers in World War II Britain* (London: I. B. Tauris, 1987).

Lucio Sponza, *Divided Loyalties: Italians in Britain during the Second World War* (Bern: Peter Lang, 2000).

Charles Stacey and Barbara Wilson, *The Half Million: The Canadians in Britain, 1939–1946* (Toronto: University of Toronto Press, 1987).

Simona Tobia, 'Questioning the Nazis: languages and effectiveness in British war crime investigations and trials in Germany, 1945–48', *Journal of War and Culture Studies* 3/1 (2010), 123–36.

Janet Toole, 'GIs and the Race Bar in Wartime Warrington', *History Today*, 43/7 (1 July 1993), 22–8.

Wendy Ugolini, *Experiencing War as the 'Enemy Other': Italian Scottish Experience in World War II* (Manchester: Manchester University Press, 2011).

Wendy Ugolini, 'The Embodiment of British Italian War Memory? The Curious Marginalisation of Dennis Donnini, VC', *Patterns of Prejudice*, 46/3–4 (2012), 397–415.

Wendy Ugolini, ' "When are you going back"? Memory, Ethnicity and the British Home Front', in Lucy Noakes and Juliette Pattinson, eds., *British Cultural Memory and the Second World War* (London: Bloomsbury, 2014), 89–110.

Clive Webb, 'Special Relationships: Mixed-race Couples in Post-war Britain and the United States', *Women's History Review*, 26/1 (2017), 110–29.

Inge Weber-Newth and Johannes Dieter Steinert, *German Migrants in Post-war Britain: An Enemy Embrace* (London: Routledge, 2006).

Wendy Webster, *Imagining Home: Gender, 'Race and National Identity, 1945–64* (London: UCL Press, 1998).

Wendy Webster, *Englishness and Empire 1939–1965* (Oxford: Oxford University Press, 2005).

Bill Williams, *'Jews and Other Foreigners': Manchester and the Rescue of the Victims of European Fascism, 1933–1940* (Manchester: Manchester University Press, 2011).

Clair Wills, *That Neutral Island: A Cultural History of Ireland during the Second World War* (London: Faber and Faber, 2007).

Michelle Winslow, 'War, Resettlement, Rooting and Ageing: An Oral History Study of Polish Émigrés in Britain', Ph.D dissertation, University of Sheffield, 2001.

Ian Wood, *Britain, Ireland and the Second World War* (Edinburgh: Edinburgh University Press, 2010).

Adam Zamoyski, *The Forgotten Few: The Polish Air Force in the Second World War* (London: John Murray, 1995).

Index